Leadership in a Small Town

26 in 26

Neighborhood Resource Centers

26 Neighborhood Strategies in a 26 month time frame
A Grant Funded by the LSTA
(Library Services & Technology Act)

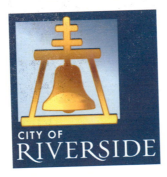

CITY OF
RIVERSIDE

Riverside Public Library

Leadership in a Small Town

Aaron Wildavsky

With a new introduction by
Nelson W. Polsby

Transaction Publishers
New Brunswick (U.S.A.) and London (U.K.)

Second printing 2012

New material this edition copyright © 2004 by Transaction Publishers, New Brunswick, New Jersey. Originally published in 1964 by The Bedminster Press.

This book is printed on acid-free paper that meets the American National Standard for Permanence of Paper for Printed Library Materials.

Library of Congress Catalog Number: 2003063399
ISBN: 978-0-7658-0579-9
Printed in the United States of America

Library of Congress Cataloging-in-Publication Data

Wildavsky, Aaron B.
    Leadership in a small town / Aaron Wildavsky : with a new introduction by Nelson W. Polsby.
        p.   cm.
    Originally published: Totowa, N.J. : Bedminster Press, c1964.
    Includes bibliographical references and index.
    ISBN 978-0-7658-0579-9 (pbk. : alk. paper)
    1. Oberlin (Ohio)—Politics and government. 2. Municipal government—Ohio—Case studies. 3. Community leadership—Ohio—Case studies.   4.   Political leadership—Ohio—Case studies.
    5. Power (Social sciences)—Ohio—Case studies. I. Title.

JS1249.O3W55 2004
320.9771'23—dc22   2003063399

For Adam and Sara, born citizens of Oberlin

CONTENTS

TRANSACTION INTRODUCTION

By my reckoning, this is the third book Aaron Wildavsky published, out of the forty or so that he produced in a life of scholarship (counting books only) that stretched from 1958, when he left the Yale graduate school and joined the faculty at Oberlin College, to his death in Oakland, California on September 4, 1993. The first two were his doctoral dissertation, *Dixon Yates: A Study in Power Politics*,[1] published in 1962, and a long essay on the 1926 Referendum published in *Studies in Australian Politics*[2] in 1958, one of the products of his Fulbright year (1954-55) in Australia. *Leadership in a Small Town* was one of three Wildavsky books that emerged in 1964, when he was thirty-four years old. The other two are still in print. *The Politics of the Budgetary Process*[3] a few years ago was voted the third most influential work in fifty years of writing in the entire field of public administration. *Presidential Elections*,[4] written with me, is now in its eleventh edition.

So, arguably, *Leadership in a Small Town* occupies less space in the minds of Wildavsky's fellow political scientists than the others that emerged in what even for him was a notably productive year. A casual glance at its contents, however, will disclose to the reader a remarkably meritorious work of scholarship, and a vintage example of Wildavsky's style as a scholar.

As Wildavsky departed for his first regular teaching appointment in Oberlin, in his rear view mirror was Robert A. Dahl's study of community power, then underway in New Haven.[5] Wildavsky's exact contemporary in the Yale graduate school, Raymond E. Wolfinger, had been spending a year of field work in the office of the mayor and with the development administrator, who was in charge locally of the nation's most conspicuous and comprehensive urban renewal program. I was also mixed up in the Dahl project, accompanying Dahl in interviews around town and digging through the community power literature in search of general propositions that we could test against New Haven data.[6]

As he did so often in his life, Wildavsky took an interest in what we were doing, and though he never formally studied with Dahl, through much informal conversation he achieved a thorough understanding of the overall intellectual enterprise, the obstacles we were encountering, the theoretical and practical hurdles in our path. His attitude was supportive, sometimes even enthusiastic.

Soon, on his arrival in Oberlin, he was confronted with the task of teaching a course on the predictably boring subject of state and local government to some of America's brightest undergraduates. Something clicked as it frequently did in Wildavsky's extremely active mind: why not organize his class into a research team and study the small and manageable town of Oberlin, which, after all, completely surrounded the college? The intellectual template, Dahl's study of New Haven, was thoroughly familiar to him. With his band of enthusiastic youngsters he could produce as close as non-experimental social science gets to a replication of the New Haven study, thus providing another—and needed—dimension to the literature.

One of the problems faced by the New Haven crew was identifying a sufficient number of political domains to investigate to get a generalizable picture of power and its exercise in New Haven. Studying too many domains—we called them issue-areas—in a city (as it then was) of 160,000 inhabitants would be beyond our resources. Too few, and general conclusions would be vulnerable to the criticism that we had missed what was really going on. We could not think of a sensible way randomly to sample domains and settled on the following solution: study highly consequential outcomes. (1) Urban renewal was obviously the biggest innovation in town, beyond dispute. (2) Public education soaked up by far the biggest share of the municipal budget. Since we already knew that at least one elected official, the mayor, was the most important player in the domains we could see, we picked a third domain, political nominations, as a way of guarding against the possibility that elected officials were planted in the community by processes we would be unaware of. There was, after all, a conception of municipal life already enshrined in the community power literature that said that elected officials were merely passive tools of economic leaders.[7] So we had to give that possibility a fair empirical test.

Wildavsky was aware of these problems and immediately saw how the scale of his project could go a long way toward solving them. In small and manageable Oberlin he would study...everything. And of course, more or less, as readers will presently see, he did.

I will not detain the reader much longer by praising Wildavsky's alertness to intellectual currents in the air around him, his capacity to conjure up imaginative solutions to problems of research, his organizational gifts, his capacity to inspire others—not limited to the small fry in the sophomore class—and the energy and focus that he brought to his scholarly tasks. But I will mention them. It will take a very neglectful reader indeed not to notice the sheer joy of discovery that leaps from these pages.

In the time—just short of three decades—left to him after the initial publication of this book, Aaron Wildavsky put his prodigious talents to work again and again, with similarly illuminating results, on a dozen different topics. In this book, very early on, he is already sailing along in top form with a report on politics in what, for four marvelously productive years, was the Brooklyn-born Wildavsky's home town.

Nelson W. Polsby
Berkeley, California, 2003

Notes

1. New Haven: Yale University Press, 1962.
2. Melbourne and London: F.W. Cheshire, 1958.
3. Boston: Little, Brown, 1964. 4th Edition, 1984.
4. New York: Charles Scribner's Sons, 1964. 11th Edition, Boulder Colorado: Rowman and Littlefield, 2004.
5. This study was reported in Dahl, *Who Governs?* (New Haven: Yale University Press, 1961).
6. This work became my doctoral dissertation in 1961 and, very soon thereafter, a book: *Community Power and Political Theory* (New Haven: Yale University Press, first edition 1963).
7. Discussed at length in *Community Power and Political Theory.*

♣🏠🏠♣ ACKNOWLEDGMENTS

In my fortunate years as a student in the Political Science Department of the Yale University Graduate School, I came to know of the inquiry into the power structure of New Haven, Connecticut, which was being conducted by Robert Dahl, Nelson Polsby, and Raymond Wolfinger. Through conversations with these men and perusal of preliminary accounts of their work, I gained some understanding of their approach and their theoretical equipment. This book was designed as a replication and extension of the New Haven study in a different community—Oberlin, Ohio. While I am grateful to Dahl, Polsby, and Wolfinger for their example and encouragement, they bear no responsibility for what is said here and they might well wish to disassociate themselves from any specific conclusions.

When I went to Oberlin College in 1958 and was asked to teach a course on State and Local Government, it was only natural that my attention should turn to the field of community power. Here was an exciting new area of study, with many unexplored possibilities, in which students could participate and gain many of the skills required by political scientists. They were asked to prepare case studies of events going on at the time, to spend time observing the activities of key participants, to administer and analyze questionnaires, and to conduct historical inquiries. In this way a substantial body of data on Oberlin, including over a thousand interviews, was accumulated. I would, therefore, like to take this opportunity to name and thank the students whose efforts made this study possible:

Gladys Allison, Michael Arian, Donald Borut, Elizabeth Bradford, Elton Burkey, Barbara Burnett, James Burrows, Barbara Chong, Charles Chomet, David Dell, John Diller, David Dorfman, David

Dreyer, Carol Dunn, Thomas Elden, Guerri Finnigan, Ronald Friedman, Jacqueline Gilley, Joan Golambos, Diane Greenwald, George Guptill, James Hamilton, Art Hamman, Philip Knox Hayes, Martin Hochman, Robert Houser, Peter Jaynes, James M. Jones, Percy Julian, David Karro, Edward Kolar, Beverly Krause, Leonard Langeland, Michael Margolis, Frank Mazurek, Glenn Nitschke, Peggy Paret, Nancy Parker, Robert Petersen, Richard Railsback, Edward Schwartz, John Shank, Morris Simkin, Judy Singer, Frank Sloan, Arden Small, Allan Spiegelburg, James Turner, Mary Turzillo, Leonard West, Christopher Williams.

The students who wrote case histories and role studies also handed in their notes of interviews and copies of documents. From these sources, together with my own observations, I prepared preliminary drafts of the chapters concerning the decisions studied and the activities of leading participants. In this work I was ably assisted by Alden Small, an Oberlin College student. Together we compiled the relevant materials, filled in gaps, re-interviewed participants to resolve conflicts in the account of events, circulated drafts to leading participants, made further corrections, and revised the case histories and role studies. Another student, Michael Margolis, helped us in putting together lists of actions taken and the resources used to accomplish various purposes. It was a pleasure to work with Messrs. Small and Margolis; my appreciation of the high caliber of their services has grown with time.

I owe an incalculable debt to the hundreds of Oberlin citizens who freely gave their time to answering seemingly endless questions by myself and my students. Their plaintive cry—"no, not again"—as hordes of students descended upon them for the "umpteenth" time was as understandable as their unfailing cooperation and courtesy was remarkable. It would be invidious to single out individuals for special praise. Let it suffice to say that their indispensable contribution went far beyond the call of duty, and I thank them one and all.

Lewis A. Froman, Jr. of the University of Wisconsin, Kyoshi Ikeda and Richard Meyers of Oberlin College, Nelson Polsby, of Wesleyan University, and Robert Presthus read individual chapters in a helpful and critical spirit. I appreciate their efforts on my behalf, especially since several of them may disagree with my interpretation of the evidence.

Financial support came from the Eagleton Institute* and the Falk Foundation and from a Ford Foundation Grant in Public Affairs awarded through Oberlin College. Without these funds, my task would have been much more difficult, if not impossible.

I have been fortunate in receiving editorial assistance from Carol Ganzel, Ann Humphrey, and Linda and Joseph Wolfe. Typing on the several drafts of this manuscript was expertly done by Estelle Berman, Helen Johnson, Helen Monslave, Sally Nishiyama, and June Wright. They all performed their tasks with distinction.

It should now be clear that the editorial "we" used throughout this volume is not a mere convention but represents the contribution of many others in the preparation of *Leadership in a Small Town*. I have tried to do their labors justice. The full measure of responsibility, however, is entirely mine.

* The studies under which this publication is based were made under a grant from the Maurice and Laura Falk Foundation of Pittsburgh through the Eagleton Institute of Politics, Rutgers, The State University. However, the Foundation is not the author, publisher, or proprietor of this publication and is not to be understood as endorsing, by virtue of its grant, any of the statements made or views expressed herein.

Leadership in a Small Town

1 RIVAL THEORIES AND A METHOD FOR CHOOSING AMONG THEM

Of all the questions which might be asked about political life it would be difficult to find one of greater interest than the ancient query: who rules over whom? It appeals powerfully to our curiosity. The "inside-dopester" in us wants to know who runs things, who makes public policy decisions in New York, Washington, Moscow, or the town in which we live. Is it a single powerful individual, an economic elite, a series of different elites, the mass of citizens, political "bosses," or some variant of these possible answers? To suggest an answer is to say much about a particular society. For if we believe that crucial decisions are made by a privileged elite outside the democratic process we are likely to arrive at far different conclusions than if we think that the mass of citizens has a considerable impact on what the society does in its political aspect. We would expect that the kinds of policies adopted, the distributions of benefits and deprivations, the degree of consent and coercion, would vary depending on who rules over whom. If we adopt equality as a goal, we would make different moral judgments of political systems in which control over decisions is shared by many rather than a few. A change from one system of rule to another would have an enormous impact on the lives of citizens.

The major purpose of this volume is to find an answer to the question—who rules?—for a small American city and to extend the answer through relevant theory to American cities in general. More precisely, we seek to find answers to the following questions: What are the relationships between the rulers (those whose preferences are carried out in decisions made by the community) and the ruled? How are the rulers (leaders) related to one another? Are the rulers the same for all policies or do they differ from one area of policy to another? How do leaders arise, and in what ways are they different from other people? What strategies are pursued by leaders and what makes them successful? How is reputation for leadership related to the actual exercise of leadership? What, in brief, is the most accurate description of the political system, the interaction among the leaders and the led?

Attempts to provide answers to these questions necessarily involve theories, that is, abstractions from life which help explain a wide range of phenomena. Political and social life are incredibly complex; yet the mind of man can accommodate only relatively simple explanations. No one can encompass all the untold millions of "facts" which might conceivably be relevant. The limitations on man's ability to store and calculate demand simple principles for the selection and ordering of the available data. Those who proclaim most loudly that they are against "theory," Keynes once said, often proceed under grand assumptions promulgated by some long dead economist or political theorist whose views of the social world they have unknowingly assimilated. The question, then, is not whether we shall theorize (in the limited sense of devising general statements to cover a wide range of phenomena) but whether our theories are more nearly correct than other alternatives.

In the search for more adequate theories of politics, it is questionable whether we have advanced much beyond Aristotle's classification of political systems into rule by the one (the monarch), the few (the coalition of nobles), or the many (the populace). Until recently, little has been done to devise a useful classification of political systems, to determine under what conditions the various types appear, to isolate the crucial variables and to describe the relationships among them, and to develop a methodology which would enable observers to determine the kind of system existing in a particular community. Single-factor explanations—economics, relationship to the means of production, formal governmental structure, national character—have abounded despite their patently unsuccessful results. Indeed, Aristotle showed himself to be more subtle, more flexible, more variegated in his approach than most of his successors. If he recognized the importance of economics as one of the determinants of politics, he also saw that the political system might be so structured as to have an independent influence upon the process of community decision.

For Aristotle, social balance was an essential quality of a community which wished to avoid the twin oppressions of dictatorship and demagoguery. At one point in the *Politics*, he devised a solution to a vexing problem. It seems that the poor were so busy trying to make a living that they could not afford to attend the Assembly, while the rich found so much profit in their private activities that it did not appear worthwhile for them to participate. This violated the balance of forces in which justice emerged from a clash of interests. Aristotle's solution was characteristically ingenious; the poor were to be paid to attend and the rich fined if they failed to attend.[1] Without dwelling on the specific merits of this proposal, we can see that Aristotle believed that there was more than one effective resource for influencing civic decisions, that he was sensitive to the consequences of differential participation of various groups, and that he conceived of a dynamic interplay in the community based on the relationships among a variety of factors. We shall make use of these insights in proposing a set of related explanations to account for the structure of power over decisions in most American communities.

Most of the social scientists who have worked on the problem of community power structure in recent decades have arrived at far different answers than we do. They have found communities ruled by economic elites; we by a variety of competing elites under conditions created by a free ballot. They have found the citizen without effective resources; we find him with many. They see little hope for peaceful change; we see much. From time to time there also appear vestiges of a much different notion which emphasizes equality of influence among the mass of citizens. It would seem desirable, in the midst of these conflicting views, to present some of the alternative answers to the questions we have posed about who rules in American communities. Then we will propose a method for deciding among them.

Rival theories

A theory of mass democracy would state that there is equality of influence among the voting citizenry and that community decisions can therefore be explained as a product of majority will. The citizens are all interested, active, and possess equally effective resources. They have opinions on all important matters that are up for decision, and they elect representatives who translate their views into public policy. A more sophisticated variant notes the existence of free elections and competing political parties interested in pleasing the electorate by proposing policies desired by a majority. The mass of citizens thus exercise influence through their use of the ballot by removing officeholders who do not please them and generally keeping the parties responsive to their wishes. Elections are considered all-important determinants of public policy.

We can take C. Wright Mills', *The Power Elite* (New York, 1956), as our prototype of ruling elite theory. Mills claims that a group of men, chiefly industrialists and military officers, united by a common background and training which is assumed to lead to common interests, are making the important decisions in American life, and that our national political institutions are but a façade. It can be seen that the conception of the power elite rests upon two basic assumptions: there is a unified group of men with similar interests who want to rule in all or most significant areas, and these men are capable of doing so through the possession of resources which dominate all others which may be used against them.

Instead of the power elite, the pathbreaking work by Robert and Helen Lynd, *Middletown in Transition* (New York, 1937), proposes a more restricted, elemental answer. The "X" family runs Middletown, they say, because of its possession of a single resource —wealth—manifested by its holding of capital and ownership of industry. The "pervasive fingers of capitalist ownership," run by this "reigning royal family," are everywhere and control every significant decision. Politics is "the same crooked old shell game" because economics control politics and politicians take orders from the economically powerful. Nothing distresses the Lynds so much as the gap between the theory of democratic control of the city's political life and actual domination by the X family. It is a sham, a disgrace, demonstrating the sheer, infuriating inability of the ordinary citizen to control what is supposed to be his government. Under these conditions, progress is hardly possible without class warfare.

A related model of the modern community is presented in the

many concepts of the mass society. The radical variant, as Kornhauser[2] has pointed out, emphasizes the culpability of the industrial elites, while the conservative variant stresses the evils of the masses. In both cases, however, the concepts center around the change for the worse which industrial society has visited upon mankind, its debilitating effects on the individual, and the availability only of extreme alternatives for starting out on an indispensable new footing. Whatever its source, the concept of the mass society breathes with a nostalgia for the past and repugnance for the present. "Things were much better then; they are bad now but they are getting worse." Man, who was once noble, is now enslaved by machines, a mere cog in a wheel, helpless and distraught, prey to any elite which offers hope of re-establishing community. Politics is nothing, a mere appendage, a screen for the economic elite (the radical view) or a cover for demogogues (the conservative view) unless, of course, it is a revolutionary or reactionary politics, designed to uproot the order which has uprooted man, led by new men with a messianic and apocalyptic view of the future as future or the future as past. In the Marxist and Leninist types, the mystique of the pure and revolutionary masses is combined, in a classic case of ambivalence, with contempt for these dregs of society. The very idea of peaceful change is deemed laughable.

Our major thesis is that the political systems of most American cities are best described as pluralist rather than as rule by all the people or by a power elite. There is no small group of people which consistently wins out in cases of conflict over a wide range of important issues. Neither is there a large mass of citizens whose views as to specific policy usually prevail by their own actions. Instead, we find that the small group of citizens which is typically influential in one issue area, such as housing, is quite different from the other small groups which largely control decisions in other issue areas such as utilities, elections, education, industrial development, and welfare activities. To the extent that some individuals are influential in several issue areas, the chances are that they are not equally powerful in all, that they suffer defeats in some, and that they are governmental officials. Power is thus fragmented among many different individuals and groups and rather widely dispersed (unequally to be sure) in the community. The answer to the question, "Who rules in X city?" is likely to be—different small groups of interested and active citizens in different issue areas, with some overlap, if any, by public officials, and occasional intervention by a larger number of people at the polls. The pluralist political system is fragmented, competitive, open, and fluid.

A second thesis is that the rise of pluralist systems in American communities is a development implying hope and promise for the practice of democracy and the development of the individual. The notion of the mass man—atomized, uprooted from his fellows and his community, utterly without means of controlling his destiny, a natural victim for totalitarian movements—though it has some elements of validity, is not accepted here. On the contrary, the opportunities which a pluralist society provides for the individual to resist aggression, for making his participation in community affairs effective, and for fruitful self-expression are stressed.

The case history method

The proper way to decide among various interpretations of the same phenomenon is to subject them to a test so that they can be proved or disproved. It must be clear from the outset that the test permits a wide variety of results and that if one set of results are obtained the conclusions will be different than if another set appears. The case history methodology used by Robert Dahl, Nelson Polsby and Raymond Wolfinger in their study of New Haven,[3] seems admirably suited to our purposes. It requires, to begin with, the selection of a number of important issues at controversy during a specified period of time. Where limited time and other resources demanded that Dahl and his associates choose a few issue areas— redevelopment, education, nominations—and defend their significance, we were not faced with that problem. The ease of working in a small town permitted us to choose every single decision (and most certainly every controversial one) of any importance from November 1957 to June 1961.

The next step is to discover those individuals who were influential in securing favorable decisions in each issue area. This was done in Oberlin by reading the newspaper and official records in order to get an initial list of names of people concerned with the decision. These men were interviewed, asked to describe their participation and that of other people, and then prevailed upon to suggest the names of others involved. In this way the researcher branched out until he had interviewed everyone who took part or until diminishing returns set in and additional interviews did not turn up new information. In particular, the interviewer sought to discover who initiated the successful proposals, who vetoed the unsuccessful ones, and who was involved in gaining the consent of others. Reliability was further insured by stationing observers with officials like the City Manager, the Mayor and school principals, and by following issues at the time they occurred. A case history was then compiled, shown to the major participants, and altered where necessary.

The final step is to compare those who are influential (the leaders) in one issue area with those who are influential in another. If the same person or group appears in all or almost all areas, then we conclude that there is a ruling elite of some kind which consistently prevails in cases of conflict with others in society. If, on the other hand, we find that everyone in the community, or nearly so, appears to be equally influential in all areas, we conclude that the town is ruled by its citizens as a mass democracy. These are the extreme possibilities. We might discover that there are a small number of leaders in each issue area but that they differ from one another so that there is no overlap at all. This would signify the existence of a highly fragmented pluralist system. Many other varieties of pluralism are also possible such as overlap between issue areas by public officials and no one else, bargaining relationships among leaders in related issue areas, and so on. The important thing is that the method permits any of these possibilities to manifest itself and that we can observe actual behavior to test the most likely hypotheses.

This is a study of leadership (power, influence, control) in community decisions. It is not a study of influence in the sense of getting other people to do things they would otherwise not do. A participant may modify the behavior of others as much as he likes, but if he does not secure a favorable outcome or alter the content of a community decision in some way, he is not counted as a leader for our purposes. Otherwise, we would be accepting as community leaders all sorts of people who have no discernible impact on decisions.

There is virtually no possibility under this method, particularly in a small town, for an important individual to escape detection. Conceivably, though this is also doubtful, an individual who has some impact on a decision might not be detected. But if this person were active in a series of cases his participation would certainly be captured. In rebuttal, it is always possible to raise the specter of decisions being made "behind-the-scenes," unknown to anyone. This is like hunting a beast who always disappears; there is no way to disprove the assertion since, by definition, the activity is not knowable. In every case we examined in which a person has been suggested as working "behind-the-scenes," the allegation turned out to be false. It would certainly surprise those active in community affairs to learn that someone, they knew not who, was really doing all these things. Only a systematic error in which case after case failed to include key events would invalidate our conclusions.

A more likely error is the inclusion of some individuals as minor leaders when, in fact, they are not. It is exceedingly difficult, on occasion, to decide which members of a body like the City Council are the leaders and which the followers. The result may be that one or two people who voted on the winning side, though they followed the lead of others, are included in our lists. Unless this kind of error was repeated in the same way in several issue areas, it would not distort the findings as to the nature of the community's political system.

The careful reader will also observe that it is not always possible to compare the influence exercised by leaders in a particular case. There is the knotty problem of anticipated reaction, designated by Carl Friedrich to cover instances where people do things because they expect counter action from others if they do not. There are subtle "meetings of the minds" where choices are made through a complex interaction and no one knows who is exercising leadership. These difficulties are not insoluble because we do not have to meet them completely. We can always distinguish, at a first level, between those who participated and those who did not. This eliminates most people from consideration. Then we can eliminate those who lost out totally, further reducing the candidates for leadership. Ultimately, we can distinguish between those who had and had not most to do with initiating a successful proposal over opposition, gaining consent for it, or vetoing the proposals of others. The distinction is sometimes fuzzy at the edges but over a series of cases it does serve to make the comparisons essential to determining the structure of leadership.

Although the scope of this investigation is quite wide, including charitable fund raising, and industrial development, as well as issues directly involving governmental bodies, we have obviously not covered the entire gamut of decisions which have impact upon community life. Social control on the job or in the family is not covered unless it is connected with a community decision. Decisions made about College building plans and personnel matters, for instance, may have a considerable impact upon many people as may the decisions of other private organizations. It is safe to say, nonetheless, that whatever the mode of decision making in these organizations, it does not alter the general structure of power in the community, for none is all-inclusive or without restraints upon its activities.

What might be called the problem of the "non-issue" must also be faced. Perhaps, it may be said, the issues which are debated in the community represent the wishes and aspirations only of the small number of activists and not of other citizens whose cultural disadvantages and lack of ability to verbalize prevent them from having their concerns put on the public agenda. If people cannot tell you what is on their minds, of course, there is no way of studying the "non-issues." We have distributed a questionnaire to a random but representative sample of citizens which asked whether there were problems in Oberlin which the individual did not feel were being met. None of the answers referred to a subject that had not been considered by some public body.[4]

No claim is made that Oberlin is representative of other cities. That would be absurd for a town with 6,000 regular residents and 2,000 students. Cities like New York and Chicago are immensely more complex. Their sheer size and population create a different magnitude of problem. But it is also possible to over-emphasize the differences and neglect real similarities. The reader will soon discover that Oberlin is wrestling with many of the same problems—housing, utilities, race relations, industrial development —that confront other cities. Even though Oberlin has a non-partisan election, its campaigns are highly competitive and provide a rough approximation of party strife. The fact that Oberlin has many independent centers of leadership—the College Administration and Faculty, the downtown businessmen, the Co-ops, residents with business affiliations out of town—makes for still greater similarity with larger cities. We will attempt to show that the same theoretical statements can account for the structure of power in those cities, including Oberlin, of which we have some knowledge of decision making. The outstanding difference seems to be that the political space, so to speak, is much fuller in large cities where virtually every conceivable interest has some kind of organizational backing, professional staff, and the formal accoutrements for engaging in policy-politics. Much more specialization is possible and, conceivably, innovation may be more difficult as the likelihood increases that every change will run afoul of some watchdog. At the same time, there are more organizations with full-time personnel who find a need to suggest changes for protection, enhancement, or merely to justify their labors. Although Oberlin is far smaller, the impression that there is more space there may also be correct in a political sense.[5]

Outline

The focus of this study is on what participants actually do to affect community decisions. It is appropriate, therefore, to begin with a survey of interest and activity in public affairs in Oberlin (Chapter 2), an overview of how much activity there is, what kind it is, and how it is distributed among different kinds of people. A description of the structure of power in the past (Chapter 3), facilitates a study of change and stability in the town's political system. The case histories (Chapters 4-15), are the basic data from which conclusions about leadership are drawn. Although an attempt is made to let the cases stand on their own feet, their primary importance is to provide raw material for the study of community power. What connects the cases is the fact that they occurred during the same period of time and dealt with decisions made on a community basis. Most decisions occasioned some controversy; a few brought about impassioned conflict as the community was deeply split. Where an individual's leadership was judged to be particularly outstanding a special study was made of his activities. This accounts for the role studies of Bill Long and the City Manager (Chapters 16 and 17).

The case histories, questionnaires, and role studies enable us to perform analytic operations which provide answers to the fundamental questions we raised about the structure of power in the community. From the case histories and role studies we can determine who the leaders were and what resources they used to control decisions. This, in turn, permits us to comment upon the use, distribution, and effectiveness (in determining community decisions) of resources like wealth, public office, skill, knowledge, control over jobs, and energy (Chapter 18). By administering identical questionnaires to leaders and non-leaders some of the essential social, economic, attitudinal, and activity differences between the two categories of people may be described (Chapter 19). The relationship between a reputation for being influential and the reality of influence can be ascertained by comparing responses to questions about who people think are leaders with what the case histories tell us about who actually exercised leadership (Chapter 20).

Rival models of the structure of power are analyzed with special attention to the implications of theories of mass society (Chapter 21). The key variables found to be operative in the Oberlin study —interest and activity in public affairs, the distribution and use of resources, relationships among leaders—are used to construct a theoretical explanation of pluralist power structure. The theory is then shown to have general relevance through citation of a host of studies in communities of widely varying sizes, locations, and populations (Chapter 22). Finally, an attempt is made to suggest a strategy of participation in a pluralist context for those citizens who wish to take part in controlling community decisions (Chapter 23).

2 THE CITIZENS OF OBERLIN

Oberlin is a small Ohio town, with 8,198 residents as of 1960. Its chief industry is Oberlin College, which is the largest employer and which holds approximately 30% of the town's total property value. The impact of the College is noticeable in the occupations of Oberlin citizens. Professional workers made up 38% of the employed, as compared with 4% in the nation. Service workers made up 8.2% as compared with 3%. Correspondingly fewer operatives, craftsmen and farmers were found. The percentage of laborers and foreign born was roughly proportionate to the national average. The high percentage of Negroes, 24.3%, is related to the original abolitionist fervor of the college founders.

In order to gain basic information about the degree of interest and activity in community affairs in Oberlin, a small survey of 101 respondents was carried out in the Spring and Summer of 1961.[1] Its purpose was to answer the following questions: Who are the active citizens? How many of them are there compared to the apathetic and mildly interested? In what ways do the activists differ from other people? The survey also included a set of social and attitudinal questions designed to suggest hypotheses which might serve to account for these differences.

To obtain as unbiased a sample of residents as possible, names were obtained through a random technique from the billing list of the Oberlin Municipal Electric Plant. This list contains, for all practical purposes, every residence in Oberlin, and is not biased against low income groups as is the telephone list, fringe areas as is the water and sewer list, or the lethargic and newly arrived as is the voting list. An interviewer visited each of the 101 residences, and asked an adult to fill out a questionnaire. In some cases, as with one illiterate, the interviewer filled out the questionnaire upon receiving instructions from the respondent.

A representation of the community adequate for the purpose of this work was obtained. Twenty-four percent of the respondents were Negroes, only .3% less than the adjusted figure from the 1960 census. The breakdowns by sex and income and neighborhood all appear to be quite representative.

Following general lines of categories developed by Robert Dahl in his New Haven study[2] the respondents were separated into active participants, voter-observers, and the apathetic. Active participants are defined as those giving positive answers to five or more out of twelve questions concerning activity. Voter-observers were separated from the remainder by their indication that they had voted in the last city election, leaving the non-voters in the category of the apathetic (Tables 1 and 2). Twenty-three active participants, forty-six voter observers and thirty-two apathetic citizens were found (Table 3).

It was discovered that in Oberlin the number of active participants increased only slightly, from 23% to 26% to 28%, when activity in state and national politics, respectively, was accounted for. Voter-observers increased from 46% to 53% and 58% when asked whether they had voted in state and national elections, respectively. This left only 14% neither active nor interested enough to vote in at least one election when state and national activities were added to local activities (Table 4). Only a quarter or less of the adult citizens of the community are active in its affairs, a larger proportion only vote, and the remainder exist in a state of voluntary disenfranchisement.[2]

T A B L E 1. *Political activity in Oberlin* by kinds of activities*

(In descending order of frequency)

	Yes† %
1. Have you ever been asked to vote for a candidate in a local election in Oberlin?	43

* All the data in these and other tables dealing with citizens are based on a random sample of 101 names on the Municipal Electric Bill list of Oberlin, Ohio, as of April, 1961.

† Number = %.

2. Do you talk to people during political campaigns and try to show them why they should vote for one of the candidates in elections for City Council in Oberlin or in elections for the Board of Education? 42
3. Has anyone ever asked you to support his or her candidacy in a local election in Oberlin? 35
4. Have you ever been asked to serve in any organization in Oberlin? 34
5. In the past year or so have you had any written or spoken contact with political or governmental officials in Oberlin? 30
6. Did you ever try to get someone to run for office in Oberlin or encourage a person to run? 22
7. Do you go to political meetings, rallies, dinners, or things like that in respect to local elections in Oberlin? 21
8. Have you given money or done other things to help in campaigns for local political office in Oberlin? 16
9. During the past year or so have you yourself done anything actively in connection with some local issue or problem, political or non-political? 16
10. Have you ever been asked to serve on a City Council Commission? 5
11. Have you ever held public office? 5
12. Have you ever held an office or had a job in a political party? 4

TABLE 2. *Political activity in Oberlin by the number of kinds of activities*

	% (Number = %)
No Activities	29
One Kind of Activity	18
Two Kinds of Activity	15
Three and Four Kinds of Activity	16
Five, Six and Seven Kinds of Activity	16
Eight to Twelve Kinds of Activity	7

TABLE 3. *Division of community by level of activity*

	% (Number = %)
Active Participants (Those responding positively to five or more of the questions in Table 1 and who also vote)	23
Voter-Observers (Those answering positively less than five of the questions in Table 1, and indicating that they had voted in the last city election)	46
Apathetic (Those answering positively less than five of the questions in Table 1, and failing to indicate or indicating that they had not voted in the last city election)	32

TABLE 4. *Participation and non-participation in local, state and national politics*

	Active Participants %	Voter-Observers %	Apathetic %
Local	23	46	32
State	26	53	21
National	28	58	14

It may appear unnecessary to test for interest in community affairs because it is obvious that the activists will score highest in that category. Although interest is a prerequisite for activity, the expression of interest does not necessarily mean that activity will follow. We need to know precisely how interest is related to activity and whether there are many people who claim they are interested but do not actually participate in public affairs.

By asking an open ended question, "What things are you most concerned with these days?" coding the answers according to type of response, and allowing any number of replies, it is possible to get an approximate notion of the things which concern our respondents according to their degree of participation. The overwhelming conclusion in Table 5 is that personal matters—jobs, money, family, children, health—are far more important for all three categories than public affairs. Within the categories, however, public affairs, though a poor second, is correspondingly more important to the activists than the others. At the same time, a little under one-third of the apathetics and observers claim to be interested in public affairs but participate little if at all.

When questions are phrased so as to try to catch rough degrees of interest in politics (Tables 6-9), we see that most activists are very much interested while most apathetics are only somewhat

TABLE 5. *Concerns of active and non-active: summary*
What things are you most concerned with these days?

	Active Participants %	Voter-Observers %	Apathetic %	% of Total Sample
Personal Affairs	39	57	53	52
Public Affairs	22	11	22	17
Both	22	13	9	14
Blank	18	20	16	18

Concerns of active and non-active* in further detail

	Active Participants %	Voter-Observers %	Apathetic %	% of Total Sample
Job, money, etc.	43	39	34	39
Home, family, children	18	35	25	29
Other personal matters	18	24	16	22
Health	13	9	9	7
World situation, war, communism	13	15	19	16
Local issues or problems	26	11	9	14
National issues or problems	18	20	19	18
Blank	13	9	16	12

* All responses coded.

TABLE 6. *Thinking about events in the last month or so, would you say that you have been very much interested in political affairs, somewhat interested, or not interested at all?*

	Active Participants %	Voter-Observers %	Apathetic %	% of Total Sample
Very	65	52	16	44
Somewhat	35	39	59	45
Not	0	4	9	5
No answer	0	4	16	7

TABLE 7. *Generally speaking would you say that you care a great deal about what goes on in local politics?*

	Active Participants %	Voter-Observers %	Apathetic %	% of Total Sample
Yes	91	67	44	65
No	9	28	53	32
No answer	0	4	3	3

interested and the observers are in-between. Along the same lines, at least one half of the respondents in each category are willing to say that they talk on some occasion about local affairs (the activ-

TABLE 8. *When you and your friends get together, do you ever talk about Oberlin politics and local affairs?*

	Active Participants %	Voter-Observers %	Apathetic %	% of Total Sample
Yes	95	76	50	72
No	4	13	41	20
No answer	0	11	9	8

TABLE 9. *Do you talk about Oberlin politics and local affairs a great deal?*

	Active Participants %	Voter-Observers %	Apathetic %	% of Total Sample
Yes	61	21	9	26
No	30	63	75	60
No answer	9	15	15	14

ists, of course, being way ahead), but only 9% of the apathetics and 21% of the observers say that they talk a great deal about local politics compared to 61% of the activists. What these figures imply is that it is not enough to be vaguely interested; if activity is to follow the individual must be very interested or care a great deal. It is not interest *per se*—even three-quarters of the apathetics claimed some interest in the previous month—but the intensity with which the interest is held that increases the probability of leading to activity in public affairs.

A glance at these tables reveal that there is a great deal of slippage between caring (Table 7), being interested in (Table 6), and going so far as to talk about local affairs a great deal (Table 9). Approximately one third of the activists, two-thirds of the voter-observers, and four-fifths of the apathetics are lost in the route from caring a great deal to talking about local affairs. The more one cares, the more one is interested, and the more one speaks about local affairs; but activists translate more of their care and interest into talking activity than do observers and apathetics in that order. Clearly, other factors must be introduced to account for the varying degrees of slippage.

Race makes little difference, but females are much less likely than males to be active (Table 10). Active participants tend to be slightly older than the average, apathetics have lived fewer than the average number of years in Oberlin, and a higher percentage of activists than observers or apathetics are married. No doubt wider participation is induced through longer residence and family contacts and needs.

Substantial differences in education, annual incomes, and ascribed class were discovered. Sixty-five percent of the apathetics received no more than a high school education, while only 26% of the active participants discontinued their education at that point. The figure for voter-observers lies between the two points at 43% (Table 11).

TABLE 10.   *Selected characteristics of activists and non-activists*

	Active Participants	Voter-Observers	Apathetic	% of Total Sample
Race				
Negro	26%	20%	29%	24
White	74%	80%	72%	77
Sex				
Female	26%	56%	53%	49
Male	74%	44%	47%	51
Average Age (years)	48.1	46.2	41.9	45.3
Average Length of Residence (years)	21.6	22.8	17.4	21.2
Married	96%	80%	69%	80
Unmarried	4%	17%	31%	19
Blank	0	2	0	1

TABLE 11.   *Education of activists and non-activists*

	Active Participants %	Voter-Observers %	Apathetic %	% of Total Sample
Did not complete High School	9	16	29	18
High School Diploma	17	27	36	27
Did not complete College	0	5	14	6
College Degree	32	20	10	20
Graduate Work	17	7	4	9
Doctorate	17	9	4	10
Business Education	4	11	4	6
Registered Nurse	4	0	0	1
Music Education	0	5	0	2

None of the active participants fell into the lowest income group, although 22% of the voter-observers, and 30% of the apathetic did. Median income for active participants was between $7,500 and $10,000, for voter-observers between $5,000 and $7,500, and for apathetics between $3,000 and $5,000 (Table 12).

Nine percent of the active participants placed themselves in the working class, as compared with 20% of the voter-observers and 44% of the apathetic (Table 13). Thirteen percent of the active participants claimed membership in the upper class, while only 7% of the voter-observers and none of the apathetic placed themselves in this category.

Considerably more information about politics is possessed by activists than by observers and apathetics in that order. Using the simplest kind of test (Table 14), we discover that activists are way ahead in naming the Mayor of Oberlin and the local Congressmen. The exceedingly low level of information possessed by apathetics is highlighted by the ability of only 19% to name Mosher as their Congressman though he was a prominent local resident, for many years publisher of the town paper. State politics appears to have receded from virtually everyone's consciousness (there are two senators representing Oberlin and either one was accepted as correct), although the activists still do better than the rest.

These conclusions are strengthened by a survey of newspaper reading (Table 15). As we would expect, more activists than observers or apathetics read the New York Times, both major out-of-town papers and the local paper, or either out-of-town paper and the local paper, or just a paper published out of town.

TABLE 12. *Annual income claimed by activists and non-activists*
(Those failing to answer excluded)

	Active Participants	Voter- Observers	Apathetic	% of Total Sample
	%	%	%	
Less than $3,000	0	22	30	17
Less than $5,000	20	24	33	26
Less than $7,500	20	35	16	24
Between $7,500 and $10,000	35	11	7	18
Between $10,000 and $15,000	20	8	4	11
Over $15,000	5	0	7	4

TABLE 13. *Class self-ratings of activists and non-activists*

	Active Participants %	Voter-Observers %	Apathetic %	% of Total Sample
Working Class	9	20	44	24
Lower Middle Class	4	11	3	6
Middle Class	26	33	31	30
Upper Middle Class	26	13	9	16
Upper Class	13	7	0	7
No Answer	22	17	13	17

TABLE 14. *Information*

	Active Participants %	Voter-Observers %	Apathetic %	% of Total Sample
Name of Mayor				
Correct	70	46	28	46
Incorrect	30	54	72	54
Name of Senator				
Correct	9	4	0	4
Incorrect	91	96	100	96
Name of Congressman				
Correct	83	57	19	50
Incorrect	17	43	81	50

TABLE 15. *Reading papers*

	Active Participants %	Voter-Observers %	Apathetic %	% of Total Sample
Either major out of town paper (Cleveland *Plain Dealer* or Elyria *Chronicle Telegram*)	26	20	22	22
Either major out of town paper and local paper	35	28	16	29
Both major out of town papers and local paper	22	17	6	13
Only local paper	0	9	4	7
Neither major out of town papers nor local paper	8	16	33	20
New York *Times* readers	22	13	6	12

It is tempting to speak of activity as largely a product of income, education and ascribed class. But these characteristics may be at least partly attributes of people who are active for other reasons. Dahl noted significant socio-economic differences among active participants in New Haven, and pointed out that the common characteristic of these people was that they tended to be active in a large number of non-governmental organizations as well as being involved in political affairs. The Oberlin study also reveals that active participants are distinguished by a general quality of activism (Tables 16 and 17). Activists in political affairs belong to more non-governmental organizations than voter-observers or apathetics, are more often officers, and attend meetings more regularly.[3]

T A B L E 16. *Organization membership of activists and non-activists*

	Active Participants %	Voter- Observers %	Apathetic %	% of Total Sample
No organizations	17	54	63	49
Less than five organizations	57	39	37	45
Five or more organizations	26	7	0	7
Officer of one or more organizations	43	24	6	23

T A B L E 17. *Attendance at meetings by activists and non-activists*

	Active Participants %	Voter- Observers %	Apathetic %	% of Total Sample
Seldom	6	18	30	17
Regularly	89	77	60	77
Always	6	5	10	6

In order to test whether the degree of activity also reflects some basic attitudes toward life and the political world the respondents were asked to react to a series of statements by checking spaces titled, "agree strongly, agree somewhat, no opinion, disagree somewhat, disagree strongly." An attempt was made to choose statements which would be closely related to the attitude—sense of civic obligation, sense of efficacy, aggressiveness—which they were designed to measure in an indirect way.

There is no mistaking the exceedingly high sense of civic obligation manifested by the activists as compared to the observers and apathetics in Tables 18 and 19.[4] They strongly believe that a person ought to participate in community affairs even if he does not like it and they strongly disagree with the idea that it is best to stay out of community affairs. There are, of course, some apathetics who share these feelings but they are far fewer. The observers are situated in the middle. The extent to which civic obligation is internalized within the individual is obviously a significant component of participation in community affairs.

Activity implies a conviction that one's actions are important and may be effective. It should come as no surprise, therefore, to learn that the activists overwhelmingly disagree with the statement that what the government does is not important for the individual and that observers and apathetics follow suit at a much lower rate. Another way of stating the relationships in Table 20 would be that most people believe that what the government does affects the life of the individual, but that many more activists believe this than others, and that approximately one-quarter of the apathetics and one-fifth of the observers actually disagree. It is difficult to know whether these apathetics and observers do not participate because they think it is not important or think it is not important because they do not choose to participate or both. No doubt the very fact of engaging in activity reinforces the activists' belief in the significance of his actions.

Following in this pattern we discover that most apathetics and observers agree that government and politics is sometimes so complicated that people like themselves cannot really understand what

TABLE 18. *"Whether he likes it or not a person ought to take part in community affairs."*

	Active Participants %	Voter-Observers %	Apathetic %	% of Total Sample
Agree Strongly	69	30	19	36
Agree Somewhat	26	37	38	35
Disagree Somewhat		13	9	9
Disagree Strongly		7	16	8
No Opinion		7	19	9
No Answer	4	7		4

TABLE 19. *"It is generally best to stay out of community affairs."*

	Active Participants %	Voter-Observers %	Apathetic %	% of Total Sample
Agree Strongly	4	4	9	6
Agree Somewhat	4	9	16	10
Disagree Somewhat	30	30	25	29
Disagree Strongly	57	41	25	40
No Opinion		9	19	10
No Answer	4	7	6	6

TABLE 20. *"A person's life is not affected very much by what the government does or does not do."*

	Active Participants %	Voter-Observers %	Apathetic %	% of Total Sample
Agree Strongly		7	16	8
Agree Somewhat	4	13	19	13
Disagree Somewhat	18	24	19	21
Disagree Strongly	74	41	34	47
No Opinion	4	7	9	7
No Answer		9	3	5

is going on, but that most activists disagree (Table 21). It is also true, however, that about two-fifths of the activists either agree strongly or somewhat that this statement is correct and that a little less than one-third of the observers and apathetics take a contrary view. This implies that while activists do definitely have a higher sense of political efficacy than observers and apathetics, the political world seems terribly complicated even to a substantial minority of those who are actively engaged in it. Conversely, a feeling that one does understand is not sufficient by itself to lead to activity for a substantial number of observers and apathetics.

These inferences are reinforced by Table 22 in which over three-quarters of the activists disagree strongly or somewhat with the statement that public officials do not care what people like them think, while only approximately one-half of the observers and apathetics share this belief. The many surveys which find that activity is related in a high and positive way to a sense of efficacy are borne out.[5]

American society appears to be characterized by ambivalence toward the exercise of power: people should not exercise power over others, but, at the same time, positive actions should be taken and things should get done in the government. Through Table 23 we discover that the entire community appears to be split on the question of whether anyone should exercise control over others but that the apathetics take a more negative view while the activists take a more positive view. Although the activists are split rather evenly a greater proportion of that group (about one-half) disagree with the statement that no one should exercise power over others compared to one-third of the voter-observers and one-quarter of the apathetics. There is thus a somewhat greater probability that individuals among the activists will prove disposed to exercise power over others. When the statement is phrased to refer directly to government activities (Table 24), our expectation is borne out as a greater proportion of activists agree strongly and fewer disagree strongly than people in the other categories that "public officials have to exercise power over others in order to do their jobs." But we also find that only the observers disagree more than they agree. It may be that governmental action confers legitimacy on the exercise of power so as to make it more palatable to citizens, especially the apathetic and the active. This, in turn, suggests the hypothesis that governmental legitimacy leads activists to resolve ambivalence toward the exercise of power and leads apathetics to accept the power-wielding actions of others.

A feeling of social adequacy may predispose individuals to become activists and the experience of activity may contribute to this feeling of adequacy. This hypothesis is supported by Table 25 in

TABLE 21. *"Sometimes politics and government seem so complicated that people like me can't really understand what is going on."*

	Active Participants %	Voter-Observers %	Apathetic %	% of Total Sample
Agree Strongly	13	17	25	19
Agree Somewhat	26	37	31	33
Disagree Somewhat	26	9	22	17
Disagree Strongly	26	22	9	19
No Opinion	9	11	13	11
No Answer		4		2

TABLE 22. *"Public officials do not care much what people like me think."*

	Active Participants %	Voter-Observers %	Apathetic %	% of Total Sample
Agree Strongly	9	9	13	10
Agree Somewhat	9	24	19	19
Disagree Somewhat	43	30	34	35
Disagree Strongly	35	24	9	22
No Opinion		9	22	11
No Answer	4	4	3	4

TABLE 23. *"No one should exercise power or control over others."*

	Active Participants %	Voter-Observers %	Apathetic %	% of Total Sample
Agree Strongly	35	22	38	30
Agree Somewhat	9	24	25	21
Disagree Somewhat	30	26	16	24
Disagree Strongly	18	11	9	12
No Opinion	4	2	9	5
No Answer	4	15	3	9

which activists agree less and disagree more with the idea that it is hard for the respondent to find anything to talk about when he meets a new person than do observers or apathetics. A majority of all three categories disagree to some extent but the activists manifest a higher proportion of feelings of adequacy in this common kind of social situation.

Not only do activists appear to feel more socially adequate, they also more frequently have definite ideas in social conversation and

TABLE 24. *"Public officials have to exercise power over others in order to do their job."*

	Active Participants %	Voter-Observers %	Apathetic %	% of Total Sample
Agree Strongly	26	4	9	11
Agree Somewhat	35	30	47	37
Disagree Somewhat	26	22	19	22
Disagree Strongly	4	26	9	16
No Opinion	4	9	9	8
No Answer	4	9	6	7

TABLE 25. *"It is hard for me to find anything to talk about when I meet a new person."*

	Active Participants %	Voter-Observers %	Apathetic %	% of Total Sample
Agree Strongly	0	9	6	5
Agree Somewhat	13	24	19	20
Disagree Somewhat	48	28	34	37
Disagree Strongly	26	28	31	28
No Opinion	9	7	3	6
No Answer	4	4	6	5

TABLE 26. *"In social conversation I frequently have definite ideas and try to convince others."*

	Active Participants %	Voter-Observers %	Apathetic %	% of Total Sample
Agree Strongly	35	17	16	21
Agree Somewhat	43	46	34	42
Disagree Somewhat	18	15	9	14
Disagree Strongly		9	13	8
No Opinion	4	11	22	13
No Answer		2	6	3

try to convince others (Table 26). Over three-quarters of the activists agreed with this statement as compared to less than two-thirds of the observers and two-fifths of the apathetics. None of the activists disagreed strongly. Public speaking may be a trying experience, and most activists say they do not enjoy it, but more than twice as many have positive feelings (39%) than do the apathetics (15%) as Table 27 shows. These figures suggest that activists are characterized by a more confident and positive attitude toward social life than are others.[6] In fact, activists apparently have more opinions of all kinds, since they consistently show fewer "no opinion" and "no answer" responses to the questionnaire.

Activity requires vigor and the data in Table 28 bear out our hypothesis that the activists would feel that they were healthier. Considering the low incomes of some apathetics, and the accompanying conditions, this may actually be the case. It may also be that these self-ratings indicate a somewhat more confident view of their personal condition on the part of the activists. Some support

TABLE 27. *Do you enjoy speaking in public?*

	Active Participants %	Voter-Observers %	Apathetic %	% of Total Sample
Yes	39	28	15	27
No	57	61	88	66
No Answer	4	11	6	8

for this inference comes from Table 29 where activists disagree much more and agree less with the statement that "it is not wise to plan too far ahead." A belief in the desirability of planning ahead indicates confidence in one's ability to control the future, although it may also reflect indoctrination in middle class mores in the values of personal planning.

TABLE 28. *Would you say that you were in good health, fair health, or poor health?*

	Active Participants %	Voter-Observers %	Apathetic %	% of Total Sample
Good	83	78	71	77
Fair	16	22	29	23
Poor				

TABLE 29. *"It is not wise to plan too far ahead."*

	Active Participants %	Voter-Observers %	Apathetic %	% of Total Sample
Agree Strongly	13	15	9	13
Agree Somewhat	18	26	34	27
Disagree Somewhat	26	35	9	25
Disagree Strongly	43	13	31	28
No Opinion		2		1
No Answer		9	16	7

In line with their greater feelings of social adequacy and their more positive approach to social life, activists are more disposed to be venturesome in argument. They disagree more and agree less with the statement, "I prefer not to take sides in arguments between people I know," than is the case with observers or apathetics (Table 30). Yet just under half of the activists agree to some extent with this statement. At the same time, activists agree to a slightly greater extent than others that "a person might lose friends if he gets too involved in community issues" (Table 31). Apparently, those who do participate are, if anything even more sensitive than observers or apathetics to the possible disruptive consequences for their social life. This feeling is also shared by a majority of the community which indicates that those who are especially fearful of losing friends or incurring hostility, and who do not have other compensations, may well prefer to limit their activities.

TABLE 30. *"I prefer not to take sides in an argument between people I know."*

	Active Participants %	Voter-Observers %	Apathetic %	% of Total Sample
Agree Strongly	18	30	42	31
Agree Somewhat	30	33	22	29
Disagree Somewhat	35	17	9	19
Disagree Strongly	9	9	16	11
No Opinion	4	9	6	7
No Answer	4	2	6	4

Compensations to the active might include pleasure from increased social interaction, opportunities to express themselves, indulging their sense of civic obligation, exercising power in a legitimatized setting, and the special interests a few may have in gaining office or favorable decisions which affect them personally. Another possible source of compensation for the disabilities of participation is the comparatively greater rate at which the activists manifest a need for achievement as indicated by their responses to the statement in Table 32. "I feel that nothing else that life can offer is a substitute for greater achievement." The observers and apathetics disagree more than they agree while the activists are evenly split, though those who disagree tend to feel more strongly about it. In his "The Fear of Equality," Robert Lane has hypothesized that the belief in equal opportunity and hard striving poses a threat to many people because it is an implied judgment that they had the chance but failed in comparison to others.[7] All we can say is that more of the activists desire to set a high standard than the other respondents. Activity in the public realm, though fraught with the possibility of failure, provides this opportunity.

TABLE 31. "A person might lose friends if he gets too involved in community issues."

	Active Participants %	Voter-Observers %	Apathetic %	% of Total Sample
Agree Strongly	13	13	22	16
Agree Somewhat	57	35	38	41
Disagree Somewhat	9	22	22	19
Disagree Strongly	4	17	9	12
No Opinion	9	4	9	7
No Answer	9	9		6

TABLE 32. "I feel that nothing else that life can offer is a substitute for great achievement."

	Active Participants %	Voter-Observers %	Apathetic %	% of Total Sample
Agree Strongly	9	9	13	10
Agree Somewhat	35	9	13	16
Disagree Somewhat	17	22	31	24
Disagree Strongly	26	33	19	27
No Opinion	9	22	22	19
No Answer	4	7	3	5

Turning now to questions designed to test views of human nature (Tables 33 and 34), we discover widespread agreement that "most people are good and kind." Opinion is fairly well split on the statement that "anyone who completely trusts anyone else is looking for trouble," but there are little or no differences between people in the categories we are using. A hypothesis which might explain this finding is that the distinguishing attitudes of activists and apathetics are to be found in their feelings toward the government and community affairs, and in their related feelings of social adequacy, rather than in more general human traits such as trust in others, suspicion, views of human nature and the like. To understand politics it may be essential to focus on it, its defining qualities, its related attributes, rather than searching in the wider realm of human behavior.

Summing up, we find that activists are distinguished by social characteristics—high income, education, perceived class—and by a set of predisposing attitudes—sense of efficacy, civic obligation, governmental importance—centering on their relationship to the civic arena. The social characteristics alone are not adequate for they leave unexplained the apathetic who share them and the activists who do not. The predisposing attitudes appear to be more satisfactory but they leave open the question of how and why these attitudes are acquired. Perhaps the best that can be done is to conceive of the social characteristics as defining the probability of engaging in life experiences which will develop the skills and indoctrinate the attitudes leading to participation. These skills—talking, writing, organizing—are not monopolized by any one group or class, the facilitating attitudes are widely propagated, and life experience is sufficiently varied to give some people who do not possess the indicated social characteristics the required experience.

TABLE 33. *"Most people are basically good and kind."*

	Active Participants %	Voter-Observers %	Apathetic %	% of Total Sample
Agree Strongly	26	30	25	28
Agree Somewhat	43	50	42	46
Disagree Somewhat	9	13	16	13
Disagree Strongly	9	2	3	4
No Opinion	9		9	5
No Answer	4	4	6	5

TABLE 34. *"Anyone who completely trusts anyone else is looking for trouble."*

	Active Participants %	Voter-Observers %	Apathetic %	% of Total Sample
Agree Strongly	9	13	9	11
Agree Somewhat	35	20	25	23
Disagree Somewhat	26	26	26	28
Disagree Strongly	26	28	28	28
No Opinion		2	3	2
No Answer	4	11	9	9

3   OBERLIN IN THE PAST

The desirability of describing the political systems of the past in order to suggest explanations for stability or change in leadership, necessitates historical investigation. But the approach described in the first chapter cannot be used because information on which to base detailed case histories is lacking. The method adopted for the decades between 1927 and 1957 is to use local newspapers and documents in order to compile extensive lists of the positions taken by the various participants and the outcomes of the issues. In this manner we can tell in a rudimentary way whether certain individuals and groups consistently triumphed or were defeated. At the very least, we can tell whether participants who were alleged to be influential by informants living in Oberlin during that period did not actually suffer defeats on important matters. Clearly, this method is by no means wholly satisfactory. It misses the dynamics of policy, is dependent upon accurate reporting, and is subject to a variety of biases. All that we claim is that this method is helpful in making the gross distinctions between political systems on which to base comparisons. If such a technique were used for the period covered intensively by this study, it would contain errors but would lead us in the right direction. In any event, it is better than sheer guesswork.

If we attempted to list the positions taken by participants and the outcomes of decision for the years between 1833 and 1927, we would need to write another volume. In order to suggest the kinds of changes in leadership which have taken place in Oberlin during its first decades, therefore, we have followed Dahl and adopted the expedient of compiling biographical information on the men who served as Mayor from the granting of the City Charter in 1846 until the form of government was changed from strong-mayor to council-manager in 1927. These men were formally the ranking officials in town. They had wide executive powers and we know from a fairly extensive body of historical writing and biographical references[1] that they made active use of these powers.

1833-1869

Oberlin was settled in 1833 as the result of the desire of an ardent reformer, John Shipherd, to do his part to save "our perishing world" from the multitude of ways in which it had departed from the true path of God. His purpose was to found a college, removed from the distractions of a secular world, in which young people would be educated in the ways of the Lord, and from which they would go forth and, by the force of example and through teaching, aid in the salvation of mankind.

The men and women who followed Shipherd held, to a greater or lesser degree, his evangelical conviction of the righteousness of his cause and the Christian duty of pursuing it, but many of them also held values foreign to him. Secularism invaded the colony early, and Shipherd's desire that the land be held in common, that profit be foregone in men's transactions, and that fancy dress and food be avoided were quickly frustrated. Yet elements of moral evangelicism, not completely absent today, persisted, especially a strong feeling of knowing and doing right, which enabled the community to take extreme positions against liquor and Masonry and for abolitionism and radical Republicanism.

Although local businessmen have always been suitable candidates for Mayor in Oberlin, the period from its founding until after the Civil War witnessed the appearance of men with strong convictions who challenged the existing order of things in their society. Isaac Jennings, author of a book on *Medical Reform*, believed that drugs were harmful and became a "no-medicine" physician, advocating vegetable diets, bathing, and abstinence from tea and coffee, and condemning tightly laced dresses. After his term as Mayor in 1849, Jennings became chairman of the Oberlin Peace League. He was a member of the College Board of Trustees for many years. Jabez W. "Deacon" Merrill, Mayor in 1851 and

1855, active in Oberlin's First Church and the American Missionary Society, was a persistent opponent of secret societies, intemperance, slavery, and tobacco. He was a trustee of Oberlin College from 1855 to 1878. James Dascomb, Mayor in 1853, was one of the first abolitionists in Oberlin, and was a member of the Liberty Convention of 1841. He was a Professor of Chemistry, Botany, and Physiology. David R. Brocaw and A. N. Beecher, who served from 1856-1859, were men of great abolitionist fervor. There are records showing them assisting fugitive slaves. Acting in his position as a leader of the community, Mayor Samuel Hendry called a mass meeting to rally the populace to the Union cause after the firing on Fort Sumter. Later, he became a member of the College Board of Trustees. John Millot Ellis, Professor of Mental and Moral Philosophy, acting President of the College, and pastor of the Second Congregational Church, presided as Mayor over a meeting which passed a resolution calling for immediate emancipation in 1862. By this time Oberlin had become overwhelmingly Republican and Ellis was a delegate to the Republican State Convention in 1865. In Mayor Samuel Plumb (1864-1865), reform and business seem to have gone hand-in-hand. He was Secretary of the Oberlin Bible Society and the builder of the gas works, organizer of the Loyalty League to combat "copperheads" and President of the First National Bank, purchaser of a saw mill and a nurse to Oberlin boys wounded in battle, incorporator of the Oberlin Woolen Manufacturing Company and vigorous opponent of President Andrew Johnson's policy of reconstruction. The next Mayor, General Giles Waldo Shurtleff, a noted orator and scholar, was wounded twice while leading his colored troops during a desperate charge. Upon his return to Oberlin, he became Professor of Latin and headed a successful campaign to raise funds needed to save the Theological Seminary. After his term as Mayor in 1869, Shurtleff served as Secretary and Treasurer of the College and leader of the Temperance Alliance and the Board of Commerce.

After Shurtleff, the list of Mayors settles down to a practically unbroken line of businessmen; civil war veterans, Republicans, temperance advocates, and pillars of the church many of them still, but they were men who knew their place in society rather than men ready to change it. Coming to Oberlin from another community, they started out in business and were successful. Soon they began to take part in Republican politics, were made officers in various local organizations, and eventually became Mayor. Though engaged in some religious and charitable work, the post-Civil War Mayors appear to have devoted themselves largely to business endeavors.

The biographical material on Oberlin's Mayors (see Chart A), as well as the various histories of the town, reveal a remarkably consistent pattern. Most of the Mayors came to Oberlin from another location. Many arrived with little or no financial resources and made themselves wealthy through their own efforts. Evangelism arrived in the company of the profit motive and never fought very hard against it. The moralist and the scholar soon gave way to the businessman as the leading citizen in the community. More so than today, the staff of Oberlin College seems to have come from the same stock as the townspeople and to have shared their values. While the exceptionally close relationship of the early years was not maintained, the ways of College and town did not materially diverge.

The position of the substantial Negro community requires a special explanation. The anti-slavery stand which Oberlin took before the Civil War made it a place free colored people could come to where their existence as permanent residents was encouraged or at least accepted. The run-away Negro found aid in Oberlin for his journey to Canada and those who wished to remain were relatively secure from slave-catchers, hidden in the free Negro population and under the watchful eyes of the abolitionists. Negroes comprised 25% of the town's population in 1860.

Although socializing and mixing with whites where common values were held was not taboo, Negroes in Oberlin made up their own community. Sometime in the 1860's separate colored churches came into existence. Whether this was, as Fairchild relates, because Negroes preferred a different style of service,[2] or for other reasons, we cannot tell. It is clear, however, that out of preference or necessity, Negroes did not participate in governing the town. They acquiesced, at least, in the standards of political legitimacy of the white community.

So far as the white citizens were concerned, there appears to

CHART A. *Oberlin mayors*

Name	Years in office	Occupation	Original home
1. Lewis Holtslander	1847-8	Businessman	
2. Isaac Jennings	1849	"no-medicine" Physician	Fairfield, Connecticut
3. O. R. Ryder	1850, 1855	Businessman	
4. J. W. Merrill	1851, 1855	Trustee of College	Pittstown, New York
5. Uriah Thompson	1852	Trustee of College	Vermont
6. James Dascomb	1853	Professor in College	New Hampshire
7. David Brokaw	1856-7	Businessman	Pennsylvania
8. A. N. Beecher	1858-9	Businessman	
9. Samuel Hendry	1860-1	Agent	
10. J. M. Ellis	1862-3	Professor in College	Oberlin, Ohio
11. Samuel Plumb	1864-5	Businessman	
12. E. J. Goodrich	1866-7	Businessman	
13. G. W. Shurtleff	1868	War hero, Professor	Quebec, Canada
14. W. H. Backus	1869-73	Businessman	
15. Montraville Stone	1874-5	Farmer, Justice of Peace	
16. George F. Hutchings	1876-7	Farmer, Businessman	
17. J. B. T. Marsh	1878-81	Editor, College Trustee	Connecticut
18. J. B. Clarke	1881-4	Insurance & Land Agent	
19. Charles A. Metcalf	1884-8	Attorney	Liverpool, Ohio
20. Arden Dale	1888-92	House Agent, Justice of Peace	Vermont
21. O. F. Carter	1892, 1904-8, 1910	Businessman	New York
22. A. G. Comings	1892-6	Businessman	Vermont
23. Alfred Fauver	1896-1904	Politician, Businessman	Eaton, Ohio
24. M. G. Dick	1904	Businessman	Ohio
25. Joseph Wolfe	1908-9,	Businessman	
26. C. P. Doolittle	1909-10, 1910-12	Professor in College	
27. J. D. Yocum	1912-18	Teacher, Businessman	Pennsville, Ohio
28. W. H. Phillips	1918-22	Editor	Iowa
29. H. F. Smith	1922-6	Businessman	

have been remarkably little open conflict within the community. On rare occasions, a conflict within the Republican party would break out. The inept handling of the gas-rate issue resulted in the defeat of an incumbent mayor in the Republican primary of 1907. But Oberlin remained a community in which the highest status could be reached by a man of the lowest origins, and those who did not rise in life apparently made no challenge to the *status quo* or leadership by businessmen.

It is not difficult to account for this state of affairs. There have been no great tides of immigration into Oberlin creating a numerically superior ethnic group which would make a bid for leadership. Nor has there been any substantial intrusion of industry which might have created sets of industrial and union leaders who were disposed to challenge the local businessmen. Originally united in their moral fervor, brought closer together in the crucible of the Civil War, sharing a Republican party identification, remaining part of a college town, the citizens of Oberlin were not disposed to challenge the existing order.

1930-1940

Of the twelve different men who were elected or appointed to City Council during this period, nine were local businessmen and three were associated with Oberlin College. Only one was a Democrat and he later changed his registration to Republican.

At the beginning of the 1930's, the Oberlin community faced the depression. Private local efforts through the Community Chest and the local Red Cross provided some relief. In 1932 the City Council set up a relief program, offering work to unemployed who were paid in kind at the stores of Oberlin merchants. Ira Porter, an official of the Peoples Bank, directed a community garden project, but experienced difficulties in getting the unemployed to care for their plots which were to provide them with subsistence. He also led the relief drive. State employment was made available, and by 1935 WPA work was done on the streets and in cleaning Plum Creek.

By far the most important action of the Council in these years was the building of the electric plant, briefly described in Chapter 5. Led by Mayor Morris and City Manager Sears, the Council took the initiative in hiring an engineer who made a survey showing the advantages the plant would have for Oberlin. A citizens committee, led by Ira Porter and aided by the support of the Business Men's Club, the *News-Tribune,* and Oberlin College, successfully publicized the bond issue. Voters decided a referendum in favor of the plant, consumers decided a rate war started by the Ohio Electric Power Company, and the courts decided a court case in favor of the city.[3]

The Board of Education proved a source of controversial decisions in this decade. In 1932 they dropped teachers' salaries by 20%, restoring them to their former level only at the end of the decade. They took the initiative in building recreation rooms in the schools, and obtained the consent of the City Council for the use of some city land for the purpose. With Ira Porter taking the lead, the Board spent a couple of years successfully fighting off attacks by interested citizens, including some College people, over the use of a room for music practice which had been designated for an opportunity class in a referendum. The Board successfully refused to rehire the teacher of the opportunity classes and eliminated them. It also withstood demands that supervision for play periods be provided.

When Russia township voters refused to pass school levies to pay for the education of their children in Oberlin schools, the Board of Education threatened to exclude them from the schools. This was sufficient to stir the township to pass a school levy, and start reducing the amount they owed to Oberlin.

Throughout these controversies, the School Board managed to retain the confidence of Oberlin voters and no levy they submitted was ever defeated.

In 1930, City Manager Sears successfully recommended turning down a request for a water line on North Pleasant Street which he anticipated would not pay for itself out of the additional rates it would bring. City Manager Zahm, who succeeded Sears, also followed a policy of opposing uneconomical extensions.

Led by Ira Porter, the Business Men's Club, together with support from the *News-Tribune,* the League of Women Voters, the

Non-Partisan Committee and the Young Men's Club, successfully advocated legislation in 1937 requiring all milk sold in town to be pasteurized.

A proposal by the Zoning Board of Appeals that the south side of West Lorain Street from Prospect Street west be made a commercial district was turned down by Council when it was presented with a petition, signed by the residents of the area, protesting the proposed action. In 1936 the voters passed a bond issue for street lighting proposed by City Manager Zahm. In 1938, when the College asked that the city pay a larger share of the cost of the Public Library, the voters passed a levy of one-half mill over the objections of the *News-Tribune*. In 1939, however, they proved they were not soft touches by turning down a levy for the Firemen's relief and pension fund.

The 1930's saw a man who still participates in town politics, Ira Porter, at the height of his activity when he was involved in numerous projects. Porter had just completed eight years of service on the City Council when the decade began, and he served on the Board of Education throughout this period. At one time or another he became the highest official of the Lorain County Bankers Association, the Exchange Club, the Business Men's Club, the Oberlin Credit Association, the Ohio Exchange Club, and the Community Chest drive. He led the relief drive, the campaign committee for the light plant, and the efforts to secure pasteurization of milk.

Porter had several *coups* to his credit. In the 1920's, while chairman of the Police Committee on Council, he often went on "booze" raids, at one time getting credit for the single-handed capture of a "boozer" with his .38. At this time, when the high school was being constructed, Porter noticed that adequate drainage was not being provided, and protested to the Board of Education. When the floors rotted out and had to be replaced three years later, Porter's reputation for alertness was enhanced. In 1933, Porter was able to anticipate the Bank Holiday, and drove to Cleveland to withdraw the funds of the Peoples Bank from their depository. The Peoples Bank was able to open the day after the banks were closed because of this measure, while the other bank remained closed for at least a week, until the College deposited a large fund to put it on its feet. In 1937, when the businessmen were trying to have Highway 20 rerouted five miles south of the town, a committee was appointed to persuade the State Highway Director in Columbus to make the proposed extension. Unsuccessful, it broke up and left. Porter, however, stayed behind and succeeded in persuading the Director.

What conclusions may be drawn from this survey of decisions in the 1930's? In the first place, it would appear that little alteration in the kind of men voted into office took place. Only three councilmen, and no mayors were College people, and only one was a Democrat. The rest were local businessmen. Second, the Negro community still lay dormant, any available bases of influence largely unused. From interviews, it appears that a small group of Negro leaders mediated between the Negro and white communities when problems arose. The first sign of the coming rise to active participation of Negroes occurred in this period, however, when Julius Burton, a Negro, ran for Council in 1933, declaring that his race should have representation. He was defeated.

Third, the vast areas of agreement, the issues which did not appear, speak eloquently of the unity of the community. The biggest issue, the light plant, found the voters in practically unanimous support of their leaders against an outside company.

Fourth, the values of local businessmen were dominant and their leadership was accepted with but a few minor exceptions. Interviews re-enforce this conclusion and suggest that the College administration and the major businessmen shared similar values and supported one another. Had the guiding spirits of the community sought new policies which disadvantaged other citizens they might well have met with resistance and suffered defeats. As it happened, the *status quo* was maintained and no one sought to challenge it. The reins of power were held in a few hands, exemplified by men like Ira Porter, but they did not reach very far.

1945-1955

Leaving aside the abnormal years of the Second World War, we turn to a decade in which signs of change in the structure of power began to appear. The relatively oligarchical pattern of former times began to give way to a highly unstructured situation in which there was no single center of power. Let us proceed to a consideration of the issues.

In the area of zoning, the period began with a rejection of a proposed change in regulations which would have permitted the Millcraft Paper Company to build a plant in Oberlin. The vetoing was done by Lynds Jones, a retired professor who was against new industry in Oberlin, a businessman, and a former College treasurer who supported the objections of a property owner who would have been adversely affected by the move. All were members of the Zoning Board. In 1946 the Planning Commission, with Ira Porter as Chairman, requested the rezoning of a part of East Lorain Street for industrial use. Jones attempted to veto but he was outvoted. The Planning Commission also recommended another zoning change which the Board approved over the objections of 61% of the property owners in the area affected. This action was vetoed by a majority of City Council. Two neighborhood groups arose in order to protest the rezoning of street corners and they were successful. In 1953 the President of the Chamber of Commerce proposed rezoning an area on East Lorain Street from commercial to industrial use. Residents protested and vetoed. Then he proposed rezoning an area in the southeast—a Negro section—to industrial use, and these residents also vetoed through the City Council.

The issue of annexation was intiated in 1950 by the residents of a large area west of Oberlin. On the Planning Commission, Ira Porter strongly supported their request as did Ben Lewis, a Professor of Economics, and J. Kutscher, a Councilman. H. V. Zahm, the City Manager, was opposed. Yet it was J. D. McLaury, a retired businessman, who pointed out to the county commissioners that the petition for annexation was legally inadequate and succeeded in vetoing the proposal. Ira Porter and Donald Love (Secretary of the College) were outvoted three to two on the Planning Commission when they attempted to veto the annexation of a small piece of land on the west side. They wanted to annex all the land on the west side and develop it as a whole. Porter resigned as Chairman because of the adverse vote.

The distribution and extension of city services were the subject of some controversy. In 1946 the residents of Follette Street, a Negro section, asked Council for water, sewers, sidewalks, and a paved road. City Manager Zahm asked them to present a formal petition and in this way temporarily vetoed their request. In 1949 Ben Lewis became the spokesman for these citizens and proposed a compromise. While councilmen were debating the cost of the project, J. D. McLaury went out and measured the length of the street to be served by the water lines. When he informed Council that the street was much longer than had been thought, three members vetoed the Follette Street request. In December, 1950, however, Council voted to advertise for bids on water lines on West Follette Street. Lewis initiated the action, but this time Porter supported him saying there might be a real estate development on West Follette. Council approved the water line in 1951.

The question of who should pay for city services beyond the city limits came up from time to time. In 1955 a policy formulated by Zahm and the City Solicitor, was passed in Council with Lewis opposed. Porter and some local builders suggested raising water rates instead of having the developer pay for the extension of water lines but they did not prevail.

Parking presented some interesting conflicts. In 1947 the Retail Merchants Division of the Chamber of Commerce requested parking meters downtown to keep people from parking all day. But City Manager Zahm vetoed their request. The retail merchants repeated their request in 1950. This time Zahm was on their side and Council consented by a three to two vote. But several merchants initiated a successful petition for a referendum and the voters defeated meters overwhelmingly.

In 1949 Porter and several businessmen requested Council to petition the Governor for removal of rent controls. Lewis was opposed, but the rest of Council, the City Solicitor and several landlords were in favor of the move. Governor Lausche temporarily vetoed Council's petition because it failed to say "no critical housing situation exists in Oberlin." In 1951, however, Lewis again lost on this issue and Porter, Fauver, and the rest of Council got their way.

There were two issues in the general area of the municipal electric light plant. In 1950 Councilmen Hill (a real estate agent) and Mosher (publisher of the *News-Tribune*) wanted to seriously consider the offer of the Ohio Public Service Company to supply Oberlin's electricity, but Kutscher, Comings, and Lewis were opposed. Porter was also against accepting the offer and spoke against it at Council. The other issue arose when J. D. McLaury declared that he was going to file a taxpayers' suit against Council to keep them from buying a new engine for the light plant, since the last one they had bought from the same company was noisy. However, Fauver suggested a compromise: Council would try to get the company that sold them the engine to fix it if McLaury would drop the suit. McLaury consented.

In 1954 the city was running out of funds. Council put a special levy on the ballot which was vigorously supported by the *News-Tribune*. The voters defeated the levy.

Fluoridation of water had been approved by Council in 1951 with no apparent opposition. When the equipment arrived in 1954, however, several citizens succeeded in getting sufficient signatures on a petition to force a referendum. The vote was very close but fluoridation was approved.

For our purposes, all we need say of the Board of Education is that except for Ira Porter (who was defeated in 1945) no member appeared to be active in any other area of decision.

A major issue of the decade, involving an important change in political structure, was the new city charter. It was initiated in 1953 by Mr. E. Maus III, the managing editor of the *News-Tribune*, who despite the opposition of City Council and its Solicitor, got enough signatures on a petition to put on the ballot the question of whether a commission should be elected to formulate a city charter. The voters approved the idea and elected a charter commission.

The charter had three key provisions. First, elections were to be nonpartisan. This was favored by men like Harold Gibson, of Gibson's Bakery, who thought it would increase the chance of Democrats and by others who like publisher Charles Mosher thought local affairs should be removed from partisan politics. Second, there were to be seven members of Council instead of five. This provision was supported by Wade Ellis, a Negro and Professor of Mathematics, and by the head of the National Association for the Advancement of Colored People, who felt it would give Negroes a greater chance for representation on Council. Third, all seven members were to be elected at the same time rather than having staggered terms as in the past. Ellis believed that simultaneous election would increase the probability of being able to elect a

Council with a "progressive" majority. With only two or three councilmen up for election at a time, Ellis felt that at least one or two conservatives were bound to win.

Ira Porter and other local Republican leaders voiced grave doubts as to the advisability of the charter. Their opposition centered around three main points. First, the continuity of the Council could be destroyed if all members were to be elected at the same time. Second, the American two-party system could only thrive if it was extended all the way down to the "grass roots." Local parties build the interest and activity in politics which is the basis of a national party. "Cutting off the local base of national parties," as Ira Porter put it, "is like cutting off the roots of a tree." And third, it was naïve to imagine that you could ever get real non-partisanship in any kind of political situation. There would always be factions, whether they have national party labels or not. Thus it was better to keep the factions out in the open by use of familiar identifying symbols than to drive them underground by making them seem "undemocratic." Of course, Republicans would stand to lose.

Nevertheless the charter was approved by the electorate in 1954. In an Appendix to this chapter we shall present data supporting our conclusions in regard to the impact of non-partisan primaries on the outcomes of local elections. Here it is only necessary to say that the non-partisan provision led to increased factional competition cutting across party lines, much greater representation of Democrats, and increased citizen participation in elections.

We are now in a position to make a few meaningful comments for purposes of comparison with later developments. No one person or group was consistently victorious over a wide range of issues. All the leading participants—the downtown merchants, the College, the newspaper, various ad-hoc citizens groups, leaders like Porter and McLaury, were defeated on matters they considered to be important. The hypothesis of a ruling elite of businessmen was certainly incorrect as the business community showed itself to be divided and as the Chamber of Commerce, the retail merchants, and a leading banker such as Ira Porter suffered defeats. The allegiance of the voting citizenry, as expressed in several referenda, could not apparently be taken for granted by anyone and shifted from issue to issue. No doubt the prevailing temper was conservative, particularly when it came to spending money, and no far-reaching projects were undertaken. The one exception, the favorable vote for a new city charter, demonstrates again that a business elite could not have been dominant for many businessmen and their spokesmen suffered defeat. Many small groups of citizens who intensely opposed measures which they believed affected them adversely were often successful. And the Negro population began to make itself heard. We find, then, a highly fragmented, pluralist community, with no one individual or faction dominant, moving slowly, with some but no great amount of innovation. The basic question to be answered was whether the new charter presaged a more innovating spirit and whether the political changes it was designed to foster would result in the election of men representing somewhat different views than in the past.

1957-

During the 1950's it became abundantly clear that there was a fundamental division among active participants in Oberlin community affairs. One element consisted of people of diverse social backgrounds, occupations, and national political views who shared a belief in planning the future of the community. They envisaged a community in which suitable new industry would create employment and bring in population to help ensure thriving local businesses. This industry would provide a tax base to support a superior school system and expanded municipal services. Business activity, industrial development, and residential housing would be regulated in conformity with prevailing notions of city planning.

The "planners," as we shall call them, were opposed by another element, with a more homogeneous business background, which held a more traditional point of view. The components of this "traditionalist" view differed somewhat from person to person, but they included a feeling that there was something about Oberlin as it always had been which ought to be preserved, and which was in danger of being lost in large and swift changes; a feeling that too large an outlay by the local government was objectionable both for its effect upon the tax bill, and upon the climate for business; and a feeling that expanded functions for local government interfered with the freedom of the individual to pursue his goals unfettered by unnecessary regulations. Another component of the traditionalist point of view may have been a desire to preserve patterns of influence which once existed and which were feared to be slipping away.

The traditionalists were not opposed to planning as such, however. It was a member of this group who initiated the studies which led to a very comprehensive housing code, and several members were among those who hired a city planner who produced the Gruen Plan, a radical program of redevelopment for the city. Both the original proponent of the housing code and those who first decided to hire Gruen disinherited the progeny of their conceptions when they turned out to involve large changes, considerable expense, and governmental action on a large scale. It is opposition to these concomitants of planning, then, which distinguishes the traditionalists from the planners.

The election of 1957 brought to Council a majority of planners and of men known to be Democrats. James F. "Bill" Long, manager of the cooperative stores, was named Chairman. Wade Ellis, Harold Gibson, and William Hellmuth, a Professor of Economics, were also Democrats. Andrew Stofan, owner of a photography shop, Fred Comings, a proprietor of a book store, and E. P. Zahm, former City Manager, were Republicans not yet committed on specific policies. The first actions of the new Council were significant indicators. Grover Severs became the new City Solicitor and Richard Dunn, a man with a strong interest and training in planning, was chosen to be City Manager. It is at this point that we begin our study of the power structure of Oberlin, Ohio, with a series of case histories describing what happened during the following three years.

Appendix to chapter 3: non-partisan elections in Oberlin

In the literature on political parties there are a number of statements concerning the results of non-partisan elections.[4] We would like to take a close look at three of the more basic propositions in the light of Oberlin's experience with non-partisan elections.

Proposition I: By doing away with party labels as guides by which voters cut their information costs, non-partisan elections advantage local notables in the community. Notables tend to be conservative, and conservatives tend to be Republican. Therefore, *non-partisan elections favor local Republicans.*

Between the years 1943 and 1954, twelve Republicans and three Democrats (counting re-elections) were elected to the Oberlin City Council. In the three municipal elections since the change-over to non-partisan elections, nine Republicans and nine Democrats have been elected. Lest one think that this is a manifestation of a general change in the voting habits of the Oberlin electorate, witness the returns in Presidential elections in this same eighteen-year period. During this time (see Charts B and C) no Democrat has ever done better than Roosevelt in 1936 when he got 43% of the local vote. Similarly, in state elections, not one Democrat has outpolled his Republican opponent for a major office in this period. One must drop all the way to the county level to find Democratic pluralities. But even on this level, there has been no significant shift in party preferences of the voters during the period mentioned. Only in non-partisan municipal elections have the Democrats made significant gains, and here they seem to have been put almost on equal footing with their Republican counterparts (just as Wade Ellis and Harold Gibson hoped they would).

CHART B. *Presidential elections in Oberlin*

Year	Candidates	Party	Votes
1936	Roosevelt	D	998
	Landon	R	1,310
1948	Dewey	R	1,513
	Truman	D	539
	Wallace	P	89
1952	Eisenhower	R	1,578
	Stevenson	D	733
1956	Eisenhower	R	1,649
	Stevenson	D	717
1960	Nixon	R	1,543
	Kennedy	D	983

CHART C. *Selected state elections in Oberlin*

Year	Office	Party	Votes
1938	Governor	R	1,324
		D	885
	House of Representatives	R	1,355
		D	768
1946	Governor	R	1,152
		D	972
	House of Representatives	R	1,494
		D	537
1950	Governor	R	1,316
		D	844
	House of Representatives	R	1,315
		D	656
1958	Governor	R	1,193
		D	885
	House of Representatives	R	1,106
		D	840

Proposition II: Parties serve as centers for building voter interest and activity in politics and campaigns. Parties serve as mediators between voters and officeholders. Through parties government is made understandable and meaningful to voters. Therefore, *nonpartisan elections will lead to increased voter misunderstanding and apathy which will manifest itself in increased non-participation in elections.*

Again the voting statistics for Oberlin do not support the proposition. For the years 1943-1953, an average of 1,279.5 votes were cast in each municipal election. In the three elections since the change in the electoral system, the average has been 1,891 votes. Obviously there has been more participation in local elections since this change. Moreover, the ratio of votes cast in local elections to votes cast in national elections has undergone a substantial increase. Thus the ratio of votes in the 1951 and 1953 local elections to the 1952 national election was 32%. In the 1957 municipal election, the first after the change to a non-partisan electoral system, however, the ratio rose to 48% of the 1956 national election. And in the 1959 local election, the ratio climbed to a dramatic 83% of the 1960 Presidential turnout. If we cast about for another ratio—votes cast/eligible voters—the increase since the non-partisan primary is also impressive. Thus the ratio of votes cast to the eligible population was 32% in 1949 and 1951 and 46% in 1959. Anyway one cuts the cake, Proposition II is shown to be false for Oberlin.

> *Proposition III:* Parties serve as centers for discovering and propounding issues in campaigns. Therefore, *non-partisan elections mean a reduced emphasis on issues and a correspondingly increased emphasis on candidate's personalities.*

The Oberlin experience with the non-partisan elections differs from that of some other communities because of the unassailable position of the Republican party and the virtual absence of any Democratic party organization. With no chance of victory at all, there was no incentive for the Democrats to make a serious organizational effort. So long as traditional political loyalties were invoked, Republicans would always win a majority of seats. By loosening party ties, that is, by permitting Republicans to vote for a Democrat without going against the party labels, the chances of victory by individuals who were Democrats was much improved. In the absence of a competitive two-party system, the non-partisan primary restored the possibility of increased competition between individuals. As Republicans and Democrats combined in various factional alignments, the competition generated greater attention to issues and led to increased participation. The old local notables were challenged by new ones who made use of non-partisanship to create a previously unknown coalition which stressed issues and altered the power structure of the community.

What happened in Oberlin does not, of course, invalidate the three basic propositions for other communities. Rather, experience in Oberlin suggests that the conditions under which these propositions apply may be more limited than had heretofore been thought to be the case. Where party competition is nonexistent or ineffective, the introduction of non-partisan primaries may facilitate the emergence of factional rivalries cutting across party lines. Hence the representation of candidates identified with the minority party may increase when the barrier of party loyalties is removed. Increased competition between factions may also lead to the ventilation of issues inhibited by single-party dominance and thus increase voter interest and turnout. Personality may count more under a non-partisan system but this need not mean a decrease in the issue-content of campaigns if this content was low under the previously existing party system or if enhanced factional rivalry provides more competition than in the past. Whereas the introduction of non-partisanship into a community with active party competition might lead to the results outlined in the three basic propositions, different consequences may occur in communities like Oberlin where the previous party system was much less competitive.

THE GREAT WATER
CONTROVERSY

The controversy over whether or not to build a new water supply system for Oberlin which reached a climax early in 1959, involved serious stakes for both the supporters and the opponents of the proposed system. Its supporters believed that an entirely new supply was necessary to avoid serious inconveniences in the coming years, while its opponents felt that repairs on the old system would make it adequate for any demand which could be anticipated for the next several years. The new supply system would be costly, but to its supporters, it was "something we have to have." Its opponents considered the proposed system an intolerable and unnecessary expense to impose upon the rate-payers and property owners. Whatever the merits of the arguments, the amortization of the bonds would come to $2,800,000, a debt which could cause controversy even in communities larger than Oberlin.

In 1957, the source of Oberlin's water was the Vermillion River, a small stream to the west of the town with a drainage area of 8.7 square miles. The water was stored behind an earthen dam in the Kipton Reservoir, which held 23 million gallons. A recently built auxiliary reservoir on the Pyle-South Amherst Road held 50 million gallons as a reserve for times of drought. It was filled from the Kipton Reservoir by gravity flow in wet seasons. A second source of supply, the Camden Bog, existed for use when the Kipton Reservoir went dry, but could be pumped for only a few hours a day.

A large conduit carried the water by gravity from the Kipton Reservoir to the small storage pond by the treatment plant on the south side of town. Parts of this conduit were the original wooden structure built in 1887; the rest was unsealed tile. In dry years much water was lost in transit through this conduit, and in wet years it was estimated that 50% of the water arriving at the storage pond seeped into the conduit along the way.

From the Vermillion River-Kipton Reservoir supply, 800,000 gallons per day were available in normal times, but only 500,000 per day could be counted on in dry years. The average daily use in 1957 was 590,000 gallons per day, and the estimated daily need of the community with its anticipated growth was 900,000-950,000 gallons for 1963 and 2,000,000 gallons for 1985.

The water treatment plant had been installed in 1903, and had not had major alterations since that time. No filtration of the water took place. After the water (to which lime and soda had been added) left the settling basin, it went to a treated water pool which, in violation of current state health regulations, was left uncovered. The water was supposed to remain in the settling basin for twenty minutes, but due to excessive demands upon the intended capacity of the plant, it remained for only two minutes, and the actual process of settling continued in the treated water pool. This treated water pool could not be drained and cleaned because no alternative route into the mains existed.

The treatment plant was operating far above the capacity for which it had been designed, and to increase its capacity further would call for major alterations. Permission to carry out these alterations would have to be obtained from the Ohio Department of Health which could be expected to refuse its assent until the whole treatment process was made to conform with contemporary health standards.

The incomplete precipitation in the settling basin and treated water pool continued in the mains, gradually causing them to clog with boiler scale and sediment. By 1957, some of the pipes could carry only 26% of their original capacity. Moreover, besides the problem of scale in the pipes, many of the mains were too small to handle the flow. In some areas the low water pressure resulting from these two conditions was a permanent fire hazard.

In spite of these deficiencies, the system had worked fairly well in the past. The water was chronically hard, but the bacteria count was considered satisfactory. However, a severe shortage was experienced in the autumn of 1953, which resulted in the closing of Crane Pool, prohibition of car washing, and the rationing of water for other uses. It even was feared at that time that the College might have to be closed. This drought resulted in the building of the Pyle-South Amherst auxiliary reservoir, but the auxiliary system did not prove adequate to solve the problem of ensuring a safe water supply.

After the drought of 1953, the water supply went through more critical periods. The community as a whole was not aware of these since further rationing did not become necessary, but they were known to members (Carl Howe, Homer Blanchard, Ed Trautz, Ben Lewis, and Carl Breuning) of the Public Utilities Commission (PUC) and others who had direct contact with people in the Water Department. These people were the more concerned because of what they called "growth factors." New housing developments were being built. The Ford Motor Company was constructing a new assembly plant in Lorain, which they anticipated would bring a spurt in the growth of Oberlin's population. And calculations of the amount of water used by the College and the amount available in the summer demonstrated to them that the old water system simply could not meet a new demand from the College if it expanded its summer operation. After preliminary steps toward a new system had been taken, the Committee's incentive to procure a more plentiful supply of water was further increased by the opportunity to attract a Pepperidge Farms Bakery and a Federal Aeronautics Administration center to the city in the spring of 1958.

Early in 1957, the first effort began to systematically evaluate the water problem and the various ways of handling it. At the recommendation of City Manager Weisbrod, a firm of engineers was hired to study the situation and suggest solutions. This firm considered three alternative sources—the purchase of water from Elyria, a city to the north of Oberlin which obtained its water from Lake Erie; a new source in the Wellington Creek-Black River area; and an expansion of the present Kipton source. However, due to a changeover in the personnel in charge of the investigations, the PUC received two conflicting reports from the firm, one recommending the Black River and the other the Kipton source, and they called for a final recommendation at their meeting on February 23, 1958. At this meeting the firm could make no recommendation, and merely submitted estimates of capital and operating costs for the three alternatives. Council then decided to dismiss the firm and declared its intention of giving the PUC direct responsibility for recommending a new group of engineers.

City Manager Dunn asked the Ohio Water Resources Board, and the Ohio Society of Professional Engineers for suggestions of firms these organizations considered competent. Further advice was sought from other sources in March 1958, and the PUC interviewed representatives of four engineering firms which had consistently been recommended to them. On March 12 they unanimously decided to recommend to the City Council that Burgess and Niple, a Columbus firm of civil and sanitary engineers, be hired to conduct a study of Oberlin's water situation. This decision was made on the basis of a reasonable cost estimate for the survey, $4,000, as well as the long experience of the company and the testimony of letters which the City Manager had secured from their other clients.

The Burgess and Niple engineers carried out their survey that summer, and submitted their report to the PUC on September 15. The report included three plans for the consideration of the PUC, together with cost estimates for each plan. Plan One consisted of supplementing the existing Vermillion-Kipton water supply with water from the Black River, to the east of town. This project would involve the construction of a dam on the Black River, a 270 million gallon reservoir near the dam, a pipeline to the site of the old treatment plant, a completely new treatment plant at the site of the existing plant, and repairs on the Kipton System. The estimated cost of construction and land was $1,705,800.

Plan Two called for obtaining the entire water supply from the Black River, which had a drainage area of 130 square miles. The costs of a dam across the river and a modern treatment plant were the same. A larger reservoir of 380 million gallons would cost more, and the type of reinforcement system for the water mains would be slightly more. However, the cost of a pipe directly to the mains on the east side of town rather than to the old plant site on the south side of town was enough less to put the total cost at $1,699,700—less than that of Plan One. The cost of water over a 25 year period with this system was estimated to be 31 cents per 100 cubic feet.

Plan Three was the alternative of buying water from Elyria. The plan for this consisted of a five mile pipeline north to Murray Ridge Road, where an Elyria line would be connected, and an underground reservoir to be filled each night and drawn from during the daytime. The cost was estimated at $789,600. The price of Elyria water and the possible disadvantages of having to depend upon a supply over which the city had no control were factors which had to be considered in connection with Plan Three.

The Burgess and Niple report was sent to the Ohio State Department of Health, which approved it. The PUC then began an extensive series of investigations to enable them to evaluate the alternatives so that they could ultimately make a recommendation to the City Council. Homer Blanchard, a builder of organs and a PUC member, was especially interested and active on the water issue. He informed himself thoroughly, provided information to councilmen, and answered questions at public meetings.

The PUC first requested the Burgess and Niple engineers to study the possibility of deferring improvements on the system. The recommendation of the firm was that the improvements be made as soon as possible. They pointed out that the current usage of 600,000 gallons per day was 20% more than the safe supply from the existing sources, and that the maximum capacity of the present plant was 800,000 gallons per day. With this supply, the city could not guarantee to meet its own much less the water needs of the Pepperidge Farms Bakery and the Federal Aeronautics Authority center.

The PUC also asked Burgess and Niple to study the possibility of making improvements on the present treatment plant and system to provide an adequate supply in the near future. The report of the engineers concluded that the present treatment plant could only be expanded to process an average of 900,000-950,-000 gallons per day, which would be adequate for only five years. The expenditure of $110,000 which this would involve would be practically useless after this period of time, for a new plant would then have to be built. Moreover, the engineers could not guarantee the safety of the water treated in the expanded plant.

To ensure a supply of 1,200,000 gallons per day, which would be needed in ten years if the projections were correct, water would have to be taken from the Black River to supplement the 500,000 gallons per day which could be counted on from the Vermillion source. The cost of these facilities for ensuring a ten year supply would be only $200,000 less than the comparable facilities suggested in Plan One, which would provide an adequate supply for twenty-five years.

The results of these investigations convinced the PUC members that patching up the present system was not a practical alternative, and that the construction of a new system could not be delayed. The only safe solution to the water problem, they decided, was in the plans submitted by the engineers.

In order to find the cost of Plan Three so that it could be compared with the other plans, a firm rate for the purchase of water had to be obtained from Elyria. Oberlin officials had been in contact with Elyria on the possibilities of obtaining Elyria water since 1956. Elyria officials had recently assured Oberlin that if an agreement were reached on price, Elyria's construction program would be accelerated to ensure that Oberlin's needs could be met.

On July 28, 1958, a joint meeting of Elyria and Oberlin councilmen had taken place, at which a firm offer was made by Elyria. Oberlin would be charged at Elyria's largest bulk rate plus 15%.

Burgess and Niple evaluated the Elyria rate schedules and concluded that a program of fixed increments was the most advantageous schedule for Oberlin. However, it also concluded that even this schedule of rates would put the cost of the water needed over a 25 year period above the cost of Plan Two. Since the rates submitted by Elyria were their firm offer, Plan Three was dropped from consideration by the PUC. Plan Two, which would obtain the whole supply of water from the Black River, thus became the least expensive alternative.

With these investigations completed, the PUC held a public meeting on November 21, to inform the citizens of the present thinking on the water problem and to give them a chance to raise objections. At this meeting, questions were asked by Ira Porter, President of the Peoples Banking Company, Chris Oliver, Superintendent of the Oberlin College Buildings and Grounds Department, and Glen Molyneaux, a proprietor of the Watson Hardware Company. Homer Blanchard answered many of their queries. The possibility of fixing up the present system for a few years more was discussed.

The PUC met on November 24 and unanimously made its

final decision to recommend Plan Two to the City Council. The reasons they gave for their decision were that Plan Two was the least expensive way to ensure an adequate supply of water for the next twenty-five years, and that stop-gap plans would waste money and be neither safe nor adequate. They also recommended that immediate rate increases be made, to put the community in a better position to finance the construction program.

The next meeting of the City Council was held on December 1, and Plan Two was embodied in resolution No. 386, and passed unanimously on the first reading. The Council decided to delay making a change in rates. When the time alloted for audience participation came, Ira Porter spoke against the plan the Council proposed to carry out. He claimed the present system could be made to work for 12 years with repairs. He presented a plan, later called the Porter Plan, which involved the construction of a 75,-000,000 gallon reservoir, repairs on the supply conduit, construction of another settling basin, cleaning the Kipton reservoir and repairing the dam, and cleaning the water mains. He estimated the total cost of these repairs would be $495,000. T. O. Murphy, a local plumbing contractor often associated with Porter, later estimated the cost of this proposal at $638,760.

Porter was questioned about the supply of water for his system. The Burgess and Niple engineers had estimated that only 500,000 gallons per day could be counted on from the Vermillion-Kipton area, and that 1,200,000 per day would be needed in ten years. Porter assured his questioners that an adequate supply could be obtained under his plan. He reported that he had traveled to the area and talked with farmers about the water. He had found out that the streams never ran dry. Moreover, enough water could be accumulated in the new reservoir during the rainy winter and spring seasons to last through the summer. When he was questioned on the discrepancy between his estimate of the available water in Vermillion and that of the engineers, he asserted that the engineers had not analyzed the possibilities of the Kipton area thoroughly enough.

Porter's proposal was the main event of the audience participation period, but other questions were asked. People were interested in the possible rates which would result from the different alternatives. At this time, Chairman Long offered to set up a public meeting if the demand for information was strong but this suggestion aroused no apparent enthusiasm.

At its next meeting, on December 15, the Council passed resolution No. 386 on its second reading. During the audience participation period, new opponents of Plan Two appeared. A local resident, a traveling salesman, protested that the rates under the plan would be too high, and declared, "We're pricing ourselves right out of a place to live in the town." He predicted that the increase in population for which the plan allowed would not take place because of the high water rates the city would have. Councilman Hellmuth replied, "They can't come if we don't have water for them."

William Gaeuman, a builder, voiced his opposition to the plan. He felt a new plant at the present site would be an adequate solution for five or ten years. By that time, he anticipated that population growth would have made feasible a regional metropolitan water district.

By the next meeting of the City Council, on January 5, 1959, more of the community was aware of the controversy taking place over Plan Two. The meeting was well attended. Ira Porter, William Gaeuman, Glen Molyneaux and Frank Green, an electrician, spoke against Plan Two. They all felt that a less comprehensive plan which would be less expensive would serve for ten years or more. They generally endorsed the Porter Plan. Letters were read from residents who felt that the increase in rates would be too much of a burden on the pensioned residents of the city.

At this meeting, voices in favor of the plan were heard from the audience. Dick Fowler, chemist for the County Health Commission, compared the expense of water with that of other less essential items used in everyday life. He exhibited a chart which compared the $24 a month which a family of four living outside the city limits had paid for water purchased from a tank truck with the $4.50 they paid when they subsequently moved to Oberlin. He asserted that at the new rate, their bill would amount to only $8.00. Mrs. Warren F. Walker, wife of a zoology professor at the College, and a member of the Water Study Committee of the local League of Women Voters, stated that a majority of her committee had voted in favor of Plan Two. Thurston Manning, Professor of Physics, and Eric Nord, President of the Nordson Corporation in Amherst, said that they supported Plan Two because the other suggestions were not based upon adequate investigations. They felt that unless the persons suggesting the adoption of a less comprehensive plan could present some figures and facts to the PUC and the Council, which were as concrete as those presented by Burgess and Niple, Plan Two should be immediately adopted.

In response to the clamor, the third reading of resolution No. 386 was delayed at the suggestion of Chairman Long, to provide an opportunity for further investigation of alternatives to Plan Two. Long suggested that the possibility of a county-wide plan be looked into, that Amherst and South Amherst be contacted to see whether they were interested in a joint system, and that Elyria be approached once more. Long also decided to call a public meeting for January 15 to review the whole problem. He asked that at this time those objecting to Plan Two come forth with facts and figures to support their proposals.

In the edition following this meeting, the *News-Tribune* printed an editorial which reported that Councilman Hellmuth, an economics professor, had calculated the amortization charges for Porter's $500,000 plan, and had concluded that the rate increase under the Porter Plan would have to be at least 70%, in contrast to the 86% increase required by Plan Two. After some details, the editorial commented, "It seems to us that neither Porter nor anyone else can just say 'We don't like the Black River Plan.' They must go beyond that and offer a definite alternative with some facts to back it up."

Porter had threatened to take the issue to the voters with a petition for a referendum. The editorial commented, "Ira Porter has made more valuable contributions to this community than we could possibly recount adequately in the space of this column . . . However, if he fails to provide a realistic alternative plan with cost figures verified by competent sources and yet goes ahead stubbornly with his referendum petition plan, he can no doubt get the signatures necessary for the petition and by appealing to voters' pocketbooks can very possibly get Plan 2 defeated at the polls. But we believe he will have capped his 50-year career of service with a tremendous disservice to the people of Oberlin. We would hate to see that day come."

Meanwhile, several alternatives were being investigated by the city officials. Chairman Long received a letter from the Lorain

County Planning Commission, asking whether the city was interested in a county-wide sewer and water plan. The PUC and Council members met with the County Sanitary Engineer to discuss a county-wide system. It was decided that any such plan lay in the remote future.

Amherst and South Amherst were contacted about a joint system and representatives of these communities expressed disinterest in such a project.

City Manager Dunn contacted Burgess and Niple to find out their thinking on getting water directly from Lake Erie. They replied that because the lake was twelve miles away, and 225-250 feet lower than Oberlin, the cost of a system using this source would be $1,000,000 more than Plan Two.

Two days after the January 5th meeting, City Manager Dunn reopened negotiations with the Mayor of Elyria at an informal luncheon. Dunn asked that Elyria reconsider its last offer. The Mayor suggested that since Elyria had already submitted firm figures, Oberlin should now decide upon firm rates which Elyria would have to meet in order for a contract to be signed.

Consequently, the PUC and the Council met on January 11 and decided to offer to pay the present Elyria rate minus 15% for 20 years. They considered this offer flexible to some degree, and were also willing to negotiate on the question of how far the Elyria water line would be extended toward Oberlin. They were not willing to offer Elyria as high a rate as Burgess and Niple had indicated that Oberlin could afford, however. The explanation for this is that some of the Council and PUC members opposed buying water from Elyria at any price, for they feared that Elyria would be able to control development around Oberlin by refusing to supply more water than the original contract called for. They also feared the Elyria Council might decide to raise rates at the end of any fixed increment contract, or at any time with a contract stipulating rates at a percentage of the Elyria rate. In the absence of an arrangement for joint control over the water supply, they preferred a system entirely independent of Elyria. Others, including Mayor Long, insisted that although these were valid objections to obtaining water from Elyria, there was a price at which Oberlin should do so, and this was finally determined to be the Elyria rate minus 15%.

Long, Councilman Comings, Dunn, Blanchard, the Chairman of the PUC and the City Engineer met with Elyria officials and explained the offer to them. They learned that one reason Elyria would not be able to meet the Oberlin offer was that the city was currently supplying two other communities with water at the Elyria rate plus 15%. Meeting the Oberlin offer would put Elyria in a poor bargaining position when these contracts came up for renewal. When the Elyria Water and Finance Committee met on January 13, they flatly rejected the Oberlin offer, and the question was closed.

As a result of this intensive work by Oberlin officials, the alternatives of a regional system, a joint system with Amherst, a direct supply from Lake Erie, and purchase from Elyria, had been ruled out by the time of the public meeting on January 15.

One hundred and twenty people attended this meeting. Chairman Long presided, Blanchard answered questions, and the issues were debated again, though nothing new was added to the controversy. At the next Council meeting, resolution No. 386, embodying Plan Two, which called for the entire water supply to be obtained from the Black River, was unanimously passed on its third reading, and so enacted into law.

On the same day, the campaign of the opposition was launched. According to state law, a petition signed by 10% of the electors in the last gubernatorial election could require that an issue be put on the ballot at the next election for decision by a vote of the citizens. Porter decided to use a petition to force a referendum on the water issue, and had one drawn up. He needed 213 valid signatures, and set February 14 as his deadline.

Porter formed a committee to collect signatures but did not contact the members more than once. Two hundred sixty-seven signatures were obtained, 200 of which were collected by three people: an employee of Porter's bank handled the petition in the bank, and gathered 50 signatures; Porter himself filled a petition with 50 signatures in one day by buttonholing people on the street. He then left town for his vacation on February 2 confident that his petition would succeed, and stayed away until February 17.

William T. Macarthy, a Negro plasterer, personally gathered 100 signatures, mostly in the Negro community. Macarthy's position appeared later in a letter to the editor of the *Oberlin News-Trib-*

une on February 26. He wrote that money spent on Plan Two would be wasted because the supply from the Black River was not dependable. "I wonder if Mr. Long has ever taken the time to do a little investigating along the banks of Black River? If he has, he would know that there isn't enough water in there in July and August to breed mosquitoes." Macarthy also argued that the times were inauspicious for large expenditures by the municipality which would raise rates. "I am not in favor of planning so far in the future with times as they are. Let's live now and try to pay the high light, water and sewer bills that you have already handed us. I feel that the rise in our bills to the tune of 500% is enough for the present, knowing that there are many of us who must ask aid in order to pay these bills."

Macarthy, who was a Democrat, also explained his alliance with Porter, a prominent Republican: "While Ira Porter and I are not on the same side of the fence politically, we see eye to eye as to how the taxpayers' money should be spent . . . Although I do not bank with the Peoples Banking Co., I must say that Ira Porter has been a friend to many little men, regardless of race, creed or color. There have been times when men have gone to him and he has loaned them money out of his own personal pocket, interest free, so we can't say he was going to gain."

Macarthy's letter and an answering letter from Fred Holloway which appeared in the March 5th *News-Tribune* illustrate the way in which the personalities of Porter and Long became mixed with issues of planning, of large governmental expenditures, and the old versus the new. Macarthy said:

> I think that we should take off our hats to Ira for having the nerve to stand up and defend the rights of the people of our town. I would like to point out that it was such men as Porter . . . who have made what these few men are trying to destroy. I am not a lawyer, but I do know that in a so-called democracy any issue can be brought before the people for their approval or disapproval. We are not living in a dictatorship, although some of the things that the present Council are doing would lead one to think that we are.

Fred Holloway replied:

> Of course Bill is entitled to his opinion. He says "that he thinks we should take off our hats to Mr. Porter"; well I don't think so and

won't. Maybe Mr. Porter has made a great contribution to this community, but time moves on and calls for progress.

Maybe the loan of some money was enough years ago when Oberlin was only a village, but we have continued to grow. . . . Now we have a City Council planning and working to bring industry where people can earn their own money and pay their own way. And yes, Mr. Long is not a native of Oberlin. Neither am I, but as citizens I don't think the people can justly and truthfully say we have tried to tear down instead of build up.

There is much more I could say, but Bill, I would much rather a man give me a good paying job than loan me some money without interest. Think about it.

Holloway's last point was an allusion to the circumstance that Bill Long made a point of employing Negroes in the co-operative stores which he managed, while there were no Negro employees in the Peoples Savings Bank.

The Porter petition aroused strong opposition. State Senator Mosher, a pillar of the Republican Party, an Oberlin resident and the publisher of the *Oberlin News-Tribune*, condemned the action as a "do nothing petition." He noted that if a petition succeeded, the new Council elected in November would have to deal all over again with the water problem, would have to seek the advice of engineers, and probably would end up with a similar program. He emphasized the benefits of a new system, and noted that the rate increase would only average $1.95 per month. Finally, he asked whether the purpose of the petition might not be to discredit the present Council in anticipation of the next election. The paper also published letters to the editor opposing the petition, including one from the League of Women Voters, which summed up the results of their investigations and appealed to the voters not to sign it. In spite of this opposition, the Porter petition obtained 267 signatures and was filed on February 16 and 17.

On February 17, City Solicitor Severs, Chairman Long and City Manager Dunn met and examined the petitions. They noted many technical errors in the signatures which would invalidate names. These included incorrect precinct numbers, signatures which differed from those on the voting records, duplications and signatures of people who were not legal residents of the city. The number of signatures in excess of the minimum was only 54 and they estimated that from 60 to 80 on the petition were invalid. Severs also believed that the form of the petition was incorrect and might be grounds for invalidating the whole petition.

Chairman Long and Councilman Ellis had discussed the problem presented by the Porter petition before this, and had hit upon the idea of conducting a campaign to remove names from the petition. A similar drive had recently been carried out in the course of a dispute in a nearby community. In spite of the fact that the Porter petition was probably invalid as it stood, Long and Ellis decided to carry out the anti-petition-petition campaign to make certain that no referendum would be held and which was more important to Long, to thoroughly discredit the Porter faction, or to achieve a "moral victory" as one of his workers put it.

That night, at a meeting of the Board of the Co-op, which Long managed, the anti-petition-petition was discussed. Mrs. Aschaffenburg, wife of a teacher in the Conservatory, and Mrs. Warren Walker, volunteered to help. Long then contacted Mrs. Robert Thomas, wife of a reporter for the *Lorain Journal,* and Dick Fowler, the chemist for the County Health Department, who had spoken out against Porter at the January 5 meeting. Ellis contacted Mrs. Margaret Baker and Mrs. Davidson. The selection of these people was aimed at countering the work of Macarthy, who had got a large number of signatures from the Negro community. Ellis, Mrs. Baker, Mrs. Thomas and Mrs. Davidson were Negroes. Fowler was a member of the NAACP.

An attempt to contact the Negroes en masse was made at a meeting at the Rust Methodist Church which had previously been scheduled by the NAACP to inform Negroes on the housing and water issues.

When the meeting was held, on February 21, an unexpectedly large number of people attended. Long spoke first and spent 30 minutes explaining the water situation. He noted that the water was necessary to attract the Pepperidge Farms Bakery and that the company had promised not to practice discriminatory employment policies. He mentioned that forms for the removal of names from the Porter peition could be picked up in the rear of the church as people left.

Subsequently, Fowler made a short appeal to those who had signed the Porter petition, and called upon Mrs. Davidson, who had signed the petition, to remove her name. Mrs. Davidson, who had previously been won over, replied that she would and asked for slips to bring to her friends. Fowler said that slips were available at the back of the church. By this time, he had a diminished audience, for many had left. No one picked up slips as the remaining few filed out of the meeting.

Long had anticipated that fifty to one hundred signatures could be removed at the meeting and was "flabbergasted" to learn that the effort put into planning a strategy for the meeting had borne no results. The next day, he contacted fifteen people himself, explained his point of view on the need for a new water system, and was able to persuade ten to remove their names from Porter's petition.

The following day, a meeting of the anti-petition-petition committee was held at Mr. Fowler's house. Long followed what he called the "organization technique" of getting "the right people to contact the right other people." A list of the signers of the petition was read, and members of the committee picked out the people they knew or thought they could approach. The goal of 60 names was affirmed and a deadline was set.

After this, Long kept in close contact with the workers. They reported to him daily and he called them once a day to inquire how many names they had succeeded in removing and to suggest more names. He reported the progress of the entire committee to each member and urged them to greater efforts. Little by little, the committee removed signatures from the petition, and achieved eight more than the goal of 60 names on February 25. Long called each worker personally to inform him of their success, and to thank him.

The campaign organized by Long and Ellis had been the most effective demonstration against Porter, but other actions were taken. One member of the League of Women Voters distributed some of Long's forms and convinced three people to remove their names from the petition. The *News-Tribune* published instructions for writing the city auditor to request the removal of a signature. Andy Stofan, a Council member, started his own anti-petition campaign.

At the Council meeting on March 2, the City Solicitor announced that due to unregistered voters, duplications and withdrawals, the Porter petition had insufficient signatures. He recommended that it not be sent to the Board of Elections. The Council voted to direct the City Auditor to reject the petition.

On March 16, another attempt of the Porter group to block or delay the carrying out of Plan Two proved abortive. At a Council meeting on that day, Chairman Long announced that doubt had been expressed over the legality of the form of resolution No. 386. The attorney Porter had consulted in connection with his petition had warned Long that the resolution might be contested on legal grounds and advised that it be rescinded and another resolution passed to avoid court action. If this had been done, the Porter group would have had an opportunity to circulate another petition. Severs, the City Solicitor, said that he doubted that the form of the resolution was illegal, and reported that the legal firm the Council was considering to handle the financing of the water program had approved the steps taken so far. He recommended that the Council proceed. The Council approved a contract for Burgess and Niple to draw up specifications, and nothing more was heard of the illegality of resolution No. 386.

After the victory of the proponents of Plan Two was final, another dispute which had been obscured in the hullabaloo of the Porter petition and the anti-petition-petition came to the surface. In its meeting on March 22, the PUC decided to recommend a rate schedule of 70 cents per 100 cubic feet for the first 5,000 cubic feet, 60 cents per 100 cubic feet for the second 5,000 cubic feet, 50 cents per 100 cubic feet for the third 5,000 cubic feet and 40 cents per 100 cubic feet for all over 15,000 cubic feet. This was the schedule recommended by Burgess and Niple, with a slight reduction in minimum price for small users.

This recommendation was passed as a resolution on its first reading at the Council meeting on April 6, after which large users of water rose to make vehement protests about the new rates. One businessman submitted a letter claiming that his water costs would increase by over $800 per year under the new rates. As a bulk customer he felt he should be entitled to a reduction. Another businessman stated that the rate increases would cost him more than $500 per year. A third spoke along the same line.

Upon questioning, City Manager Dunn stated that an alternative schedule had been submitted by Burgess and Niple with a fifth step for large users. This schedule had not been adopted because it would cost the city $4,000 in 1962, a year which he said was crucial in the bond amortization program. Chairman Long stressed the need to demonstrate to the bond buyers that the city would be able to meet payments.

Councilman Comings asked whether the schedule was similar to others in Ohio, or whether other communities had a rate for large users. Councilman Zahm asked whether experience might prove the proposed rates brought a surplus and might make possible future reductions. Long replied that in five or six years a reduction might be possible, or a surplus might be allowed to accumulate for future needs.

Long then asked whether someone wanted to move that the new rate schedule be passed on suspended rules as an emergency measure. City Solicitor Severs said that this could not be done. Ellis, who had been known as an opponent of all emergency actions, demanded the reason. Severs cited a passage in the city charter which prohibited the passing of rate ordinances as emergency measures.

Debate over rates within the context of Plan Two had been going on for some time. At the December 1, 1958 meeting of the City Council, when it considered Plan Two for the first time, Councilman Zahm had inquired about consideration for large users. Dunn had replied that there was nothing hard and fast about the proposed rates. He had then written to Burgess and Niple asking them to study changes in rates to make them ". . . more attractive to industry." The firm had supplied him with a schedule which moved the fourth step from 15,000 to 35,000 cubic feet and added a fifth step of 35 cents for purchases over 50,000 cubic feet. They estimated the loss of revenue from this rate would not necessitate a change in financing arrangements.

At the January 19th meeting, Councilman Hellmuth had said that something might be done to ease the burden on the 415 minimal users. Burgess and Niple, at Dunn's request, had replied with a set of five possible rate schedules.

About that time, when the Porter campaign was attracting attention, one of the businessmen had contacted Comings and Zahm to see whether large users would be given consideration in the new rate schedule. Both of these Councilmen assured him at that time, or so he believed, that something would be done for the large users and he received the impression that the entire Council felt the same way. Another businessman had been given a similar assurance at one of the open hearings.

The PUC had discussed minimum rates in several meetings subsequent to Dunn's receipt of the minimum rate schedules. They apparently felt hampered by commitments made by Council members. The principle was expressed on several occasions that "political considerations should not be taken into account." At one point they decided against any deviation at all from the original rate schedule Burgess and Niple had suggested. However, Councilmen, especially Councilman Ellis, pushed for a reduction for minimum users. Carl Howe, of the PUC, felt that the $7.00 minimum might be difficult for some people to pay, and favored a "gesture" toward the small users. At the last meeting before they submitted their recommendation to the City Council on April 6, the PUC members adopted the reduction which Burgess and Niple had suggested which would cost the city least. The major consideration for the PUC members was that the rates show an adequate income to finance the bonds. The reduction from $7.00 to $6.30 for the minimum users would not substantially reduce the proceeds of the sale of water.

No one had pushed for concessions to the large users before the PUC, however, and when the three businessmen heard the recommendation submitted on April 6, they felt they had been betrayed and abandoned. They had refrained from joining the Porter campaign because they thought they had promises that their interests would be considered. When they went to the meeting, however, they found that the Council unanimously supported the PUC recommendation, including the two Councilmen whom they claimed had given them assurances. These two Councilmen voiced weak expressions of sympathy for the large users, but stated they thought the need of financing the new water system was the overriding consideration.

After the meeting, these three businessmen discussed their plight on the sidewalk in front of the City Hall. They spoke of the defection of the two Councilmen they had counted on, and one speculated that the real reason Long was pushing the water program was his interest in converting the old water works with its holding pond into a recreation area. He also felt sure that the present plant was only pumping eight hours a day, and the others agreed with him that no emergency actually existed, although the present plant had defects. This businessman continued that he had heard that Burgess and Niple were getting a 7% fee for their report and that he had heard that the original firm had been fired because their views differed from those of the Council. He then suggested they institute proceedings for a taxpayers' injunction. One of the other two participants in the conversation protested that he did not want to get involved in anything until he knew the details. The first said he would consult his lawyer. The second encouraged him to get all the necessary details, and the third wondered how long this procedure would delay action by the Council.

Each began to work separately. One contacted all the Councilmen except Hellmuth, who was out of town. Another spoke with Zahm, the third saw Comings and Zahm. He also contacted his attorney and discussed the possibility of starting a taxpayers' suit on the grounds that the rates were unfair. Such a suit would delay the solution of the issue long enough for it to become an issue in the November election. They also discussed the possibility of getting the rate question placed upon the ballot. The attorney then approached Long and Comings with the news that an injunction and referendum were being considered seriously.

As a result of these pressures, a special session of the City Council was held on April 13, at which the three once again voiced their objections. Councilman Zahm presented water rates from Wellington and New London, showing that other communities gave reductions to large users.

Chairman Long reported that the PUC had considered sliding the rate down to 35 cents at 40,000, 50,000 and 60,000 cubic feet at its last meeting and had informally decided that no change should be made. At this point, one of the businessmen objected that Councilman Zahm had been informed that the PUC would not discuss water rates at its last meeting and so had not attended. The Council passed the rates on their second reading at this meeting, but with the understanding that the PUC would reconsider the case for selling water at 35 cents per 100 cubic feet over 30,000 cubic feet per quarter.

After the meeting, another of the three convinced Lewis Tower, the Business Manager of Oberlin College to write a letter to the PUC asking for consideration for large users.

The PUC met again on April 19 to discuss the cost to the city of rate reductions. In the course of the meeting, the costs were recalculated, and an error was found in the figures of Burgess and Niple. Instead of a loss of $5,000 to $6,000 per year, reductions would cost only a little more than $1,000 per year. An air of relief passed through the meeting of PUC members and Councilmen. They decided to grant the reduction though Zahm declared that the policy of appeasement irked him. The rate was dropped from 40 cents to 37½ cents per 100 cubic feet at 35,000 cubic feet, and to 35 cents per 100 cubic feet at 100,000 cubic feet.

Most PUC and Council members were glad to make a concession which averted a possible delaying action which could have opened up the entire water question at the next election and to clear their consciences of unredeemed past promises. The concession to the large users was token. The yearly bill of one, which would have been approximately $1,000 was reduced by $22. The yearly bill of another was reduced by $24.

The new PUC recommendations were submitted to the City Council on the following day. Councilman Ellis asked whether the city could afford the loss of approximately $2,000 with the reductions for both small and large users. Dunn answered that all future expenses could not be known, and suggested that other means of finacing could absorb the cost of the reduction. When Ellis asked who benefitted from the reduction, Dunn named 25 users, of which 18 belonged to the College. At this meeting, in spite of Ellis' resistance, there was no question but that the final compromise had been reached. The new rates were passed on their first reading without opposition, and were passed in the following two meetings to become an ordinance.

When various city officials were questioned on this concession to three vociferous individual users, they agreed that since the city could make a small reduction without jeopardizing the financing program, the concession was justified by its effect of preventing a possible court action, which could have delayed the whole program.

From an issue which generated considerable passion and participation, we now turn to one which was resolved by the specialists elected and appointed to deal with it. The Light Plant decisions, with their roots deep in the city's past, may serve as an example of the difficulties encountered even when making seemingly "technical" decisions far removed from the public view.

The subject of one of the oldest of Oberlin's recurring issues is municipal ownership of the local supply of electric power. It is noteworthy that in all the controversy and passion aroused by this issue in the last seventy years, not once have Oberlin's citizens and public servants been lured from the pursuit of the lowest possible electric bill by arguments about the "tendency of municipal ownership to breed corruption in local politics," "moral obligation" to a private exploiter, or the inherent inefficiency of a "one-horse outfit." This is noteworthy because seventy years of controversy seem to show us quite plainly what the real issue is, and where to look for the deciding factor when the issue crops up.

The issue was first touched off in 1890 by a report of the lighting committee of the Village of Oberlin which recommended the construction of a municipally owned electrical system to provide more adequate illumination of the streets than the gas lighting system, which was then operating seventeen nights a month when the moon was in the dim part of its phase. Oberlin did not get electricity until two years later.

By then, the controversy was evidently in full swing, for the following year the supporters of municipal ownership failed by six votes to obtain the two-thirds necessary to pass a referendum to build a village plant. Thus a private plant was built.

The local company was soon in receivership, though the plant continued to supply electricity. In 1912, it was sold to St. Louis interests. The expiration of the franchise in 1918 was the occasion of a terrific row in which the company lost so much good will that only six out of the 316 voters opposed a municipal plant in 1919. The company succeeded in delaying construction through recourse to the courts until 1922, when they negotiated a settlement highly unsatisfactory to the city.

By the time the franchise expired again in 1928, the electric company had changed hands three times and had come under the ownership of the Ohio Electric Power Company. Accepting a rate reduction which still left rates higher than those of nearby towns, the Council renewed the franchise with a provision allowing them to reopen the rate question.

The College appears to have opened the final struggle against the private company when a representative proposed to the Council in 1932 that a study of the possibility of building a municipal light and power plant be made. City Manager Sears and Mayor Morris strongly supported the plan, and a utilities engineer from Cleveland was hired.

The engineer carried out his study and recommended that the city construct its own light plant. His report showed that Oberlin was paying much more than other cities for electricity, which everyone knew. It also spelled out the costs of a municipal plant, and showed that much lower rates could pay for such a plant and allow a $100,000 reserve to accumulate by 1948, while saving power consumers $1,196,000.

The Council then submitted an ultimatum to the Ohio Electric Power Company to meet the rates in the report. This was refused, and the Council passed the necessary ordinances and resolutions to build a light plant. At this time, Oberlin accounted for about 10% of Ohio Electric's sales, and as the report showed, Oberlin rates were yielding a large profit to the company. Ohio Electric decided to fight back.

As its predecessor had done in 1918, it began by throwing away what good will it had in Oberlin. When a representative attempted to convince Council that the city had no moral right to start a rival system while the company held a franchise, he was laughed down, for the report had revealed that a highly questionable method had been used to calculate the fair return on the company's Oberlin investment. A representative then threatened to cut off electric service from the local bank and oil company. A local banker, Ira Porter, had been appointed chairman of a citizens committee set up by Council "to conduct an educational campaign on behalf of the proposed bond issue." His committee provided speakers for clubs and other groups which wished to consider the question of municipal ownership in Oberlin, and advertised in the *News-Tribune*. Porter himself later bought $10,000 of the original issue of light plant bonds. Finally, an election on the issue resulted in an 11-1 margin for a municipal light plant.

Arbitration was then carried on, in which the company gave a substantial reduction, but still maintained a profit rate of between 12% and 17%, depending upon whose figures were accepted. This was too little and too late. The city quickly disposed of the legal barriers the company attempted to raise, and built its light plant. A final attempt by the company to get its customers back by underselling the city was defeated. By 1940, the engineer's report had been clearly shown to have been conservative, for the plant had contributed nearly $85,000 to the city's general fund in six years.

Since 1934, municipal ownership of the light plant has been challenged occasionally. In 1950, two councilmen, John Hill and Charles Mosher, wanted to solicit an offer from the Ohio Public Service Company to supply Oberlin's electricity, but were in a minority. In that year, a taxpayer's suit was brought by a J. D. MacLaury to prevent buying a new engine for the plant, but his objection was to the piece of equipment rather than to municipal ownership. The last attempt to scrap the plant was brought about by the necessity to expand output by a third. The opponents were easily defeated, and a 2,500 KW generator was installed.

In 1959, a new controversy, the subject of this paper, was started by the necessity to expand the plant still further. A dispute involving a departmental interest broke out between the manager of the light plant and his superiors. This conflict illustrates the problems raised when a municipal body must deal with technical data and place its trust in an expert when making a decision.

Early in 1959, City Manager Dunn, the manager of the municipal light plant, Howard Reichenbach, and the Public Utilities Commission (PUC) began to consider the city's ability to meet the expected electrical demands of the new Federal Aeronautics Administration center which had recently been attracted to Oberlin. This center would be in charge of directing air traffic in the Cleveland area, and could be expected to require large amounts of electricity. The expectation was confirmed when Mr. Reichenbach returned from a conference with FAA officials in New York, and presented the outlook for power demand for the next five years.

With the necessity of supplying more power than the present plant could generate, Council decided to have a complete "feasibility study" made of the alternative ways of meeting the new demand. Three alternatives were to be explored: selling the generating and distribution systems to the Ohio Edison Company; closing down the light plant and buying power wholesale from Ohio Edison for distribution by Oberlin authorities; or expanding the municipal plant to meet the new need.

The Public Utilities Commission, an advisory board consisting of five members appointed by Council, was authorized to make a survey. This commission investigates and debates all matters concerning the maintenance, operation and improvement of the city utilities, and submits recommendations to Council.[1]

The PUC received the names of competent engineering firms from professional sources. Six of the firms suggested were requested to bid on the job of preparing the study. The PUC interviewed representatives of all the firms and decided to hire the J & G Daverman Company, of Grand Rapids, Michigan, which not only submitted the lowest bid, but had the greatest experience with municipal diesel plants.

In the course of carrying out his study, R. J. Daverman, the company representative, asked the Ohio Edison Company to make an inventory study of the light plant and submit a bid for the entire Oberlin electric distribution and generating system. He also asked the company to submit proposals for supplying power wholesale to augment Oberlin's existing generation and for supplying the city's entire power requirement. The Ohio Edison Company refused to consider supplying power to Oberlin at a wholesale rate, but submitted an offer to purchase the entire Oberlin system for $2,000,000. Daverman then completed his report, comparing the two possibilities of plant expansion and sale to Ohio Edison, and submitted the report to the PUC on March 20, 1960.

The Daverman report was even more optimistic about the advantages of municipal ownership than its predecessor, the engineer's report. Noting Oberlin's location in the "Industrial Center of America," and the rapid growth of the nearby industrial cities of Elyria and Lorain, the report took what it called a conservative approach, and assumed that Oberlin's future growth would at least parallel the national average growth of 8% per year. To support this assumption, it added to Oberlin's historic 4.86% annual growth in demand, the expected demand of the FAA center, the expected Pepperidge Farms Bakery, the new buildings being constructed by the College, and the increased requirements of the new Water Works. It also took note of the new Gilford medical instrument plant, and the increasing use of air conditioning.

Using this growth projection, Daverman analyzed the costs of expanding and operating the system, and predicted that the cost of municipal electricity to the community as a whole (electric bills minus surplus revenue or income accruing to the Oberlin government), would be less than Ohio Edison electricity. In ten years, the accumulative difference would be $2,502,000. Under the current rate structure, which was substantially lower than that of Ohio Edison except in the largest category, the municipal operation would accumulate a surplus of $1,850,000 for the city in 10 years, or $2,076,200 with interest. These calculations took note of the fact that the light plant surplus was paying for $20,000 of electricity for street and traffic lights, and $12,000 for services performed by light plant employees beyond their regular functions. The "intangible factor" that Oberlin residents would lose an annual payroll of $100,000 was also pointed out. The recommendation called for steps to expand the light plant.

The PUC studied the report and asked Daverman to calculate the advantages of using a smaller growth rate. This was done, and the results were still highly favorable to a municipal operation. The PUC drew up a draft resolution supporting the report, and submitted the report and their resolution to the Council on May 2, 1960. All members of the PUC supported the Daverman report and recommended a price of $6,500,000 if Council should still wish to sell the light plant.

At this meeting the only opposition to the report came from Councilman Davis, a staunch opponent of the municipal light plant. He considered the price of $6,500,000 too high, and pointed out that a price for selling the plant had not been seriously negotiated or considered. Long, on the other hand, felt that the price was about half of what should be asked if they were considering selling the plant. PUC member Trautz suggested that both submit figures to support their assertions, which Long later did. Bickering over an asking price for the plant was merely a byplay between Long and Davis, however, for after the Daverman report, selling the plant was not seriously considered.

The proposed resolution, which could have been passed on one reading, was changed to an ordinance requiring three readings in order to give interested individuals an opportunity to examine the report and raise questions. It was passed with only Davis opposing at the following three meetings.

At these meetings, Davis remained almost alone in his protests. John Cochrane, manager and owner of the Ben Franklin Store, Lewis R. Tower, Business Manager of Oberlin College and Ira Porter, former president of the People's Bank, showed up to oppose expansion. At one meeting when Porter protested that the projections of the report were over-optimistic, PUC Chairman Carl Howe, a physics professor, reprimanded him for failing to attend meetings at which the PUC had studied the report.

The PUC held a special meeting on May 23 at which questions by a representative of Ohio Edison were heard. He pointed out some omissions in the Daverman study which would raise costs above the figure estimated, but admitted that Ohio Edison could not charge as low rates as the municipal system. Councilman Davis wondered whether the city had adequate funds to cope with a major disaster, and asked whether arrangements existed for buying power in an emergency.

Since no other opposition to expansion of the light plant appeared, Council directed the PUC to hire an engineer to carry out the project.

The PUC again interviewed representatives of the bidding firms, and decided to hire Daverman. There were two bids lower than his, but the PUC members had developed confidence in Daverman's abilities because his report had been so satisfactory to them. They were aware, moreover, that the firm had had more experience with municipal diesel plants than the other companies, and concluded that it was worth paying slightly more to secure an engineer in whom they had confidence.

All of the Council agreed with the PUC's decision except Davis, who protested that an engineer should not be permitted to bid on a contract which was the result of his own recommendations. Such a practice, he thought, encouraged engineering companies to submit biased reports in order to increase their chances of getting the contract for construction. However sound Davis' contention may have been, it was opposed to the traditional practice of the city in situations like this. The engineering firm which had carried out the water study two years before received the contract for construction as a matter of course, and the original engineer's report was done with a guarantee that he would be awarded the construction contract. The City Council decided to accept the PUC recommendation, and hired Daverman on August 1, 1960.

Daverman proceeded to draw up specifications of a new engine for the light plant, and presented them to the PUC on November 7. No objections were raised at this time, but later in the week, Reichenbach and Craig, the plant superintendent, came to the City Manager to protest that under Daverman's specifications, either a four-cycle or a two-cycle engine could be installed. The plant, at that time, was using only two-cycle engines; Reichenbach and Craig, who had had no experience with four-cycle engines, were apprehensive about using them. Moreover, they had had very good relations with the two-cycle company which had kept records on the plant operation much more complete than the city records. These records had been of great use to Reichenbach in the past, and he wanted to continue the association with that company.

In order to quiet their doubts, Dunn suggested that they take a trip to upper Michigan to examine some municipal plants which used four-cycle engines. As it happened, Reichenbach had been making an intensive study of the engine situation, had collected data from many sources, and had decided on his own that a field trip would help him gather first-hand information to either affirm or discredit the data in his possession. The plant superintendent expressed a desire to go along, but Reichenbach was reluctant to grant this request because Craig was in poor health (he died a week after the trip) and it might be difficult to take care of him should he become ill. Yet Craig appeared to have his heart set on visiting these plants, particularly one noted for its efficiency. At that time, a representative of the two-cycle company, a particular friend of Craig's, happened to come by on his routine weekly visit to the Oberlin powerplant. Craig suggested that the two-cycle representative go along and Reichenbach, not wishing to disappoint a dedicated engineer who might not have another chance, decided to grant his request. The presence of this second man would make it easier to handle the situation if Craig should happen to fall ill.

Reichenbach agreed to this arrangement, however, only under several definite conditions. He explained that he would give an unbiased recommendation on the purchase of the new engine and that he wanted unbiased information from the plants they were to visit. It was agreed that Reichenbach would pay both his and Craig's expenses. The two-cycle representative agreed to drive and pay his own expenses, and also agreed that he would at no time divulge his identity or his connection with an engine company to any person they would contact. He was introduced as a friend in order to make certain that the powerplant employees who were to be interviewed would give unbiased answers to questions. Moreover, Reichenbach and Craig were to choose the plants to be visited, the order of the visits, and the questions to be asked. All these conditions were met and the two-cycle representative acted as chauffeur and nothing more as he was supposed to do.

The three men visited four or five powerplants, asking about cost, efficiency, and over-all performance of the engines used. One of the plants they visited had been suggested by Daverman. It was using a four-cycle engine. One of the engineers at this plant was in a position to compare the two types of engines, for he also ran a plant which used two-cycle engines. This man related how four-cycle engines had been forced upon a staff which had wanted two-cycle engines, with disastrous results. The cost of maintenance of the four-cycle engines, he said, was ten times as high as that of the two-cycle engines.

When Reichenbach returned from this trip, he was firmly convinced that four-cycle engines were not desirable. He wrote a three page letter to the PUC strongly opposing consideration of four-cycle engines.

In the week following the trip, it became known to city officials that the representative of the two-cycle engines had accompanied Craig and Reichenbach on their trip, although no effort had been made to hide this fact. Most believed that Reichenbach's intentions had been good and that he had not realized that such an action might be considered out of place by others who were not fully aware of the circumstances and who were not cognizant of his high reputation for integrity. Some members of the PUC, however, were suspicious of the purposes of the trip. Thus Reichenbach discovered that an action taken for what he knew were the best humanitarian motives was badly misconstrued. He knew that neither he nor those who accompanied him had committed any impropriety, but it soon became apparent that a prejudicial factor had been introduced into the coming decision on the new light plant engine.

On November 27, the PUC heard Reichenbach's objections to the four-cycle engine. He argued that since the plant was using engines of a single type, they had been able to use a single supply of replacement parts in the past. This convenience would be sacrificed if a four-cycle engine was purchased. He also pointed out that the plant staff had been trained at city expense to work on two-cycle engines, and they would have to be retrained. He asked that if makers of four-cycle engines were not prevented from bidding, they should at least be penalized in some way. At this point, PUC Chairman Howe suggested that Reichenbach go to Grand Rapids to discuss his objections with Daverman. He agreed to do this.

Before Reichenbach left, he received a letter from the two-cycle salesman stating that Daverman's specifications were "sketchy" and "slanted" to favor four-cycle engines over two-cycle engines. The letter accused Daverman of ignoring the wishes of plant managers on occasions in the past.

When Reichenbach talked to Daverman, the engineer defended the use of four-cycle engines but said that he was willing to alter the specifications to exclude them if the PUC desired that this be done.

At a meeting of the PUC on December 4, Daverman told why

he thought both types of engines should be considered and Reichenbach told why he opposed the four-cycle engines. The Council
and PUC members present decided to allow both makers of two-
and four-cycle engines to bid. Some of these officials found Reichenbach's arguments unconvincing. Others reported that they had
not been interested in Reichenbach's arguments. They had hired
Daverman because he was an expert, and intended to follow his
advice.

The four engine companies who could make engines which
fitted the specifications were asked to bid. Two stipulations were
made to the bidders. At the request of Nord, who had become
suspicious of salesmen, the company representatives were requested not to speak to Council and PUC members who would
have to vote on the bids. There is evidence that two of the four
companies did not adhere to this stipulation but they did not receive the contract and there were no repercussions.

The second stipulation was that the bids be "evaluated" bids
rather than "initial cost" bids. This was an attempt to award the
contract to the company the engines of which would produce
power at the lowest cost rather than to the company with the lowest price engine. This required the companies to estimate future
operating and maintenance costs, and was criticized as subject to
bias.

When the bids were submitted, the four-cycle engine had the
lowest evaluated bid, and the PUC decided to award the contract
to that company.

The PUC recommendation was submitted to the Council,
where Councilman Blanchard objected that he still was not convinced that a four-cycle engine was better than a two-cycle engine.
At the request of Councilman Comings an ordinance which required three readings was substituted for the resolution to buy a
four-cycle engine, so that he and Blanchard would have time to
investigate further. After a meeting was arranged with the four-
cycle salesman, Blanchard was satisfied that the engine was well
suited to the requirements of the plant and decided not to oppose
it.

At this time, serious charges were whispered about that a certain
individual (not on Council or PUC) who was known to hold
stock in the four cycle company had influenced this decision, or

possibly even the decision to hire Daverman, who, it was alleged, was partial to four-cycle engines. These charges appear to be without justification, and their circulation made no difference in the final decision.

Reichenbach felt that the decision of Council was a personal defeat, since he had opposed the four-cycle engine so strongly. He anticipated that his men would be disgruntled at this turn of events, and he believed that the powerplant would have an inferior machine. He resigned on the spot, but was later persuaded to reconsider, and has since resumed his duties. The Council, City Manager and the PUC did not want to lose the services of an exceptionally able technician and administrator who probably could not have been replaced by anyone of comparable skill and dedication. They respected him, and they valued his work, but this did not mean that they were unwilling to substitute their judgment for that of the expert.

In a broader sense, the case of the light plant engine was but a symptom of the growing effort to recruit citizens who would develop specialized knowledge and take an abiding interest in an important but circumscribed area of community activities. It was the existence of a group of citizen-specialists on the PUC and City Council which made this conflict possible. Had there been no small group of laymen who felt competent to challenge the views of the acknowledged local expert, or at least to choose among different experts, the views of the manager of the light plant would probably have prevailed. The conflict we have just described might, then, best be viewed as part of the price paid for a deliberate effort to increase, in however small a way, the amount of citizen participation in community affairs.

The Housing Code decision, to which we now turn, is far different in kind than the one we have just concluded. For the code had much greater impact on many more people, and was much more exposed to public view, than was the question of what kind of engine the light plant should have. Moreover, as the area of policy changes, so do many of the participants and the kinds of resources they bring to bear in the arena of decision. Bargaining extending into sections of the community rather than a growing consensus among specialists becomes the order of the day.

The question of how far the demands of long range planning and regulation can be carried out without infringing upon the right of the individual to use his income and opportunities as he sees fit is one which is argued again and again in the process of making political decisions in Oberlin. In the controversy over the passage and enforcement of a code of minimum housing standards, the question took the form of a debate over the extent to which the municipal government should be allowed to regulate the living conditions of individual family units in order to prevent the growth of slums and to help ensure healthful living conditions for the residents of Oberlin.

The dispute over the Housing Code took place between January and April, 1959. It should be remembered that this falls within the period when the water question was being fought, and that the segment of the community which ordinarily takes notice of the activities of the City Council, as well as those usually active in community affairs, were dividing their attention and energies among an unusual number of controversies.

When John Cochrane, manager and owner of the Ben Franklin

Store, and member of Council, proposed the appointment of a Committee on Minimum Housing Requirements in July of 1957, some sections of the community were already aware that slum conditions existed in Oberlin. Welfare and church groups, such as the Social Action Committee of First Church, the United Church Women, and the League of Women Voters, had long been interested in the problems of dilapidated housing, outside toilets, lack of sewers or water, rat infestation and related problems. Cochrane stated that he had been concerned about "the lack of regulations with respect to building and housing requirements which most of us considered basic necessities," and, indeed, Cochrane's motion was the first official recognition of the problem by the City Council.

After passing Cochrane's resolution, however, the Council decided to defer the actual appointment of the Housing Committee until after the election that fall. The committee was appointed at the meeting on January 20, 1958, along with other commissions and committees, from a pool of volunteers for community service. It originally consisted of 21 members, including social workers, interested wives of members of the faculty of the College, medical men, contractors and businessmen.[1] There were three Negroes on the Committee. George Simpson, Professor of Sociology at the College, was named chairman. At its organizational meeting the committee expressed its purpose: "To propose legislation to regulate minimum standards for sanitary housing in the City of Oberlin."

The Housing Committee divided itself into four subcommittees. At the March 20, 1958 meeting of Council, Douglas Johnson and Richard Haller, of the Subcommittee on Public Housing and Finance, recommended that a building and loan company be attracted to Oberlin, and that a low income housing project be considered.

The work of the Survey and Code Subcommittee was to take longer to complete. Mrs. Blair Stewart, wife of the Dean of the College, and Mrs. Samuel Goldberg, wife of a mathematics professor, together with the five other members of their subcommittee, prepared a survey of Oberlin housing conditions to help them draw up a code. In the first of her publicity articles on the code, Mrs. Goldberg explained, "Exact information on what is standard for Oberlin . . . is unknown. What may be accepted practice, the status quo in other cities, may be unreasonable or below par when considering our own living standards. Therefore, as is the case with most cities, a housing code must be tailor-made to fit the individual city."

The first indication of the extent of the ambitions of the committee was given in this article. Mrs. Goldberg said, "A housing code covers more than a few obvious signs of substandard conditions. Proper light and ventilation, minimum space per occupant, and other requirements that cannot be determined from the outside of a house are included in a modern code."

The survey was carried out in May, 1958, by the seven subcommittee members, with the help of three other members of the Housing Committee. Seven streets in different parts of town were chosen in an attempt to get a representative sample of conditions, and each was assigned to one member. Armed with letters of introduction from Mayor Bill Long on city stationery, they made an intensive investigation of 107 dwelling units, filling in a questionnaire with information on the type of dwelling, the kind of construction, the number of occupants, the rent charged, the income of the family, the kitchen, bathroom and heating facilities, the means of disposing of garbage and rubbish, the floor and window area, and the means of egress available.

While the survey was being carried out, Mrs. Bruce Hawkins, a social worker, became interested in the work of the committee. She was subsequently asked to do a study of the social problems in Oberlin. Her report contained the information that about 15% of Oberlin's houses had no private bath, no running water, or were substandard in some other way. A common finding was that water was carried from houses several hundred feet away, and that an outside privy was used.

In the fall and early winter of 1958, the subcommittee organized a second survey, which was intended to cover the rest of the city with a questionnaire similar to that of the first survey, but less detailed. One event of this second survey was a "Help Day" organized by Mrs. Goldberg and Oberlin College sophomore John Tropman who had declared at a Council meeting the previous spring that he would like to help organize an activity which would show that college students took an interest in the community in which they lived for four years. About 200 students scattered over the city on September 27 and managed to survey 732 dwelling units. The rest of this second survey was carried on by committee members and members of the League of Women Voters, until 1,164 units, approximately ⅘ of the city's estimated 1,500 dwelling units, had been inspected in the two surveys.

The results of both surveys revealed 22 cases of obvious overcrowding, including cases where 11 occupants lived in a four room unit, 9 lived in a two room unit, and 6 in a unit with one bedroom. Twenty to thirty outside privies were discovered, though not all of these were due to the unavailability of city water and sewers. A seven room unit was found which was heated by one space-heater, and other startling conditions were discovered. On the whole, however, there was not as much substandard housing as some members of the committee had expected.

With the results of the two surveys at hand, the subcommittee set about drawing up a code. Practically all of this task was left to Marcia Goldberg who obtained and examined much material on urban renewal from City Manager Dunn and Councilman Ellis and through her own efforts. The proposal for the code which was submitted to the City Council was completed in January, and was approved by the general committee during that month. It was based substantially upon the model code of the American Public Health Association, with modifications based on 8 or 10 other codes, and the results of the surveys. Mr. Severs, the City Solicitor, rewrote some sections and added a preamble and a subsection creating the post of Housing Inspector, but most of the code was the result of Mrs. Goldberg's efforts.

The proposed code was very comprehensive. It gave authority to a Housing Inspector who was directed to make inspections. Every unit was required to have a kitchen sink properly connected to water and sewer facilities, a bathroom affording privacy with a flush water closet and lavatory basin, and hot water heating facilities capable of supplying water at a temperature of 120 degrees F. Each dwelling unit had to have at least 150 square feet of floor space for the first occupant and 100 square feet for every other occupant; each room had to have a total window area of 10% of its floor area; each room had to have at least two electrical outlets;

and each window or door used for ventilation had to have screens in the summer.

There was a section on responsibilities of owners and occupants which included the provision that "Every occupant of a dwelling shall keep in a clean and sanitary condition that part of the dwelling, dwelling unit, and premises thereof which he occupies and controls." Procedures for condemnation were set forth, and the Housing Inspector was given power to require elimination of violations, with a fine from $50-$100 per day for noncompliance.

The code was presented to the Councilmen in a briefing session in January, and a public hearing was arranged for January 22. Before this meeting, the *News-Tribune* published a summary of the code, and announced that copies of the proposed ordinance were available at the office of the City Clerk. Mrs. Goldberg wrote an article to prepare people for the presentation of the code, in which she pointed out the place of a housing code, a building code, and zoning ordinances in creating "a suitable living environment for all of Oberlin's citizens." She described the areas covered by the code, told of the surveys, and affirmed that poor conditions had been found.

At the meeting, which was attended by about 60 people, a tirade of opposition was encountered. John Wood, the owner of the Ross Lumber Company, and John Oldfield felt that their right to privacy would be invaded under the code. Wood later expressed the opinion that the entry of the inspector was illegal and would be considered so in high courts. He felt the code as a whole was paternalistic, idealistic, and overly ambitious.

A property owner predicted that if the code were enforced, 50-75 homes would be condemned. This, he felt, would make necessary a program of low-cost housing. A television repairman expressed the opinion that the code should be put on the ballot at the next election, since it concerned the whole city.

City Manager Dunn, defending the code, said he did not want wholesale condemnations, but that he felt that Oberlin needed minimum standards to help meet the need to keep houses habitable. Mayor Long suggested the possibility of creating a fund of from $5,000 to $20,000 from which people could borrow to make improvements.

Fred Holloway, a Negro factory worker, said frankly that although he wanted to fix up his home, he had been unemployed for the past six months and did not have the money to do it. Because others had similar problems, he felt the code would not do much good without some system for financing improvements such as Long had suggested. Holloway later pointed out that he could not borrow because he was unable to put up security. He added that he did not like the power the inspector would have.

The public meeting was a shock to the Housing Committee, for much of the opposition came from the people they felt would be benefited most by the code. The members of the committee discovered that the very people whom they felt needed help did not welcome having repairs and improvements forced upon them. Mrs. Hawkins commented that the meeting was "such a let down, but revealing too."

The public meeting caused the Council members to give serious consideration to the implications of the code. After their regular meeting on February 2, they held a two-hour study session and went over the code, section by section. They took no action, but generally agreed that the code was overambitious in some respects. The right of the Housing Inspector to enter a building without a warrant, which had been challenged at the public meeting, was discussed. They also debated the possibility of limiting inspection to rental dwellings and inspecting owner-occupied buildings only when they changed hands. The requirements for window screens and electric outlets were questioned, as was the requirement that habitable basement space, which would include basement recreation rooms, comply with the same standards as above-ground rooms. A principal topic of discussion was the necessity of making available some sort of financial assistance to home owners who would be forced to make repairs.

At the Council meeting on February 16, it was apparent that the Council Members had given further thought to the problems involved in enforcing the Housing Code. Councilman Zahm declared that he would have to vote against the ordinance in its present form, and suggested that the Councilmen and the Housing Committee work together to revise the code.

After considerable discussion, the Council acted upon Zahm's suggestion and appointed two of its members, Comings and Ellis, to meet with George Simpson, Laura Stewart and Marcia Goldberg of the Housing Committee to make adjustments in the code which would satisfy public opinion. Ellis asked that the public approach Comings and himself with their objections to the code.

A subcommittee of the Housing Committee was formed and asked to study the problems of financing repairs, new housing, and relocations which the enforcement of the Housing Code would make necessary.

The three members of the Housing Committee met with the two Councilmen sometime after this meeting and agreed on a few minor changes in the code. They reduced the number of electrical outlets required in a room from two to one, dropped the provision that screens be on every window used for ventilation, and exempted basement rooms from the necessity of complying with the code. At this meeting, the two Councilmen seemed willing to accept the code generally as it stood, however, and no basic changes were made.

The code was discussed again at the Council meeting on March 16. Chairman Bill Long read a letter from George Simpson, Chairman of the Housing Committee, which mentioned that the committee had made an intensive survey of housing conditions, held several public discussions on the proposed code and revised it. The Committee now felt that the code was quite workable, and urged its unanimous passage by the Council. Simpson was in the audience, and rose to add, "I hope the Council will take some action on this problem now. If Council does not, I think we might as well forget about trying to exercise any control for years to come . . . We must be reconciled to seeing housing conditions get worse and worse."

The Council members, however, seemed more reluctant than ever to pass the code without reducing the hardships which would be caused by its enforcement. Fred Comings suggested that the code be passed without its enforcement clause until an arrangement for financial help was worked out. Zahm objected that he did not want to pass something which could not be enforced.

Councilman Hellmuth suggested that the date when the ordinance would take effect be changed from "immediately" to September 1, 1960. This would give owners two building seasons to make the changes in the dwellings they owned which would be necessary to bring them into compliance with the code.

If this were done, Councilman Comings asked, could a provision be added to the code which would make it retroactive to prevent new violations from being committed before the effective date? He was especially concerned that overcrowding be stopped immediately. City Solicitor Severs pointed out that to make the code retroactive to the present date, a special census would have to be taken immediately. This was deemed unfeasible.

Stofan suggested that the code be passed and inspections started immediately but that enforcement be begun on January 1, 1961. Hellmuth pointed out that if this were done, whatever date was set for the beginning of enforcement would be amendable once the code was passed. This idea, which would leave the final decision to put the code into effect to a new Council, seemed to reassure Zahm and Stofan, the two Councilmen who were most concerned about the proximity of the effective date. Council directed the City Solicitor to draw up an amendment to section 14 of the Housing Code, which simply stated the date upon which the ordinance would take effect in the original code proposal, to permit inspection to begin soon, but delay enforcement of the code provisions until January, 1961.

A further outcome of this meeting was the formation of another committee to study the possibilities of obtaining financing for home repair and remodeling. The committee was made up of a heterogeneous assortment of 19 citizens, among whom were Mrs. Goldberg, Councilmen Gibson, Ellis, and Long, City Manager Dunn, and Fred Holloway. These people met twice, but few had concrete suggestions to make, except Bill Long, who thought that some kind of arrangement might be made to help people in rental units secure down payments for home mortgages. This would create vacancies in rental units into which those presently living in substandard dwellings could move. The committee failed to solve the problem of financing any scheme, however, and did not meet again.

The next meeting of Council was held on April 6, and ordinance no. 113, the Housing Code, was passed on its first reading, 6-0. (Hellmuth was out of town.) However, the code was not in the form which had been decided upon at the last meeting. Instead of the amendment to section 14, which would have delayed enforcement until January 1, 1961, and which could have been altered to delay enforcement further, at a later date, an addition was made to section 3.02, which detailed inspection procedures. The section read in part, "The Housing Inspector is hereby authorized and directed to make inspections to determine the conditions of dwellings, dwelling units, rooming units, and premises located within the corporation limits of Oberlin." The clause added was, "Inspection will be made: (a) Only at change of ownership or occupancy. (b) At the direction of the City Manager. (c) At the request of the City Health Department." Section 14 read, "This ordinance shall be in full force and effect from the earliest period allowed by law."

The change which had been made between the two readings removed what seemed to be an authorization for the Housing Inspector to inspect at his discretion, and limited the occasions for inspection to changes in ownership or occupancy, or at the direction of the City Manager or the Board of Health. In effect, the new provisions made the City Manager, rather than the Housing Inspector, the responsible official, and was designed to give Council, which has the formal power to instruct the City Manager on policy, closer control over enforcement.

The explanation for the change is to be found in the variety of pressures to which Councilmen had been subject since the first public meeting; for besides the opinions expressed at the various public meetings, citizens had contacted Councilmen to voice their objections to the code.

One of the two chief objections had been that the inspection required for enforcement involved an invasion of privacy. John Wood, who had voiced his opposition at the January 22 public meeting, felt that the inspection section constituted "illegal entry," and contacted Long, Comings, and Zahm to inform them of his opinion.

The other main objection to the code held that forced compliance would cause hardships for those who could not afford to make the necessary repairs. Fred Holloway served to illustrate the problems presented by the code. Long especially considered Holloway an example of others who were in the same position, and contacted him for his views. Holloway later approached three other Councilmen to state his position to them.

Other objections to the code concerned specific points. Chris Oliver, Superintendent of Buildings and Grounds at the College, and a regular visitor at Council Meetings, pointed out some practical difficulties to Long, Comings and Stofan. He noted that the space requirements would be troublesome for a family with 10 or 11 children and that the provision requiring a watertight foundation was unfeasible due to Oberlin's clay conditions, which caused foundations to move and crack.

Harold Gibson, a Councilman, reported that another cause of opposition was that many people misunderstood the provisions of the ordinance. For instance, section 6.05 of the proposed code required that "Every dwelling shall have heating facilities which are properly installed, are maintained in safe and good working condition, and are capable of safely and adequately heating all habitable rooms, bathrooms and water closet compartments in every dwelling unit located therein to a temperature of at least 68 degrees F., at a distance of three feet above floor level." People construed this to mean that they must heat their homes to 68 degrees at all times, and protested that they did not want to be told how hot to heat their houses. Some who misunderstood the requirements of the code came to Councilmen, who explained the proper interpretation, and some of these were converted to supporters of the code. Others continued to dislike the code.

Some of the opposition to the code may have been for reasons not directly connected with the code itself. Bill Long, who was currently playing a chief role in the water controversy, expressed the opinion that some people indulged in diehard opposition to anything the present Council did because individuals had made enemies in the past over other issues. He pointed out that, although city elections are nonpartisan, four known Democratss outnumbered the three Republicans on the City Council, a situation which was considered disastrous by some in heavily Republican Oberlin.

Long also felt that those who feared integration anticipated that if the code forced Negroes to seek better living quarters, they would try to obtain housing in the white neighborhoods in the better parts of town. These types of opposition, if they exist, are difficult to detect, however, and no specific examples of overt partisan or segregationist opposition could be found.

A final category of complaint was on more general grounds. John Cochrane, the former Councilman who had initially proposed the studies leading to the code, said, "Perhaps they have gone too far, or rather, farther than I had in mind." In his opinion, the code was unenforceable because it was too idealistic. One businessman felt his house did not meet the requirements of the code and went to a Council meeting to protest vigorously. He thought that the code was "just asking too much." He did not oppose the code altogether, but felt that if it were revised so that it were less stringent, it would fit Oberlin's needs better.

The active supporters of the original proposed code were limited to members of the Housing Committee. Marcia Goldberg wrote newspaper articles concerning the code and participated in several forums which were held to acquaint community groups such as the NAACP and the League of Women Voters with the code. Both she and her husband were personal friends of Bill Long and often checked with him on the progress of the code.

Laura Stewart, who had been primarily responsible for organizing the surveys, attended the various forums with Long and Mrs. Goldberg.

George Simpson, Chairman of the Housing Committee, felt that the code was not unduly severe and worked for its passage. He often accompanied committee members when they spoke to groups. He was a main speaker at the meeting of the NAACP which considered the code (and the water question) at the Rust Methodist Church on February 21.

All these people had, on occasion, expressed their feelings to the Councilmen, who, as a result, were fully aware that the ordinance could not be passed as it was without dissatisfying many people whom they were not prepared to defy, and without ignoring arguments to which they were frankly sympathetic. At the same time, all Councilmen agreed upon the need for an effective code, and some of them felt strongly that the code which was passed should be very nearly that proposed by the Housing Committee. Council leans heavily upon the appointed committees and commissions to investigate community problems and watch over various areas of local government action. In order to preserve the usefulness of such committees to Council, they felt that it was necessary to give them their support and approve of their work as much as possible. The close personal connections of Long, Ellis, and Hellmuth with Mrs. Stewart, Mrs. Goldberg, and Mr. Simpson served to make these Councilmen particularly aware of this need.

Of the Councilmen, Zahm and Stofan were the most opposed to the code as it was initially proposed. Zahm's chief objection was the financial hardships it would place on some people and he advocated the development of a program of financial assistance for home improvements. Stofan was most concerned to protect the right of the individual to privacy and opposed the invasion of homes by an inspector.

Gibson and Comings were the most uncommitted members of the Council. Comings still wanted a stopgap to prevent further overcrowding before the code became effective, for he anticipated that new industry would locate in Oberlin before 1961, and bring in more people. He also held reservations toward the enforcement section, and desired an arrangement for financial assistance to needy home owners.

Long, Ellis and Hellmuth were most in favor of the code as it stood. Of the three, Hellmuth had the fewest reservations. He was on a sabbatical leave to the University of Wisconsin during this semester and, because he was absent most of the time, he was least exposed to citizen opinion.

Long was active in selling the code to the community. He often attended the forum meetings with members of the Housing Committee to speak for it.

Long and Ellis, who also supported the code, realized the difficulties which it would cause for poor families in substandard housing and they were active but unsuccessful in trying to find an arrangement for financing home repairs.[2]

The agreement reached at the March 16 meeting to postpone enforcement until 1961 seemed less satisfactory as the week went on. Nothing would be done for almost two years, and then the same problems would present themselves. Gibson finally suggested to Comings that the Council members get together to talk over the problem privately. They spoke to Zahm, who fell in with the suggestion. On March 25, the six Councilmen met privately and discussed more their own objections to the code, criticizing various items. Comings noted that most of the objections to the code were on minor points, and that the principal objections to the financial hardships which would fall upon the poor homeowners, and to the arbitrary invasion of privacy by the Housing Inspector, involved the way in which the code would be enforced. This was no new discovery, but Comings suggested that the problem would be solved if the proposed code, which seemed to place responsibility and authority to carry out a systematic inspection program of all residences in Oberlin upon the Housing Inspector, were altered to remove any discretion from him, and provide for inspection only upon a change in occupancy or ownership, or at the direction of the City Manager.

This solution in effect exempted those who owned their own homes from inspection for the time being. This was a group which contained those who had objected most to the code, and, incidentally, many of those whose homes were in the worst condition, while giving the city a large degree of immediate control over landlords who rented dwellings, the occupants of which changed frequently. This solution was quite close to the suggestion made by Ellis at the February 16 meeting that the code be enforced for rental units and not enforced for owner-occupied dwellings. This solution also reflected the feeling which Fred Holloway had expressed at one meeting, and which had been generally agreed with, that the landlord who rents his premises to others has a more pressing obligation to bring his property up to minimum standards than the man who owns his own home.

Comings' solution had other merits to the Councilmen. It preserved the body of the code intact, which seemed desirable in order to support the Housing Committee. It also preserved a tool with which slum conditions could be combatted more actively at some future date when there was more support for such a campaign. Meanwhile, it allowed for some enforcement to take place immediately. At the same time, by putting discretion in the hands of the City Manager, over whom the Council has direct control in setting policy, it allowed the delay in beginning full enforcement which seemed so necessary at the present time. The Councilmen found this solution quite satisfactory, and agreed to substitute it for the compromise they had accepted on March 16. The third provision, allowing the City Health Department to request inspections was inserted somewhat later with the concurrence of all the members. It was not a change which would effect the political consequences of the new settlement.

Long afterward expressed the opinion that this second compromise did not sacrifice anything of substance. "What you're really doing is playing around with words, since the City Manager would be in charge of inspection in any case." Insofar as it seemed to represent what was possible to accomplish with the alignments which existed at the time, he was right; but the compromise was a sacrifice of some of the aspirations of the Housing Committee.

At this special meeting, one other change was made in the code. Harold Gibson said, "I personally brought down the ceiling height to six feet, six inches." He knew a man who had just built a new home with ceilings of that height. If he were to comply with the requirement for a ceiling seven feet high, Gibson estimated the alteration would cost him approximately $5,000. He declared he would refuse to vote for the code if this alteration was not made. "The code may be well-meaning, but this was ridiculous—the man was five feet six inches!"

Word of the new compromise circulated slowly. On the same day as the luncheon meeting, Comings encountered Ruth Tumbleson, a professor at the Oberlin School of Commerce and the secretary of the Housing Committee, and asked her what she would think of a change in the inspection section which would provide for inspection at a change in ownership or occupancy, or at the direction of the City Manager. Mrs. Tumbleson later told an interviewer that she had not given the idea much thought at the time, but that the committee had expected that some things would have to be changed to get the code through. Her opinion was, ". . . if that was the best they were gonna' do, it was the best we were gonna' get."

Someone called Mr. Simpson and asked him if the change were acceptable. Mr. Simpson told him that the committee would not oppose it. He later expressed the opinion that it was a reasonable compromise, although he would have liked to have seen the code passed in its original form. He was glad that inspection and enforcement could begin immediately instead of in 1961.

At the April 6, 1959 Council meeting, the Housing Code finally received its first reading. Chairman Long asked Comings, who had been appointed together with Ellis at the February 16th meeting to meet with members of the Housing Committee to modify the code, to give a brief summary of his work. Comings complied, and mentioned that he had suggested a change in the code which would result in immediate enforcement. He explained the additions to section 3.02. The code was then read with the new provisions included in the body of the text. Gibson moved that ordinance no. 113 be passed on its first reading, Stofan seconded the motion, and it was passed 6-0.

Laura Stewart, Marcia Goldberg and Ruth Hawkins, who had been most involved in the preliminary work and the drawing of the code, were not informed of the change until after the Council meeting. On Tuesday, April 7, George Simpson called Mrs. Stewart and Mrs. Goldberg and informed them of the change. Both women resented getting their information on the change at second hand. Mrs. Stewart felt the big weakness in the compromise was that there would never be a complete inspection of houses in Oberlin. She was glad that some enforcement would begin immediately, for she had feared that a new Council might table the code, and leave them with no code at all.

Mrs. Goldberg admitted that she had been quite upset about the change at first. Later, she thought the matter over, talked to Bill Long about it, and finally became philosophical about the change. "Council has done pretty well by us," she said, and anyway, "I'm kind of tired of the whole thing."

Mrs. Hawkins was surprised that the code had been changed, and said, "I'm not too happy about this, but it was the best and only step Council could have taken." She felt that the opponents of the code had won a substantial victory, and anticipated that enforcement would not be carried out very vigorously under the new provisions.

Many of those who had opposed the code were pleased by the compromise. Fred Holloway and John Wood, as well as Cornelius Wright, President of the NAACP, agreed that the code was now satisfactory to them. Mr. Robert Thomas, a Negro resident of the city, and a reporter for the *Lorain Journal*, told Comings that "you fellows have done a fine job on this" at the meeting on April 6. The code passed its second and third readings in a routine manner and became an ordinance.

The battle over the code cannot be completely separated from the decision over enforcement which necessarily had to follow it. It would not be misleading to say that the victory of the supporters of the original code was won at the cost of its immediate enforcement, for it was partly because of the feeling stirred up in the controversy over the passage of the code that the Councilmen did not venture to begin enforcement immediately.

The actual efforts to modify the proposed code were of two sorts. The proponents of the code were able to defend it successfully against attempts to alter its provisions in ways which would weaken it as a tool for improving the housing in Oberlin. The concessions made on basements, screens, electrical outlets, and ceiling height were minor, but essential. This victory was a qualified one, for the opponents of the original code were fully satisfied with the outcome of the battle. They had not opposed the code as such as much as they had worked to prevent the effects they thought the code would have in causing higher rents, forcing expensive repairs, and making homeless the poorest people in the worst dwellings. Since no enforcement took place for nearly a year after the passage of the code, their desires were temporarily satisfied. An area of agreement existed or had been created in the course of the controversy. This consisted of the willingness of the proponents of the code to delay enforcement, and the willingness of their opponents to have a code, providing that their interests were protected in its enforcement. With the formula devised by Fred Comings, the Councilmen were able to create at least a temporary solution within the area of agreement.

Although different degrees of support for the code existed among the Councilmen, as the case developed they acted as searchers for a compromise between the different points of view in the community. Some may have been working to save the people from the code, and others to save the code from the people, but they acted as a unit throughout, and took the role of middlemen.

That they were able to do this was probably not entirely unrelated to the circumstance that the water controversy was raging throughout this period. The water issue was one in which those who had been community leaders in the past were more deeply involved than they were in the Housing Code, for it caused a clearer-cut division between the planners and traditionalists among them. The heat generated by this dispute was particularly intense, because the alternatives were such that the winners could satisfy most of their desires, while the losers would suffer total defeat. In the water issue, all of the Councilmen were ranged on one side, with their differences submerged, in order to defend a water system they believed essential to the community. The fact that they were attacked as a body, and that more of their resources than they had anticipated were being spent on their Council duties in order to defend the water system, may have been factors in inducing them to take the position of middlemen rather than partisans in the housing issue.

The coincidence of the two issues also may have prevented more spectacular happenings from having taken place in the housing issue. Ira Porter, a principal actor in the water dispute, opposed several provisions in the code, and some suspected that he might petition for a referendum on the code as he did on the water system. However, he refrained from taking any part in the housing controversy. He explained that he "had abused the Council so on this water thing" that "if they ever heard that I was planning to circulate a petition it would pass as an emergency matter." He apparently felt that his participation in the water dispute had exhausted his effective resources.

7 ENFORCEMENT OF THE HOUSING CODE

✤ ✤ ✤ ✤ When Oberlin's Housing Code was passed in April,
✤ ⛪ ⛪ ✤ 1959, it resembled closely the original proposal of the
✤ ⛪ ⛪ ✤ housing committee, which had been formed to draw
✤ ✤ ✤ ✤ it up. Preservation of the main part of the code,
however, had cost changes in the enforcement section. Instead of creating a Housing Inspector with more or less independent authority, the change limited him to inspections (a) at changes of ownership or occupancy, (b) at the direction of the City Manager, or (c) at the request of the City Health Department. These changes reflected strong feelings which had been publicly expressed by citizens who thought that the work of the housing inspector would involve invasions of privacy, that homeowners would be forced to make expensive repairs against their will, that an undue hardship would fall upon those without the means to carry out the repairs required of them, and that homes would be condemned and people thrown out on the street. The new provisions were designed to enable the City Council and City Manager to proceed slowly in putting the code into effect.

Actually, they made no attempt to enforce the new code immediately after its passage. The newly created post of Housing Inspector was left vacant and no program of inspection at changes of ownership and occupancy was started. From April, 1959 until February, 1960, the only inspections made occurred when one or two people registered a complaint about a condition of which they were aware, and the City Manager investigated. Other than those particular complaints, the City Manager heard no demands for enforcement.

On the night of February 21, 1960, a tragedy occurred which brought the problem of substandard housing to the attention of the entire community with shocking force, and altered its attitude toward the Housing Code. It marked the beginning of the enforcement of the code and of several other lines of attack upon poor housing.

Nine Negro children aged six months to eight years were alone in a sparsely furnished four-room apartment in a flimsy two-unit dwelling on Lincoln Street, while their mothers watched television in the other apartment. Both families were receiving welfare aid. The electricity in one apartment had been turned off for a month after three months of arrears had accumulated.

Apparently a candle used for illumination in the kitchen of the rear apartment ignited the oil around a leaky heater, and the rear apartment was immediately turned into a raging furnace. Two children escaped, running outside and around to the front apartment shouting that the rear section was on fire.

When the fire department arrived, men entered the apartment immediately with air packs, and located the remaining children while the fire was being extinguished. All seven were dead.

As the tragic news was circulated the next morning, the community experienced a profound wave of emotion, well expressed by the *News-Tribune*:

> Initial response by almost every Oberlinian was certainly one of extreme shock. Death by fire is never pleasant, and to inflict it on seven helpless youngsters is horrifying indeed. But as the first shock of the news passed, the horror seemed to change into a variety of reactions. Some people felt genuine pity for the children and for the parents, too. Offers of help began to come in soon after the news of the fire became general. Others found it difficult to feel compassion because the victims were who they were—little children in circumstances which would forever make theirs an uphill battle for survival. Did life hold any more promise for them than death?
>
> . . . People felt a deep sense of *guilt* that such a thing had happened in enlightened Oberlin. Guilt that they as individuals had not helped keep such slum conditions from continuing, or worse yet, that they as individuals had been blissfully ignorant of the existence of these miserable dwellings.

The desire to do something, *now*, was the most remarkable feature of the new mood which enveloped the community. But what could be done? Beginning enforcement of the Housing Code was an obvious step, and it became a foregone conclusion that this would be done.

The *News-Tribune* took advantage of the new feeling in the community to press home the fact that objections to the code which had been expressed in the past would have to be overridden. It asked some hard questions:

> Has the horror of Sunday night's fire made Oberlinians willing to open their homes to inspection, and to force inspection of those who are unwilling? . . . Are we willing to brush aside cries of "discrimination" if we decide to concentrate inspection on the poorest housing in town, and those homes happen to be occupied by (but not necessarily owned by) Negroes? . . . If a landlord says "But I can't afford to repair the house because the income is so low" are we willing as a city to say to him, "OK, then, board the place up"? . . . Are we willing to physically throw families out on the streets if they move undetected into housing branded inadequate by the housing inspector? . . . Are we as individuals willing to ante up the $20,000, $50,000 or $100,000, either through the city government or by means of subscription to some non-profit corporation perhaps, which will be needed?

In this time of extreme emotion the community turned to the elected officials for leadership. Eric Nord, newly elected Council Chairman, received many telephone calls from citizens indicating that they expected leadership to be part of his role, though his office was minimal. An investigation at the time revealed that he received far more calls than other Councilmen, including Bill Long, who had just stepped down from the chairmanship of the Council.

The City Council met informally the Tuesday after the fire, and met once or twice more during the week. The main topic of discussion was the steps to be taken in beginning enforcement of the Housing Code. "This is the thing we want to do something about immediately," said Nord, "to make sure that there is no new occupancy of completely inadequate dwellings." The Councilmen also called a public meeting for the following Monday night to discuss the steps which could be taken to meet the housing problem.

The meeting was scheduled to be held in Sturges Hall, a College

Building, seating about 200. Sturges was soon jammed, and the meeting was moved to the nearby First Methodist Church, where nearly 300 citizens finally assembled. Held over a week after the fire, the meeting was characterized by emotion. Speakers who had never participated in public affairs would rise to make suggestions and comments, and many lapsed into incoherency, bewildered and unable to express themselves.

Mayor Nord led the meeting. Commenting that the problem of substandard housing had long been in existence, but had remained "below the level of community attention," he noted that many still did not appreciate the magnitude of the problem. He analyzed community opinion as divided into three parts: those who thought that strict enforcement of the housing code would be sufficient to take care of the problem; those who saw the whole situation as too complicated for any solution; and those who felt that a start, however small, must be made.

At Nord's request, Bill Long outlined the housing enforcement problem. He divided housing into four categories: the modern, owner-occupied homes which only needed a watchful eye to see that violations such as conversion to multiple occupancy dwellings did not take place; housing with major code violations, where the owners have the financial ability to bring them up to standard, which require only strict enforcement; houses in essentially the same condition, the owners of which are unable to get credit to make the needed improvements; and houses which cannot be brought up to standard and which should be demolished. Long promised that Council would not follow the three usual solutions to the housing problem: doing nothing, isolating the worst cases, and hoping for the best; beginning strict enforcement while leaving families to solve the problem of where they should live after they had been evicted from substandard quarters; or turning the problem over to the welfare agencies and forgetting about it. He promised that inspection of the worst housing would be started. He noted that Oberlin could not take care of new families moving in, but declared that all families living in the city at the time were the responsibility of the community. The combined efforts and financial assistance of both government and nongovernmental bodies, he continued, would be required to meet this responsibility.

Long outlined steps which could be taken. As the *News-Tribune* reported them, they were ". . . exercise of police powers in areas of health, fire and housing; extension of utilities under conditions which the people living on the streets can afford to meet; new home construction and appropriate sale terms for low income families seeking to establish standard homes; maintain close relations with the townships surrounding Oberlin in order to insure that we do not dump our problems on them and that they do not permit conditions to develop which some day we may inherit."

A new commission, Long continued, was needed to coordinate and direct all activities associated with housing. It should be empowered to use governmental as well as non-governmental funds. If it had proper leadership and substantial funds, it could work out a program and take steps towards the ultimate goal of the elimination of all substandard housing.

At this meeting, the Council took four official actions. It directed the City Manager to take immediate steps to enforce the housing code; it directed the finance committee to include a sum in the next year's budget sufficient to hire a part time housing inspector; it approved the appointment of Mills Clark, a retired real estate developer, Thurston Manning, a professor of physics, William Stetson, proprietor of the Sport Shop, Robert Thomas, a Negro reporter for the *Lorain-Journal*, and Mrs. Margaret Baker, a Negro housewife, to a housing advisory board, and it passed a resolution providing for a new Housing Renewal Commission.

Private initiative had taken steps which were revealed at this meeting by Harold Peterson, public school music instructor. He related how six couples of First Church had met and pledged $600 "as evidence of our concern and responsibility." The wives of this group had made some telephone calls following the meeting, and brought the total of pledges up to $1,500. This money was available to Council, he said, to support any action it might wish to take.

Eric Nord announced plans for the formation of the Oberlin Housing Foundation, Incorporated, to be a loan fund made available to private individuals who would otherwise be unable to obtain loans for home improvement. Nord suggested that shares might be offered at $50.

Individuals made many comments during the meeting. E. A. Trautz, vice president of the Oberlin Savings Bank and manager of the South Amherst Branch, felt that financing by subscription was unrealistic. He thought that all should share equally in this burden, and suggested a tax. David Anderson, a physics professor, said, "I object to the constant refrain that we're overburdened with taxes. The rate looks high but the assessment basis is low. Taxes are a very modest part of most of our budgets." Bruce Hawkins, a physics professor, agreed. "Wasn't everyone assessed for the Lorain Street sewer? Some do not have sewers yet. Then I do not see why the rest of us cannot be assessed to put sewers in for them. I am willing to contribute yearly till the problem is solved." Russell Reynolds, General Manager of the National Association of College Stores, suggested the immediate step of taxing every light meter $1.00 per month. City Solicitor Severs noted the limitations on the expenditure of public funds. "I haven't found any way to take public money to subsidize an individual in the improvement of his property. I think we'd be in real trouble if we tried it."

Others suggested the use of volunteer labor. Mrs. E. U. Carter, a Negro proprietor of Carter's Rest Home, said, "There are plenty of people here who would give $100 in work or money. I'm willing to put in money and I'm a great solicitor." Fred Owens, a compositor for the *News-Tribune* printing plant, said, "I have energy and no money. I'm willing to give my time, to be directed by the committee, to do work on houses that are bad. Let's inspect, then get together and do something right now instead of waiting for a big project in a year or two."

Councilman Davis read a prepared statement on the problems of substandard housing in the city. He maintained that even without the housing code, city officials had had sufficient authority under fire and health laws to have prevented the catastrophy. "The crux of the matter is that of enforcement, and the failure to have acted, rests upon all of us, citizens, Council and law enforcement officers alike." He went on to call for some large effort, either public or private, asking only that it be carried out under the guidance of someone with proper experience in the field, and that instead of a dole, it be an effort based upon sound financing to help people to help themselves.

James Lancaster, an attendant at the Elyria Country Club, suggested that Council could provide a valuable service by extending utilities to sparsely settled areas. Living on East Hamilton Street without water or sewers, he said, he and seven or eight other families were paying assessments and getting nothing for them. Davis agreed. His first concern, he said, would be for those who had houses, but who are without paved streets and utilities. Ordinarily when one buys utility services, he said, part of the rate includes a charge for unprofitable extensions. "Utility rates aren't right if they don't have that in them." Long made a motion which was seconded by Davis, directing the City Manager to report in 60 days on all dedicated streets in the city that didn't have pavement or utility lines.

Council then appointed City Manager Dunn Housing Inspector, and directed him to serve in that capacity one day a week until a regular inspector was named. Davis objected that it was improper to designate an administrative officer's time, but withdrew his opposition when Hellmuth explained that enforcement would be "no good" without such a provision.

The first activity of the newly formed Housing Foundation, together with the Housing Renewal Commission, was a general clean-up campaign starting April 4. Citizens were encouraged to clean their own property and cart away their rubbish. The city furnished a collection truck and put a man on full time duty at the dump. The volunteers on the labor committee were organized to respond to requests for special assistance in cleaning up and carrying away refuse. Groups of college students, high school students, and adults armed with rakes and cartons dispersed to clean up areas where committee members had noticed that refuse remained.

These are the last activities resulting from the fire which were carried out by private initiative except for an undertaking of the Housing Foundation. In May, this organization found its first major project, a house which needed finishing. This enterprise is further described in the chapter on Negroes and Low Cost Housing. Further activities of the Housing Renewal Commission may also be found in that chapter.

Immediately after the fire, City Manager Dunn condemned the fire-gutted houses, and what remained of these families were taken into other homes. He made a series of inspections of known sub-standard houses, condemning them when they were vacant. He also inspected dwellings whenever his utility billing records revealed a change in ownership or occupancy. By November, he had condemned as unfit for human habitation fourteen dwellings, including two upstairs apartments lacking two exits, which were owned by the Co-op.

In the meantime, Dunn made efforts to get a part time housing inspector to take over the job. He finally decided to hire the Lorain County Health Department to make inspections.

Dunn and the Inspector assigned by the Health Department, George D. Bragg, worked out a program of door-to-door, street-by-street inspections in the southeast section, where the worst dwellings are located, in addition to inspections made at change of ownership or occupancy, and those made upon complaint. Dunn anticipated protest over his focus on this almost exclusively Negro section and checked with Negro leaders before the program was started. They agreed that the city would get the most for its money by concentrating on that section and Dunn's policy has elicited no protest from Negroes to date.

Bragg checks all the houses for all items covered in the housing code, using a check-off sheet. Letters announcing condemnation and the necessity of repairs go out over the signature of the City Manager, with time limits set by him. Bragg reinspects dwellings with violations to determine whether necessary repairs have been made.

At the April 3, 1961 meeting of Council, Dunn presented a brief summary of the inspector's work: 71 inspections, 25 houses requiring repair and 8 condemnations, four of occupied buildings. The latter figure, Dunn indicated, raised a question which had been avoided before—when the Housing Code was originally passed there had been an agreement that condemnation be applied only to unoccupied houses.

After the regular session on April 17, a closed meeting was held to consider the condemnation question. Bragg presented a vivid description of the conditions in which many extremely low-income families lived. Dunn then informed the members of Council that he was awaiting their instructions as to whether he should order eviction. Council wrestled with this problem until Long suggested that a straw vote be taken. The outcome was a 3-3 tie (Comings was absent) with Long, Hellmuth and Ellis opposing eviction. At this point, Davis proclaimed that there was not one courageous man in the room and walked out. A few minutes later he returned to get his coat and Hellmuth told him that if he would propose eviction in a public meeting, he would second the motion and vote for it, insuring at least a 4-3 victory. Davis picked up his coat and left the room, deigning no reply.

To date, Council has taken no definite action, and Dunn has ordered no evictions. Bragg's report for April, May and June, 1961, shows a total of 84 inspections made, broken down as follows:

3 dwelling units unsuitable for human occupancy and unoccupied.
6   "   "   "   "   "   "   but occupied.
6   "   "   reinspected correcting violations.
5   "   "   "   not correcting violations.
20   "   "   requiring corrections.
44   "   "   in compliance with code.

At the end of his report, Bragg noted that unsolved problems remained. Some way to aid occupants of substandard housing to move to suitable housing was needed. Financing for rehabilitation of other dwelling units was needed. Finally, he asked again for a time limit for vacating dwelling units designated unfit for human habitation.

Out of the fire came many things, some transitory, some lasting. One lasting result may come from the investigations of the Housing Renewal Commission described in "Negroes and Low Cost Housing"—low-cost dwellings financed by the federal government. Another lasting development is an atmosphere permissive of inspections and of the enforcements of the Housing Code. If the final step has not been taken—the eviction of unfortunates living in substandard dwellings and unable to afford better quarters— the less extreme enforcement measures are being carried out. The Housing Foundation still exists, but most of its capital was tied up in an unfortunate investment until recently.

The transitory result of the fire is the pressure to do something which sprang up from the wave of emotion which temporarily swept the community after the fire. The Housing Commission has nothing new to offer. The capital improvements plan the City Manager offered (he actually had prepared it before the fire) awaits the passage of a new income tax or additional income producing measures.

The normal state of apathy and non-involvement in governmental matters has settled once again upon the community, after having been lifted by the tragedy long enough for a few citizens to become permanently interested in Oberlin's housing problems, and for a few changes to take place.

8   NEGROES AND LOW-COST HOUSING

In our day it is difficult to discuss the issue of housing without also talking about race. We have seen how enforcement of the housing code became involved with race because most of the substandard dwellings were in Negro neighborhoods. Now we turn to some of the continuing efforts to deal with the housing problems created by low incomes, cultural differences, and racial prejudices.

Since Oberlin was founded in 1833, its population has consistently contained a much higher percentage of Negroes than does the typical Ohio town. In 1950, 24.5% of Oberlin's population were Negroes, whereas only 6.5% of the population of the entire state consisted of Negroes. The relative Negro population seems to have declined slightly in the last decades of the 19th century, but since then it has increased slowly.

The Negroes in Oberlin seem always to have formed the lowest economic class, and occupied the worst housing. By 1957, between 85% and 90% of the city's Negroes were concentrated in the southeast section of town.

Oberlin's Negro population began to play a significant part in local politics only recently. In 1933, Julius Burton, a Negro, participated in the Republican primary, claiming that members of his race ought to be represented in Council. But it was not until twenty years later, in 1953, that a Negro held an elective position in Oberlin. In that year, Wade Ellis, a Negro mathematics professor who conducted a campaign to get Negroes registered and to teach them how to vote with a portable voting machine, and Mrs. Eva Mae Crosby, a Negro attorney, school teacher and real estate developer, were elected to a fifteen-member Charter Commission.

The Charter Commission successfully carried out some changes in the organization of Oberlin's governmental structure which made it easier for minority factions to gain representation on the City Council. (A large part of the credit for these changes belongs, incidentally, to Ellis. When he ran for Council in 1957, he was the sixth of the seven successful candidates. He ran again in 1959, and so increased his vote that he placed second.)

Ellis' arrival in Oberlin seems partly to have coincided with, and partly to have caused, an awakening of some of the Negro community to political consciousness. At the same time, the changes wrought by the Charter Commission helped bring into power leaders who have been sympathetic to the problems of the Negro community. These changes in Oberlin's political balance have produced an atmosphere in which groups interested in benefiting Negroes through governmental action have an opportunity for successful action which does not seem to have existed previously.

Nevertheless, grave handicaps to action persist, for the Negro community today is split into at least three segments. One consists of those who are contented with the job security provided by the College, or the less secure but higher paying employment in nearby industries and construction projects, and who cherish the acceptance given them by the whole community as long as they demand no further privileges.

Another element resents what racial discrimination appears to exist in employment, finance, and housing, and is willing to make an effort to change this state of affairs. These people are active in registration drives and electioneering, on various committees and organizations, and in trying to secure municipal improvements in the Negro areas.

By far the largest segment of the Negro community, however, is apathetic. Most of the Negroes in Oberlin have a low level of education and are employed in unskilled labor with low wages. They lack political awareness; the possible gains of political action, if realized at all, seem distant and unattainable. They are not aware of a relationship between their own actions and the policies of the local government. A man whose home had been condemned was asked why he did not protest to the City Council that the action was contrary to the established enforcement policy. He replied, "Well, ——, that is the law and there is not much a man like me can do. The white people downtown just run things like they want to, and they will not give a poor colored man like me a break." Another man, asked why he didn't vote for Ellis, replied that Ellis was a Democrat. He was a Republican, he said, because the Republicans had freed the slaves.

As yet, the Negroes themselves have been unable to organize for effective action. The eight Negro churches have not been interested in local politics. All but one of the ministers have other commitments than their Oberlin churches. The exception is the Reverend Fred L. Steen of the Mt. Zion Baptist Church who has been active on the City Health Commission, which administers state funds for medical care for indigent persons, and on the committee appointed by Council to study discriminatory practices in housing. He is a member of the NAACP and the ACLU, and was a candidate for the Board of Education in the 1961 election. Of the others, some hold full-time jobs, some serve other congregations as well as their Oberlin ones, and one is a student. Nevertheless, the Negro churches have on occasion served as a channel of communication to the Negroes. In the 1959 election, some ministers reportedly endorsed Ellis from the pulpit. Organizations such as the League of Women Voters and the NAACP have used church facilities for public meetings, and the Open Occupancy Housing Committee circulated petitions in the churches.

The local NAACP has not been very active. It successfully carried out a boycott of one local store in an attempt to secure the employment of a Negro, yet the response to this action from the Negro community was decidedly mixed. Some active Negroes criticized the boycott, for the store had employed Negroes in the past. Others felt the action discredited the Negro and jeopardized his position in the community, and apologized to the manager for the action taken in the name of their race. Since this one skirmish the NAACP has retired from the field. Its most obvious handicaps are the refusal of some of the active Negroes to join it, its leaders' lack of political experience, and the conception which prevails among its members that its role should be "non-political."

There have been charges of discrimination in three areas:

employment, finance, and housing. Some racial discrimination in employment practices undoubtedly exists in Oberlin. The two local banks have yet to hire a Negro. Bill Long's Co-op makes a point of employing Negroes, and several are employed for maintenance and clerical work by the College and city, but Negroes hold positions in few other white-owned businesses. On the whole, there is little opportunity for action in the employment area, for most of Oberlin's businesses are small and hire only a few friends and relatives.

Charges of discriminatory financial practices have been made against the local banks. One instance reported to a Council Committee concerned a Negro who wished to build a house in a predominantly white area and was refused a loan in a local bank, yet was able to obtain one from a bank in Lorain when he later applied there. Representatives of the banks, however, steadfastly maintain that the criteria by which they grant credit deal only with ability to pay, and this may well be the case. Many Negroes do not have the resources to obtain a bank loan.

Housing is the third field of discrimination. Here real estate agents and landlords openly follow the racial policies which are practiced by their profession in most parts of the United States. With the exception of one house, all of the real estate developments in Oberlin in recent years have been either all white or all Negro. The exception is College Park, an expensive development undertaken by the College to provide residences for members of the faculty. Wade Ellis lives there, and two or three lots are owned by other Negroes.

Housing is also the area where there is the greatest incentive to attack discriminatory practices. Negroes have shown increased interest in obtaining housing outside of the southeast section of town in recent years for the Negro population is growing, as is the rest of Oberlin's population. A factor which has aggravated the housing problem for Negroes is the housing code passed in 1959. Enforcement has started, and the unoccupied dwellings which have been used by Negroes in the past have been declared unfit for occupancy. The code makes it more difficult for families to double up in one house.

Several years ago Mrs. Eva Mae Crosby founded a corporation which has a development in the northwestern part of town. The purpose of the corporation was to give Negroes an opportunity to buy a better kind of house than they had previously been able to do. Mrs. Crosby wanted her development to be integrated, but up until the present date only Negroes have bought her houses. She is currently reserving one house for potential white buyers who have not yet materialized.

Mrs. Crosby encountered opposition to her development. In 1950, North Prospect Street was developed by a white man. The city put in a turn-around at the end of the block, and the Planning Commission reserved the right to break it in the future when further development seemed to warrant it. In 1956, when Mrs. Crosby began developing the upper end of North Prospect Street, the sixteen residents of the older development formed the North Prospect Street Park Association and purchased a strip of land 4.57 feet wide, at the end of their *cul de sac*. Their expressed purpose was to protect their street from further traffic. Later, the park association refused to allow Mrs. Crosby to put a water line through the park to connect with the 6″ main on North Prospect, and she was forced to put a 6″ main through Union Street, an approach street which would never have houses, to connect to the main on Hollywood Street. When water pressure on Hollywood Street was lowered by this arrangement, the city threatened to condemn the park, and Mrs. Crosby subsequently received permission to connect her water line to the North Prospect main.

Further, there has been continued resistance on the part of the park association to the efforts of Mrs. Crosby to provide easy vehicular access to her development. This resistance has been represented solely as the natural concern of property owners anxious to keep their street free of traffic, but whatever the motives of the members of the North Prospect Street Park Association, their actions have been interpreted by many as resistance to a new Negro settlement in a hitherto white section of town. Later, after a bout in the courts, City Council appropriated a strip of land connecting Mrs. Crosby's development with North Prospect Street.

Now let us turn to community efforts to meet the housing problem. After the mass meeting which followed the fire that killed seven Negro children, Eric Nord, Harold Peterson and Bill Long took steps to organize the Housing Foundation. Constitut-

ing themselves the "steering committee," they drew up a statement of purpose.

> The purpose of this corporation shall be to promote, encourage and
> implement the improvement of private housing in the City of Ober-
> lin and, in furtherance of such basic purpose, to cooperate with
> public bodies and with other private organizations:
> (1) To assist individuals and organizations in arrangements for the
>   financing necessary to effect such improvements.
> (2) To guarantee loans by existing financial institutions and others
>   where necessary to enable needy persons of limited means who
>   could not otherwise do so to improve their properties.
> (3) To loan money at interest on the security of the mortgages, or
>   otherwise, where necessary to finance needy persons of limited
>   means who could not otherwise do so to improve their prop-
>   erties.
> (4) And otherwise to engage in such programs and take such ac-
>   tion as shall be necessary or desirable to effect such purposes.

They announced a pre-organizational meeting for Sunday,
March 6, 1960 publicized by the *News-Tribune*, which provided
a blank on the front page which could be cut out and sent in, to
indicate an interest in buying stock. The meeting drew ninety-
two people and about $5,000 worth of stock was bought.

That same week the organizers of the Housing Foundation succeeded in raising some $8,100 from about seventy stockholders.
Directors were elected at an organizational meeting on March
13.[1]

Eric Nord, while acting as chairman, appointed the volunteer
labor committee to see how many offers to donate time and labor
could be utilized.[2] The *News-Tribune* gave publicity to this
group, and published another sign-up blank on the front page
for those wishing to volunteer labor. At a meeting in the community room of the People's Bank on Sunday, March 20, sixty people
assembled to volunteer their labor. With written offers, the assembled number of volunteers reached 150. At this meeting more
members were added to the committee.[3]

A man who seemed a good subject for the efforts of the Foundation was found on West Lincoln Street. He had started to build
a house, but had run out of money and left the house unfinished

while he lived in a definitely substandard metal dwelling nearby. The Housing Foundation loaned him the money he needed to finish the house—almost the entire capital—and many high school and college students and townsmen contributed labor to the project. The directors of the Foundation had expected that when the house was finished the man would obtain a mortgage on it from a bank and repay them. However, by the time the house was finished, the man had lost his job and become entangled in other difficulties, which caused the banks to refuse to grant him a mortgage. Consequently, the capital of the Housing Foundation appeared to be indefinitely tied up in its first project, providing a discouraging example of the difficulties in coping with the problem of substandard housing.

Soon after the fire, on March 7, 1961, the City Council created a Housing Renewal Commission and appointed to it Robert Thomas, a Negro reporter for the *Lorain Journal*, Betty Martin, Principal of Eastwood School, Douglas Johnson, an architect, the Assistant to the President of Oberlin College, and Arnold Schwartz, a plastics manufacturer with a business located out of town. Their mandate was to investigate ways of alleviating the housing problem, so as to bring every unit of housing in Oberlin up to standard. It was informally understood that this body would coordinate all the activities in the community involving housing. A study was made of the housing problem, and a report was given to Council. The Commission concluded that the only way to get the very low income element into acceptable housing would be through a program of public housing. A program subsidized by the Federal Government could be carried out through the Lorain County Metropolitan Housing Authority, under which the Authority would buy a site delineated by the city and build the housing units, and the city would provide the utilities. The rent would be used to pay off a forty-year loan, and a fee would be paid to the city in lieu of lost taxes. At the end of forty years, the housing would belong to the city.

The Council passed the resolution of need required to apply for the subsidies, and authorized the Housing Commission to gather the information necessary to support a request for aid. A survey was then conducted under the auspices of the Lorain County Metropolitan Housing Authority, and the results revealed that, of the 146 families eligible to live in this low-rent housing, 100 said they would be willing to occupy it, 33 said they would not, and 13 said they did not know whether they would.

The survey was sent to Washington, and an authorization to request 200 units of subsidized housing was returned. Council approved the project in 1962.

These are the various efforts only indirectly connected with discrimination which have been made to cope with the problem of providing low-cost housing for the poorest citizens in town, many of whom are Negroes. They have not, as of this time, made a substantial impression on the problem. Attacks directly upon discrimination stem both from the heightened interest in enabling Negroes to obtain better housing which resulted from the fire, and from civil libertarian and religious convictions.

The Willowbrook Farms development was the direct cause of the anti-segregation movement. This development on newly annexed land on the east side of town was scheduled to add 264 houses to the community when it was completed. Soon after the sales office was opened, word got around that no Negroes would be able to buy. Negroes had gone to open houses and had been given evasive answers and had failed to obtain appointments for further interviews.

The Reverend Edward Jones of the Christ Episcopal Church was stirred to do something by this situation, and held a conversation in a downtown restaurant with Councilman Bill Long and Don Pease, co-editor of the *News-Tribune*. These three men drew up a list of people who might be interested in discussing the Willowbrook Farms segregation policy, and contacted them.[4] The twenty-six members first met in May, 1960, at Christ Church and discussed the problem at many meetings thereafter. Robert Thomas pointed out that segregation was not limited to Willowbrook Farms, but existed in other developments in the community.

The committee spent much time discussing the causes of the problem, and decided to petition the City Council to pass an ordinance to prevent discriminatory housing practices. Chairman Jones appointed Milton Yinger, Bill Miller, and Donald McIlroy, to prepare a short declaration.

This committee reported three statements and the following one was adopted unanimously:

117 *Negroes and Low-Cost Housing*

Believing that we are not being true to our religious and democratic heritage if residence in any neighborhood is restricted to certain racial and ethnic groups on purely arbitrary grounds, we, the undersigned, declare our intention to practice the principle of equality with respect to housing, and we declare our desire to see people given the right to acquire residence without prejudice as to their race, religion, or national origin. Moreover, we petition the Council of the City of Oberlin to consider such legislation as will be necessary to eliminate discrimination in housing.

Bill Long moved that ministers of Oberlin churches be asked to preach on the statement, and newspapers be asked to mention it when the drive for signatures was begun.

In January, the petition was circulated in both local banks, and in several of the churches. Five hundred and fifty-eight signatures were obtained in this manner, and the petition was presented to Council on January 16, 1961.

At some point in the Committee's activities, an attempt had been made to attract the manager of the Willowbrook Farms development to a meeting at which he could be questioned on his segregation policy. The committee arranged to have a letter written by four of the most prominent citizens of the city, Mayor Eric Nord, President of the College Robert K. Carr, Congressman Charles. A. Mosher, and Professor Milton Yinger, asking him to lunch at the Oberlin Inn. No answer was received.

Thus, when the petition campaign had been successfully carried out, the committee decided to make a more direct attack upon Willowbrook Farms. A subcommittee was formed which found out that the development was using Federal Housing Administration (FHA) loans, and that there was a federal law against discrimination where they were used. Bronson Clark, a builder who had had experience with integrated housing out-of-town and who was serving as chairman of the subcommittee, consulted the FHA representative in Cleveland and found out that while the law was not being actively enforced, measures could probably be taken if a discriminatory situation were brought to their attention.

With this information, the subcommittee, with Arnold Schwartz as new chairman, began to devise a way to test whether Willowbrook Farms would sell to a Negro. A Negro family was found which declared it was willing to live in Willowbrook Farms, and two white families who had no intention of buying a house were located to play a part in the plan.

One Sunday, the three families separately went to look at the houses and expressed their interest. On Monday night, the first white family went to the office and paid a $10.00 fee for a preliminary credit investigation; then the Negro family went. To their surprise, the fee was accepted from them also. The other white family entered while the Negro family was there and after they had left inquired whether there would be very many Negro families in the development. They were told, "No, not any."

That night, the subcommittee met to discuss the unexpected turn of events. They decided that the Willowbrook Farms management might suspect their plot, or might simply be playing it safe. They decided to see whether the Negro's credit would be approved.

Eventually, one of the white families received notification that their credit had been approved. The other white family called and was told that its credit was all right. The Negro family went to the office and learned that their credit too had been approved.

The next step in purchasing a house was to put up a $90 deposit. It was suspected that the Negro would not be able to get this back if he was finally refused admittance to Willowbrook Farms, as the committee fully expected he would be. At a meeting of the full committee, the sum was raised by contributions of the members. However, at this point, the Negro involved said that he had understood that the committee would make the entire down payment on the house for him. This had in fact been discussed by the committee, but had been decided against, for they reasoned that such an action would make them appear to be gratuitous troublemakers rather than citizens interested in helping someone who needed help. Since the down payment was not forthcoming, the Negro withdrew from the scheme, and the attempt to prove Willowbrook Farms would not sell to a Negro fell through. As of yet, no Negro has bought at Willowbrook Farms, but neither is an instance known of any Negro being turned down outright.

Another activity of the Open Occupancy Housing Committee was the formation of a Placement Subcommittee. This subcommittee, with Bill Long as chairman, was delegated to find which houses that were for sale could be purchased by Negroes. Long was particularly interested in this in order to be able to assure officials of the new Federal Aeronautics Administration (FAA) that their colored employees would be able to obtain decent housing if they wished to move to Oberlin. Long now knows of three houses in white neighborhoods on the west side of town which can be bought by Negroes. Their prices are between $14,000 and $25,000, too high for most Negroes already living in Oberlin. Long and Councilman Ellis have made attempts to induce Negroes to buy these houses, but so far they have not been successful. Long reports that many Negroes are reluctant to place themselves, and especially their children, in a situation of racial tension.

The committee has talked of founding a finance company, or inviting one to come to Oberlin, to make loans easier for Negroes to obtain. They also have considered financing an integrated housing development. However, the committee is not eager to get into the banking business, and nothing has been done about these suggestions.

At the January 16 Council meeting, when the petition sponsored by the Open Occupancy Housing Committee was presented, a resolution to form a committee to study the problem of discrimination in housing was passed. At the next meeting fifteen citizens were appointed to the committee.[5] George Simpson, who had previously been chairman of the group which drew up the Housing Code, was elected chairman. The first action of the committee was to purchase books on open housing and donate them to the public library. Then, the chief activities of the committee were to interview various people acquainted with housing in Oberlin in order to find out what kinds of discrimination exist, and to study the statutes of thirty-four American cities in an attempt to discover what sort of legislation would be most appropriate for Oberlin.

The committee learned about various devices which can be used by residents of a development to prevent people they consider undesirable from becoming their neighbors. In Eric Nord's development, any lot sale or resale has to be approved by three of the nearest five lot owners, and if the sale is refused, those protesting the sale must buy the lot themselves. Nord testified that this provision was not intended to be used for racial or religious discrimination, but could be used that way. He stressed the need for public education on the problem and said that if it could be proven that the coming of Negroes did not lower property values in a neighborhood, much of the problem would be solved.

In William Gaeuman's development, Robin Park, there is a three-man regulatory board elected by lot owners, which must countersign all transfers of property. No relief is provided if the counter-signatures are refused. Mr. Gaeuman pointed out that all of his lot owners approve of this provision and wish to extend its application to the future development of Robin Park. Those who do not own property, he asserted, were the ones who advocate open housing, because they have nothing to lose by doing so. Gaeuman protested that the discussion of racial discrimination was injuring the interests of the developers by driving many prospective buyers away from Oberlin. He expressed the opinion that an ordinance would not be enforceable, and declared that if it were passed, he would continue his present practice and carry his case to the courts.

At another meeting it was hoped that a representative of Willowbrook Farms would be present, but the elusive gentleman was out of town. Eventually he flatly refused to attend any meetings of the committee. However, Mills Clark and Kenneth Clark, both local builders, were present. Kenneth Clark testified that several of the tenants of his new apartment house on East College Street had asked whether the other apartments would be open to Negroes. He had told them they would not be, and believed that most would not have rented them if he followed an open occupancy policy. A law which made discriminatory practices illegal, he thought, would give landlords something to point to and make it easier for them to follow an open occupancy policy.

Mr. Clark expressed doubt as to whether the majority of people in Oberlin desired integrated housing, and pointed to the Crosby and his own Gladys Court developments which are presently all Negro. He stated that an official of the new Federal Aeronautics Administration Center had told him that FAA personnel would not buy his houses unless he would guarantee not to sell to Negroes.

Mr. Clark pointed out that much of the inability of Negroes to obtain good housing was due to their low income rather than to prejudice. Builders, he said, make the most profit on the construction of residences. In his opinion, legislation against discrimination would not help the Negro much, but would serve to prevent builders from constructing low-cost housing.

The committee also interviewed local real estate agents, and learned that when a Negro asked them about a house, they showed him only houses in the colored section. The agents pointed out that in many instances, the seller specified that the sale was restricted to whites. They also asserted that when Negroes move into an area, property values fall, and estimated that the difference between similar houses in white and mixed neighborhoods was about $4,000. One agent declared that colored people were not interested in integrated housing, or they would be attending the meetings of the committee, and most felt any ordinance would be unenforceable.

While the interviewing was being carried on, a subcommittee had been examining various ordinances, and on May 8 recommended that the (proposed but not enacted) Cleveland ordinance be the basis of the recommendation to Council. The ordinance finally recommended prohibited refusal to sell or rent because of race, religion or ancestry by owners of three or more dwelling units, apartments, or building lots. It also applied appropriate prohibitions to real estate agents and lending institutions, and provided for enforcement procedures. The aggrieved individual would register a complaint with the Housing Renewal Commission. The Commission was authorized to use persuasion, and if that failed, to hold a public hearing and issue such orders as appeared warranted by its findings of fact. Appeal to Council was provided for, and a penalty of $100 or thirty days imprisonment was set for failure to obey the order of the Commission.

A few changes were made in the proposed Cleveland ordinance aside from those necessary to make the ordinance fit Oberlin's system of government. Ownership of three units, rather than four as in the Cleveland ordinance, or five, as in the Pittsburgh ordinance, made one liable to a charge of discrimination. The Commission was given power to compel the attendance of witnesses, and could hear the case even if the respondent refused to attend.

This ordinance, together with a recommendation that it be

passed which had been voted for by 9 of the 10 committee members present at their last meeting, was submitted to the City Council on June 6.

John Strong, a member of the committee, submitted a minority report opposing the legislation. He pointed out that the committee, which had been chosen from volunteers, did not represent all areas of opinion; that the committee had spent little time considering possible negative results of legislation; that the ordinance seemed to invade the area of "thought"; that all materials studied by the committee had dealt with cities with populations of more than 1,000,000; and that College Park had open housing, and only one Negro lived there, and three owned lots. Strong was in favor of seeking state legislation to remedy the situation.

Mr. Simpson, the Chairman of the Committee, retorted that "Civil rights are not correlated with the size of cities." He gave the following reasons for adopting an open housing ordinance:

> For all practical purposes, Negro families are restricted to a few sections of Oberlin. Some Negro families prefer not to live in a segregated neighborhood.
> Also, the property for which Negro families are permitted to compete is a small and inferior part of the total housing supply.
> Here, as elsewhere, Negroes obtain poorer housing even when they pay the same or higher rents.
> Housing restrictions on the basis of race constitute a serious infringement of the civil rights of Negro citizens of Oberlin.
> An ordinance of the kind proposed by the committee would put moral as well as legal pressure on the community to relax the racial restrictions on housing which exist in Oberlin at the present time.

Ira Porter, former President of the People's Banking Company, objected to a clause in the preamble of the proposed ordinance which indicated that discrimination took place in the making of loans. "Whether or not anyone believes it, every consideration is given to loan applications. They are granted on the basis of value of property and ability to pay." William Davis, Councilman and Executive Vice President of the Oberlin Savings Bank, seconded this sentiment.

Morgan McDonald, the Negro proprietor of a watch repair shop who soon after the meeting announced his candidacy for City Council, also spoke to oppose the legislation. He derided people who wanted to move to a better neighborhood. "Clean up your property . . . The house doesn't make the people, the people make the house. And no law can make anybody love anybody."

A public hearing on the proposed ordinance was held on June 21. About 150 people were in the audience, which was heavily in favor of the ordinance. Over half were Negroes. Simpson introduced the ordinance with a description of the work of the committee and their findings, and reiterated the arguments in support of the proposed legislation which he had presented at the previous Council meeting. In an effort to anticipate objections, he expressed the opinion that the 1954 Supreme Court decision in *Brown versus the Board of Education* indicated that the ordinance was constitutional. He cited a sociological study as evidence that property values did not necessarily decline when Negroes moved into a neighborhood, and he denied that an absolute right of property existed upon which the law would infringe. The Council, he said, would have to weigh property rights against community rights. He concluded that he felt a resolution instead of an ordinance, a compromise which had been suggested, would have little effect.

At this meeting Ira Porter, John Strong, Morgan McDonald, Ernest Chamberlain and Lee Ross spoke against the legislation, arguing chiefly for the property rights of the individual. Porter expressed the opinion that Oberlin was losing potential residents to surrounding areas and hurting its economic position by advancing ahead of nearby communities.

The majority of those who spoke favored the ordinance. Among these were a man who felt that it was important to support Oberlin's ideals. He declared that Oberlin's Negroes would feel much less at home if the ordinance was not passed. When Strong asked, "If one were against the code, would you say he is anti-Negro?" Many in the audience said, "Yes." At one point, when the argument was given that the problem was purely one of economics, someone shouted that this was an argument for an FEPC (Fair Employment Practices Commission) too.

After this study was completed, the fair housing ordinance was revised to cover ownership of five or more units and was passed by

City Council. Ira Porter then filed a citizen's suit to have it declared unconstitutional. The Lorain County Court of Common Pleas ruled in favor of Porter, and the District Court of Appeals has tentatively agreed to hear the city's appeal.

The controversy over the Open Housing Code has raised many problems in the community. In spite of the five-unit exemption from the code, many people feel that it violates property rights. Some of these are apparently not prejudiced or excessively concerned over property values, but men who feel that the matter is one of the conscience, which should not be and cannot effectively be legislated against. Others, however, think that failure to pass the ordinance would be a betrayal of Oberlin's tradition and ideals. The developers and real estate agents are against the law, and no one can say what percentage of the community is opposed to it. As one woman remarked, "Those who simply don't want to live next to Negroes stayed away from the meeting."

In all of the efforts to break down barriers of racial prejudice, whites who wish to carry on the fight have faced the problem of Negro apathy. While Negros are conscious of discriminatory housing practices, not one has been willing to provoke the censure of "contented" Negroes and brave the racial tension which a determined attempt to buy a house in a white neighborhood would create. Many Negroes want to improve their condition and bring up their children in a good neighborhood, but so far no instance of a Negro using all the resources available to enter a white neighborhood has been found.[6] The understandable unwillingness of those Negroes who could afford to live in a better environment to take the step which would lead them into a situation with unknown but ominous prospects has frustrated most attempts to combat the effects of prejudice. In this situation, many whites who could be attracted to a struggle against discrimination see no reason to tilt windmills for Negroes who do not wish to take the steps necessary to help themselves.

More demand for equal treatment may be developing in the Negro community, however. An unusual number of Negroes turned out for the public meeting on the Open Housing Ordinance. When a Negro announced his candidacy for Council, taking a position against the ordinance, and declaring that he would not want to live among white people and could not see why other people of his race did, he received a volley of protests from Negroes, including one letter asking him to leave town. Thus the situation is in flux with change dependent upon the rise of leadership within the Negro population as well as upon the behavior of whites.

9 ENFORCEMENT OF THE ZONING ORDINANCE: THE GIBSON CASE[1]

The story of the proposed but never completed Gibson apartments forms an important chapter in the continuing conflict between (as one side would have it) the old ideal of enterprise by the rugged individual and the new ideal of community development guided by the local government according to present-day principles of city planning; or (as the other side would have it) between individual liberties and the principle that the end justifies the means in pursuit of the common good. In this case, the role of Oberlin activists became neither one of creating support in the community nor of reconciling different points of view, as in the water and housing controversies, but rather of searching out and wielding the various legal weapons which were available to them. Their actions were no less important on this account than the decisions of the courts; nevertheless, the courts constitute an outside power in the struggle which may prove decisive.

Bert Gibson is the head of a family which has long been prominent in Oberlin. Together with his two sons, Allyn and Harold, he owns and runs Gibson's Bakery, an enterprise which was established around 1885. The Gibson estate also owns a block of 6 lots on West Lorain Street, subdivided in 1955, which has a frontage of about 99 feet and extends back for over four hundred feet. On the south and west sides of the lot is College property, and the College owns the rest of the block to the east. This lot was occupied in 1958 by the old Gibson house in the front, two new houses in the rear, and a hen house in the west side. For many years Bert Gibson had planned to build an apartment house where the hen house, from which he derived a small income, then stood. This plan was ready to come to fruition in 1958, and late in May he applied for a building permit to erect an apartment house with twelve suites. At that time, Gibson was told by the City Manager that he wanted to look over the plans. Ten days later Gibson called on the manager and was told that the manager would like to show the plans to the Planning Commission.[2] Harold Gibson then stated that the City Manager was in error in presenting the plans to the Commission because that body had no legal authority to review them.

When City Manager Dunn was confronted with the Gibson application, he had found himself in an awkward position. He personally was a believer in the principles of city planning, and the Gibson apartment building would violate several of the current standards of good planning. It would not be able to provide what he felt was adequate off-street parking and open area access would be over the narrow, undedicated road which had previously served as the Gibson driveway, and the lot would be crowded, with 807 square feet of space for each family instead of the 2,000 square feet minimum now recommended by city planners. There seemed little Dunn could do, for the existing zoning law did not prohibit any of the features he objected to. Though a new law was being formulated which would embody the principles of modern planning, it had not yet been passed.

As for Harold Gibson, he had made a practice of attending many commission meetings in his duties as a councilman and he knew that there was a committee working to revise the zoning ordinance applicable to various areas in Oberlin. He did not know, however, what the criteria for building in the various locations would be when and if a new zoning ordinance was passed.

Dunn was determined to stop the erection of a structure which he felt would have harmful effects upon the community as a whole and upon the College. Accordingly, he denied Bert Gibson his permit on the grounds that the proposed apartment dwelling did not comply with the existing requirement that any new structure must be 30 feet back from the road. The plans showed the apartment building 150 feet from Lorain Street, but only six feet from the undedicated Gibson driveway.

Gibson decided to appeal Dunn's decision to the Zoning Board of Appeals, a five member commission with authority to hear appeals from the refusal of building permits and to grant variances where the strict interpretation of the zoning ordinance imposes unusual difficulties or particular hardships. Council appoints one member each year and has power to overrule decisions of the Board. The Zoning Board of Appeals has tended to view its role as that of defending the citizen against the power of the government and the rigidity of the zoning laws, and in past years has refused few of the appeals brought before it.

At the time of the Gibson appeal, Thomas Piraino, an official of the Nelson Stud Welding Company, and an active participant in community welfare and civic associations, was chairman.[3] Piraino felt that the first question to answer was the legal one of whether the Gibson plans conformed to the Zoning code. If this question was answered in the affirmative, then he felt that the Board should overrule the decision of the City Manager. If this question was answered in the negative, then the Board could proceed to consider whether a variance should be granted. Hence Piraino asked City Solicitor Severs for a ruling on the legality of Dunn's action. At a special meeting the members of the Board decided that their decision would rest entirely upon Severs' opinion, in spite of the members' dislike for Gibson's plans. Meanwhile the case had started to receive attention, and the members of the Board received several calls from Councilmen asking them how they would vote.

At a public meeting of the Zoning Board of Appeals on August 1, Severs' opinion was heard and adopted by the Board. He ruled that since Gibson Drive was not a dedicated street, the only setback requirement which had to be met was that of Lorain Street. However, there was a question whether the building might not be too far back. If there was a uniform setback, the building would have to comply with this setback. (A uniform setback existed if building on more than half of the frontage conformed to some standard.) The city engineer was ordered to make a survey to determine whether a uniform setback existed.

On August 14, he reported that six homes did conform to a uniform standard, being between 27 and 32 feet from the road. Gibson could argue, of course, that the five foot variation did not constitute a uniform setback. He did not have to do this, however, for two buildings belonging to the College were 49 feet back, and another was 75 feet back. Together these occupied over half of the frontage in the block. Consequently the Zoning Board of Appeals overruled Dunn and ordered him to issue a building permit to Gibson.

Following this meeting, T. O. Murphy, a local plumbing contractor, Paul B. Arnold, a member of the Fine Arts Department at Oberlin College, and Bronson Clark, a builder, members of the Planning Commission, a body charged with planning the orderly growth of the city, decided to file a protest of the decision of the Zoning Board of Appeals with Council, an action they could take under the zoning ordinance as private citizens.

The protest was based upon several grounds: (1) The building would front on an undedicated street, (2) It would isolate the two houses already on the lot, (3) The lot was too small, (4) There would be no room for the proper parking facilities and means of access,

> (5) A complete revision of the Oberlin Zoning Ordinance is being prepared at this time to insure the orderly growth and development of the community, which is designed to prevent such unwise building as the proposed Gibson apartment building, the new ordinance is to be submitted to City Council in the near future for their acceptance and for its enactment into law; a mere matter of priority of the time of the Gibson proposal should not be allowed to violate the principles of land use that will govern the ordinance; (6) finally, the construction of an apartment facility in the midst of an area occupied by college buildings is poor planning, and it is within the Council's right to uphold proper planning in this regard and deny the permit.

On August 21, the *News-Tribune* printed a long editorial opposing the apartment building because in the paper's opinion it would violate the standards of modern city planning. The editors appealed to Gibson not to build it on his lot, but to find another site. However, they held out little hope for any legal remedies the Council might resort to as a result of a protest. In their opinion, further delay in granting a permit would be questionable tactics, but if Gibson adhered to his plans, it would be hard to blame anyone for carrying on the fight against him.

That night the protesters, Gibson, his attorney, council members, and Dunn met to talk the matter over. The attorney protested that the clause under which the protest was made did not apply to the Gibson situation, but no agreement was reached.

The Council met to consider the protest on August 25. Meanwhile, Bill Long, a known proponent of city planning, searched for further legal means of combating the Gibson apartments. He discovered that Gibson had not presented subdivision plans for his lot to the Planning Commission for approval, and presented this evidence at the council meeting.

At this meeting, Dunn was asked why he opposed the building. He said, "I feel it is completely overcrowding a normal residential lot and setting a bad precedent." Bronson Clark and Paul Arnold added that the Planning Commission had refused to approve five or six plans to subdivide deep lots for construction in the rear of the lot in the past two years.

Gibson's lawyer challenged the Council's right to review the decision of the Zoning Board of Appeals. "The application either complies with the law or it doesn't." Severs, however, ruled that the Council had the right to review any action of its board and commissions.

When the vote was taken on the motion to reject the action of the Zoning Board of Appeals, Long, Hellmuth, Stofan, Zahm, and Comings voted for it, and Gibson voted against it. He explained that he felt bound to vote in spite of his relationship to his father because he felt that the Council had a moral and legal responsibility to uphold the Zoning Board and the decision of the City Solicitor.

Gibson realized that he was jeopardizing his political career by voting in a case in which his father had an interest, and, for emphasis, was told precisely this by Bill Long. But he was under conflicting pressures—the desirability of not voting at all conflicted with his point of principle. He resolved the conflict by deciding that a man must stand up for what he believes and he voted accordingly.

Dunn sent a notice of "permit denial" to Gibson. The legal grounds at this time were those that Long had suggested—that the plans for the apartment at the time of subdivision had not been presented to the Planning Commission for approval. Harold Gibson believed that this was not necessary because the city did not have a Master Plan and this requirement was established by statute, an opinion subsequently upheld in the courts. A second ground was also given: "Construction of an apartment on that site would run contrary to the basic aims and purposes of good planning."

Thwarted by the local government's decision, Gibson filed suit in the Lorain County Common Pleas Court on September 2. He appealed for a ruling on the right of the City Council to review the decisions of the Zoning Board of Appeals. On November 22, the suit was dismissed on the grounds that the statute under which Gibson filed did not apply to a legislative body such as Council.

Gibson also initiated an action in the District Court. His request for a mandamus was refused, because he "had adequate remedy at law by appeal."

Meanwhile, in November, the new zoning ordinance had been passed. It included a provision that the minimum lot size per family had to be 2,000 square feet in a multiple dwelling structure. Under this provision, Gibson's plans would be illegal.

Gibson filed a new plea with the Court of Common Pleas after the decision of the District Court, on the new grounds that he had complied with the zoning ordinance then in effect. Gibson had found the right grounds at last, for this appeal was granted. The decision appeared to rule out any attempt by the city to apply the new zoning law to Gibson.

The Council debated whether they had grounds for appeal, and whether they should appeal at meetings on April 6, and April 10, 1959. Harold Gibson protested the holding of the latter meeting, saying that the matter had been settled when no action was taken at the previous meeting. Bronson Clark and Paul Arnold were present to argue for an appeal, and Gibson's attorney presented his case once again. At this special meeting, a basic difference in attitudes of the Councilmen, hitherto united except for Gibson, was discovered. An appeal would have to be made on the grounds that since no substantial construction had begun, and no use of the land which did not conform with the new zoning law had been established, the permit could be refused under the new law even though the application had been made under the old law. Severs assured the Councilmen that the legal question of whether an applicant could be bound by regulations passed after his application was sufficiently unsettled to give them a case, but Zahm, Ellis, and Gibson maintained that the denial of the permit because of regulations which had been passed since the application would be morally, if not legally, wrong. Denial would in effect, they felt, be an *ex post facto* law.

Long, Comings, and Stofan, on the other hand, believed that since Gibson's plans represented a clear violation of what they considered principles of good planning, the city had an obligation to exhaust the legal possibilities of thwarting them.

When the vote was taken, the result was three for appeal and three against. Hellmuth was absent on his Wisconsin Sabbatical. Since there was no majority for appeal, the motion was defeated. Apparently Council had decided not to appeal and Gibson had won.

However, under the rules of procedure followed by the Council, a question could be opened for another vote if someone who had voted on the winning side so moved. Bill Long was determined to take advantage of this possibility. The next day he called Hellmuth, who had opposed the Gibson apartments from the beginning, to see whether he could return for the regular Council meeting on Monday. Evidently Harold Gibson also knew of Hellmuth's intention to return, for he phoned him and tried unsuccessfully to convince him that an appeal should not be made.

Immediately after his telephone conversation with Hellmuth, Long called Stofan and Comings and asked them to meet him. They agreed to try to get Zahm to re-open the case and he did agree to make the necessary motion. He had voted against an appeal because he thought Gibson was legally entitled to his permit, but he disliked the proposed apartment house as much as they did.

The regular meeting was held on Monday, and Zahm moved to reconsider the appeal question. Hellmuth, Long, Comings and Stofan voted to appeal. At this meeting Gibson protested, "I believe in good, sound planning, but I believe laws are drawn up and then people are asked to conform. That is the only proper sequence." Hellmuth's comment was that ". . . the power of government should be used to the best long-range interests of the city."

Before the appeal was filed, Long attempted another move against Gibson which did not succeed. By the May 18, 1959 Council meeting, Solicitor Severs had not completed his brief for the appeal and had not filed. The deadline was May 28, but it was apparent that if the appeal were not filed by May 22, the case would not be heard in the coming session of court. This would mean the decision would be delayed until October. Long moved the passage of a resolution appealing to Bert Gibson to withdraw his application for a permit. The time necessary to present the resolution to Gibson and obtain his answer would delay the filing for the appeal beyond the 22nd.

Long noted that the Gibson plans were contrary to all the principles the Council had been trying to formulate into law and he concluded with his opinion that the city was entitled to use all the legal means available to block development which was not in accordance with present city planning regulations. In spite of this statement, Long only mustered one other vote, that of Ellis, for his resolution. Gibson, Stofan and Zahm voted against it. Comings and Hellmuth were absent.

Stofan then proposed a motion which instructed the Solicitor to file the appeal by May 22, and which provided that the appeal be withdrawn if he were unable to complete his brief by then. Ellis thought that assigning a deadline for the City Solicitor in this way was an unwarranted interference with Mr. Severs' professional prerogative. He also opposed the second part of the motion which would forego the appeal if Mr. Severs was unable to file by the 22nd. Though he had voted against an appeal, he felt a new decision not to appeal would be wrong in the absence of two councilmen who had voted for it.

Stofan split his motion, and Ellis moved to amend the first part by adding "if at all possible" to the instructions to file by May 22. Long voted with Ellis. Gibson also voted for the motion to amend which may seem inexplicable in view of his interest in either getting a quick trial or having the case dropped. He had originally thought that it was completely understood (as it appeared to be) that the city would push for quick action when the case was sent to the Court of Appeals. Instead he found delay. He did not know in advance what Stofan's motion would be and found himself in a dilemma. He agreed with Ellis that the city should not drop the case because he believed that it should be decided in the courts. So he voted to get it into court as quickly as possible. The motion to amend Stofan's first motion failed, for four votes are needed on a motion to amend a motion.

Part one of Stofan's motion was passed, with only Long opposed. Ellis then attacked the second part of the motion, which would withdraw the appeal if it were not filed by May 22, and Long and Gibson voted with him to defeat it.

In a letter to the editor which appeared in the *News-Tribune*, Long explained his motion and votes at the meeting and questioned Gibson's ethics in voting.

The City Solicitor was not able to file his brief before the original deadline set by Council, but he did file in time to secure a decision by August 27 from the District Court of Appeals which upheld the City's refusal to grant a permit to Gibson. The court noted precedents where regulations which had been passed after a permit had been applied for or even granted, were enforceable if no substantial construction had begun at the time it became effective. If construction had not begun, no nonconforming use of the land (automatically exempt from new zoning regulations) could be established.

Gibson appealed this decision to the State Supreme Court, which reversed the District Court on May 19, 1960. The court ruled that since Dunn had refused to issue the permit, Gibson had been denied the opportunity to establish a nonconforming usage on his property. Since this was the case, he could not be refused his permit on those grounds. Since Gibson had established his right to the permit under the old law in the Court of Common Pleas, and Council had appealed under the new law which was now declared inapplicable to Gibson, the Supreme Court issued a mandamus to Dunn.

Dunn issued the permit to Gibson on May 27, 1960, almost two years after Gibson's application. At this time, he turned his calendar to November, and noted that the permit expired on Monday, November 28.

During the summer, nothing was done on the site of the proposed apartment except to tear down the old chicken house. However, Gibson did obtain bids for the construction of the building, and made several attempts to secure financing, including obtaining a Dunn and Bradstreet credit report. He finally received a commitment from the First Akron Corporation to finance his enterprise, posted $2,000 in good faith, and made investigations about insurance for the building. He was hindered by illness much of this time.

Dunn noticed the date on his calendar about a week before the permit was due to expire, and spoke to City Solicitor Severs about it. They agreed on Saturday, November 26, that Gibson should be notified that his permit had expired on Monday, November 28, rather than Sunday, November 27. Dunn also told several Councilmen of his intention to notify Gibson that his permit was void when the proper time came.

On Monday the 28th, Dunn sent a letter to Gibson by registered mail, declaring that his permit was void under Ordinance 30AC, which said that in order to maintain the validity of the permit, "work" must have begun within six months after its issuance.

Then he and Andy Stofan, no longer a Councilman, but still proprietor of the local photography shop, went to the Gibson property and photographed the empty lot. While they were taking pictures, someone saw them and informed Gibson. Evidently suspecting what had happened, Gibson immediately called Anthony Palkovic of the Palkovic Excavating Company who came out that afternoon, dug a ditch for the sewer line for the apartment building, and began digging for the foundation.

Someone in the Oberlin College Service Building, next to the lot, saw the digging and informed Dunn. Dunn and Severs met that evening and decided that the proper step was to send a cease and desist order to Gibson. This was done on Tuesday. Later that day Palkovic applied for permission to make a water tap for the apartments which was refused. That night Gibson's lawyer met with Dunn and Eric Nord, the new Mayor, but could not persuade them to relent.

Consequently, Gibson appealed to the Zoning Board of Appeals for a second time on January 19, 1961, asking that Dunn's action in declaring the permit void be reversed, and that the cease and desist order be cancelled.[4] Four meetings of the Board took place. At the first, sworn testimony was given by Dunn, Allyn Gibson, and a representative of the First Akron Corporation. At the second meeting, perplexing legal problems presented themselves to the members of the Board. There was the question of whether Gibson might not have had all day Monday the 28th to begin "work" under Ordinance 30AC, since the 27th, chronologically the date of expiration, was a Sunday. It was also an open question whether the activity of Gibson in the six months since the issuance of the permit, obtaining a credit report, arranging financing, and obtaining bids, might not be considered "work."

As a result of these legal complexities, Flanigan, the only person trained in law on the Board, led the discussion. His opinion was that the legal questions were sufficiently in doubt so the Board ought to base its decision upon what he called "the equities" of the situation. Since the law failed to provide a clear standard of justice, a common-sense standard should be used.

Discussion of what the "equities" of the case were, and of the personalities involved in the case, was vigorous. Flanigan and Gilford were most concerned with Gibson's rights according to the equities, while W. E. Parker had been convinced by cases cited by Solicitor Severs that Gibson's time limit had clearly legally expired when he was notified by Dunn. Broadwell and Hicks remained undecided on the question.

Before the final vote, a meeting was held at Broadwell's house to discuss the presentation of the Board's decision, but Hicks and Broadwell remained undecided. Long spoke to Gilford about the case, and regrets neglecting to try to persuade Hicks and Broadwell.

The final public meeting was held on January 18. Flanigan read a statement (to which Gilford subscribed) pointing out that Gibson had won a long and expensive battle in the courts, and that the city had resorted to a very technical remedy, which it had not previously used ". . . in order to accomplish what it could not do in the courts. Since the legality of the remedy utilized by the city in this case is subject to reasonable doubt in the minds of this board, it is our opinion that the individual personal rights of the private citizen must be protected and that these personal rights should take precedence over the rights of the city unless or until an adjudication of the legal questions can be made."

When Gilford seconded the motion to reverse Dunn's actions, he declared that he felt that the building was undesirable, but pointed out that the city's actions appeared to many as persecution of an individual. "You can't justify good to the city by using this kind of means." Broadwell and Hicks voted with Flanigan and Gilford.

Mayor Nord, invited to speak at this meeting, agreed that the city should be careful not to abuse the rights of individuals, but the charge of using technicalities could be made against Gibson too. Nord believed that Gibson had known the new zoning ordinance was pending, and had rushed to apply for a building permit before Council could pass it. "It seems to me a matter of whose technicality is the lesser."

By January 26, Arnold Schwartz, a plastics manufacturer, whose business is located some 50 miles out of town, Chairman of the Housing Renewal Commission, had contacted Dunn about making an appeal. He felt that Gibson had been legally right in the first case, but was wrong in this instance. Schwartz, together with Bronson Clark and Paul Arnold, two who had signed the corresponding letter in 1958, subsequently submitted a protest on the grounds that (1) the Zoning Board had no authority to act in matters pertaining to building permits, and (2) the ordinance was self-executing, so Gibson's permit had expired independently of Dunn's notification.

As in the case of the first letter of protest, a rumor exists that this letter was inspired by a councilman. Although this has not been verified, Hellmuth has asserted that had it not been done by someone else, he would have seen to it that a protest was filed.

The protest was considered by the Council on February 6, 1961, where Severs gave his opinion that the Zoning Board had overstepped its jurisdiction by (in effect) extending Gibson's permit. Flanigan replied that the Board's jurisdiction had not been questioned by the city, and that the Board could give as much weight to Gibson's interpretation as to Severs'. Severs confirmed this. Gibson's attorney contended that actual construction did not have to start in six months in order for "work" to have begun. He then charged that Dunn had "run out" and "harassed my client" by taking pictures. Long retorted that Gibson was being saved from "an uneconomic investment," a statement which may have been correct in view of the difficulties encountered by the owners of an apartment house constructed since that time. Council voted 5-1 to appeal. Councilman Davis voted against, asserting that it was an open question whether six months had legally expired, and claiming that Council should uphold its boards and commissions. He did not want to spend another $1,000 on a court case.

Gibson promptly appealed, and the case is pending in the Court of Common Pleas. The city's revocation of the building permit has been switched from Ordinance 30AC ("work begun") to Ordinance 70AC, ("construction begun"), which was passed earlier, in order to strengthen their case, and because there is some doubt over whether Ordinance 30AC was in effect when Gibson applied for his permit. This may provide further interesting complications, for the two ordinances may contradict each other on this point.

The Gibson case is a remarkable example of the use of the legal merry-go-round. Gibson was in court five times in order to get his permit, and spent approximately $2,500 in costs and legal fees. The city spent $1,800. Getting his permit took Gibson almost two years. Then he found himself faced with another ride around the courts. The legal weapon has proved to be effective in delaying construction indefinitely.

The tenacity of Bert Gibson is matched only by the stubborn refusal of his opponents to admit defeat and their ingenuity in devising legal ways of throwing the case into court. Although Dunn grasped at a straw in refusing the permit for inadequate setback, enough doubt existed to start the legal process. Bill Long found a legal excuse for the reversal of the Board in Gibson's failure to present his subdivision plans to the Planning Commission. Severs was able to find the legal area of doubt which gave them a case for an appeal in Gibson's failure to establish nonconformancy. After the permit was issued, Dunn took an unprecedented action in enforcing the six months limitation on the permit. The legal weapon may have been bobbled at this point on the question of the legal expiration date. Another possibility existed for Gibson in the vague terminology concerning what he had to do to maintain the validity of his permit and in the seeming conflict between the ordinances. Again, initiative was exercised in arranging for a protest, and a new rationale for reversing the Board was devised.

The Zoning Board of Appeals showed its orientation toward individual rights in its use of a strict legal interpretation to support Gibson in the first appeal, and in its abandonment of legalism in favor of "equity" in order to support him in the second. In this second instance, three of the members of the Board were apparently picked by the planners as men who thought the same way they thought about planning, but the Board, in spite of their sympathy for planning, felt individual rights were paramount. In the comparable instance when an open legal question existed over Gibson's failure to establish nonconformancy, the Council defined the demands of planning as paramount.

Appendix to chapter 9: revision of the zoning ordinance

Since early in the 1950's several citizens of Oberlin had been convinced that a general revision of the city's zoning ordinance was needed to bring it more nearly into line with current practices throughout the country and to make it more effective in guiding the future growth of the city according to the canons of "city planning" which they considered desirable. Chief among this group were Paul Arnold and Andrew Stofan. But before 1955 there was no body empowered to undertake such a major project except the City Council and that group was too busy even to consider it. In that year, however, Oberlin voted for a city charter which included a provision for the establishment of a City Planning Commission. Such a body was immediately appointed with Paul Arnold as chairman, and the first order of business was a study of the zoning ordinance with the purpose in mind of suggesting any revisions deemed advisable. But as the early enthusiasm of this group faded the project bogged down in its earliest stages. This was the state of affairs when Oberlin got a new City Manager, Richard Dunn, in the early spring of 1958. Dunn's immediate interest in the idea of a new ordinance seems to have provided the spark needed to reactivate those interested in this project. On April 21 of that year, upon formal recommendation of the Planning Commission, Council passed a resolution setting up a special five man committee to draft the new ordinance.[5]

Shortly thereafter the controversy over Bert Gibson's proposed apartment house began. By September of that year he had won his litigation and the city had reluctantly awarded him his building permit. Although the special zoning committee had been active all this time, it had not yet come up with any proposals which were definite enough for Council action. Spurred on by what they considered to be the shortcomings of the present ordinance as made clear by the Gibson case, by a desire to prevent another such incident from arising, and by a need to demonstrate their good faith in claiming during the Gibson affair that a new ordinance was on the way, the committee went into high gear and presented the first part of the new code for Council approval on September 22. (Incidentally, this first completed section covered class B-residential housing, the precise category in which Gibson's building had fallen.) City Council approved these revisions on the first reading by a vote of 7-0.

On September 25, the *News-Tribune* carried a feature story on the proposed revisions, explaining them in detail and endorsing them wholeheartedly. At the second reading on October 20, the City Council again voiced its approval, this time by a vote of 5-1. The one opponent was Harold Gibson who thought that the revisions were discriminatory in that some semi-public buildings— hotels, hospitals, and tourist homes—were not to be covered. At a public meeting on October 27, the only opposition came from Gibson again who raised this same point. When informed by the City Manager that the proposed changes conformed fully to standard practices and that state statutes provide the regulation he feared would be missing, Gibson changed his stand. The resolution passed on this third and final reading by a unanimous vote.

By April of 1959 the remainder of the new zoning ordinance was also completed. Sections 1 and 2 of that ordinance defined the terms to be used and stated its general purposes. Section 3 itemized the restrictions for R-1 or single family dwelling areas. It listed the types of accessory buildings which are permissible, stated the off-street parking facilities required, gave the front and side setback requirements and the minimum floor and lot areas, and set down maximum standards for the "intensity" of lot use. This last term referred to the percentage of a lot which is covered by buildings. Section 4 stated the regulations for R-11 or multiple family dwelling areas. These parallel those for R-1 areas but were less stringent. Section 5 dealt with commercial district limitations. Section 6 governed proper usage of industrial areas. Sections 7 and

8 gave the exceptions and provided for appeals, and the rest of the ordinance dealt with amendments, enforcement, and penalties for violation.

There were a few scattered complaints at this time from people who objected to some specific aspects of the redrawing of the zoning map which accompanied this new ordinance (Bert Gibson not included). These complaints were not directed at the ordinance itself, however. The story was concluded when Council accepted the whole ordinance by a unanimous vote early in May of 1959. The matter does not seem to have been at all a controversial one. Even those who supported Bert Gibson's legal position approved the new ordinance. Opposition was literally non-existent. Under the management of Richard Dunn and Paul Arnold the proposed changes were steered through to adoption without a single hitch.

10   THE COMING OF THE FAA

✤✤✤✤ Until now we have dealt with decisions which come
✤🏛🏛✤ within the formal province of the City Council and
✤🏛🏛✤ its commissions and employees. As we move into the
✤✤✤✤ area of private activity with community-wide impact,
there is a marked change in the participants. Bill
Long remains, a leader in two projects, shut out in another, but
there are many new participants—a federal agency, local businessmen, citizens with some cash to invest—and familiar ones like
John Cochrane appear in a new role. The economic entrepreneur
enters the scene, though no one can fail to note the essentially political skill in coalition building which each of the projects requires.[1]

On April 26, 1957, a memorandum was sent from the Director
of the Office of Air Traffic Control and from the Director of the
Office of Air Navigation Facilities to their administrators. Its subject: Establishment of Adequate Quarters for Air Route Traffic
Control Centers. The memo covered location and siting of centers, space requirements and the financing of new quarters. It set
processes in motion which eventually resulted in a phone call on
January 16, 1958 from Frank Van Demark, Program Engineer of
the Federal Aviation Agency (FAA)[2] to James F. (Bill) Long, who
had taken office as Chairman of the City Council of Oberlin on
January 1. Van Demark informed Long that Oberlin was one of
several places being considered for the erection of a new Air
Route Traffic Control Center for the Cleveland area. Oberlin was
far enough away from the metropolis to be out of the direct target
area in the event of an enemy attack, and the direction of the prevailing winds would minimize nuclear contamination in the area.
A building with 50,000 square feet of space, several stories high,

costing about $1,500,000 would be needed, which could be built by the government, or preferably, financed locally and leased to the FAA. About 100 families with an average yearly income of $7,000-$8,000 could be expected to come to Oberlin to work at the installation. What he wanted to know, Van Demark said, was whether Oberlin would be interested in having such an installation built there.

Long immediately replied in the affirmative. For some time, people in the community had been talking about the increased revenues for schools and the local government which would result if a few clean, quiet industries were added to the tax rolls. Long himself was a principal advocate of attracting industry to broaden the tax base.

Van Demark went on to outline what would have to be done. He wanted a meeting arranged for January 22, six days later, at which people who could give information on the local power, water, sewer, street and telephone systems would be present. He also wanted someone who knew the housing and school situation, and some people who could facilitate matters in the local and federal political arenas. Long agreed to set up a meeting. He went to work immediately. He told the story of the telephone call to Councilmen Fred Comings, William Hellmuth and Andy Stofan, who together with himself made up a majority on the City Council. They were enthusiastic and agreed to attend the meeting. He then requested the attendance of the manager of the municipal light plant, the city engineer, and the city employee who was in charge of streets. He contacted the Northern Ohio Telephone Company which agreed to send its equipment superintendent and the manager of the Oberlin Branch Office.

Kenneth Roose, Chairman of the School Building Committee and Harry Koss, Superintendent of Public Schools agreed to come at Long's request. State Senator Charles A. Mosher, who was prominent in the Republican Party and close to Representative A. D. Baumhart, also arranged to be present. Long then asked John Hill to line up a few pieces of land which were available for sites. Hill located three sites. All the parties involved were asked to keep confidential the information that Oberlin was being considered.

On January 22, Van Demark came with the Chief of Property

Management for FAA and the Chief of the Cleveland Center, which was to be moved to Oberlin. Two men from the Ohio Bell Telephone Company accompanied them. They were shown the sites that Long and Hill had lined up, and were taken to the meeting. There they were assured that all the city's facilities would be adequate. The city was planning to expand its water facilities, a new trunk sewer had just been installed under Lorain Street, which ran past the site favored by the FAA men, and the municipal light plant would be able to supply the 1500 kilowatts of firm capacity which the center would ultimately need. A new 2,500 KW generator was about to be installed which would give the plant a firm capacity of 5,300 KW, and further expansion could be made if necessary. Long said, "Whatever they want, we told 'em we had it."

Hill assured the men that there would be adequate housing for any FAA employees who wished to remove to Oberlin. Eighty-five units were under construction at the time, and 150 were in the planning stage. If more were needed, he was sure that private construction could be arranged.

Roose was not sure what the effect of an influx of families would be upon the school system. He said that a study would have to be made before it could be established whether or not Oberlin schools could take care of the FAA children.

The telephone company seemed to be the most serious obstacle at this meeting. Special equipment would be needed to connect the FAA center with the remote radio installations and other associated air traffic control facilities. The new, special system was not then available to the local telephone company and required special engineering and procurement.

When the FAA men left the meeting, they seemed pleased at Oberlin's facilities. They said that they would recommend Oberlin for the site for the new installation.

On January 27, Long received a call from Van Demark, who gave him revised estimates of the water and power which would be needed. Long checked out the new figures and replied that the supply would be adequate.

By February 3, the telephone company and the FAA had worked out arrangements for the communications facilities which would be needed, and on that day, a man in the regional office wrote to the Washington headquarters. He reported that all the technical difficulties could be solved, and that adequate housing was available. Finally, he recommended that the regional office be permitted to relocate the Cleveland Center to Oberlin as quickly as possible, "in view of the prompt action taken by the City of Oberlin and the need to relocate to adequate quarters."

Meanwhile, the school officials had been calculating the effect of the FAA upon the school system. They shared the planners' desire for new industry, but the results of their studies worried them. They drew up a report which predicted that with natural growth, 300 more children would be in the schools by 1960. One member of the Board of Education noted that if 300 new FAA families came in as well (the estimate of the size of the installation had grown since the telephone call the month before), 600 more children would be added to the system. The borrowing capacity of the school system would be $600,000 in 1960, enough to build 18 classrooms for 540 children. There would be no quarters for 360 of the expected increase. Building costs were not the only expense, more teachers and supplies would be needed.

At an informal meeting Long arranged between the City Council and school officials, Superintendent Koss and Roose went on to discuss what might have to be done to teach all these children. Larger classes would have to be held. Perhaps the junior and senior high school grades would have to go on double sessions. Kindergartens and accelerated classes could be discontinued and the auditorium and cafeterias could make do as classrooms. Perhaps classroom space could be rented, or sessions could be stretched to ten or twelve months. When these predictions had been presented, Roose emphasized the Council's responsibility not to let these things happen. If Council invited the FAA, he said, it was committing itself to getting funds for the schools. Long agreed that Council had an obligation to the school system, and said that Council would do all in its power to obtain federal aid. Council voted unanimously at this meeting to invite the FAA if federal aid to the schools were available. Another vote was taken to determine whether Council wanted to invite the FAA even if no aid were forthcoming. This vote was affirmative, 5-2, with Hellmuth and Zahm dissenting.

Investigations of the possibility of obtaining federal aid had already begun. Senator Mosher had been in contact with the State Superintendent of Schools and had found out some details. He then contacted Representative Baumhart in Washington who referred him to P.L. 874 and P.L. 815, providing for federal aid to school areas impacted because of federal government installations.

Long co-signed letters to the State Board of Education and to the FAA, saying that the Oberlin invitation was based upon the expectation that federal funds could be obtained for the schools. Van Demark put Long in contact with the regional representative of the U. S. Department of Health, Education and Welfare. Van Demark met with HEW and General Services Administration officials and set up another meeting in Oberlin to discuss the school needs. Efforts to obtain federal aid ceased for the time being, however, when it was learned that grants were made only after it had been established that a school system had been impacted.

A disturbing incident occurred after the invitation to the FAA had been sent. On the 20th, Van Demark notified Long that an agent of the General Services Administration would call to get the option on the Lorain Street site. Long contacted Hill, whom he had instructed to obtain an option from Clare Van Ausdale, the owner of the land desired by the FAA, and learned that he had got only a verbal commitment. Fearing that they had made a disastrous slip, he hurried to see Van Ausdale, who, to his relief, sold him the option on the land.

Soon after the meeting on the 16th, Long was informed that efforts had been started to have the center placed in Medina, a community 22 miles southeast of Oberlin. Long contacted Mosher and asked him to recommend to Representative Baumhart, in whose district Medina was located also, that the installation be built in Oberlin. Long then began a program of telephoning. About every three days he called high FAA officials, asking whether he could announce the coming of the new installation to Oberlin. When an official would protest that someone else was responsible for the decision, Long would call him too. Finally, on February 26th, he was instructed to announce that an FAA installation would be erected in Oberlin.

Long is inclined to take a restricted view of his role in bringing the FAA center to Oberlin. All he did, all he could have done, he notes, was to clear away the obstacles which might have delayed or prevented the FAA decision to come to Oberlin. He gave a direct affirmative answer to Van Demark's query about Oberlin's interest. He had sites ready to show the FAA men. He arranged for all the people who could give the FAA men the information they wanted to be present at the January meeting, and managed to create the impression then that if Oberlin were chosen, there would be no problems. Thereafter, he was at their service if they needed something else done.

Within the community, he worked to persuade people that it was desirable to have the FAA. As previously mentioned, most of the community was predisposed to welcome industry of the proper kind. The only people who were afraid the FAA was not the proper kind, a few who thought it would bring low-flying jets, had their fears quickly allayed. Those who were concerned about the impact of FAA children upon the schools did not want to prevent the coming of the FAA, but wanted assurances that the consequences they dreaded would not be allowed to occur. Long, who thought the influx of families in the $7,000-$8,000 income bracket would be good for the city whether or not their taxes would pay the full costs of the education of their children, took care to emphasize that they would be paying more of the school bill than most parents who had children in school. He also arranged the meeting at which the school representatives were assured that Council would help them find funds, which apparently satisfied them, for Roose reported, "If we could get funds from the government, that was very good, but if we couldn't, we knew that we could raise funds some other way."

The only area where Long stepped beyond removing obstacles was in his attempt to influence federal officials to decide upon the Oberlin site. A Democrat, he had been very critical of Congressman Baumhart, and had no access to him; although State Senator Mosher made attempts to influence Baumhart, it appears that the congressman only recommended the Oberlin site after he had heard that Oberlin had finally been selected. Long's telephone calls may have had some effect in speeding up the announcement of the site in order to forestall the efforts of Medina, but they were admittedly shots in the dark.

What is important to note is that although all Long did was remove obstacles, this is exactly what was not done in other communities, and is what seems to have made the difference. Little was heard from one town, the first choice of the Cleveland Center men, who had preferred a location near their radar equipment. Medina began efforts only at a late date. Long's initiative and activity were exceptional, and Andy Stofan, the popular Chairman of the previous Council generously admitted, "If this had come up when I was mayor, I don't think we would have gotten FAA."

11 THE OBERLIN IMPROVEMENT
AND DEVELOPMENT
CORPORATION

With the exception of the City Manager, James F. (Bill) Long has been the most active participant in governmental affairs in Oberlin since 1957 when he was elected to the City Council. Long, however, had also been active in business enterprises in the city. The offspring of his efforts in this area shall be examined in this essay.[1]

The cooperative store in Oberlin had been started by students of Oberlin College in 1938 to provide themselves with better laundry service than was then available and to obtain lower prices on books and study materials. It grew and attracted enough members from townspeople and local farmers to put in a line of groceries in 1941. For a time it prospered, moving frequently to better locations, but in 1948-49 the organization had suffered a setback. Its financial status had deteriorated, apparently due to poor management, and it failed to obtain loans to buy a locker plant and a new location for the store. The manager resigned, and the Co-op Board of Directors began hunting for a new man. They were put in touch with Long, and he agreed to take the manager's job on a temporary basis.

For the first few months, the Co-op account did not have enough balance for Long to cash his paychecks, and he re-invested his salary in the enterprise. Meanwhile he set about restoring the Co-op's finances. He introduced new lines of merchandise, arranged to buy larger bulk lots of goods, and spent more money on advertising. Under his guidance, business recovered, and he decided to stay on as manager. In 1952 the Co-op moved the grocery department to a modern store on the outskirts of town where there was ample parking space.

In 1952, the Co-op Bookstore was moved into space in the Oberlin Inn. When this building was torn down, no adequate store space was available in town, and the Bookstore had to be set up in the basement of Bostwicks, a clothing shop. Negotiations with the owners for the purchase of the store were under way when it suddenly was sold to John Cochrane, a local businessman who was reputed to dislike the Co-op. He offered to lease space in the building to the Co-op if it would abandon the book trade, much of which it had won away from privately owned businesses. The offer was refused, and Long and Kenneth Roose, an economics professor and the president of the Co-op, began looking for a spot upon which to build.

In December, 1955, Long and Roose negotiated the purchase from C. A. Barden of the land on East College Street upon which the bookstore was built. They organized Oberlin Stores[2] to put up the money for the land and to build the store for lease to the Co-op. At the time of the purchase, Oberlin Stores acquired an option to buy the rest home on the adjacent corner lot, part of which could be used for a driveway. The two men decided to eventually buy the two houses adjacent to the rest home on Pleasant Street for later use as parking space. These plans led them to think about the business potential of the area, and they discussed the possibility of buying the land to the south and southwest of the bookstore location for a shopping center and the Co-op food store in the future. They were pleased by the opportunity this would give them to contribute to the redevelopment of the downtown area, which they wanted very much.

In the spring of 1956, several parcels of land in this area became available for purchase, and Long tried to interest Oberlin Stores in buying them for a future shopping center. Some of the members did not want to enter the project since the properties would bring no immediate income, so Long and Roose, acting as individuals, took options on the lots in the center of the area. Then, in order to bring more of this land under their control, they decided to invite State Senator Charles A. Mosher, publisher of the Oberlin *News-Tribune*, to join the shopping center enterprise. Mosher had the money they needed to acquire more land, and he expressed interest in downtown redevelopment in the columns of his paper. Furthermore, he was not connected with the Co-op and his participation would help dispel a possible impression that the enterprise was promoted by Long and his friends for their own benefit and would help ensure wider support for it in the community.

Mosher fell in with the project and took an option on a lot in the area. Soon after it was rumored that Oberlin College was planning to discontinue use of Westervelt Hall, a pre-civil war building which was adjacent to this land and which fronted on Main Street. Mosher placed a bid on it with the college but when the trustees of the college met for a final decision on the sale, they decided they needed the classrooms provided by Westervelt. Mosher's bid was turned down.

During the summer, the group got in touch with a shopping center developer through a cousin of Roose who was engaged in large scale real estate development. The shopping center company was unenthusiastic about Oberlin as a site. It mentioned that a well-known department or food store was considered necessary to make a shopping center successful. Mosher, who agreed that the center would be unsuccessful without a large chain store, became pessimistic about the success of the venture and refused to aid in taking up the options which he, Long and Roose had acquired.

Long remained optimistic. He thought that if he could find the tenants for the shopping center, it would be profitable. Roose was away on a year's leave when the options fell due late in 1956. Long let two of them go and extended his option on the largest, central parcel of land. Further efforts failed to pursuade Mosher to put up the amount necessary to purchase it, and Long mortgaged his home and bought the land for $25,500 in March, 1957. When Roose returned to Oberlin in September 1957, he and Long formed Oberlin Improvement, Incorporated, to hold the property Long had bought in March and another vacant lot he had acquired to connect it with Pleasant Street, which runs parallel to Main.

Long and Roose once more cast about for a man who desired to modernize the business district and was able to provide the money necessary. They approached David Anderson who already was involved in Oberlin Stores and brought him into the corporation. The resources they now possessed enabled them to buy all the property on the west side of South Pleasant Street, from East

College Street to the vacant lot they already owned, including the two houses next to the rest home, and a small structure which had served as a church. When they tried to buy the Falkner Block, a series of five small stores on Main Street which abutted their property, they met with a refusal. This obstacle was overcome when Falkner's nephew went into the real estate business. Falkner commissioned him to sell the block of stores in order to start him off, and Long heard of it. The corporation bought the property for $45,000.

Meanwhile, Long had been elected to the City Council and had been chosen Mayor. In this capacity he had been negotiating with the Federal Aviation Agency (FAA) and the Pepperidge Farm Bakeries to locate plants in Oberlin. The two installations were to be located on East Lorain Street near the New York Central Railroad tracks, with 80 acres of land between them. Long had acquired the option on the parcel of land upon which the FAA wished to build for $100, in order to be able to assure them that the land was available. The FAA had used the option to buy the 10 acres they needed for the plant site, and had left Long with the option for the remaining 30 acres. He saw this land and other land between the two plants as an ideal site for an industrial park, an enterprise to ensure orderly growth and to raise Oberlin's tax base. In the March 13, 1958 issue of the *News-Tribune*, he announced this idea to the public.

Later in the spring, Long called a meeting[3] and proposed to a group of Oberlin's business leaders that an industrial development corporation be formed on a non-profit basis to hold the land between the FAA and the Pepperidge Farm sites. This was often done in municipalities, he explained, to attract desirable industries. He also proposed that the control of the corporation follow the Co-op plan of one vote per person, regardless of the size of his investment.

Many of the businessmen reacted unfavorably to the proposals. They felt that such an enterprise should be run on a profit basis and that the principle of equal control would be unfair to investors. The only decision reached at this meeting was to await the appointment of an industrial development committee of the Oberlin Business and Civic Association (OBCA), an organization similar to a chamber of commerce.

153 The Improvement and Development Corporation

This committee was organized soon after, with Long as chairman, and spent a great deal of time drawing up a constitution and by-laws for the corporation. It was to incorporate Long's non-profit and equal vote ideas, and was to be organized and financed by the OBCA.

On June 12, the proposals were presented at a meeting of the committee and the board of directors of the OBCA. Porter and Murphy, who were not directors but who attended the meeting, said that the necessary money could not be raised to finance a non-profit corporation which gave one vote to every stockholder. Long would not give up those provisions, because that "would transfer control to men of money." Director Ben Lewis, an economics professor, supported Long. No decision was taken at this meeting, due to the absence of two directors.

At a second meeting, held two days later, directors Ben Lewis and Lewis R. Tower expressed the opinion that the OBCA ought not to become involved in the ownership of property at all. The Association, they felt, was representative of the whole community, and some people might oppose bringing in industry. With some opposing the non-profit, equal vote aspects of Long's plan, and others the idea of an OBCA-sponsored industrial park, the Board of Directors unanimously decided that the committee should cease its efforts. At the next meeting of the organization, the directors were asked to reconsider, but they refused. Long's comment was, "They don't know how to get anything done."

Shortly after the attempt to create an OBCA-sponsored holding company had fallen through, a well-heeled local businessman approached Long and suggested that they form a private company for profit. Long refused, for he had acquired the option in his capacity as Mayor, and felt that it should be used for a community project, or not at all. He let the option lapse.

At this time it became known that a builder of low-cost housing developments was interested in the land, and two further attempts were made to remove the property from the market and place it in a holding company for industry. Fred Comings, a councilman, suggested that the city council buy the tract of land, but other council members felt that such an action by the city would be improper, and the idea was dropped. Then City Manager Dunn approached T. O. Murphy privately and suggested that he buy the land himself and start an industrial park. But Murphy felt that the price of the land was too high and refused to pay a share of the cost of a sewer which would benefit the property, but which was not on it, and Dunn's attempt also failed. The rest of 1958 passed with the dream of an industrial park still unfulfilled.

Meanwhile, a local resident, Saul Gilford, had organized a corporation for the manufacture of medical instruments. This took place quite separately from the events we have been describing, except that Roose was a director of the new corporation. Gilford's new industry was the type most people considered desirable for Oberlin. It would be small and clean and would employ skilled labor.

Gilford looked for a suitable site for his plant in Oberlin. Aside from the undeveloped area where the industrial park had failed to materialize, the only land suitably zoned lay along the New York Central tracks on the south side of town. This section contained ancient abandoned buildings and Gilford did not wish to erect his new factory in such a setting. He decided to look for a site in Wellington.

When Long heard of this decision, he felt that his aspiration to make Oberlin an attractive location for light industry was at stake. If Gilford, a local resident with the ideal type of industry, could not be induced to stay in Oberlin, how could industries from the outside be drawn in? He suggested to Roose that they bring Bronson Clark, a Cleveland real estate developer who resided in Oberlin and controlled the Prospect Development Company in Oberlin, into Oberlin Improvement, Inc. Clark was known to share Long's and Roose's goals for community development, and the Prospect Development Company had $13,000 in cash which could be used to make the down payment on the 50 acres of land which Joe Artino owned between the Pepperidge Farms and the FAA sites. Gilford could then build his plant in Oberlin. Roose was reluctant to jeopardize the downtown holdings for a new venture into industrial development, but Long reminded him that the corporation's primary commitment was to community improvement rather than profit. It was apparent, he pointed out, that if Oberlin Improvement did not act, no one would; and Gilford and subsequent industries would be lost to Oberlin. Thus persuaded, Roose agreed to the venture. Bronson Clark was contacted, and he fell in with the plan, agreeing to be bought out with shares of Oberlin Improvement.

Having carried plans for an industrial park to this stage, Long went back to Roose and proposed that they make an attempt to buy the other 30 acres of the land between the FAA and Pepperidge sites. He talked to Clare Van Ausdale, the owner of the property, on Thursday, February 12. Van Ausdale said that he would sell the land for $37,000 ($5,000 more than the price had been the previous year) if Long could raise the money by the following Monday, February 16. Long and Roose went to work the same day.

First, Roose approached Arthur (Kenny) Clark, a local builder and head of the Oberlin Development Company, which had $8,100 in cash. Roose had had contacts with him before and knew that Kenny Clark also favored community development and might be willing to sacrifice immediate prospects of profit. Kenny Clark proved willing to participate in the plan. The same day, Roose called Leonard Barr, an Oberlin resident who was president of Gregory Industries, an out-of-town firm, but Barr was not enthusiastic about entering an enterprise with so little promise of a profit and did not commit himself.

That evening Senator Mosher was contacted again and was won over by the argument that if Oberlin was ever to be attractive for light industry, action must be taken now to keep the Gilford plant. He pledged $15,000 which he would raise by borrowing on downtown properties. Roose called Barr again in the morning and persuaded him to pledge $5,000. Barr, Roose commented, "makes a lot of noise about profit," considering it a "way of keeping score," but was ready to come in when the chips were down.

With Barr's $5,000, Mosher's $15,000, $8,100 from the Oberlin Development Company, and $3,000 which remained of the Prospect Development Company's cash after the down payment on the Artino land, they had $31,100 of the $37,000 they needed. When efforts failed to bring in some of the people who had declined to participate when the scheme was before the OBCA, they called a meeting of interested people for Sunday morning, February 15, at the Oberlin Inn.

This meeting was attended by John Daly of the Lorain County Development Committee and City Manager Dunn as advisors.[4]

Although the planned enterprise had $143,000 worth of assets from the three companies, and the $20,000 pledged by Barr and Mosher, they still needed $6,000 in cash to buy the Van Ausdale land. Long and Roose managed to generate enough enthusiasm at the meeting to obtain pledges of $19,000 from those present, raising the assets to $182,000.

Some changes in organization were agreed upon at this meeting. Oberlin Improvement was not organized to be able legally to make investments of this size, and the two Clarks wanted to form a new corporation out of Oberlin Improvement, Oberlin Development and Prospect Development, in order to avoid the capital gains tax they would have to pay if they sold their holdings to Oberlin Improvement. Leonard Barr suggested that the new corporation should be controlled by votes alloted in proportion to the size of the investment. Long was sorry to lose control over the downtown land he had accumulated, and still favored equal voting as the ideal form of such a community project, but he agreed to the new organization with this feature. In any event, the stockholders who agreed with his view that the corporation should be operated to attract suitable industry to Oberlin rather than to yield a large profit, would hold the majority of shares.

Van Ausdale's property was bought, and Long, Roose, Barr, Bronson and Kenny Clark, and Severs drew up the plans for the new corporation. Long and Roose continued to recruit more members, in the belief that as many members of the community as possible should take part. They sold more shares to the value of $13,000 to 80 individuals, bringing the total issue to $195,000 and the number of stockholders to 98.

An organization meeting was held on March 12, and Anderson, Barr, Kenny and Bronson Clark, Long, Mosher and Roose, who each held $10,000 or more of stock and together held a majority of the issue, were elected to the Board of Directors. Roose became president; Barr, vice-president; and Long, treasurer. On May 1, 1959, the final legal steps bringing the Oberlin Improvement and Development Company into existence were taken.

The corporation arranged to have the factory built for Gilford Instruments and is currently leasing the site and factory to that corporation.[5] Oberlin Improvement and Development advertises in the *Wall Street Journal*, the *Journal of Commerce*, and *Barron's*, and sends out brochures to prospects. People have given Long, who is the only active member of the corporation, dozens of tips on enterprises looking for a site, and he has checked them out. However, only one other factory, the Muller Packaging Co., has been erected in the industrial park. The plant, constructed in 1962, is owned by Oberlin Improvement and Development and rented to Muller. Eric Nord was the prime mover in getting this industry for the industrial park. A lawyer in Elyria asked him whether he knew of a spot for an industry. Nord suggested Oberlin, and set up a luncheon to which he invited the lawyer, the president of the Muller Corporation, and Long. They negotiated the terms, and Oberlin now has a plant which specializes in the flexible packaging of easy-mix recipes in vinyl, foil, paper and other "roll" materials, and which has some of the nation's biggest food producers for clients. The process, which is highly mechanized, employs 30 people, and the manager reports that he has "thousands" of job applications on file.

Long himself considers the industrial park "unsuccessful" so far, and attributes the failure to Oberlin's location which is somewhat removed from the main stream of commerce and to the selectivity of corporations. Two plants which would have located in the park, a rubber fabricating concern and a metal processing plant, have been turned down because they were not interested in buildings of the quality desired in the park, and merely wanted an inexpensive site.

Meanwhile, Long has been trying to do something with the downtown lots owned by the corporation. He has found a major food chain—Fishers—which is prepared to locate at a shopping center on that site. At the annual stockholders meeting in March, 1961, the issuance of up to $100,000 worth of interest-bearing bonds to help finance shopping center construction was authorized. After an extraordinary series of delays, which would have crushed a different man, Long finally began construction of the shopping center in 1963.

12 A HISTORY OF THE OBERLIN OFF-STREET PARKING CORPORATION

The problem of how to provide adequate parking facilities for the Oberlin business district has been a recurring one in the community for almost 20 years. Various committees sponsored by the city council and by local civic or business organizations have studied the problem at frequent intervals in that period, but until 1958 nothing concrete ever resulted from their deliberations. This abridgment of the report issued by a 1956 special city council committee is representative of the conclusions reached by these committees.

I. Assuming no charge for parking.
   A. Merchants as individuals or in a group purchase land and build a parking lot for use of their customers as is done by shopping centers.
   B. Merchants form a corporation which would build the lot. Operating expenses and dividends would be met through participation fees paid by merchants.
   C. City purchase land and build a lot and then recover the cost through beneficial assessment of the merchants involved.
   D. City finance a lot and recover the cost through a general assessment.
II. If a parking charge is allowed.
   A. An individual buys land and operates the lot as a profit-making enterprise.
   B. A merchant association or corporation buys land and builds a lot and then recovers the cost through a parking charge.

C. Use parking meters in the lot. Lot would then have to be leased to the city with net income to city being returned to the association or corporation as rent.

III. Combine one and two.

    A. Merchants buy land and build lot. Users of lot would pay a fee unless their parking ticket were validated by a participating merchant. In this case operating expenses would be met partly by participation fees from merchants and partly by the revenue from parking charges.

The outstanding features of this report are that there are many possibilities, that no attempt is made to examine their feasibility, and that no recommendations are made.

In 1957 the situation began to change. Oberlin merchants disbanded the local Chamber of Commerce and replaced it with a new organization called the Oberlin Business and Civic Association. The new OBCA sent each member a questionnaire asking him to check local problems which the committees might study and also on which committees the member would be willing to serve. Membership on a committee was not to be limited but was to include all who professed willingness to serve. Subsequently, a number of committees were established, two of which were those for Business District Modernization, and Parking, Traffic and Highways. In May of 1958 these two groups began to meet jointly because their chairmen, Paul Warner and John Cochrane, respectively, realized that the most pressing problem facing both of them was the provision of off-street parking facilities in the downtown area.[1]

Meanwhile, the city administrations had not been entirely inactive in this area. On June 2, 1958, city manager Richard Dunn presented to the city council a résumé of the plan for a municipally financed off-street parking lot which the former city manager had devised in 1956. This plan called for a 287 space parking lot to be constructed at an average cost of $900 per space and to be financed by an annual beneficial assessment over a twenty year period of four mills on the property owners involved. The average cost would be about $150 per year per property owner. At this meeting, John Cochrane's suggestion that council not take any action until it had a chance to consider the findings of the OBCA committee was accepted. At the same time, through the urging of Harold Gibson, the council appointed a special committee to study the problem and the possible solutions to it.[2] It was assumed that the group would work closely with its OBCA counterpart. A report was to be prepared by September first of that same year.

During July and August, the OBCA group continued to meet regularly, but no concrete action resulted. Finally, on August 18, 1958, the group drafted a letter to the City Manager asking him to clean up the existing off-street parking facilities as a first step in the right direction. The specific suggestions called for grading and resurfacing the areas where pot-holes or ruts made parking impossible, removal from the parking area behind City Hall of the old impounded cars then stored there, and the marking of parking lanes on the larger areas through use of discarded poles from the Municipal Light Plant on which white lines could be painted to mark individual spaces. On September 30, the city's special committee for parking submitted its report to the council. No recommendations accompanied the report, and after it was submitted, Gibson asked that council refer it to the OBCA group for their approval or modification before taking any final action. This suggestion was accepted and council laid the matter aside to await the OBCA recommendations.

On March 31, 1959, the OBCA group held its final meeting. Richard Dunn was present to report on the suggestions submitted by the committee to him in August of the previous year. He stated that the city budget allocated only $10,000 a year for all street maintenance and improvements so that any large scale municipal program for off-street parking was out of the question. He did, however, indicate that he would do all he could with the funds available. As of December, 1961, all the suggestions of that committee have finally been implemented. The final report of the OBCA group made no recommendations to the city council as the council had anticipated. This lack of a recommendation can partly be traced to the fact that the committee chairman, John Cochrane, was reluctant to see the city undertake the solution of the problem, for he considered it to be outside the proper scope of public action. The other businessmen on that committee concurred in this judgment. Although nothing stood in the way of council renewing its efforts in this field on its own, it chose to let the matter rest.

Several factors seem to be important in explaining council's inaction. One stressed by city manager Dunn is that the high cost of installing extensive off-street parking facilities put such a project far down on the council's priority list of the city's needs. One stressed by Cochrane is that council realized that a city-financed project would be so far removed from the proper sphere of public action that it would not be acceptable to the community as a whole. And finally, Bill Long, who was then mayor of the city, stressed that it was generally recognized among city officials that public action would not be necessary, for a privately financed project would surely soon be initiated. At any rate, the failure of the OBCA group to submit a recommendation to the council was undoubtedly based in part on the realization that the council was not particularly anxious to receive one.

By this time, John Cochrane became convinced that some kind of parking program for the downtown area was a real necessity. There were less than 300 on-street parking spaces in the area and employees used up many of those. Cochrane felt that much business was lost to shopping centers where ample parking space was available. With such centers becoming ever more numerous, the Oberlin situation would only worsen unless parking facilities could be provided. He began to think seriously in terms of a private corporation to build and maintain the needed facilities. He called a series of meetings of some of the local merchants with whom he had close associations to get their reactions to the idea of founding such a corporation. Bill Long, manager of the prominent Oberlin Co-operative Association and mayor of the town, was not invited to attend. His omission was based on the antagonism between him and many of the other local merchants in regard to basic political philosophy. These meetings were the most definite step anyone had ever taken in Oberlin in regard to the parking problem.

During the same summer the formation of the Oberlin Industrial Development Corporation was made public, one of the announced aims of which was the construction of a shopping center in or near Oberlin. Some people have argued that Cochrane's pressing forward for immediate action on an off-street parking corporation during that summer was motivated by a belief that such a corporation would either nip in the bud the shopping center idea or would put the downtown merchants in a much more competitive position if the proposed shopping center were erected. Opposed to this line of reasoning is the position of city manager Dunn and others, that the drive for a parking corporation grew out of the deliberations of the OBCA Committee, and that once that group had started the ball rolling, the idea was carried on through to completion with little or no regard for the OID.

The merchants who attended these meetings expressed approval of Cochrane's plan on a theoretical level, but many were skeptical of its chances in a practical sense. The problems of how to acquire the needed land, how to raise sufficient capital, and how to maintain the completed lot at a cost not prohibitive to local businessmen were mentioned often.

Cochrane was sure that all of these stumbling blocks could be surmounted. Since no one objected to the idea of a corporation *per se*, Cochrane was convinced that once it became a reality the merchants would participate enough to make the corporation successful. Jim Molyneaux, manager of Watson's Hardware and a good friend of Cochrane's, expressed particularly keen interest in the plans. He soon was just as convinced as Cochrane of their practicability. Within a few weeks he had become nearly as active as Cochrane in gathering support for the corporation idea. In October of 1959, Cochrane, on his own, purchased a piece of land behind the Apollo Theatre on East College Street. This not only demonstrated his faith in the off-street parking idea, but also was a tangible beginning to his efforts to make the parking corporation a reality.

In the winter months of December, January, and February, Cochrane and Molyneaux were busy contacting the owners of the properties in the downtown area, the tenants in that area, and some other interested citizens as to the possibility of their buying stock in such a corporation. The purpose of this new organization would be to purchase land in the downtown area, raze some of the buildings there, and build and operate an off-street parking lot or series of lots. Again, the Co-op was not contacted. Many of those approached agreed and so the final plans were drawn up. On April 28, 1960, the formation of the Oberlin Off-Street Parking Corporation was formally announced to the public. There were 25 original investors with an initial capital subscription of over $50,000.[3]

The Corporation obtained the financial backing of a Cleveland bank in which one of its backers is influential. Ground was immediately broken for a parking lot in the rear of the West College —South Main Street block. Simultaneously, Cochrane and Molyneaux contacted each of the businessmen in that block to solicit their participation in the use of the lot. There were to be sixty parking spaces available, and each merchant was asked to rent, at $180 per space per year, as many spaces as the corporation felt to be his fair share. The participating merchants were authorized to stamp the parking tickets of their customers, thus entitling them to 2 hours free parking. Otherwise, a charge of 25¢ was to be levied. (The Co-op stores and the A and P market, as well as a few others, refused to subscribe. The Co-op based its refusal on the fact that no stock of the corporation was available for its purchase and on its belief that the eight spaces which it was asked to lease was not a fair number.) The $100,000 plus mortgage of the corporation and its operating expenses were to be paid through the rental incomes of the corporation-owned properties, the participation fees, the income from the users of the lot, and from any further sale of stock (approximately 15 additional investors have been taken in since the original 25).

On August 15, 1960, the off-street lot was opened to the public. With space for seventy cars, it relieved much of the strain on the existing parking facilities. In May of 1961 a second lot was opened behind the South Main-East College block. It added space for an additional 100 cars. Over sixty of the spaces were absorbed by employees of the participating merchants, so that only about half of the total is available for customers. But the use of the lot by these sixty employees means that sixty extra spaces on the street are thus made available to shoppers.

There is some feeling among the officers of the corporation that they have not received the full co-operation of the city government in the establishment of the off-street facilities. They mention particularly the slow service provided by the light plant in relocating light poles within the lot area and the reluctance on the part of the city manager and the city council to allow the corporation to mark the lot exits and entrances with clearly visible signs. Both the city manager and the previous mayor deny these charges. They admit that the service provided by the municipal light plant in regard to the off-street lot was slow, but they deny a bias against the corporation. They mention first that formal requests were not submitted soon enough to guarantee immediate action by the plant's service crews. They also stress that the nature of this project is such as to place it far down on the light plant's priority list. Most of the work of the plant's servicemen is carried out in emergency situations dealing with power failures, so that a routine job such as that in regard to off-street parking must necessarily wait until the men are available. These statements can be seen either as valid reasons or as bald-faced rationalizations, but they don't shed much light on the question of municipal "feet-dragging."

However, there are two other considerations which are perhaps more helpful. First is the fact that the city has already spent over $10,000 of its own funds in promoting the off-street facilities, specifically in regard to light poles, sewers, resurfacing alley-ways, and removal of debris. Granted that most of this money would have had to be spent eventually anyway, it is still significant that the city chose to spend it immediately in support of the parking corporation. The other consideration is the speed with which the city council approved the corporation's request in April of 1961 for permitting two-way use of the north-south portion of College Place so that this normally one-way street might still be available as an exit for the West College off-street parking lot, even though the east-west portion of College Place was blocked. Council might have ignored this problem as one of its members, Bill Long, tried to do, but it instead acted immediately, some heated debate notwithstanding, to open College Place to two-way traffic.

The question of the "proper" size of the signs of the off-street lot is an even more ticklish one. The small signs on East College were originally approved jointly by Dunn and Cochrane with Paul Arnold of the college art department acting as an adviser. The sign attached to the blinker caution light on South Main was installed on the initiative of Dunn. Both Molyneaux and Cochrane expressed appreciation at the time. Now they feel that the sign is inadequate. They also want larger ones put up on East College. On the other hand, Dunn has not been altogether consistent either. He gave the corporation a free hand in marking the College Place entrance but then objected to the large arrow-shaped sign that was installed. Dunn views large signs as "aesthetically objectionable." The representatives of the corporation see large signs as an important way of publicizing the presence of the off-street parking facilities. The best locations for the signs are either attached to the light poles or hung over the streets. Dunn controls the use of both of these locations and thus his opinion has prevailed. Remembering the Gibson case and anti-petition-petition, it seems hard to believe that conditions could have remained so favorable for the corporation had the city manager and the chairman of the city council really been actively opposed to its project.

A major project, such as this clearly was, is concrete evidence of the potential of private initiative in meeting community problems. With only minimal support from others a few individuals were able to convince almost an entire business community that off-street parking was not only theoretically desirable but also possible in practice.

MULTIPLES OF SIX:
NOMINATION AND
ELECTION IN 1959

The Oberlin election of 1959 was the most vigorously fought of any in the memory of the oldest resident, and if we can trust the history books, of all such events, going back to the 1840's. The community was facing a serious decision. The traditionalists cast down the gage and the incumbent planners accepted the challenge; the question was who would secure the essential mark of legitimacy required to either move ahead with the major decisions of the past two years or to abandon or curtail them.

Nominations

In order to qualify as a candidate a person had to file a nominating petition signed by 28 voting residents before the August 5 deadline. Virtually anyone could get sufficient support to run under this system.

Shortly before the August 5 deadline for filing, an editorial in the *Oberlin News-Tribune* decried the fact that no one had announced his candidacy. Several days before the deadline, Ruth Tumbleson, an unsuccessful candidate in the 1957 election, and Fred Comings, an incumbent, were the first to file. In the following two days, six citizens, supported by a Citizens Committee for Better Government; five incumbents, and five others filed their petitions and became candidates for City Council. There were now 18 candidates. Let us reconstruct as best we can the factors involved in their decision to run for office.

Though they may occasionally attempt to influence some community decisions, most people do not utilize their resources of time and energy to anything like the full extent. Apathy is the rule and activity the exception. But as the planners won one victory after another and the irritating figure of Bill Long appeared everywhere to infuriate the traditionalists, considerably greater efforts appeared necessary to some citizens in order to turn the tide. At first, grievances against the way things were going were vented only verbally. Gradually, the complaints mounted as those who voiced them found a receptive audience and were joined by others with fresh grievances. Finally, all that remained was for a spark, a center of leadership, to seize upon this disaffection to create an organized opposition.

As the nominating deadline approached, four couples—The Glenn Molyneaux Jrs., the Charles Smiths, the Bud Arnolds, and the Robert Fauvers, long leading figures in Oberlin—at a social engagement found themselves in agreement that the existing sorry state of affairs had to be stopped. As the evening progressed, they talked up enthusiasm for doing something about the present City Council. They went through the phone book and picked out those who they thought might be sympathetic to a change and invited some 25 people to a meeting at the Oberlin Inn. The stage was set for action.

There was immediate agreement that things were bad and getting worse. Bill Long and his cohorts had to be stopped before they ruined the town. But as one participant put it, people came with a "got to get somebody to run but not me" attitude. Eventually, one woman suggested that several businessmen run as a group to support the beliefs they had just stated. She suggested names of people in the audience but none of them wanted to run because they realized how much time and effort it would require. After much discussion and amidst pulling and hauling, six men agreed to be candidates on an "I'll run if you will basis." They were John Cochrane, owner of the Ben Franklin Store and a former Councilman; William Davis, formerly treasurer of Oberlin College; Paul Warner, President of the larger of the two banks; Frank Parsons, owner of the town dairy; Glenn Molyneaux Jr., proprietor of Watson's Hardware, and Charles Smith, owner of Smith's Furnishings and Floor Coverings. The selections were made partly on willingness to serve but also on the basis of what those present considered a representative selection of the community who would appeal to the electorate; well-known merchants, a prominent banker and financial expert, all honest, hard-working businessmen.

There were, of course, many reasons for the establishment of this group. One individual believed that the water issue touched off the formation of the citizens group because it meant that the town would be in debt for twenty-five years. "We chose six candidates who would give us progress in a businesslike manner, not in idealistic plunges." Then there was a personality problem with Bill Long. "He is shrewd and capable, very dynamic; in fact he is too dynamic, he catches people asleep. He has his fingers in too many pies." This person felt that Long had used his position on City Council to benefit the Oberlin Industrial and Development Corporation (OID) by getting the city to extend water lines to his industrial park. "Long represents the Co-op group which is in competition with private enterprise. This makes for resentment of local businessmen since Co-op does not have to pay corporate taxes and can get money from the Government to expand easily. The Co-op is open to all, not just to members as it should be." Especially annoying was Co-op's purchase of the two competing bookstores in town. Long's ability to secure access to large sums of money was dangerous because he "represents a socialist group, using radical means of business enterprise to promote his own business with the backing of co-opers."

A second informant spoke of "a feeling and a fear by many people that the city has embarked on a program that was too much money for the community to afford. A group was bent on making radical changes in the community set-up not to the best interests of the community. Long is a very aggressive individual, energetic and a natural doer."

A third respondent simply added that the citizens group was "trying to keep Oberlin a small college community. They were not in favor of increased population of 10 or 15 thousand; it would spoil the climate now extant." A fourth was concerned because "The Mayor (Long) did everything and the City Manager was just a figurehead. Heard all over that people were dissatisfied . . . Long is trying to run the town. . . . He is a 'snooper' and went into Watson Hardware, made a report to the City Manager who issued an order [on upstairs occupancy]. Co-op acquired too many businesses, against private enterprises. Lots of people just don't like Long personally."

As a whole this group was disturbed at the ability of Bill Long to pyramid his resources by going from business to government to other business back to government in order to gain additional strength with which to change the community. The citizens group hoped to mobilize previously unused resources in an effort to halt this unfavorable state of affairs before their opponents had become so powerful that they could not be stopped. In the traditional view of students of community power the outcome would be obvious— the business and banking dominants in the citizens group would surely triumph. But others were determined not to let this happen.

As for the incumbents, Andy Stofan, who received the most votes in the previous election, publicly announced his retirement from office. He felt that he had served his time and perhaps did not relish the thought of the brickbats that were certain to come his way in the campaign. He did, however, choose Bill Stetson, owner of a sports shop, as his "successor" and convinced him to run.

The announcement by the Citizens Committee quickly and effectively rallied the other members of Council. They looked at the coming election as a referendum on their record and they wanted to see through, improve and protect the new legislation that had been passed during their term. Their decision to run was prompted and strengthened by requests from fellow members of Council, editor Don Pease and publisher Charles Mosher of the *News-Tribune*, and friends whose opinion they respected. Bill Hellmuth, a professor of Economics, received requests from several city employees and from colleagues like Clyde Holbrook, Ralph Turner and Elbridge Vance. Wade Ellis, a Negro and a professor of Mathematics, received many words of encouragement. Bill Long had not planned to run, hoping to devote more time to his various business activities. But as Chairman of Council he felt obligated to defend it and he gave in to the strong urgings of Bill Hellmuth, Dave Anderson, a Physics professor and neighbor, George Simpson, a professor of Sociology and others. In the background, the City Manager, Richard Dunn, urged several incumbents to run.

Harold Gibson, another incumbent, found himself "caught in

between Long and his group and the Solid Six—not liberal enough for Long and too liberal for the conservatives. I am concerned for people who lose in overall city improvements; there should be some sort of compensation." While agreeing with the planners in principle and in most of his votes, he hoped to use his office to protect lower income groups and to tone down extreme actions by devising ordinances tailored to the individual situation.

"I am running because of my great interest in the town, there is no other reason," said Phip Zahm, a former Oberlin City Manager. He had also hoped to devote himself more to his new gas station but responded to appeals to defend the Council's record.

Perhaps the most interesting examples of recruitment occurred as the result of strategic considerations. For some time past, the City Council elected in 1957 had made special efforts to recruit and/or identify individuals to serve on city commissions with the hope of attracting good people, securing their support, and getting them interested so that they might run for office. It was particularly advantageous to recruit Republicans who were in general sympathetic with the planning approach at the local level, but who were irreproachably conservative in national policy orientation. Homer Blanchard, a builder of organs, and Eric Nord, manager of a factory in a nearby town, were two such men.

Impressed by the work of Blanchard and Nord on the Public Utilities and Planning Commissions respectively, the planners encouraged them to run for Council. On the weekend that the Solid Six (as they were called) decided to run, Bill Long concluded that additional measures would have to be taken. And if some planning minded conservatives like Blanchard and Nord ran they might take the sting out of the Solid Six's charges of radicalism, irresponsibility and high tax rates. Long called Blanchard, vacationing near Pelston, Michigan, and prevailed upon him to run. Then Long, Comings and Stofan contributed funds for a plane trip to Pelston where Blanchard signed in order to "guarantee progress rather than see reactionaries on the Council."

Nord was approached in a different way. He was sensitive to involvement in "politics" and Long thought it undesirable to approach him directly. "For grounds of political expediency," one participant declared, "it was better not to get too many people tarred with the brush of Long." Instead, Long asked two friends of his who knew Nord, Professor David Anderson and Leonard Barr (a wealthy businessman with his operations out-of-town) to approach him. They thought Nord was an excellent choice, and, with some insistence, persuaded Nord to be a candidate. Nord later told an interviewer that he "was asked to run by a group of responsible people who were not politicians." [1]

Organization of the campaign

Since everything happens at once during a heated campaign, it is difficult to present a blow-by-blow account of the shifting focus of events without presenting a confusing picture. One can, nevertheless, present a coherent view by rather artificially dividing the subject into "organization" and "issues."

At the initial meeting of the Solid Six's Citizens' Committee, previously mentioned, Robert Fauver acted as Chairman. [2] They set a budget of $400, which Ira Porter raised by soliciting contributions in small amounts from the Citizens' Committee.

The publicity program consisted of advertisements in the *News-Tribune* and handbills containing the group's platform. "We decided to use the newspaper medium because it reached the most people and was widely read," one of the participants reported. In addition, many members of the committee wrote letters to the Editor, particularly after it became obvious that the *News-Tribune* was on the other side.

Ester Sperry handled the reproduction of campaign literature. Copies of the platform and of talks by the Solid Six were made for distribution and sent through the mail to registered voters. Posters were displayed in store windows.

Mr. and Mrs. Arnold were in charge of personal solicitation. "We had to build an organization for a house to house canvass. This was done by precincts and there were about 35 to 50 people who worked on this activity. We enlisted these people primarily by calling those we felt would be interested. If we were uncertain, we would ask, 'How do you feel about the current Council election?' If we got a favorable answer, we asked them to work. The house to house canvass was conducted on Monday, November 2, so that the materials we handed out were in the voters' hands just before they voted and would be fresh in their minds."

Mrs. Cooley did some work in precincts five, six and seven (located in the higher incomes area) where she discovered that most of the people already made up their minds. She would talk to the people but they would say, "We like you, but we don't agree." She had much better luck in the other four precincts. "We knew at the beginning that it would be rough, Mrs. Cooley said. "We encountered a lot of apathy but worked hard and stimulated interest."

Much of the campaigning by the Solid Six, like the rest of the candidates, was concentrated in two open meetings held by the League of Women Voters and one held by the National Association For the Advancement of Colored People. These affairs were attended by candidates for the School Board as well, and the three or four minutes allotted to each candidate led to a nearly universal feeling of frustration. This, however, was the usual method of campaigning, and for many candidates, it was the only one used.

Bill Long possibly was the first of the incumbents to start campaigning. He used his small pay as Chairman of Council to insert a series of columns entitled, "The Long and Short of It," as advertisements in the local paper. He did not directly support his own candidacy but defended the outgoing Council's record and answered attacks by the opposition.

At one point Long tried to institute a public debate, in which he could use his talent at repartee to advantage, by issuing a challenge in a letter to the Editor of the *News Tribune*. He declared that the Solid Six had made

> rather serious charges against the present City Council and particularly against me as Chairman of that Council. I hope you will agree that fair play in politics demands that these charges be supported by facts and public discussion so that the voters may have the proper information on which to judge the truth or falsehood of your statements.

But the Citizens' Committee rejected this proposal saying that "If Mr. Long has any special comments to make with respect to specific issues, we will be happy to answer same through the columns of the local paper."

In a sense, Long had laid the groundwork for his campaign in the past several years although not necessarily with an electoral contest in mind. During this period, he had made a point of hiring Negroes in the Co-op Stores and had established working relationships with a number of other Negroes in town. He had become known as a supporter of equal opportunities in housing and in jobs. Through his friendships with members of the faculty, particularly Samuel Goldberg, Kenneth Roose, William Hellmuth and David Anderson, and his espousal of policies which they preferred, he had built up a following in the academic portion of the community. His vigorous leadership in Co-op affairs had made him known among many of its six hundred members. Finally, he had attracted the confidence and support of many commuting businessmen (that is, men who lived in Oberlin but had business connections out-of-town) through the OID and through his championship of measures to raise the tax base, improve city facilities and the like.

During the campaign, Long used these associations both in support of his own campaign and in behalf of others. He brought Blanchard, who was not well known, to various gatherings, and talked him up as much as possible. He also gave warm support to Comings and Hellmuth. He was, however, unwilling to support Gibson and Zahm, and he believed that Ellis, with whom he had some differences of temperament, would win anyway. He did speak in favor of Nord when he thought it would do some good, but in general, he considered that Nord's chances were better as an independent who was respected in town.

Although Nord did not request them to do so, his campaign was handled by Leonard Barr and David Anderson. "At first we had to get the rank-and-file voter to know his name," Anderson stated. "Later, this wasn't too important for he got publicity in the paper. I also talked to some of my good Democratic friends on the faculty to convince them that though Nord was a Republican, he knew that the world was round."

The campaigns of the rest of the candidates can be rather simply described. They went to the public meetings, submitted answers to the questions posed by the *News-Tribune*, and had a few friends solicit votes for them. If they were fortunate, some of their friends got together when newspaper ads seemed to be the thing to do and inserted one for them. Some had letters to the Editor written on their behalf.

In an absolute sense the organization of the election campaign was quite rudimentary. Most of the charges and counter charges took place in the pages of the *News-Tribune*, through letters to the Editor, comments on issues posed by the paper, and paid advertisements. Only the Solid Six did much campaigning and after a while they avoided those who might disagree with them. Except for Bill Long's column and brief statements at public meetings, there was little organized activity. In the Oberlin context, however, where there was rarely any organized electoral activity whatsoever, the 1959 campaign stands as a landmark of its time.

By the time the campaign was running to a close, many people were tired of it. There was abundant reading matter in the *News-Tribune* and the handbills were cluttering up the wastebaskets. Talk was beginning to be heard about the impropriety of inserting too many advertisements in the paper. It was time for a vote.

When the reports of expenditure required by Ohio law were filed by the candidates and their supporters, the following results were compiled by the *News-Tribune*:

Bill Long

Biggest individual spender in the Council race was Bill Long, who reported spending $243.61 of which $228.46 was for his weekly advertising column, 'The Long and Short of It'; he spent $10.25 for having placards printed and $4.90 to have letters typed. Long provided all but $10 of the money himself. The rest came in anonymous gifts of $5 and $2 and a $3 donation from Robert Tufts.

Harold Gibson

Harold Gibson reported spending a total of $30.24 of *News-Tribune* advertising. He received no outside financial support.

Andrew Stofan

Andrew Stofan's statement said he spent $76.74 of his personal funds supporting the candidacies of seven Council hopefuls. All but $6.18 was for political advertising.

Bill Hellmuth

Councilman William Hellmuth spent $22.02, almost entirely for two advertisements in the *News-Tribune*. He received contributions ranging from $1 to $3 from seven persons, and paid $10 himself.

Ruth Tumbleson—Gerald Scott

Mrs. Ruth Tumbleson reported spending $7.50 for mimeograph

paper and stencils, and Gerald Scott submitted a statement for $2.10 for newspaper advertising.

Wade Ellis

Though Wade Ellis reported no personal expenditures, two reports from others listed money spent on his behalf. Burrell Scott reported spending $14.94 for campaign posters supporting Ellis, and a group of supporters each gave $1 to pay for a $17.64 advertisement in the *News-Tribune*. Mrs. Eva Mae Crosby filed the report.

Glenn Molyneaux

Glenn Molyneaux reported spending $47.07 mostly for political advertising and printing, for the candidacy of his son, Glenn Molyneaux, Jr.

Citizens' Committee

The Citizens Committee for Better Government which supported the group of candidates tagged "the Solid Six" listed total expenses and receipts of $373. Of the amount $239.99 went to the Oberlin Printing Company for political advertising and posters, $85.41 was paid to Ester Carson Sperry, public stenographer, and $47.00 was for postage.

The Citizens Committee report listed contributions from the following: T. O. Murphy, $10; I. L. Porter, $25; Robert Fauver, $25; P. H. Ohly, $10; John Loflin, $10; G. H. Cowling, $10; Dr. C. J. Cooley, $25; Gerald Stang, $10; V. W. Rosa, $10; Maurice Schubert, $25; Glenn Molyneaux, $25; Frederick Artz, $25; John Hill, $20; M. L. Tobin, $25; J. H. Kutscher, $6; Jr. R. Haylor, $10; H. G. Klermund, $25; A. E. Bradley, $5; Dick Olmstead, (sic) $25; and John Cochrane, $22.

Virtually anyone who can muster even minimal support should have no difficulty in raising the small amount needed for a campaign. And it is doubtful whether spending a lot more money would have done any of the candidates much good. There is such a thing as diminishing returns in the political world as well as the economic, and approximately $500 was about the upper limit. Several winners got by with much less.

Issues

One can try to talk about issues by observing what was written and said during a political campaign. But all that the surface noise may represent is what the active participants wanted to talk about, what they wanted others to talk about, what they felt others wanted them to talk about, or what they could not help talking about. So far as the mass of citizens is concerned, they may have little or no interest in "the issues" as defined by others; in fact, there may be no subject which is available for political discussion that may engage their interest. Their interpretation of various issues may differ radically from that of the activists and they may be using similar labels to refer to quite different things. There is some reason to believe, as we shall see, that general notions of the issues penetrated fairly deeply into the community. But it is well to remember that we are dealing with what the activists talked about and that, in the absence of voting surveys, guessing what was in other people's minds is a hazardous business.

With Robert Fauver planning the strategy and John Cochrane doing most of the public speaking, the Solid Six posed the overriding question before the community in these terms:

> We believe that Oberlin should have the right to choose between the realistic-conservative approach which we represent, and the autocratic-radical approach to Oberlin's problems as expressed by Bill Long's faction and as emulated to a degree by the present City Council. (Cochrane speaking to the City Club, October 6, 1959)

The incumbent Councilmen replied individually in various ways but their comments added up to the contention that the issue was progress and planning versus stagnation and decay. They sought to portray the Solid Six as rather crotchety, hidebound types who would rather be swept aside by the times than do anything to direct the course of events. An advocate of the Solid Six, Sue Arnold, reflected the impact of this attack in a letter to the Editor where she protested that the six candidates "are being called a future Council which would do nothing. It is said that these six are against progress in Oberlin, that they are, in fact, hoping to keep out new interests and have no desire to plan for the future of Oberlin."

Bill Long publicized planning issues in his column. He pointed to a 1946 report by a city planner which raised questions about land use for housing, stores and industry, and suggested action to prevent serious damage from undesirable developments. Thirteen years later, Long declared, a city council had finally got around to doing some of these things. But all the Solid Six had to offer was "a whispering campaign of nonsense about dictatorship. . . ."

The cost of governmental services and the tax levies necessary to support them were considered of paramount importance by the Solid Six. In the platform they issued, they criticized the present Council for increasing water rates and favoring "a drastic increase in special assessments." And they pledged themselves not to impose new taxes or special assessments except by petition of property owners, to attempt to reduce expenditures, to consider citizens with limited means in taxation, and to encourage industry only if this did not involve increased utility and tax burdens. The financial issue was joined with their dislike of Bill Long through a pledge to "discontinue the policy of using city funds for the benefit of any special interest group." Specifically, they challenged the use of some $30,000 by Council "to extend water lines which will primarily benefit private developers," a reference to a water pipe running down to the OID Industrial Park. The financial issue also merged with "style" issues such as their complaint over emergency passage of the water ordinance.

The opponents of this slate of candidates opened a vigorous attack on its platform by trying to show that it was ill-informed, distorted and downright misleading, better interpreted as a personal attack on Bill Long, rather than as a reasoned assessment of the city problems. Mosher, Pease and Williams of the *News-Tribune* sought to take the high tax issue out of the campaign quite early by referring, in advance, to what was likely to be "very loose, uninformed talk" some of which could "degenerate into emotional nonsense." They began by pointing out that Oberlin's city tax was $10.02 per year on each thousand of property as evaluated and

A PLATFORM
For Better Government
In Oberlin

1. **WE PLEDGE** that no new taxes or special assessments will be imposed by vote of Council for a period of two years except by petition of property owners.

   The present council has drastically increased water rates and are favoring a drastic increase in special assessments.

2. **WE PLEDGE** to return the administrative responsibility to the City Manager and his Staff under the direction of Council as is set forth in the city charter.

   The Chairman of the present Council has acted not only in the capacity of Chairman of the City Council but has in addition taken on many of the administrative functions of the city manager's office. Oberlin has clearly expressed its desire to operate under a city manager type of government.

3. **WE PLEDGE** to discontinue the policy of using city funds for the benefit of any special interest group.

   The City is spending over $30,000 of tax money to extend water lines which will primarily benefit private developers.

4. **WE PLEDGE** that we will encourage new industry only in such a manner and to the extent that such encouragement will not drastically increase the utility and tax burden of our citizens.

   The City, in order to encourage the development of an industrial area, has over-extended Oberlin's present capacity for water, sewer and electricity.

5. **WE PLEDGE** the passage of a fair and enforceable housing code.

   The present housing code, if enforced, could be used by the unscrupulous to either blackmail violators on a selective basis or drive hundreds of our citizens out of their homes.

6. **WE PLEDGE** that there will be no large expenditure of taxpayers' money without offering an opportunity for a referendum.

   The present council has committed the community to over $1,700,000 plus over $1,000,000 in interest for the extension of the waterworks without giving the people an opportunity for a referendum. They did this by passing the ordinance to proceed under an emergency clause which precluded any referendum.

7. **WE PLEDGE** that we will examine critically all items included in the proposed budget with the object of reducing city expenses.

   The expenditures from the General Fund from 1956 thru 1959 (estimated); have increased from $107,000 to a proposed budget of $170,000. Electric Fund expenditures for the same period have increased from $325,000 to $425,000.

8. **WE PLEDGE** that at least two policemen will be on duty each day and each night.

   On many occasions the city has had only one policeman on duty during the day or night.

9. **WE PLEDGE** that we will take into consideration the pocketbook of those citizens with limited means when considering the tax load.

   Oberlin citizens should have all of the advantages they need, but the dreams which some define as needs will be examined realistically, conservatively and be processed in a democratic manner.

10. In keeping with the above items of this platform, **WE PLEDGE** that we will not represent any special interest group but will endeavor to perform our duties to the best interest of all of the citizens of Oberlin.

Respectfully Submitted,

| JOHN A. COCHRANE | GLENN I. MOLYNEAUX, JR. | CHARLES C. SMITH |
| WILLIAM P. DAVIS | FRANK V. PARSONS | PAUL A. WARNER |

that only $4.17 went into the city's general fund, the rest going for rubbish collection, state police pension funds, maintaining Westwood Cemetery, and other such purposes. All that any Council could do was to increase or decrease the proportion going to the general fund. Actually, the existing tax was a fraction lower than it had been in 1956. The editorial went on to state that

> No council since 1955 has advocated or counted on any city tax increase. And so far as we are aware, not one of the 18 present candidates for Council favors any attempt to increase the city tax rate or anticipates any need to do so in the near future. It seems to be the unanimous view of *all* the candidates that the city of Oberlin must continue to operate within the income now available from its present tax structure. Thus, the city tax can hardly be considered a real issue in this election.

The editorial mentioned figures which purported to show that residents could save very little—$25 to $100 a year at most—by moving to lower tax areas. Even when one counted in the large school tax, which no one was challenging, the savings by moving elsewhere would be quite small. True, business taxes included inventories and thus businessmen were likely to be "more concerned about any new property tax proposal than are those people who pay the tax only on residential property." Finally, the editorial issued a warning: "We believe the Oberlin voters should beware of any candidate who may advocate or promise lower property taxes while at the same time opposing the promotion of industrial development here." The two positions were antagonistic, it contended, because the most likely chance to avoid higher taxes in the future was to increase the tax base by selective development. The *News-Tribune* doubted that most citizens would choose the more drastic alternative of letting "the old town go to seed." This blast did not prevent the Solid Six from trying to make the tax rate a major issue.

In a letter to the Editor all the present Councilmen replied to the charge about using funds for the benefit of special interests by declaring that the 14 inch water line was part of the total plan for water improvement voted the previous year. This portion was being built at once because the FAA building required greater flow and pressure than could be had from the existing line, and because this action would avoid having to dig up the road again in the near future. The only plant then in the Industrial Park could get its water from an existing connection. "Finally," and this was expected to be the crusher, "the cost of extending the water lines north from Lorain Street along the FAA drive and along Artino Road has been paid for entirely by the private developers and not by the City."

In their platform, the Solid Six charged that general fund expenditures had increased from $107,000 in 1956 to a proposed budget of $170,000 in 1959, and that this evidenced the need for a critical examination of all budgetary items. In response to this argument it was repeatedly pointed out (once by Editor Mosher in his column) that the two figures were not comparable. The lower one represented actual expenditures and the upper one was just a bargaining figure presented to the County which would be severely reduced as was the practice in preceding years.

At a public meeting, John Cochrane raised his points about the drastic increase in water rates, Council's unwarranted emergency ordinance, and his opposition to special assessments without consent. Bill Long, prepared by some research into Cochrane's past record as a Councilman, showed that during the period from 1954 to 1957, when Cochrane was in office, water rates had gone up 116 percent, sewer rates, 500 percent, and that he had moved once in 1954 to pass an emergency ordinance to provide $300,000 for improvements in the sewer line on Lorain Street by assessment of land owners without holding a referendum. Long repeated this in his weekly advertisement asserting that his purpose was not to disparage Cochrane but to honor him for doing what had to be done, for getting the facts and acting accordingly. His conclusion was that the signers were opposed not to what had been done or to the methods used, but "to who has been doing it. And this, as I see it, is the sad but nonetheless real reason for all the talk which is so disturbing to our otherwise quiet community."

Cochrane replied to the accusation in a letter to the Editor. He was willing to assume that Long's figures were correct without checking on it. Yet Cochrane still felt that the Council's action was unjustified. The difference was that on the matters which he had moved on an emergency there was little opposition. The voters, he believed, should not have been denied the right to pass on a $3 million proposal for a new water system.

Sometime in October, a water plant employee in Elyria contacted members of the Solid Six and told them that the city was still interested in selling water to Oberlin. At the same time, an older citizen interested in the question also saw officials in Elyria and passed on the information that they were willing to sell treated water at cost plus 15%. In response to this information, but without first hand knowledge, the group formulated a letter to the City Manager supplying this information with a request not to sign a series of contracts implementing the water ordinance until after the election when the new Council would confer with the old to see what should be done. The letter was postmarked 3:00 P.M. on October 14, 1959. On the morning of October 14, John Cochrane handed copies of the letter to reporters from the Oberlin, Elyria and Lorain newspapers. The reporter for the Lorain paper asked the City Manager what he intended to do about the letter but Dunn knew nothing about it. After a flurry of telephone calls and talks with Cochrane and Warner, Dunn was handed an unsigned copy of the letter addressed to him.

At noon, the Councilmen held an informal strategy session on the letter. As they talked they came to the conclusion that it would be unwise to hand the opposition a ready-made issue enabling them to claim that Council had ignored an opportunity to hear a citizen plan to save money on the water plant. Instead, a special meeting was called for 7:00 P.M. on the fifteenth.

Around 10:00 A.M. on the fifteenth, Dunn received the letter from the Solid Six. At the same time, Cochrane, Fauver and Warner were meeting for the first time with Mayor Stewart in Elyria. The Elyria officials said they wanted to sell but were not too specific about the arrangements.

At the special Council meeting that evening, Warner, Cochrane and Davis handed out news releases saying that they had been talking to certain people in Elyria and that Oberlin could save half a million by halting its proposed water program until after the election and then dealing with Elyria. Council members pelted the three delegates with questions about whom they had spoken to and what the Elyria offer was supposed to be; they received no answer except the comment that the names and conditions could not be revealed at that time. Bill Long asked if Cochrane would serve on a committee with Blanchard, a respectable conservative gentleman, and bring back a proposal which Council could act upon. Cochrane replied that he would be willing to go anywhere with Blanchard but this did not lead to anything concrete. Eric Nord expressed the Council's opinion when he said that "What you three gentlemen are saying here tonight means nothing unless you are willing to say who it was you talked to and what it was they proposed by way of an offer to Oberlin. Unless you are willing to reveal this information, you are acting in bad faith. . . ." Bill Long then read a letter from the Mayor of Elyria saying that he had given the Oberlin people no promises but had only offered to sell water if a satisfactory price could be obtained. Comings was in favor of waiting a few days to enable the Six to come up with a proposal, but the other Councilmen decided to move ahead with the water program immediately.

News-Tribune publisher Charles Mosher, who was politically aligned with Republican backers of the Solid Six, expressed his feelings on the request for postponement of the water contracts in his column:

> I would like to believe their prime motive really was to prove that Oberlin could save the expenditure of half a million dollars, as they claim. But their obvious care to notify all the newspapers first, and then send their request to Council and the City Manager a day later, only as a sort of afterthought . . . . [dots in original] that was not only rank discourtesy, it had all the earmarks of being merely an election tactic, aimed only to please the voter crowds in the grandstand.

The Housing Code received brief attention in the campaign as (horrible) pictures were painted of families thrown out into the street and (brutal) government officials forcing their way into the homes of (peaceful) citizens. The code might do as an ideal, the Solid Six proclaimed, but it would cost far too much to implement. When G. Molyneaux raised the question at a candidates' meeting, and referred to several provisions he regarded as too extreme, Fred Comings rebutted with the statement that Molyneaux was referring to the original proposed code and not the final version and that inspection would take place only on change of occupancy. Comings then read a list of the doctors and businessmen who had served on the committee preparing the code. Little was heard of the issue after that.

When the *News-Tribune*, as was its custom, asked a weekly question of all candidates on a particular issue, police protection did not generate much excitement. Most candidates pointed out that the 1960 budget called for hiring an additional person at a cost of approximately $7,000 a year. The incumbents said they accepted the City Manager's estimate that this would be sufficient and Long added that it was inconsistent for the opposition to charge that the Manager's opinion was being disregarded and then to do so themselves on this issue. The Solid Six said essentially that they did not disagree with the City Manager but that an extra policeman could be provided by squeezing the water out of the existing budget.

Much more heated were the "town versus gown" and "oldtimer versus newcomer" issues which usually are kept at the whispering stage. When Mrs. Brigette Cooke, wife of a college professor, wrote a letter to the Editor in praise of Bill Long, Glenn I. Molyneaux, "The Old Man Himself," responded by asking her "how many years she has lived in Oberlin and how much actual cash of her own. . . . she has placed in our fine city? Does she intend to live out her normal life in Oberlin or in case her husband gets a substantially better offer, will she move and kiss us 'goodbye' and permit the rest of us to hold the bag?" Clyde A. Holbrook, a senior member of the Religion Department, replied in professorial style, "Fortunately, your readers seldom are affronted by such an embarrassingly crude exhibition of provincialism and bad taste." The exchange serves to highlight resentments which undoubtedly exist but which usually are submerged in surface politeness.

Although they did not raise the town and gown issue at all, members of the Solid Six made a point of including references to their long associations with the town. "First of all," Glenn Molyneaux Jr., said, ". . . I was born and raised here in Oberlin. . . . I plan to live and work in Oberlin for many years to come. . . ." William Davis mentioned the members of his family who had lived and gone to school in Oberlin. What these men considered the inexplicable defection of Fred Comings, son of an old business family in Oberlin, bothered them a great deal and made it rather difficult to characterize the Long faction as Johnny-come-latelys or birds-of-passage.

Most heated of all was the controversy over "Longism." "Why not abolish Council and let Bill Long run the whole town?" William Davis asked this question of the citizens assembled at the League of Women Voters' open meeting. This was a much kinder statement than those circulated privately. Feelings ran high as his enemies pictured Long as a combination village idiot and mastermind, a modern carpet-bagger determined to rule or ruin, a dictator, the source of all evil and insidious plots, whom anyone ought to be able to see through, but whose slick talk managed to fool the uninformed. For his part, Long did little to dispel the rumors of his omnipotence in the early part of the campaign. He confined himself to saying that his enemies should be talking about what was good for the community instead of the phony issue of what was bad about Long. Toward the end, he began to publish satiric jabs making fun of those who thought that everything that happened was his fault.

What Long did do was to suggest that in the old days a few men, meeting for coffee in a local restaurant, had secretly made all the Council decisions and that body just ratified them. If a question about money arose, it would be handled by a local banker or by "six solid businessmen" or by the city solicitor who then was Robert Fauver. However, the present Council made its decisions democratically on the basis of what was said and not who said it. Facts were gathered and subjected to rigorous logical scrutiny; the public was informed and community discussion encouraged; decisions were made "even when the action may be unpopular with some people." It was this method of democratic discussion and nothing else, Long assured his readers, that led the Council to arrive at so many unanimous decisions; for when citizens discussed these matters without partisanship they would see that logic and clear thinking led to the right choice.

Long himself came to believe that much, if not all, the opposition to the policies he favored was really a reflex action against him and had little or nothing to do with the substance of the disputes. What happened, of course, was that he and his policies became inextricably intertwined so that support and attack of one became support and attack of another. One issue can serve as an example where he and his policies seem to merge.

For some time, Long had come to believe that the downtown business district was in bad shape both financially and aesthetically. There were too many small businesses competing with one another and too little parking to accommodate people. As new shopping centers continued to be built in surrounding areas, they would draw off business unless the downtown area was modernized and consolidated. One result of the existing situation was low taxes which deprived citizens of necessary services. In his column, Long declared in a typical statement, "The question for the city is whether this area is to develop or deteriorate only according to the whim of those who own real estate, or whether the city is going to state in no uncertain terms that the center of the city is also the concern of those who have to look at it, and provide it with services." Why tax payments were so low that one merchant paid only 23 cents a day, and these paltry sums were said to "represent unbearable tax burdens." The need for action was clear.

> This area must be converted into an attractive shopping district with adequate walking and parking facilities, designed to blend harmoniously with the nearby cultural and residential areas, and able to pay the costs of the services it requires from the city.

Naturally, the downtown merchants, represented to some extent by the Solid Six, were furious at Long. But they would have been angry at anyone who had suggested this plan in no uncertain terms.

The issue of bringing new industries to town formed part of the larger controversy over planning. No one was against planning in the abstract. But the incumbents and independents were in favor of selected light industry and the Solid Six were skeptical if not hostile to changes which they felt would alter the nature of the community. Long was vehement in his insistence that City Council should take an active part in bringing in industry while the Solid Six were bitterly opposed to this. Council might possibly consider plans drawn up by the Chamber of Commerce, they argued, but it should be a legislative body, not a dictatorial mechanism for compelling people to move about.

The last issue to be discussed here revolved about the *News-Tribune* endorsements. This kind of criticism in the United States is usually directed against the alleged partiality of conservative newspaper owners to Republican candidates. With some irony, the same sort of charges were leveled against the *News-Tribune*, published by a leading Republican, for supporting "radical" candidates, several of whom were known to be Democrats.

Mosher was in a difficult position. His career aspirations lay in continued service as a Republican State Senator, or, if the rumors proved to be correct, in running as successor to the Republican member of the national House of Representatives. By coming out for Long and against the Solid Six, he would risk losing support from officials of the Republican Party in Oberlin, particularly Ira Porter, and voter displeasure at the polls. In addition, the newspaper might well lose advertising from the banks and businessmen. Yet Mosher had become increasingly committed to the planning orientation of Council and strongly believed that Long was an influence for good in the Community. He decided to follow his conscience.

Two or three weeks before election day, Mosher met with co-editors Don Pease and Brad Williams to consider endorsements. Each had lists and they discovered that all agreed upon five men —Long, Comings, Hellmuth, Nord and Blanchard—but not on the others. In their editorial, Long was commended as the unquestioned leader of the present Council whose spark contributed greatly to their accomplishments. "With his colorful, informal brash manner, he has offended the sensitivities of many an Oberlinian (us included) but the fact remains that he has been a singularly effective leader of City Council." Comings was hailed as a valuable counterbalance to Long who had interpreted the traditional Oberlin point of view with a forward-looking spirit. Bill Hellmuth was praised for his quiet logic and work on city finances which had saved much money. Blanchard and Nord were commended as men who had contributed much to the work of city commissions and whose down-to-earth, if not conservative, judgments would be most useful. Gibson and Zahm were given credit for their good work as incumbents, but, perhaps for lack of time, they did not quite measure up. Gibson particularly was scolded for believing that he could divorce his private interests from his role as

Councilman. Ellis had been a good Councilman, the *Tribune* thought, but sporadic and inclined to quibble on small matters. But these objections were admittedly "small, carping ones." As for the Solid Six, they did not merit support as a bloc because their ideas were "sterile" and factional voting was dangerous. Nevertheless, as individuals, they had many good qualities and any two would make a good addition to the five already endorsed.

The full force of Mosher's feelings came through in his column, "Voice from the Cellar":

> Now let's be brutally frank: I think it is apparent to nearly everyone in Oberlin that there is an unfortunate amount of factional pique or envy, and of personal animosity in the drive back of the 'Solid Six' slate. That has created an unhealthy mood in the community, in sharp contrast to the spirit by which the present Council members have put aside personalities and have worked together, in their attempt to decide all matters carefully on the basis of complete, impartial information and inviting all shades of public opinion.

Mosher was terribly disappointed in the Solid Six Platform which he thought had many distortions, easy slogans and inaccuracies. "Whoever is the behind-the-scenes coach and quarter-back for the Solid Six," Mosher concluded, "has done a surprisingly inept and bumbling job. I had expected better of them."

The editors and publisher were pilloried in the letter section of their paper the following week. "I wonder if you realize that your personal opinions can be ballooned up far beyond their inherent worth, by the position of public trust you hold?" Bill Davis asked rhetorically. The Citizens Committee for Better Government had feared this and had resorted to paid advertisements in order to get a hearing in the community. Davis wondered whether Long's endorsement had anything to do with the circumstance that "one of you [Mosher] is a large stockholder in one of his companies [OID]." "Has it occurred to you that your superior five includes no local businessmen other than the two from the Co-op, although ten of the remaining sixteen candidates belong to this class?" Privately, there were some cancelled subscriptions—"Don't send this dirty rag any more"—some harsh words, many hard looks and a drop in advertising by some local businessmen. (But despite opposition from some Republicans, Mosher was later nominated and elected to Congress where he votes as a conservative Republican.)

The outcome

The planners won a sweeping victory in the 1959 election with six of their number and only one of the Solid Six victorious. Eric Nord came in first with Wade Ellis and Bill Hellmuth in the top range of the 900's. Fred Comings and Bill Long were next near the bottom rung of the 900's, followed by Homer Blanchard. Bill Davis was the only Solid Six member to win. He was at the lower range of the 800's just beating out Paul Warner and John Cochrane of his group. No one else came close.

The absence of demographic data on a precinct-by-precinct basis makes interpretation of the returns rather hazardous, but some simple operations can prove revealing. Since Oberlin is overwhelmingly Protestant and has no significant ethnic divisions, two of the most likely factors to influence the vote are race and income. Inspection of the community reveals immediately that precinct four is almost entirely Negro; that precinct three is predominantly Negro with white faculty located on East College Street and in Shipherd Circle, although Negro Professor Wade Ellis has a house there; and that precinct one is a mixed neighborhood about one half Negro. Only a handful of Negroes live in other precincts. It is evident from Charts D and E that Wade Ellis did extremely well in the Negro precincts roughly in proportion to the percentage of Negroes. His overwhelming vote in precinct four leaves little doubt that a racial factor was involved. Bill Long also gained a large number of votes from Negroes in much the same proportion as Ellis though at a lower level. Hellmuth also scored but did somewhat better in precinct three, where he lived and where faculty were fairly numerous.

Income presents more difficult problems but it can also be handled in a rough and ready way. Interviews with real estate men and members of the Sociology Department as well as personal inspection reveal widespread agreement that precincts five and six are the wealthiest in town. The houses there are in the $30,000 to $40,000 range. The occupants are generally the high income people who work or have businesses out-of-town, and the upper ranks of the professorial class. Precinct seven (containing some faculty and many local business people) is somewhat between the high income section and the middle and lower-middle income precincts, numbers two and eight. Three is difficult to classify having a sprinkling of upper and middle income faculty as well as lower income Negroes. Precincts one and four are the low-income areas though there are some middle income Negroes living there.

We are now in a position to say that Bill Long received his primary support from the low-income Negro precincts, one and four, and secondarily from the high income-white precincts (five and six). Wade Ellis drew heavily from the Negro precincts, which also were low income, with a modicum of votes elsewhere. Nord, Comings and Hellmuth did especially well in the high income precincts and moderately well in the middle income precincts, with the last named scoring significantly in the low income Negro precincts as well. Blanchard just squeezed in by scoring heavily in the high income precincts, gaining some support in the

CHART D.   *Precinct returns*
1959 City Council elections returns

	Pct	Pct	Pct	Pct	Pct	Pct	Pct	Pct	Oberlin	
For City Council (7)	1	2	3	4	5	6	7	8	Total	Rank
Homer D. Blanchard	66	87	107	86	177	131	98	89	841	6
John A. Cochrane	95	107	100	80	97	90	130	101	800	9
Fred A. Comings	75	100	144	100	157	136	117	97	929	4
William P. Davis	94	110	99	93	113	97	107	104	816	7
Wade Ellis	109	94	193	276	93	74	66	65	970	2
William F. Gaeuman	31	31	34	63	22	59	35	22	297	17
Harold D. Gibson	73	45	95	115	23	25	54	53	483	16
Wm. F. Hellmuth Jr.	83	108	140	119	169	129	112	98	956	3
James F. Long	89	89	147	176	141	112	88	75	917	5
Glenn Molyneaux Jr.	78	69	71	67	36	42	77	68	508	14-15
Eric T. Nord	73	112	122	105	191	149	120	115	987	1
Frank V. Parsons	113	106	114	115	56	69	90	108	771	10
Gerald P. Scott	26	22	70	125	3	4	16	11	277	18
Charles C. Smith	66	68	73	76	38	43	70	70	509	13
William C. Stetson	53	75	107	86	94	64	73	73	625	12
Ruth L. Tumbleson	61	59	64	55	81	70	54	62	508	14-15
Paul A. Warner	97	112	99	90	106	85	111	104	804	8
Edgerton P. Zahm	68	76	115	122	82	71	83	68	685	11

Oberlin News-Tribune, November 5, 1959

Precinct 1	
Parsons	113
*Ellis	109
Warner	97
Cochrane	95
*Davis	94
*Long	89
Molyneaux	78

Precinct 5	
*Nord	191
*Blanchard	177
*Hellmuth	169
*Comings	157
*Long	141
*Davis	113
Warner	106

Precinct 2	
Warner	112
*Nord	112
*Davis	110
*Hellmuth	108
Cochrane	107
Parsons	106
*Comings	100

Precinct 6	
*Nord	149
*Comings	136
*Blanchard	131
*Hellmuth	129
*Long	112
*Davis	97
Cochrane	90

Precinct 3	
*Ellis	193
*Long	147
*Comings	144
*Hellmuth	140
*Nord	122
Zahm	115
Parsons	114

Precinct 7	
Cochrane	130
*Nord	120
*Comings	117
*Hellmuth	112
Warner	111
*Davis	107
*Blanchard	98

Precinct 4	
*Ellis	276
*Long	176
Scott	125
Zahm	122
*Hellmuth	119
Gibson	115
Parsons	115

Precinct 8	
*Nord	115
Parsons	108
*Davis	104
Warner	104
Cochrane	101
*Hellmuth	98
*Comings	97

* Elected to City Council

middle income areas, and holding on in the lower ones. Taken as a whole, therefore, with the exception of Ellis, the planners had their electoral base in the high income precincts. Then they split; Ellis and Long, and to some extent Hellmuth, gained low income Negro votes while Nord and Comings gathered middle income votes.

Solid Six candidates made their best showing in low income precinct number one, middle income precincts two and eight, and to a lesser extent in precinct seven, which is middle and high income. Only Frank Parsons came within the first seven in the most heavily Negro precincts, four and three, and only Davis managed this in both high income precincts, five and six. It is also apparent that at least one other member of the Solid Six might have defeated Blanchard had their votes not been split among Warner and Cochrane.

Looking at Chart E we can see that high income precincts five and six had all of their preferred candidates elected, Wade Ellis being the only one not in their top seven who won. At the same time, Long and Ellis could not have won without extraordinary support from the low income-Negro precincts. It would be fair to say that the election returns reveal a victory for the upper income voters allied on one side with lower income Negroes and on the other side, though to a much lesser extent, with middle income voters.

A reasonable interpretation would be that Nord, Comings, and Blanchard received votes both from those who identified with the planners and those who (though critical of Bill Long) regarded these candidates as solid, conservative citizens. Hellmuth had a reputation for quiet, effective service and also for serving the interests of Negro citizens. Long may well have suffered for his outspoken positions, but by placing himself in the forefront he may also have deflected criticism from the other planners on the ballot. He made up for this presumed loss by his activities on behalf of Negro employment and housing. This also was the pattern of his 1957 victory.

Members of the Solid Six tended to blame their defeat on the newspaper. They had hoped to keep the *News-Tribune* on-the-fence, since the paper reached more people than any other medium of information and too many people accepted its opinions without thinking. In view of the beating they took from Mosher and company, the Solid Six felt that they had made a good showing.

There is no adequate way of determining whether the endorsements in the *News-Tribune* were influential in determining the final results or not. Voting studies in national elections have shown how misleading it can be to assume that anything which appears in a newspaper necessarily gets across to the reader, and how often unwelcome information and advice is not only rejected but cast out of the realm of consciousness. Certainly, Ellis won handsomely despite lack of endorsement and Kenneth Roose lost his bid for a seat on the Board of Education despite a glowing endorsement. In the absence of more reliable information, it would appear wise not to replace the myths of the past with a new one centered on the newspaper.[3]

The victorious candidates were not impelled to much electoral analysis. The planners interpreted the election as an approval of their program and a mandate to do more of the same.

Through the bare election returns, one can, in general terms, say something about the kinds of people who voted for a particular candidate, but it is rarely possible to say anything conclusive about what an election means in terms of support or rejection of specific issues. A candidate can win an overwhelming victory while a majority of the voters are opposed to every single position he takes.[4] But this writer did attempt brief interviews with some fifty citizens, white and Negro, all incomes, college and town, just before the vote, in order to ask what they thought it was all about. Forty-two gave some answer which could be interpreted as having general issue context. Twenty-two thought that the election was between those who were for and against progress. Nine thought that the main issue was high taxes and Bill Long, the two mentioned in the same breath. Six felt that Long's dictatorship was the issue. Three thought that the place of the Negro was important. Two believed that a man's right to privacy was being attacked by the Housing Code. The others said things like "I don't know" or "some people like to feel like big shots" or "something about a drought."

Without any pretension of having made a scientific survey, there would appear to be some reason for interpreting the election as a victory for the planners and their approach without necessarily implying very much specific about particular issues. Indeed, the election campaign conforms largely to the requirements of the more extreme democratic theorists who demand that there be at least two opposing groups of office seekers with clearly differentiated platforms, ready and willing to put their views into practice if elected. Thus, it does not appear strange that many if not most voters saw some issue context in the election and that this played a part in their choice. Even their identification with, or antagonism toward, various candidates implies something about the kinds of personality and style they prefer in government, which in itself may be an indicator of issue preference.

14   CO-OPTATION

A study of co-optation was undertaken in order to determine how people got appointed to the various city commissions. In many cases the individuals on the commissions did not know who was instrumental in appointing them. And those who did the appointing did not always agree on precisely who had suggested which person. But it was possible to get agreement on which individuals did most of the successful recommending—Bill Long, Bill Hellmuth, Richard Dunn (though he was rather careful), Don Pease, Eric Nord, Fred Comings, Wade Ellis and to a lesser extent Harold Gibson—and on the criteria which were used in making the appointments. There are two interrelated but separable questions: discovering who might be interested enough to serve and choosing among these people on the basis of certain decision-rules.

The members of City Council who formally choose commission members, and those who advise them, are well aware that only a few in the community are interested enough to serve on a commission. Before anything else can be done, the interested few must be identified. This is accomplished, first of all, by adherence to a basic rule: those who are most likely to be interested and active are those who are already interested and active in some sphere of public affairs. Thus the councilmen and their advisers look first at the people who ran for Council and were defeated. Next come those who show an interest in state or national affairs or who have otherwise been engaged in some public activity. Finally, each councilman or adviser looks to his personal acquaintanceship for an individual who has expressed interest or who is in his judgment the type of person who would become active if he served.

Lest these informal processes miss individuals who are willing to serve, announcements are put in the *News-Tribune* stating that anyone who is interested should submit his name to the City Manager or a Councilman. This device proved so successful that it has been used every year. It also provides a convenient argument in case anyone should complain about the composition of the commissions: why didn't you put yourself forward when you had the chance?

Interviews with commission members reveal that most of them are interested and active to some degree although the rate of activity varies considerably. Most but not all believe that their work is important and is likely to have an impact on what the city does. There are a few, however, who differ. They feel that someone has to do the dirty work and they are performing their civic duty by serving on a commission. They find either that what the commissions do is insignificant or that there are some good reasons why they should not be a member. One businessman said, "There is always the chance that you will make an enemy and that hurts business." One Chairman said, "The only reason that I was elected chairman was because I missed the first meeting and I could not decline." He is surely not the only one who has had this experience. Thus it appears that while the expectations of the appointing body have generally been met, it is difficult to find people who will be both interested and active.

As for criteria for appointees, an obvious one is that they have some knowledge or skill which would be useful in their respective jurisdiction. The members of the Public Utilities Commission should have some knowledge about some aspect of a light plant or water system. There is usually a representative of the science department of the college on the PUC because he can contribute technical assistance that is not possessed by most citizens. It is also desirable to have some people who are acquainted with some aspect of city planning serve on the Planning Commission. There is an architect and a retired contractor serving on the Planning Commission presently. On the Housing Renewal Commission it is desirable to have a building contractor serve so that he can make practical suggestions that will help the city. The Recreation Commission should have some people who are qualified to know what is a good, interesting, program for the different age groups. It may also be beneficial to have a social worker or someone who knows how to deal with racial problems. Someone with this type of background would be useful on the Housing Commission too because it deals with racial matters. An individual with a background in economics would also prove very useful in almost any one of the commissions. The city is always interested in knowing how it can do something for the most reasonable price possible. Though experience is desirable, the Council realizes that it is not always possible to meet this criterion. The system of staggered appointments makes it easier for Council to appoint someone who is interested but inexperienced because a body like the PUC can perform its duties while one person is becoming acquainted with the situation.

To the technical criterion is joined a political one; every effort is made to balance the commissions by seeing to it that certain groups are represented and that others are not over-represented. In practice this means that an attempt is made to appoint one Negro to every commission and to appoint no more than one or two college people. If self-selection were to take place, the fear is that too few Negroes and too many college people would be chosen. There is also recognition by some of the need to have businessmen and merchants represented. These two categories are politically so diverse, however, that the kind of person selected is more important than the group in which his occupation puts him. Other groups which might be considered—housewives, professionals, out-of-town businessmen—seem to find their way on commissions so that no special effort is necessary. (Religion, by the way, has never been considered in making appointments.) The justification for this "balance" criterion is rather evident. Since the policies of these commissions are likely to affect their fellow citizens, it is felt wise to have people with similar characteristics in a position to represent their preferences. When the time comes to sell decisions to the citizenry, it is felt that the chances of success would be better through this broader representation. In any event, opponents could not say that a vital group had been excluded.

The policy opinions of the available pool of people are given consideration in choosing commission members. This is in part a conscious choice; councilmen and their advisers want people working with them who will share their views; they do not wish to be sniped at by people who have inside information and who to some extent share their legitimacy. The policy-agreement criterion, however, also comes as a by-product of other factors. Since personal acquaintance is a major source of recruits, and people usually associate with those who share their views, it is not surprising that appointees tend to share the policy preferences of the men who pick them. Self-selection plays a part in that individuals who agree with the faction in power are more likely to put themselves forward and to be willing to serve if asked. Supporters of the "solid-six" would not have felt comfortable serving on commissions chosen by their opponents. Moreover, the opposition tended to downgrade the value of the commissions because they were opposed to the policies that were being promoted by several of them. Had the Solid-Six won the 1959 election, the Commissions would have lost much of their importance as there would have been less desire to look for ways of altering the *status-quo*. It is a great source of weakness for the traditionalists in Oberlin that they do much less recruiting than the planners.

It should not be thought that the leaders among the planners recruit only those who agree with them in every detail. On the contrary, they try to make use of the commissions as an experience for converting opponents and doubters to their cause. The planners feel that immersion in the facts of the situation will prove therapeutic, and that men who participate in making recommendations will feel bound to support them. Where they draw the line may be best explained by an example: they would accept a person (though not more than one or two) who felt it might be a good idea to sell the electric plant but who expressed willingness to consider alternatives; they would not take a person whose mind was closed on the subject.

The political criterion takes on added importance for the planners, however, as they have come to view the commissions as recruiting and training grounds for future council candidates. Bill Long (Recreation Commission), Eric Nord (Planning Commission), Don Pease, Homer Blanchard, and Thomas Griswold (Public Utilities Commission), have all served in this capacity before their election to City Council. Not only did this experience prove valuable after they were elected, these men also felt that their service gave them something of an advantage in getting themselves known and in discussing the issues. Moreover, their initial activity drew them in to still other activities; activity breeds activity. Some believe that service on a commission should be made a prerequisite of running for office. Bill Long, for one, would be willing to amend the Charter to require this. The fact that people serve on a commission gives other activists an opportunity to observe them in action so that choices of candidates do not have to be made in the dark. The use of commissions as a recruiting, training, and converting ground is a basic strategy of the planners, one which they have used to advantage. They would think twice before nominating a person to a commission who might run a successful campaign against them next time. The fact that their avowed opponents select themselves out of consideration, however, means that this kind of choice rarely has to be made.

The planners seek the support of the commissions by appointing people who appear to share their policy preferences and by contact during the year. If persuasion fails, however, there is nothing the planners or their Council majority can do. The work of the Zoning Board of Appeals is evidence of this. Indeed, commission members are in a position to exercise considerable leverage because, as we have seen, Council is reluctant to go against their recommendations too often lest they damage the usefulness of this key device.

15   THE UNITED APPEAL

The adage that "he who pays the piper calls the tune" is no doubt accurate in many circumstances. But suppose there are many who pay and that those who pay the most are not disposed to get together to try and exercise influence. Suppose, in fact, that they prefer to avoid controversy. And suppose further that others are interested in being leaders. Might it not then be true that these others call the tune, though they do not pay or pay little? Observe the situation in the United Appeal as we turn to the area of community welfare services.

Oberlin residents contribute to causes dependent upon voluntary donations in several ways. Churches are supported through the contributions of their members, and often use their position as a legitimate recipient of donations to solicit for causes of interest to themselves. School groups and the Girl Scouts generally mobilize their armies of children once a year to sell cookies, garden seeds, and magazines. (A few groups, including the Boy Scouts and some churches, used to take advantage of the offer of the state legislature (now rescinded) to contribute a portion of the sales tax revenues to non-profit organizations industrious enough to gather and sort the sales tax receipts given with most retail purchases in Ohio.) Collection cans for various health organizations and funds are present in local stores to gather stray change. Christmas seals are sold to carry on the fight against tuberculosis and once a year, the Oberlin resident finds it impossible to walk through the business district without a red poppy for the disabled veterans displayed conspicuously upon his person, unless he has the moral stamina to ward off five or six assaults by teams of school girls.

The success of all these efforts to procure funds depends largely upon two factors. Some, such as the health funds and the church groups, enjoy widespread recognition as good causes, and thus, a built-in capacity to move hands toward pockets. Others are able to recruit many hours of unpaid labor to sell seeds and count stamps. Girl Scouts and poppy salesgirls seem to combine these two resources successfully.

Some causes dependent upon funds from Oberlin lack significant amounts of either resource, however. Chiefly little known welfare agencies, together with assorted other causes, they are dependent upon the annual community-wide fund-raising drive known as the United Appeal (UA). Since most of them are not in a position to raise money effectively through their own efforts, or prefer the "give only once" approach, their budgets depend upon the abilities of the campaign organizers to obtain the annual goal, and upon the decision of the United Appeal organization to grant them all or part of their requests.

Scope of the UA

The United Appeal organization was formed in 1955 out of a smaller Community Chest organization. A United Appeal is designed to include solicitations for national, state-wide and county causes, while the old Community Chest merely attempted to include the local charities. In Oberlin's case, the attempt to broaden the organization to include national organizations was only partially successful. Eventually, the funds for polio and crippled children were included in the UA through a special arrangement with the Junior Women's Group and the Rotary Club which enabled these organizations to keep their identity. The Salvation Army was included with the understanding that 80% of its allocation would go to the national organization, and the Red Cross, a highly desirable prize for the United Appeal because of its established support, consented to join when the UA agreed to grant its full request each year. Three health organizations, the Heart, Cancer and Tuberculosis Funds, refused to join.

Organization of the UA

The United Appeal is chiefly an organization of fifteen sponsoring bodies in the city, including seven churches, seven business and service clubs, and Oberlin College. The general committee is made up of two representatives from each sponsoring organization, with alternately expiring two-year terms, and (an innovation in 1961) ten or more individual members selected at the annual meeting on April 1, who also serve two-year terms. Each year, the general committee elects a president, vice-president, secretary and treasurer, who are not necessarily members of that body. In practice, the secretary and treasurer are permanent officers, for they are re-elected each year, and receive a small stipend for their services, and the vice-president of one year becomes the president of the next year. The general committee also elects four of its members to the executive committee, where they serve for two years. Together with the officers, the campaign chairman and the past president, *ex officio*, they make up the executive committee.

The chief function of the executive committee is to review the requests of the various beneficiary agencies for appropriations and to establish the goal for the fund-raising campaign. The agencies must submit applications for appropriations to the president. In a procedure which was begun in 1961, members of the executive committee and the general committee split up into three budget review committees, which hear the agencies' representatives present their cases. When the three committees have completed their task, the full executive committee meets and draws up a budget. Agencies which have had their requests cut may appear at a special session to explain why their full request should be granted. After this session, the budget is submitted to the general committee at a public meeting, at which time they may either accept it, make further cuts, or restore funds to an agency. Any citizen may speak for or against an agency's appropriation, but usually few changes in the executive committee's recommendation are made.

The fund-raising campaign is conducted in October, in accordance with established practice, and in order to benefit from national United Appeal advertising. Prior to 1961, one of the four service organizations, the Kiwanis, Rotary, Exchange, or Oberlin City Clubs, appointed a member to be third assistant campaign manager each year. He became second assistant the next year and finally became campaign manager the fourth year of his tenure. As campaign manager, he organized the drive and carried it out with the aid of his assistants, the service organizations, the other sponsoring organizations and any other help he could recruit.

The 1960 campaign was divided into separate divisions to solicit from the faculty and administration of Oberlin College (the students have their own charity drive), schools, organizations, special donors who can be expected to give large sums, business firms, the outlying townships which are included in the drive, and the residents of the city. To contact the people in the last two categories, eight local team leaders were selected for the house to house canvass of the city and six were put in charge of the three townships and Kipton Village. They, in turn, were in charge of more than 150 volunteers who did the actual canvassing from door to door. These canvassers were assigned specific residences to visit, so that people who fell under one of the other divisions, such as the college employees, were not visited twice. The customary practice is to ask the head of each family to fill out a pledge card committing him to remit specific sums periodically. A "fair share guide" is sometimes distributed with the pledge cards to aid the donor in deciding what portion of his income would be an appropriate donation.

In 1961, the method of selecting campaign chairmen was changed, and the president of the United Appeal was given power to appoint the campaign manager, a first assistant and four other assistants to conduct the campaign.

This innovation was suggested in January, 1960, by the Vice President of the United Appeal. It was felt at that time that by limiting themselves to the 160 members of the four service clubs for campaign chairmen, the UA was losing the services of others in the community who might have the required talents. The representative for Sacred Heart Church on the general committee, for instance, had served as campaign chairman for the United Appeal in Lorain, where he worked. Under the old system, he was not a possible campaign chairman for Oberlin, since as an out-of-town businessman, he did not belong to any Oberlin service club.

Robert Singleton, vice president of the Nelson Stud Welding Company in Lorain, and long a representative of First Church on the general committee, suggested that a committee be formed to study the whole question of membership on the general committee. This committee was eventually appointed, with Pease as a member, and it came up with the suggestion that ten or more individuals be elected to the general committee in addition to the representatives of the sponsoring organizations. This was written into the constitution in 1961, during Pease's term as president.

An element of continuity in the United Appeal and Community Chest has been provided by H. W. Barone, vice president of the Oberlin Savings Bank, who has been treasurer since its beginning in the 1920's. He took the position at that time because it was a paying job and he needed to supplement his income. As activity begun for other reasons often leads to genuine interest, Barone offered to continue in the post and has been re-elected year after year. He has not, however, been an active decision-maker in the last few years.

Reviewing financial requests

A continuing problem for the United Appeal has been working out a satisfactory way of reviewing the requests of the beneficiary agencies. Over the six years of the existence of the United Appeal, goals for the drive have risen, and in three of those years, the fund raising campaign has failed to reach the top. Twice, in 1956 and 1959, there were spectacular failures, while in other years, the goal was reached only through determined efforts stretching weeks after the initial drive. In addition some townspeople have expressed the opinion that the goal is consistently too high.

Members of the executive committee report that there have been demands from some members of the public interested enough to show up at hearings that the goals be lowered. Members of the Rotary Club have been the most persistent in protesting the quantity of money the UA tries to raise. These men have declared that the UA is a soft touch for anyone who comes along, that "do-gooders" have caused it to go "hog-wild" and have stressed that more money is taken out of Oberlin than it receives in benefits. In 1960 and 1961, the Rotary Club did not submit requests for their Crippled Children Fund, but asked that their name be kept on the pledge card. They have indicated that they thought their action should enable the United Appeal committees to lower their budgets.

Executive committee members feel obligated to appropriate enough money to support continuing programs, and find reducing requests a difficult task. Caught between the need of agencies for funds, and the awareness that high budgets not only are extremely difficult to raise, but also arouse opposition to the whole program, the United Appeal has searched for ways to make intelligent estimates of what is needed to support a program independently of the request submitted by the agency.

Formerly, all the appeals of agencies were heard by the executive committee in one or two long evenings. When the executive session was held to decide the amounts to be granted, the members would have little idea of the needs of some of the agencies. Discussion would often center on considerations such as the personality of the representative, and the cuts made would have little apparent rationale. In 1959, the general committee passed a resolution calling for the executive committee to hold five hearings at which not more than three beneficiaries would be heard at once. Four hearings were actually held that year, and it was considered a great improvement in procedure. That year, however, only seven cuts in requests were made, compared with thirteen the year before, and the budget reached the highest figure before or since, $45,476. It was undersubscribed by over $3,000.

In 1960, Don Pease, who had attended meetings as a reporter for the *News-Tribune*, and who had been impressed by the unbusinesslike procedures followed at the time, became vice president. Concerned with satisfying himself that no "boondoggles" were being supported by the UA, he made a point of questioning all representatives closely about their agency's use of money. At times, he found that representatives could not answer all the questions on finances he asked, because they did not expect to be questioned closely on the details. In one instance, a representative did not even appear to make a presentation at the scheduled meeting.

In 1961, when he became president, Pease initiated some new procedures. He bought some reporting forms from the United Community Welfare Funds, which broke down expenses in a standard fashion, and required figures for the expenditures of the previous year, the present year's requested allotment and the estimated expenses of the following year. These forms were sent to all the beneficiary agencies and they were asked to return them before the hearings. Acting on a suggestion from Douglas Polhemmus, Pease divided the executive committee and general committee into three subcommittees and had each of them review the financial forms of the proportionate number of agencies. This procedure has enabled members of the executive committee to become familiar with the budgets of some of the agencies they review and to question their representatives closely. In spite of innovations and a determination to keep the budget down, however, the 1961 goal is slightly above that of 1960. Tracing its formation will give us an idea of the problems faced by an executive committee determined to reduce expenditures.

When all the presentations of all the beneficiary agencies had been heard, the executive committee met as a whole to draw up the budget for the year. The polio fund had not submitted its usual request, and the Rotary had again declined to submit a request for its Crippled Children's Fund. Therefore, the committee, under Pease's leadership, tried to draw up a lower budget than that of the previous year. They attempted to do this by cutting all requests back to the figures granted in 1960. In this manner, nine requests were lowered.

In addition, the committee decided to take a $500 bite from the $6,500 sum which had been allotted to Allen Hospital for the care of indigent patients. Pease reported that they were looking for something which could be cut, and that a big sum was easiest to reduce (Allen Hospital is the biggest beneficiary of the United Appeal). Allen was the more tempting because controversy over how this money was used had occurred the year before. The Hospital simply bookkeeps the United Appeal contribution into its general fund, and estimates that it is just about enough to cover unpaid bills. In 1960, the theory had been put forth by Pease and W. Dean Holdeman, Rotary Club representative and Dean of Men at the College, that the United Appeal contribution should be used strictly for the purpose for which it was granted, namely that of paying the bills of indigent people. At the hearing that year, the executive committee had suggested that the Hospital authorities set up an account for the expenditure of the UA money, to ensure that it would not be used to pay the bills of "deadbeats" or be used for general operating expenses. The money was alloted to the hospital with the suggestion that the books show that the money was used for indigent patients of the Oberlin United Appeal Area. The hospital authorities felt that they could not justify the expense of a collection agent to handle this detail. When the Allen Hospital request was submitted in 1961, without having separated the costs of indigent patients from other costs, their grant was cut by $500, although there was some opposition.

Another cut was made in the request of the County Council for retarded children. They had been receiving $840 to support school classes, but they only asked for $425 this year because the state had made some money available to them. They also asked for $1400, however, in order to establish a new workshop. When it was learned that there was a possibility that this money could be obtained from the state, the executive committee decided not to grant it.

A young man, full of enthusiasm, had appeared at the hearings to ask for $100 for the Cystic Fibrosis Foundation, applying for funds for the first time. The organization he represented was not affiliated with the national organization. It was learned that representatives of this foundation also were looking for a campaign chairman in Oberlin in order to make a separate drive. They really had not expected the UA to support them but had decided it would do no harm to try. Wary of little-known organizations and sensitive to the accusation of being soft touches, the executive committee decided to refuse this request.

Pease's innovation, the financial forms, yielded grounds for another cut. Upon examining the form returned by the Visiting Nurse Association, it was discovered that they were carrying a sizable bank balance, and $1,000 was cut from their request.

The executive committee also debated a cut in the allocation to the Village Improvement Society (VIS). This society was set up many years ago to administer a trust fund donated by Charles Martin Hall, a chief benefactor of the College. Since the founding of the Community Chest, the Society run by members of the older generation of influentials in Oberlin,[1] has asked for and received $500 each year to be used in its program of maintaining a park with foot-paths and foot-bridges along Plum Creek. The Society has bought most of the houses on the north side of East Vine Street, though some of the former owners have life tenancy. The ultimate plan of the Society is to level these houses when the last life tenant departs, complete the remaining parts of the park and deed it to the city. Since most of the required properties have now been obtained, and since the trust fund continues to grow at each interest period, the UA executive committee has been tempted to cut it in the past. In 1956, the entire amount was cut from the Society's request by the executive committee, only to be restored by the general committee when Ira Porter defended it before them. In 1958, a similar attempt to reduce the amount to $400 was made, and Porter again spoke before the general committee. He noted that the Society had made the same request for $500 for fifteen years, even though costs had risen considerably in that time, and said that Society members were unable to understand why the amount should be reduced.

In 1960 the appropriation was questioned but passed, and in 1961, Pease and others wanted to cut the Society's appropriation. The Society had donated money to the Oberlin Historical Society to help them to move an old house which was to be made a museum. The UA has a policy of not giving to agencies which pass the money on to other agencies. The executive committee agreed that the merits of the Village Improvement Society were less than those of some of the other agencies, but it could be argued that the moving of the building for the Historical Society was a legitimate function of the VIS, which might have assumed the total cost. In the absence of a black and white case against the Society, the majority wanted to avoid the protest they were sure Porter would make at the general committee meeting, and voted to grant the usual sum. This was the only decision on which the executive committee split. The supporters of the Village Improvement Society are leaders of the element which had been defeated in the water issue and the election of 1959, and members of the executive committee were anxious to avoid the appearance of mixing "politics" with the United Appeal, which might lose the support of that part of the community for the fund drive.

In all, the executive reduced twelve of the seventeen requests for funds it had received at its budget meeting, in the manner indicated, and eliminated one. The agencies were notified of the cuts that had been made, and were given an opportunity to demonstrate why their original requests should be restored at a special hearing. Four succeeded in persuading the executive committee to restore all or part of their requests.

The Center for the Sightless had requested $850, and had been cut back to $800, the amount it had received the previous year. In his appeal, the representative of the Center noted that the $50 increase was for a special expense, and probably would not be repeated. The request was granted. The Center, it must be noted, is an agency with some popular support. When it was considered in 1960, Pease had suggested that its allocation be cut. His suggestion failed when Dean Holdeman pointed out that Oberlin residents received more benefits from this county-wide charity than the Oberlin United Appeal paid for.

The Family Service Association, which provides counselling for problems of marital and parent-child relations, and for problems of mental illness, old age, and vocational adjustment in the family, had applied for $2,705 and had been cut back to $2,200, the amount they received the year before. When the representative of this agency appeared, he was able to impress the committee with the efficiency and business-like management of the organization, and a compromise figure of $2,350 was granted.

Pease had met with the president of the Visiting Nurse Association, which provides nursing care to patients referred by local physicians, and which operates health and hygiene classes for Brownies and Girl Scouts. The president feared that if the $1,000 were cut, the action would serve as a precedent for lowering its allotment in future years. Therefore, the executive committee made the full grant but $750 due the Visiting Nurse Association for the 1960 drive was withheld.

The policy of cutting all requests to the amount granted the previous year proved unwise in the case of the Health Commission. Several years ago, this agency had been part of the Oberlin Community Welfare Council, which coordinates community welfare activities. At that time, the State had wanted to run a pilot study in organizing health services, and members of the Welfare Council had applied for the grant and organized a separate agency, the Health Commission. The state funds ran out in 1961, and the Commission applied for $5,500, substantially more than the $3,650 it had received the previous year, to support its part-time case worker. Executive Committee members were dissatisfied with the Health Commission in several ways. It was sharing quarters with the Welfare Council, but had a separate telephone. The State money had been granted with the understanding that the social worker of the Health Commission would not be expected to do secretarial work, but both the Health Commission and Welfare Council Social workers were spending part of their time on this type of labor. Executive committee members felt that one social worker could be eliminated if cheaper help were hired to do the secretarial work. The Visiting Nurse, they felt, could be moved into the same office. In addition, at least one member felt that the Health Commission used too much of its resources for favorable publicity, instead of its work. These doubts about the Commission, and the desire to keep the budget down, caused the executive committee to cut the Health Commission grant to the $3,650 it had received in 1960, thus eliminating its case worker.

When notified of this decision, John Cochrane, a supporter of the Health Commission, telephoned every member of the executive committee to protest the cut. He appeared at the hearing with three supporters and demanded to know why they had decided to take an action which was the death-knell for the Health Commission. There was a chance, he said, of getting more money from the State if the Commission could show it had local support. At the executive committee meeting after the hearing, a member proposed that the Commission be given all it asked for. This sentiment was revealed to be that of most of the executive committee members when Pease tried to find a compromise figure, and the full request of the Health Commission was granted. Cochrane was a "solid six" candidate in 1959, and in discussing the Health Commission item in both 1960 and 1961, Pease had felt compelled not to probe as deeply as he would have liked, for fear of creating the impression that he was using his position on the United Appeal to take a swipe at a political opponent. He was in a weak position, then, when he tried to arrange a compromise after the hearing in 1961. The Health Commission and the Village Improvement Society seem to be the only areas where community politics affect the United Appeal decisions, for defeats suffered by their supporters in the politics of government act in favor of these agencies in United Appeal politics.

The $500 reduction in the allocation to Allen Hospital was restored at the meeting when the general committee reviewed the budget submitted by the executive committee. At the preliminary hearings, Kenneth Roose, an Economics professor, had spoken for the Hospital. He felt the executive committee was taking a narrow view of the community obligation to the Hospital, and pointed out that in many communities most of the expense of the Hospital was supported as a charity. Frank Van Cleef, resident trustee of Oberlin College, and a trustee of the Hospital, spoke before the general committee. Pointing to the recent reorganization of the Hospital from a College-City enterprise to an independent organization, he said, "The Hospital has had $6,500 for a good many years, and has always just broken even. It has always had the College back of it till this year. I would hate to boost rates again—which only means more troubles for the marginal patients. It seems pretty hard to select the Hospital to be the one thing to be cut, the first year we try to run it as individuals." Pease replied that it was the opinion of the executive committee that the United Appeal should be providing funds to pay the Hospital bills of indigent patients, rather than contributing to the Hospital's operating expenses. The general committee, however, voted to grant the full request of Allen Hospital.

At the general committee meeting the Village Improvement Society came up when Dr. David DeLong, one of the ten new "members at large," asked, "Does the executive committee feel that this $500 is as important to the people of the community as it might be to Boy Scouts, Girl Scouts, or others dealing with the health and welfare of the community?"

Pease admitted that this item had been debated by the executive committee, and Porter rose to defend it. He said that the Society had never increased its request, and went on to outline the plans for Plum Creek. The general committee decided to keep the item.

At the end of the meeting, when the total budget had risen above the amount raised in the 1960 drive, due to the addition to the Allen Hospital allocation, Porter again rose, this time to point out the dangers of having too high a goal. "If we keep the total up and don't quite make it, it affects every agency. We shouldn't go on fooling ourselves. It's all right if we go out and make it."

Conclusions

Now that the history and some of the decisions of the Oberlin United Appeal are before us, we are in a position to examine the theory that in charity drives, the few who make the largest donations decide where the money goes.

When the drive for funds took place in the fall of 1960, the *News-Tribune* published a list of 48 members of the "Hundred Club," those who pledged $100 or more to the United Appeal. Certainly no more than these 48 people can be considered the economic "charitable" elite of Oberlin.[2] A person whose name does not appear in this listing either does not aspire to the prestige attributed to riches or is not rich. The activity of the Hundred Club, then, will be our test of the influence of the rich in the Oberlin United Appeal.

In May, 1961, the *News-Tribune* published a list of people on the three budget review committees. Three of these nine people are members of the Hundred Club.[3] The others are not.[4] The executive committee, then, is made up of a substantial but not predominant portion of members of the Hundred Club. (The secretary and treasurer are also members of the executive committee but were not involved with the budget review this year.) Singleton was the originator of the plan to alter the make-up of the general committee but the committee of eight which studied and recommended his proposal had only three members of the Hundred Club. The other constitutional change, considered by this same committee, was in the procedure of recruiting campaign managers. This was not proposed by a member of the Hundred Club. Pease's innovation of the financial forms seems to have been carried through without any suggestion or opposition from the Hundred Club, or anyone else. Influence in matters of procedure, then, seems to be available either to the Hundred Club, or to an outsider like Pease. Probably the most appropriate hypothesis is that in an organization depending upon voluntary efforts, little opposition is encountered by a person who has a plan to forward the agreed ends of cutting costs, conducting a better campaign, widening community support, and giving more careful study to agency expenditures. He needs only energy and initiative to put this sort of idea across.[5]

In the sphere of allocations, with Pease being most persistent, the executive committee was able to reduce the budgets of nine of the thirteen agencies they attempted to cut. Of the six agencies which had their budgets partially or fully restored, the Center for the Sightless, the Family Service Association and the Visiting Nurse Association seem to have triumphed by persuading the committee that they needed the money.

In the case of Allen Hospital, the Health Commission, and the Village Improvement Society, we do encounter the support of the Hundred Club. Cochrane, champion of the Health Commission, Van Cleef, trustee of Allen Hospital, and Ira Porter, Donald Love and T. O. Murphy, of the Village Improvement Society, are all members.

This, however, does not imply that the members of the Hundred Club exercise exclusive control over the area of allocations, for a more parsimonious explanation is available. Any agency which can muster a supporter or two to speak for it at the executive committee hearing or the meeting of the general committee (and this includes practically all agencies) can get at least its "fair share" of the appropriations, based on the appropriation of the previous year and any other claim for which it can establish some sort of legitimacy.[6] The members of the committees are volunteers, carrying out a task about which most of the community knows and cares very little. They are not so vitally concerned with cutting the budget that they will withstand the demand of an interested citizen or two for his agency's "fair" allotment. They stress sociability, wish to avoid conflict, and thus find it difficult to resist anyone who can threaten to make a fuss. It is not the wealth of these protestors, or their contributions— few on the committee were even aware of the figures—but their presumed ability to make an issue if turned down which guided the general committee. All three appeals by Hundred Club members involved some sort of "fair share" argument. Cochrane's agency needed to continue to hire its social worker to carry out a program it already had established. Van Cleef and Porter only wanted the usual sums for their agencies, and Porter's influence upon the executive committee was due to his proven ability to use the "fair share" argument before the general committee. To upset prevailing practice means risking controversy, courting hostility and incurring wrath, and this the committee members were unwilling to do.

The roads to influence, then, are more than one; elite and non-elite can travel them, and the toll can be paid with energy and initiative as well as wealth.

16   THE OBERLIN CITY
         MANAGER

The case histories tell us what the participants did and how they did it. And the survey of interest and activity sets these events against the background of the pattern of participation in the community as a whole. Men like Bill Long and Richard Dunn emerge as more active and influential than the man in the street or even the citizen who participates in community affairs now and again. What are these men like and how can we account for their leadership participation? The role studies which follow are designed to illuminate these questions. In the concluding chapters we shall try to specify more precisely how leaders differ from other people.

The City Manager of Oberlin, Ohio, is appointed by the City Council (a vote requiring a five out of seven majority) and remains in office at the pleasure of the Council. He can be removed by a similar vote, providing that he is given previous notification and a chance to defend himself. He is the chief executive officer of the city and formal head of its administrative branch. According to the City Charter, which defines his legal responsibilities, the Manager is empowered and required to do the following things:

1. Appoint and remove all officers and employees of the city except those appointed by Council;
2. Prepare the budget annually, submit it to Council, and be responsible for its administration after it is adopted;
3. Prepare and submit to Council, at the end of the fiscal year, a complete report on the city's finances and administrative activities for the preceding year;
4. Keep Council advised of the financial condition and future

needs of the city and make such recommendations as seem desirable;

5. Perform such other duties as may be described by this Charter or required of him by Council, not inconsistent with this Charter;
6. Attend all meetings of Council unless excused;
7. Attend any and all commission meetings he chooses and enter into discussions, though he may not vote.

These formal statements tell little about what a city manager really does. He may utilize the footholds which the above provisions give him and actively recommend, discuss, and carry out a wide range of policies. Or he may stick to the bare letter of the Charter and carry on a sort of holding operation, content to patch things up, wary of taking initiative or stirring up controversy. What he does finally depends on a myriad of factors: his personality, his training, the purposes for which he was hired, the opportunities and constraints in his environment, his definition of his role in the community.[1] The manner in which City Manager Richard Dunn was hired, how he conceived his job, and what he did during the period from February to May, 1961 can serve as an example leading to a better understanding of the functions which the Manager performs in the Oberlin political system.

In the process of discussion after the City Manager resigned the morning after the new City Council was elected in 1957, the Council agreed that, above all, the new appointee must be a young, vigorous, professionally qualified person with interest and experience in planning. The Council did not want someone who would just drift along but, rather, someone who would take the initiative in foreseeing problems before they arose and in suggesting solutions. His educational background was to be in public administration with some training in planning. His experience should be in a community comparable to Oberlin, should involve planning, and should be gathered under the supervision of a city manager of high caliber. The Council wanted a person capable of supervising others, delegating responsibilities, and making professional job analyses. His personality should be such that he could handle complaints dexterously, make a good impression when representing the city, and live happily as a member of this kind of community. His general appearance and credit rating as well as his family status were to be scrutinized. The question of religion was frankly faced but it was agreed that this could not under any circumstances be taken into consideration. Turning to the crucial area of council-manager relations, three major questions were posed: "Which of the candidates is best able to think with Council and participate in the making of decisions? Which is best able to bring in facts and information on which Council can base its decision? Which is best able to carry out the decisions of Council?" Most of these criteria were written up into a job specification presented to the new Manager when he was hired.

Seventy applications were received in response to an ad in the journal of the City Manager's Association, and these were quickly weeded down to ten on the basis of age. On the basis of experience and education in planning, this number was reduced to three and the applicants were interviewed. The men were literally grilled about their experience and notions of planning for a community like Oberlin. When Dunn was interviewed, Long recalled, "I was a real bastard. I tried my darndest to make him get mad. He didn't crack." So Dunn passed the "public-relations" test. He also had a degree in city planning and experience in planning in Oak Park, Illinois, with a city manager of high repute. Just to make sure, Long called citizens and members of the local government there and received glowing reports. Dunn was hired.[2]

To say that an official like Richard Dunn tries to do what is best for the community is true enough but is not very helpful. Men's opinions differ considerably on the community's good. It is far more useful to speak of his concept of the good and his view of his role in achieving it.

Dunn views his role as that of an active participant in helping elected officials and interested citizens derive goals for the community and move toward their realization. This is not strange, considering that he is a city planner by profession and interest. There is no need to convince him that Oberlin ought to have the trademarks of contemporary planning—zoning, housing, building ordinances, off-street parking, selected industry, and the like. The significant question is how far to push his preferences when they conflict with others. Dunn has chosen to support the collection of planners whose ideas come closest to his and who are most receptive to his views. Although to publicly campaign for one faction against another would violate his notions of propriety for City Managers, this does not prevent him from trying to sell his ideas in private, from gaining citizen support for them, from trying to recruit citizens who he believes will help the community (and him as well), and from generally fulfilling the expectations of those who hired him as an active planner. In the final analysis, Dunn really cannot be impartial, for a more restricted role would bring down the ire of the planners rather than the traditionalists. Well did he know that a defeat for the planners in the 1959 election would mean an end to his term of office, a circumstance which shows how far the City Manager inevitably becomes a part of Oberlin's political life.

In the following pages are a series of capsule case histories in which City Manager Dunn was a participant during a cross-section of time, February to May, 1961. This should suggest the range and quality of the City Manager's job.

Personnel

The Charter provides that the Manager hire and fire all city personnel, except those appointed by Council, subject to civil service regulations. All that the city Civil Service Commission now does regularly is to administer entrance examinations for all uniformed personnel—fire and police. Since the Manager may choose among all those who attain a minimum grade, and is not required to select the high scores, his achievement of internal control is not hampered by Civil Service procedures. Unlike police commissioners in many large cities, the Manager has a direct hand in training the uniformed personnel and thus has a chance to educate them in practices that he may desire to be performed.

The Charter also stipulates that neither the Council nor any of its members shall direct the appointment or removal of any person by the City Manager except at the latter's request. This formal provision suggests that the Manager is to have complete independence in appointments and removals. Nevertheless, the literature of public administration suggests that formal powers will not necessarily prevent internal and external challenges to the executive's control. These incidents will illustrate the point.

Negro in City Hall When Bill Long first interviewed Richard Dunn, he received assurances that the future City Manager had no qualms about hiring Negroes, as, indeed, he did not. At the same time, Dunn saw no reason to go out and recruit people just because they were Negroes, especially since there were a good number on the city's labor force (though not at City Hall.) During the past three years, Long has reminded Dunn of this statement several times and has requested him to employ a Negro at City Hall. Each time, however, Dunn stated that either job vacancies or Negro applicants were lacking, except for the one case where a Negro was offered a job but refused it.

In the winter of 1961, Ted Wood, a Negro reporter for the *Elyria Chronicle-Telegram*, complained to Councilmen Wade Ellis and Bill Long about the lack of a Negro employee at City Hall. Long talked to Dunn and was informed that a vacancy existed on the clerical staff and that the City Manager would hire a qualified Negro to fill it. Long then encouraged two Negro women to apply for the job, and, as a result, a Negro was hired.

Appointment to New Positions At the Council meeting on April third, discussing the annual salary ordinance, which prescribes changes in the pay scale for the coming year, Bill Davis criticized Dunn for having created and filled a new position, second clerk in the light plant office, without first having informed Council. In the discussion that followed, Bill Long pointed out that Council could lose control of funds if the City Manager employed additional personnel without its approval. Action on the ordinance was delayed until the next meeting.

After the meeting had ended, Dunn privately informed Chairman Eric Nord that he would not put up with this kind of criticism and that he wanted his position on this matter clarified. Nord met informally with Long, Hellmuth, and Blanchard and they decided that the Manager should confer with Council if heads of new departments were to be appointed and with the Mayor (the Chairman) if any other new positions were being filled. At the next Council meeting, this compromise was accepted by all present, including Davis, and the salary ordinance was subsequently passed.

The two cases of external influences on the administrator's

power of appointment illustrate two of the strategies for influencing appointing of officers noted by Sayre and Kaufman. The first is to "emphasize the type of appointee" and the second "is to establish the rules under which the appointment is made." [3] The next is a case of internal opposition.

Police Suspension On the evening of Tuesday, February 7, the Civil Service Commission heard the first appeal in its history. The appeal was made by a police corporal who had been handed a disciplinary one week suspension by the City Manager.

The immediate cause of the discipline occurred on New Year's Day, when the policeman had released a person (in jail because of an accident charge), before the clerk of courts had signed property bond papers, and without himself signing a property envelope containing a description of the prisoner's valuables left at the station. In a letter to Dunn after notice of the suspension, the corporal contended that the penalty was inequitably heavy since the infractions were rather trivial, and stated that he would take the case to the Commission.

There was, however, more involved than neglect of duty in a single instance. For some time the City Manager had noted a general deterioration in the quality of work performed by several members of the police department. Sloppy dress and behavior, poor preparation of court items, complaints from citizens, and information concerning inefficient performance prompted Dunn to impose the penalty after milder forms of discipline had been tried without success. This, then, was indictment for past as well as present action.

Because publicity of the suspension might place the City Manager in a bad light and extend unwarranted sympathy to the policeman, and because it was felt problems of the police department should remain within the department, Dunn tried to keep this matter quiet. He was not successful, however, since the *Chronicle-Telegram* soon began printing stories about the suspension with exactly the slant feared. As the days went by and Dunn refused to explain the suspension, the Elyria and Lorain papers made a field day out of it, hinting at some exotic goings-on. On February 6, the Council backed the Manager.

The Civil Service Commission heard the case the following

evening. The police corporal and Dunn appeared and stated their cases, the latter admitting that the disciplinary action pertained to other infractions besides that on New Year's Day, but claiming that the policeman was lucky in not having been suspended for previous incidents. The Commission approved Dunn's action in a unanimous decision.

One of the difficulties related to the establishment of control by a top administrator, as Sayre and Kaufman point out, is the failure of subordinates to be impressed by his reputation and position, particularly when he has not come up through the ranks.[4] Having never been a policeman, Dunn does not receive undivided loyalty from the rank-and-file who feel that he does not understand their problems. For his part, Dunn thought that he might handle the publicity angle differently next time; he might have done better to make some innocuous statement at first to cut off all the newspaper speculation.

Public relations

Ordinarily Dunn's pleasant manner serves to ward off from himself the hostility of irate citizens, and the exercise of discretion in the carrying out of city business keeps individuals from considering themselves unbearably imposed upon by the local government. On one occasion, however, Dunn found it desirable to take extraordinary measures to make amends to a citizen for an inconvenience caused by the city.

At the council meeting of February 20, Mrs. Mary Randleman who lived at the end of Hovey Lane, an undedicated road in the northern part of town, rose to inform those present that the laying of the new reinforcement water main had caused the entrance of her driveway to cave in, and had left the road in a nearly impassable condition. When told that the city could not repair an undedicated street, and that the contractor had returned the road to the condition it was in before he dug it up, she replied that she didn't expect the Council to do anything, but was registering a protest anyway. She reappeared at the March 6 meeting to protest again.

In the March 9 issue of the *News-Tribune*, a letter to the editor from Mrs. Randleman told of the dependence of her family upon the road for coal, medicine, newspapers and travel to and from work, and cited the danger of being cut off from fire protection and ambulance service. "The City Manager and the Council sneer and in a manner call me a liar, but fellow citizens, put on your mud boots and take a good look at our lane." The same issue printed a picture of Mrs. Randleman standing in a sea of mud in front of her home.

The next issue of the *News-Tribune* printed two pictures of Dunn and Bill Long "acting as private citizens," lugging baskets of coal on foot down the snowy lane, and of Mrs. Randleman standing over Long and shaking her finger at him as he tried to dig a four-wheel drive jeep out of a trench. The paper reported that the two men had gone to bring coal to the isolated Randlemans and had gotten stuck twice. Peace was made at the end of the lane over coffee, home-made biscuits and jam, when Dunn, who could not send city equipment to the undedicated lane, promised to make the contractor who had laid the water line do some more work on the road.

Finances

The Charter charges the City Manager with the preparation and submission of the budget and with reporting to Council on the city's finances. This is an onerous task but also an essential one with large potentialities for exerting control. The City Manager is the only person with the time and knowledge necessary to formulate and present budgetary items and he guards these functions zealously. His word is likely to be final on a myriad of small matters and to carry weight on others which occasionally reach the Finance Committee or the Council. The most significant restrictions facing the Manager come from the limited financial resources of the city. Richard Dunn faces the same problem as almost every other municipal executive: how to raise revenue for the city's ever-increasing responsibilities in a way that is politically palatable. Here are three cases showing the City Manager grappling with these difficulties, often in routine fashion, sometimes in unexpected ways.

Appropriations Ordinance In August, preceding the fiscal year beginning July 1, Council acts on an expense budget prepared by the Manager. In January of the following year, the budget is presented before the Lorain County Budget Commission which must review the expenditures and then allocate a portion of the local government fund to the municipality. This fund is part of the state budget which is apportioned annually to each county on the basis of population and property value and which is to be distributed by the County Commission to the local governments under its jurisdiction.

Representatives of the various localities appear before the Budget Commission and state their case for their share of the fund. This year Dunn in attendance with the town's auditor presented his request for the same amount that was received the preceding year. (The word had gotten around to the various finance officers in the county that no more than the preceding year's allotment could be expected since the Commission would have to distribute money to the newly created Metropolitan Park District.)

Quite a bit of bargaining sometimes occurs in an attempt to influence the Commission's decision, but all that Dunn did this time was to send in a copy of the budget and a letter and speak before the body. Apparently, this was all that was needed, for Oberlin received the sum requested—$21,800.

The next step in the budgetary process was approval by Council of the final budget, in the form of an appropriations ordinance. If the various expenditures in the original budget had not been altered, Council would have been acting on the same budget passed in August. In the intervening period, however, the City signed a contract with the State of Ohio for the widening and surfacing of Lorain Street, a state route, and Oberlin was required to pay for 5% of the total cost, 6,000 dollars. Since Ohio law prevents a greater total expenditure than that certified by the County Commission, $6,000 had to be subtracted from the original budget. The City Manager accomplished this in conjunction with the auditor (but without the advice of department heads) and before presenting the revised budget to Council, spent about two hours explaining the changes to the two members of the Council Finance Committee—Hellmuth and Blanchard. Formally, the two men were to advise the City Manager, but because of the short time period allotted and the knowledge which Dunn possessed, no revisions were offered. On March 27, Council passed the appropriations ordinance with Davis in dissent.

Revenue Study Committee   At the March 27 meeting, before the vote on the appropriations ordinance was taken, Davis queried the City Manager about the cost of improving Oberlin streets, which the Councilman believed to be in miserable condition. Dunn proceeded to give a rather lengthy and detailed description of the need for streetwork, listing the cost of each improvement which he felt was necessary. Davis suggested that the total expense— approximately $7,000—should be pared from other items in the budget by the City Manager before Council approved the ordinance. All other members of Council objected to Davis' recommendation. While the battle raged, Dunn remained silent and finally the appropriations were authorized as he had suggested.

After the vote, Nord proposed and Council approved a motion that a committee be formed to study the entire matter of financing capital improvements, He believed that streets were not the only items that would require large capital expenditures in the future and in the motion stipulated that the committee seek means of raising $150,000 annually for this purpose. This figure was $50,000 less than that included in the capital improvement program recommended by Dunn in 1959, but was, as far as the City Manager was concerned, at least a step in the right direction.

Dunn participated in the work of the Revenue Committee, delegated by Council to work in conjunction with the School Board in order to assess the needs of the whole community. At the second meeting, those present decided not to place a tax increase before the voters at the coming November election. The School Board was already planning on confronting the electorate with a five mill property tax increase, and it was felt that another request for the taxpayer's money would hurt the Board's chance of victory. This decision went contrary to the wishes of Mayor Nord who was out of town at the time.

The Revenue Committee then began an intensive investigation of various sources of funds for Oberlin. Dunn, who favors a local income tax, gave the Committee information on this subject in the form of written material from the Ohio Municipal League and also made available for inspection the capital improvements program which he prepared. He also acted as liaison between the Revenue Committee and the Public Utilities Commission, informing the Revenue group of the city's future requirements in the utility field. The Revenue Committee recommended a one percent city income tax and Eric Nord ran for Council on a program pledged to the enactment of this measure. He was elected but the tax was decisively defeated in referenda held in 1962 and 1963.

Payment for Sewers At the April 3rd meeting of Council, Presti's restaurant requested that it be allowed to tap-in to the city's Lorain Street sanitary sewer, running directly in front of the building. The restaurant, located at the intersection of Lorain and Pyle Road, lies outside the city limits. Council was faced with the problem of setting sewer rates for non-residents, a situation which had occurred only once in the past and for which no definite rule had been determined. After considerable discussion, bringing no concrete decision, the matter was referred to the Public Utilities Commission.

Taking advantage of his right to be present at all committee meetings, Dunn participated in the PUC's deliberations. He suggested to the Commission that (1) a lump-sum be charged Presti's for the equivalent cost of the presently existing 200 feet which fronts the property—a practice followed in other cities, and (2) that a premium be added, a precedent established by the City in imposing an increment to rates for the water service extended outside the City limits. The Commission accepted Dunn's recommendations but decided that the 10% premium which Dunn suggested was too low and settled on the figure of 25%. The PUC also proposed that the service be discontinued unless the entire Presti property had been annexed to the city within five years.

When at the next Council meeting, Dunn presented the PUC's recommendations, Long moved to substitute for the annexation provision a stipulation that Presti's agree to pay for its share of the cost of constructing water and sewer lines along the Pyle Road side of the property in the event that residents in this area petitioned for annexation and for the utility services. Since Long believed that annexation of Presti's would come sooner or later he wanted to protect the city against refusal by Presti's or future owners of the property to pay for Pyle Road water and sewer line extension. Council passed the PUC's proposal with Long's substitution six to one, Davis opposed.

On the night of April 24, Oberlin was hit by a heavy downpour in which a storm sewer pipe, lying underneath the basement of Glenn Molyneaux's Watsons Hardware Store, blew out because of excessive pressure. The sewer, which drains Tappan Square, and also serves a store as well as the Off-Street parking lot, is very old and Dunn suggested at the May 1st Council meeting that a new sewer be constructed, running through Carpenter Court to South Street, thus avoiding Molyneaux's store. The expense of this project was estimated to be $3500 and Council requested Dunn to bring in, at the next meeting, a recommendation for apportioning this amount.

Because funds were limited and the city would be unable to bear the full responsibility of financing, the City Manager, to expedite matters, decided to include only four parties in the sharing of the costs—$700 each from the city and the college, and $1,050 each from Molyneaux and the Off-Street Parking Corporation. At the Council session on May 15, Dunn reported that only the college, in the person of business manager Lewis Tower, had agreed to pay the amount stipulated. Councilman Davis stated that Dunn's method of financing was unfair and suggested that the drainage area served should be the standard by which cost would be allocated. Making some rapid calculations, Long figured that under this formula the college would bear 13/16th of the total cost and the city none. The college again proved willing to pay.

Planning

The boundary line between what is private and what is public is often thin and tenuous. What the government does affects private persons and what they do may have a profound impact in the government. This is particularly true in cases involving the location of industry, parking facilities, and the relationship of the business community to other segments of the population. The City Manager grapples with these problems, taking the initiative or standing to one side if that will help, always seeking to move toward his preferred goals for community development while mitigating opposition as effectively as he can. Whatever the outcome, he keeps trying. That is his job.

Industrial and Commercial Development   In 1959, the Oberlin Improvement and Development Corporation (OID) was formed. Because Dunn is interested in the development of the Oberlin community, and because several members of the OID have worked with him on other issues (e.g. Long and Solicitor Severs), the City Manager has utilized his personal (though not his official) resources to assist the Corporation.

Dunn is concerned with the industrial park primarily because its full development would add greatly to the city's tax rolls. He gave the OID information that he possessed about similar parks in other cities and was able to offer suggestions relating to sewer requirements and the layout of lots and streets. Dunn has not, himself, attempted to bring industries to the City, but he has known about this and been asked to give advice whenever the OID is considering signing a contract with a firm.

The City Manager has felt for some time that the Oberlin business district was in a state of decay and would require changes to prevent a further deterioration. He was therefore most interested when Long informed him that the OID was planning a shopping center. When the Corporation received a report from an architectural firm in regard to the layout of the center, Dunn took it upon himself, with Long's consent, to modify the plan, spending a few evenings at the drawing board at his home.

After two years of discussing the type of stores that the shopping center should have, Long and Dunn have come to the conclusion that a large supermarket would serve as a necessary magnet to draw customers to the area. To obtain stores to surround the supermarket, Long contacted West College Street merchants and unsuccessfully asked them to move to the center. It is now hoped that out-of-town firms will come to the center.

Recently, as a result of several discussions, Dunn, Long, Roose and Arnold (both College professors), and Nord drew up a prospectus outlining the group's line of thinking concerning the city's commercial area. Written by Dunn, it describes the history of College Place and the conservatory (related in the next section), supports the idea of a shopping center and suggests that all stores on West College and South Main be combined under one ownership.

College Place and the New Conservatory College Place is a small, L-shaped street, running south from West College Street along the Co-op Bookstore and then making a 90 degree turn to continue west to Professor Street.

In 1957, before Dunn came to Oberlin, the College decided to build a new conservatory in the area around East-West College Place, a plan which required that a portion of the street would eventually be abandoned. Because it was generally agreed that North-South College Place should continue to be used, that an exit from this street should be provided, an access route replacing East-West College Place had to be found. The original proposal would have extended North-South College Place to a point south of the new building and then east to Main Street over the land adjoining the telephone company. But the company constructed a garage on this spot and thus made this plan unfeasible.

In January, 1960, discussions between Dunn and College officials, particularly a member of the Board of Trustees, Van Cleef, led to the agreement that the College would be given East-West College Place in return for which it would extend North-South College Place south of the Conservatory and then west to Professor Street. But again difficulties arose—concern was expressed by the college about the amount of traffic which would encircle the conservatory.

In November, President Carr called a meeting of adjoining property owners, city officials including the City Manager, and representatives of the College. Dunn, who had had several discussions prior to the meeting with Van Cleef, Bill Long, and the Lorain Metropolitan Planning Commission, presented three alternatives to the November conference: first, the January agreement; second, Long's recommendation that North-South College Place be closed off entirely and converted into a pedestrian mall;

and third, the College's new proposal, that North-South College Place be extended to a new East-West street to be constructed over a small portion of the Off-Street Parking lot and over the land now occupied by the Pizza House. The last alternative was accepted by those at the meeting.

Dunn and Long hope that the sudden appearance of a new conservatory, and shopping district will have the effect of awakening the town and particularly the merchants to further changes that could be made.

College Place and Off-Street Parking At the April 17th session of Council, Robert Fauver, representing the Off-Street Parking Corporation, requested that North-South College Place be converted from a one-way-south to a two-way street. He gave as his reason the inconvenience incurred by several of Off-Street's patrons when trucks, delivering construction material to the new conservatory, and workers' cars parked along the curb, prevented use of East-West College Place as an exit from the parking lot. Dunn, who had received complaints of a similar nature previously, believed that very little delay had confronted the motorists and that the Corporation was just using this as an excuse to obtain two outlets on College Place. After Council defeated a motion to grant Fauver's request for which only Nord and Davis voted, Dunn offered a suggestion that North-South Place be made two-way, but with the restriction that a left-turn north to College Street be prohibited. Council, however, did not approve this suggestion, but, instead, directed the City Manager, with Nord and Davis dissenting, to make a two-week study of the problem to see if there really were blockages. Fauver, who felt that this was hardly sufficient, tried to capture something for his clients by proposing that all parking on North-South Place be eliminated. (He could not request the same on East-West College Place because this was now owned by the College.) Council unanimously passed the request.

The next day at the Oberlin Business Council's weekly Tuesday morning meeting, feelings were still hot, despite the study to be made by Dunn and the concession received by Fauver. John Cochrane and Molyneaux were particularly disturbed and threatened to circulate a petition. After the session, Bill Stetson, president of the group, called up the City Manager, related what had occurred and asked if he and several others could talk to Dunn that morning. Dunn agreed and before the meeting began he phoned Tower and asked him to be present at the meeting in order to dispel a story that the College was to tear up College Place immediately which he believed to be false.

At the session, in addition to Dunn and Tower, were members of the Business Council. Tower explained that the College had no intention of destroying East-West College Place at this time, and offered a concession previously suggested by Dunn to prohibit parking by all trucks and workers' cars on the Place by requiring them to park on the grass area. The Business Council contingent went away with its anger partially mollified. A few days after the meeting, Dunn received a copy of a memorandum (which he requested that Tower send to the contractors) to the effect that no blockage should henceforth occur on the Place. During the ensuing two weeks Dunn visited the controversial street on his way home to meals. At the May 1st meeting of Council, the City Manager reported that he had observed no impediments to traffic and suggested that not only was there no need for a two-way North-South College Place, it was also unnecessary to remove parking from that street.

Fred Comings, general manager of the Co-op Bookstore which would benefit from the reinstatement of parking, backed Dunn, but Bill Long, who is general manager of the entire Co-op operation, opposed the City Manager. Long claimed that this was a matter of principle; namely, whether or not the City was going to encourage off-street parking. Council took no action to reinstate parking and it remained off North-South College Place.

Education

The formal separation of the Board of Education from the City Council is an important fact of life in Oberlin as in many other communities. If the Council was responsible for education, the criteria for decision might involve a comparative evaluation of various city needs, but the Board is free to consider its own requirements. By and large, the two sets of decision-makers go their separate ways. But there are some instances where joint consultation has obvious advantages.

School Parking Lot   In January, Dunn received word from Superintendent of Schools Duncan that the members of the School Board were considering constructing a gravel parking lot for student drivers at the new high school. The lot was to adjoin Pleasant Street, which would then serve as the point of exit and entry. Dunn was quite disturbed about this plan, for the street which would be traveled upon by the high school motorists was narrow and already overcrowded with busses, trucks, and automobiles. He explained the problem to Duncan and said that he would bring the matter before Council unless the parking lot proposal was dropped. The Superintendent replied that his hands were tied; the members of the School Board were definitely in favor of the idea. Dunn then stated that he would informally discuss the situation with the few Councilmen whom he hoped he could persuade to present his argument to the School Board on an informal basis. He also assured Duncan that if the school promulgated a no-driving rule, the Oberlin Police Department would be able to enforce the regulation.

The strategy outlined to Duncan was successful. The Manager explained the difficulties created by a Pleasant Street parking lot to Nord and one other Council member, and the two legislators proceeded to convince the President of the School Board that Dunn's argument was correct. On April 10, it was announced that students would not be permitted to drive to school, thus avoiding the necessity of a parking area.

Recruitment of Teachers   Dunn is a member of a small group which meets regularly to discuss various subjects. When the group, which includes Don Pease and Bill Long, decided to talk about teacher recruitment, the group invited Duncan to speak about the procedure he followed in this annual project.

Duncan had with him a digest distributed to potential teachers describing the City of Oberlin, the College, and the public school system. The group decided that the pamphlet was poorly written and did not present in an attractive manner the advantages of living and teaching in Oberlin. With Duncan's consent, they wrote a new propaganda piece and had it printed in large quantities. The writers were ready to bear the cost of the printing, but the School Board later consented to cover this expense.

Extension of contracts

When a private firm signs a construction contract with the city, it agrees to finish work within a certain time period. Included in the contract is a clause stating that a penalty payment, usually $200 per day, will be assessed if delay in completion of the construction results in damages to the city. Council occasionally is requested to waive the penalty stipulation and may do so if it wishes. During the period under consideration, two such requests came before Council.

At the May 20th session of Council, the City Manager presented a letter from an engineering firm asking that a 101 day delay in completing a section of the low-level dam and pumping station at the new waterworks be forgiven. Dunn explained that the delay had not resulted in any damage to the City because the project was of no value until electric power reached it, and this had not yet happened. All present except Long voted to approve the firm's request.

On May 15, Dunn petitioned for a delay of 56 days for contractors for the new water treatment plant. The deadline had been April 5 and the plant had been functionally finished eight days later but some outside work still had to be done. In presenting the application, Dunn stated that the request was reasonable since bad weather had impeded progress and the firm had been extremely cooperative in every aspect of its relationship with the city. The Manager believed that it would damage the city if contractors came to feel that reasonable requests were not granted.

Long, however, felt that good use could be made of the $11,200 ($200 x 56 days) which would accrue to the city in a penalty payment and after City Solicitor Severs stated that this may have been a case in which there was actual damage, the Councilman moved to deny the request. The vote was a tie, 3-3-1, as Ellis and Hellmuth joined Long in opposition and

Davis abstained because he did not want to be involved in any phase of the waterplant.

Blanchard proposed that the delay be granted, but withdrew the motion when Hellmuth moved to direct the City Manager and Solicitor to confer with the contractors and report back to Council at the next meeting. This motion passed 5-2 with Long and Davis (who apparently changed his mind) in dissent.

Conclusions

These are, of course, not the only issues in which City Manager Dunn was active. Enforcement of the housing code, new water system, and many other matters come within his purview. Indeed, it may appear that he is omnipresent, an active participant in all that goes on in Oberlin. This would be an exaggeration, though an excusable one. He did not participate in the reorganization of the United Appeal, a small labor dispute,[5] and the drive for open housing for Negroes, the controversy over who should sell school workbooks, and other issues.

What accounts, then, for his selective participation? Like most other people, the City Manager is not interested in everything, especially if the affair at hand does not involve official duties. He feels that he should not spread himself too thin, and he fears that excessive use of his resources would work against him. And in some areas he just does not have the resources to influence the results as in many school matters and welfare activities.

It is clear that Dunn is influential in many of the issue areas in which he participates; what he does has an impact on the outcome. But it is equally clear that he suffers a number of defeats; he must secure the consent of others, particularly Council, in order to prevail, and others can mobilize against him. In fact, careful reading of the case histories will show that many of the outcomes he desires are accomplished without opposition, as in the instance of the zoning ordinance. For the most part his official position and knowledge is sufficient to carry the day. Such potential opposition as does exist is either uninterested, uninformed, or not sufficiently active to challenge the Manager. So long as he has the support of a majority of Council for his activities, this is presumably the way things are supposed to be.

Six of the seven members of Council (Davis excepted) frequently support the City Manager. Dunn considers Long his closest ally and talks to him either on the phone or in person five or six times a week. Nord, the Mayor since 1959, converses with the City Manager two or three times per week. Communications between these two men is impeded because Nord's business is out of town. It is also true that Dunn and Long are closer in the sweep of their planning objectives than are Dunn and Nord.

Hellmuth and Blanchard speak to Dunn once or twice a week, usually in regard to their special interests, finance and public utilities, respectively. Comings talks to Dunn about the same amount and Ellis less, mainly because they seem to have trouble reaching one another.

As closely as Dunn and Long work together, there is bound to be a certain amount of strain in their relationships because they have different responsibilities, different roles to play as City Manager and Councilman, and disagreements are bound to arise. Although they differ on contract penalties, parking in town, and the College Place situation, among others, all of these are minor matters which do not impede the cooperation they both find so useful.

The City Manager is interested, active and has the resources of his office with which to influence the course of decision-making. He is, after all, the only individual in town whose full time job it is to help make decisions over a wide range of community affairs. Other city employees are specialized to the particular areas in which they work and they lack his formal powers and his broad contacts. Everyone else (except for retired persons whose energy levels cannot be expected to approach his) has primary work responsibilities in his or her job and can engage in community affairs only as a part-time activity. As a matter of course, therefore, we would expect a City Manager who takes a broad view of his responsibilities, in a town without full-time elected officials, to be the most general activist and to appear in more decision areas than anyone else.

Long's activity has been invaluable to Dunn in many ways. Long serves as a sounding board upon which Dunn can present his ideas and get a reaction which he respects. This is a source of inspiration, guidance, and comradeship to sustain the Manager in the necessarily shifting and rocky fortunes of public affairs. Where other men, even devoted ones, are sporadically concerned with community policies, Dunn knows that Long is continuously concerned, always approachable, and ever-ready to spring into action. When Long was Chairman, Dunn knew that he would move matters up for decision and that things would get done if it were possible to gain consent from others. And for a considerable period of time it proved possible for Dunn to remain in the background while Long carried the ball in public and deflected the criticism for their joint projects to himself.

A citizen like Bill Long, who rivals the Manager in the breadth and intensity of his participation, is not to be considered a normal manifestation of the civic spirit to be expected of all good patriots. On the contrary, such activity and such a person are extraordinary phenomena, unusual in the extreme, deserving of the most careful study. Casting aside the notion that every citizen ought to be or can be a perpetual whirlwind of activity, attention can be centered on the interesting case of the perpetually active citizen.

17 BILL LONG: PORTRAIT OF AN ACTIVIST

✤✤✤✤
✤🏛🏛✤   In this chapter we turn to the fascinating question
✤🏛🏛✤   of how the remarkable individual gets involved in
✤✤✤✤   community affairs, how he makes his will felt,
       how he operates, and what satisfactions he gets
       from his activities.

James F. "Bill" Long was born on January 7, 1913, in Baltimore, Maryland, the second oldest of six children in the family of a produce and seafood distributor. After attending high school in Baltimore, Long joined his father's business for a period of four years. During that time he came under the influence of clergymen from the Evangelical and Reformed Church who preached the social gospel with much fervor. Long became interested in the typical ideological concerns of the reform movements of the 'thirties, bringing about greater economic justice, reducing racial prejudice, ending war. From this period we can date his passion for conversion, for getting other people to see the light, not only on religious but on social matters. With the intention of studying for the ministry, he enrolled at Heidelberg College, Tiffin, Ohio and studied history and English until his graduation in 1940. By that time, however, he had lost his theological bent (though not his reformist ardor) and gave up a fellowship to the Yale Divinity School in order to take a position with the Ohio Farm Bureau and Cooperative Association, thus transferring his "missionary" activities to the cooperative movement. Six months later, he moved to Wooster, Ohio, as organizational and education director for that area. He was married in 1942 and has four children.

The coming of the Second World War found Long faced with a crisis because of his pacifist convictions. He initially registered as a conscientious objector but in the light of Nazi activities, his loss of religious conviction, and his own active temperament, he decided that he could not maintain this position and went into the Army. He was in the Medical Corps from 1942-1946, went to Officers Candidate School and served as an administrator and a detachment commander at a hospital. He found that he had administrative talent and liked the work. He could never stand to watch mismanagement and, indeed, has never found an organization run by others which was handled as well as it could be.

After the war Long rejoined the Farm Bureau in Bucyrus, Ohio. In 1948 he attempted to pioneer a cooperative store in Lorain, and when CIO officials sponsoring it became less than enthusiastic, he moved to Oberlin to take charge of the Co-op stores.

Most people receive their primary satisfactions through their jobs, friends, families, hobbies, and not through participation in the seemingly esoteric and threatening realms of public affairs. Like them, Bill Long was so busy during the years from 1949 to 1952 trying to put the Co-op bookstore and foodstore on their feet that he had little time and inclination to do much else. But his work as manager of the Co-op bookstore brought him into contact with many people in the community, especially with college professors with whom he had to deal many times in the procurement of text books. Samuel Goldberg, a Professor of Mathematics, became a close confidant of Long's. Professor Kenneth Roose, who was to become his most intimate associate in the Oberlin Improvement and Development Company and Professor William Hellmuth, who was to serve two terms with him on City Council, were both presidents of the Co-op. Interested in discussing national affairs, debating religious questions, and exploring such exotic areas as game theory, Long soon found that he had more in common with faculty members and their friends among the "out-of-town" executives, than he did with the downtown merchants.

At the same time his business activities brought him into conflict with leading members of the local business community. Upon discovering that the head of the People's Bank, Ira Porter, was hostile to the Co-op, Long transferred the organization's funds to the other bank in town. On one occasion he had difficulties in arranging essential loans and was able to survive only by going out of town for some Co-op funds and raising additional amounts through internal subscriptions. When he wanted to move the Co-op stores to advantageous locations, he was temporarily blocked, he believed, by the actions of John Cochrane who controlled the necessary leases. The stage was set for conflict but it took time to mature.

One day, as a result of prodding from the wife of an Oberlin College math professor, he decided to attend a meeting of citizens for the purpose of organizing a recreation committee in Oberlin. He soon found that there was a lot of talk, most of it terribly confused, in his opinion, and beside the point. Being irrepressible, Long then asked a series of questions to try and clarify what the participants were trying to do. When an unofficial recreation committee was set up pending the results of the campaign for the new charter in 1955, Long was asked to serve. After the charter was approved, and an official commission of five was appointed by Council, Long was chosen again. A year later it transpired that no one else sought the job of chairman of the Recreation Commission, and that Long's activity seemed to make him the logical choice. As he put it, "I'd just as soon run it if I'm going to be on it." The incident illustrates a typical process of self-selection: an individual manifests interest in and shows some capacity for a particular chore; he is immediately drawn in by others who are looking for people willing to work. The incident also shows certain of Long's most prominent characteristics, his impatience with what he considers sloppy thought and procedure, and his desire to run things more effectively as he views effectiveness.

When it became known that Long was willing to do things, he became drawn into other activities. A committee to promote fluoridation had been established and someone told its chairman that Long was good at writing advertisements (he had done some snappy ones for the Co-op). Ken Roose brought Long in as a member of the Board of the American Civil Liberties Union.

During this period Long was a member of the NAACP as well, reflecting his life-time interest in eliminating racial prejudice. He hired Negroes in the Co-op, gave them positions of responsibility, and sought to set an example for the community. He was thwarted by the unwillingness of the NAACP to take positive action, such as threats of picketing, to improve employment opportunities, and he constituted himself a one-man committee to prod and goad them into doing things. He would, on occasion, taunt his own employees about the Negro community's lack of action and its inability to use the ballot to reward friends and punish enemies. Looking back on these events, Long perceives a considerable change in the Negroes' willingness to vote and, to a lesser extent, to act in a manner to benefit members of their race. But he takes no credit for this, ascribing it, instead, to the determination of about a dozen Negro families in Oberlin.

In 1951, Long was still only mildly interested in town politics. A friend suggested that Long run for Council and he agreed in a lukewarm manner provided that the friend got the required signatures on the nominating petition. The "campaign" consisted of one speech at a meeting. Long was soundly defeated.

By 1957, Long was much more interested and active in city affairs. He had a network of acquaintances, knew his way around, and had had some dealings with the City Council, serving as chairman of the Recreation Commission. When Dan Kinsey came up with the notion that the existing waterworks would eventually be abandoned and that the reservoir, together with a large arboretum owned by the College, would make a splendid city recreation area, Long did the organization work and pushed the idea, getting Councilman Andrew Stofan interested. Meeting opposition from other councilmen, Long arrived at the conclusion that this negative attitude reflected fear that a municipal swimming pool would involve interracial activity. (He was not aware then of the discussions within the Public Utility Commission related to the water problem.) During 1957 Long had begun to venture in the realm of real estate. Together with Ken Roose he had acquired some land near the new Co-op bookstore and the two men had made preliminary planning efforts to redevelop this area as a community shopping center. This led to reflection on problems concerning the community as a whole especially with regard to economic factors related to growth. It was the combination of these two interests: recreation and community planning which led to Long's decision to run for Council.

Although Long came in third out of the first seven, he was named chairman of the Council. This came about because neither Stofan nor Comings, the two vote leaders, wanted the job whereas Long was more than willing. Among other things, he stressed the need for an early selection of a chairman to take the lead in choosing a new City Manager, the old one having resigned on election day.

During the pre-election period and in his first few months in office, Long had an opportunity to attend many Council and commission meetings, experiences which changed his views about the difficulties which the city was facing. He had previously thought that there were a number of irreconcilable reactionaries, "old buzzards," running the town to suit themselves, determined to protect their own interests. In the election campaign he had complained about decisions being made by small groups at coffee time, all of them businessmen or their allies. But as Long came to observe their behavior he decided that while such groups existed, they were ineffective, did not know how to get things done. He found their procedures "hit and miss" rather than systematic. Their meetings rambled on without sharp questions being posed or determined efforts made to get all the relevant information. Most important of all, Long decided that there was no real attempt to plan, to anticipate problems, and as a result Council reeled from one to another half-hearted attempt to meet immediate crises. He determined to change all this.

Since serving on Council, Long has wandered far afield in gathering basic information about the problems a city faces. He reads extensively on city planning, drawing his basic philosophy from architect Victor Gruen, architect Eliel Saarinen's book entitled *The City*, and Lewis Mumford's recent book *The City in History*. For month to month stimulation in this area he is a regular reader of *Architectural Forum* and *House and Home*, two of the trade journals for builders.

Long sees his role as an initiator, builder of support, gainer of consent, and decider of wide-ranging policies. His task as a councilman and citizen, as he views it, is to be continually active on a broad front and to see that decisions are made (after public discussion) which he believes are wise. Naturally, he identifies his own views with the common interest. A passive role as registrar of other people's sentiments or keeper of the city's consensus is not for him. He feels his job is aggressively to promote policies (such as a new water system) desirable for the city and to veto others which threaten these goals. When other people propose policies he prefers, as in the housing code, he may be content to do his part in gaining consent and leave it at that. When serious opposition appears, he is ready and willing to take his side to the public and to present the case with full force. He not only recognizes the right of others to dissent, but he prizes discussion and takes pride in arranging the fullest possible opportunity for debate. Indeed, he has an almost mystical view of truth emerging from what others would call the market place of ideas, a feeling not unconnected, perhaps, with his zest and talent for debate.

Long does see certain limits in his role. Although clear in definition, they are rather fuzzy in practice. He does not deem it proper to interfere in administrative matters within the province of the City Manager. But he tends to view the area of policy, belonging to Council, as wide enough to do what he wants. Whenever possible, he will back up the City Manager and refer matters dealing with working conditions, traffic tickets, and that kind of thing to him. Long's close relationship with Dunn no doubt helps in this regard. Indeed, Long has insisted upon and largely secured an open, critical relationship with Dunn, in which both feel free to criticize the other and disagreements take place. It is mutually profitable, however, for both men to minimize their disagreements and their zealousness in defining their spheres of action helps prevent encroachments.

Dunn, and, especially, Long are pragmatists. They have held many discussions over what constitutes "administration" in a city like Oberlin, and have come to the conclusion that it is a combination of City Manager and staff, Council and its chairman, and Boards and Commissions. The way to get things done, they agreed, was to use this machinery in any possible combination in order to achieve the desired results.

The degree to which self-interest creeps into human affairs is difficult to describe with precision. The notion that what is good for General Motors is good for the country is well nigh universal. And if we need a reminder, Reinhold Niebuhr has insistently pointed out the degree to which self-love can contaminate the highest human aspirations. So far as he is conscious of his own interests, Long tries rigorously to exclude them from his official acts. He is not averse to taking actions which apparently run counter to his immediate interests, such as bringing in a chainstore to compete with the Co-op or opposing parking on a street near the bookstore. And when the downtown shopping center developed, requiring Council action for parking space, he announced that he would not vote and would not run for re-election in order to avoid possible conflict of interests. It remains to be seen whether he is correct in his assumption that his moves for industrial development and his complementary Council actions are both in the general interest.

For Long the explanation of his leadership is rather simple. He puts in a lot of time and energy, he is persuasive and he knows how to do things in business and local affairs. This is not a bad short explanation. For our analytic purposes, however, it is desirable to essay a more detailed and systematic discussion of his resources (his bases of influence), the attributes and positions he uses to make an impact on community decisions.

There is no doubt that Long devotes more time to community affairs than anyone else in Oberlin except for the City Manager who works at it full time. He is constantly thinking about city problems, working out policy alternatives, talking to people, taking action. As one resource can be converted into another, the nature of his job permits him to spend more time, and make more effective use of it, than would otherwise be the case. Although he spends much time working, he is free to attend to city affairs when the occasion demands. He is not tied to a particular schedule, and he uses various economizing devices to make the most of the available time. Working at the produce counter in the foodstore, he can talk to people about town problems. Going to and from the two Co-op stores, he can see people and have brief discussions. He keeps a list of things that need doing in his pocket, attends to them in spare moments, thinks about them whenever he can, catches people on the run.

Where other people have hobbies like golfing and fishing, Long is pretty much of a "cause" man and has been for most of his life except for the time spent in the Army. Prior to his college days the cause was working for what he calls the old-fashioned concept of the Brotherhood of Man under the Fatherhood of God. After college and war service the cause was the cooperative movement. In Oberlin, up until his election to Council, it was the Oberlin Co-op. But after election it became the city with its many problems and complex relationships.

The pattern of Long's social life differs from that of other citizens. He does not like chit-chat or discussions about the weather. He does not socialize for the sake of going out or just to meet people. One result is that his evenings are largely "free" for community business. Another is that what social life he does have, and it is not inconsiderable, tends to revolve about his interests in the city. A good example is the origins of a study group in which he now participates. One night at a social gathering at Dunn's house attended by the Don Peases and the Longs, the three couples began speculating on the possibility of establishing a group where they might engage in discussion of philosophical subjects not necessarily connected with city problems, topics like religion, the purpose of life, and so on. Later they expanded the initial group to twelve.[1] During the 1960 national convention period, four meetings were devoted to presentations about the rival candidates. City questions did come up sporadically and the individuals present had a chance to communicate about these before or after the discussions. One night some group member raised the question of quality in the schools and Long suggested getting Superintendent Duncan down. The offer was accepted, and a lengthy discussion ensued. One result was the new brochure advertising the school system which we have previously mentioned. Another was that School Board member, George Hoover, who visited the group one night, made a very favorable impression and probably generated support in a circle which previously had suspected him of being a poor board member.

The time which Long spends is not a sacrifice for him; this is what he enjoys doing. He will think nothing of writing six drafts of a speech or report, revising continually in odd moments, to satisfy his desire to excel and to make the best possible impression for the policy he is proposing. He is a political man.

Time and interest are not enough; one also must have the energy to pursue one's objectives. It is an understatement to say that Long is phenomenal in this respect. Apparently tireless, he continually spews forth ideas and works at them. Of middle height, in good health and rather chunky, he manifests remarkable resiliency. Inevitably he comes in for his share of rebuffs, as in the early days of the industrial development campaign, but he can take a lot of punishment and come back for more. He enjoys the give and take, the rough and tumble of public affairs. What all this energy signifies for his personal psychology is beside the point for present purposes; the fact is that it exists and must be taken into account like any other imposing natural phenomenon.

Information is a prerequisite of influence. Ordinarily one must know that events are taking place and know something about them in order to affect the outcome. Bill Long is probably the best informed person in town (over the widest range of issues) other than the City Manager. There are some who know more than he does about specific issues, such as Homer Blanchard on the light plant, but none who can rival him over the general field and over those issues, like industrial development, of which he makes a particular specialization. As regards information in the sense of knowing what is happening, Long tries to learn as much as possible. He sees or phones the City Manager constantly, talks to other councilmen, city employees, and commission members, converses with customers in his stores, and seeks out others who are in a position to inform him. Though subject to much heckling, he occasionally goes down to the restaurant where the downtown businessmen hang out for coffee, and frequently manages to discover what they are doing, a technique that is handy at times when strategic moves depend upon knowing who is on what side, who is wavering, and who can be persuaded.

Referring now to information in the sense of knowledge about issues, Long is uniformly better prepared than his opponents. No doubt this must in part be a subjective judgment. But it is one which is supported by the evidence in this book and by many of his opponents who recognize a deficiency on their own parts in that respect. Typical of Long's emphasis upon being informed are the research he did on John Cochrane's record as councilman for use in the 1959 election campaign, and his familiarity with the various water plans useful in rebutting Ira Porter. Long's intelligence is high and he has a quick mind. But he is also willing to spend time and energy building up a storehouse of information. His answers are always based on some kind of evidence, and even if his opponents are correct in saying that his conclusions are highly fallacious, it is difficult for them to meet something with nothing.

Bill Long's position as Co-op manager provides him with many resources—control over jobs, access to money, a friendly clientele, a "dispensable" occupation, status as a businessman—which he has exploited with considerable success. (Unlike most retail merchants, Long's clientele is a "committed" group, held to him in part by the Co-op ideology.) It must not be thought that Long can use jobs in the traditional sense of patronage; he cannot and does not. But he can employ Negroes and, whether intended or not, this may be useful to him at election time and in raising his prestige among those interested in providing equal opportunites in employment.

By serving people at the Co-op stores and working with Co-op Board members, Long becomes identified with them and he gains a popularity which may be translated into votes, letters to the editor, or even more active support on various issues. We already have spoken of the value of his job as a listening post, information center, conversion hall, and general focus of activity which he can leave when he has to attend to other matters. Yet it is perhaps in a negative sense that being manager of the Co-op has been most helpful. Long has a reasonably safe job utterly outside the control of bankers, businessmen, college officials, or any others who might conceivably threaten him. He cannot be controlled through his job. Had the Co-op been unable to raise capital, the refusal of the local banks to lend might have proven fatal as Long was faced with the choice of losing his position, of knuckling under or leaving town. But this did not happen. His success in building the Co-op from a $30,000 a year business in 1949 when he came to a $750,000 a year business in 1960 has raised his prestige. It is only fair to add that this further infuriates his opponents among the downtown businessmen who cannot abide the thought that a "radical" with so "difficult" a personality has made a success of even a subsidized business like the Co-op.

Legitimacy, the acknowledged right to hold public office and exercise its functions, has obviously been a valuable resource for Long. It has given legal cover for his multitude of activities, given him access to information, a forum for publicity, a means of persuasion, and public acknowledgment of support (whatever that might mean) from the voters. Most important, his position as Councilman gave him one vote out of seven and the widespread expectation that it was proper for him to try to convince other members to support his views. While the position of chairman is chiefly an honorary one, it had extra advantages for Long during the two years that he held it. It enabled him to establish a special relationship with the City Manager by making it customary for them to discuss all matters appearing on the agenda, a practice which Mayor Nord continues, though to a lesser extent. The position of chairman also legitimatized the notion that leadership should come from that direction. And in chairing the meetings Long was able to expedite matters on the agenda and see to it that the debate was carried on according to his conception of proper procedure.

Popularity is a difficult resource with which to deal. All we need say here, however, is that so long as he won victories at the polls, Bill Long's opponents could not do much to stop him. His popularity among Negro and high-income college people as well as out-of-town executives was an indispensable base for his influence.

That resource called skill is an important part of what makes Long an effective leader. Being intangible, it is often neglected, to the detriment of the study of politics. Properly used it may seem effortless and appear to require no explanation. Nor is it possible to show on every occasion that a less skillful person might have failed and a more skillful one might have succeeded. For the sake of convenience we shall speak here of technical skill, skill in persuasion, skill in coalition-building, and skill in devising strategies.

The ability to manage two stores, to run a development corporation, to juggle mortgages, to understand financial operations, has enabled Long to do things which other men could not. His skill as a business technician has served him well.

He has, moreover, proved himself to be an exceedingly persuasive person, capable of altering the views of others. He presents his case fluently, with a wide array of factual material, emphasizing the public interest involved, stressing the real coincidence in goals between himself and the other person. He is adept at feeling out the kind of arguments which will have attraction to specific individuals. He appeals to a sense of reasonableness by denying that his statements are perfect but asking whether the other person has anything better to suggest, because if so, he would certainly like to hear about it and give it serious consideration. The policy alternatives (or some selected set) at his fingers, Long marshals them in verbal columns so that one or two emerge as clearly desirable if not the only possible solutions. Whatever else happens, he is certain to present a barrage of arguments, sometimes assuming volcano-like proportions. Although some doubt has been expressed as to whether Long really convinces others or merely wears them out, these techniques are effective. And for those who are disposed to agree with him, Long's proclivity for explicit statement provides them with ready-made rationales, prepared for use when challenged, to justify their position. In a community where leaders exercise virtually no coercive authority over followers, a talent for persuasion is no mean asset.

Skill in building coalitions is perhaps the supreme art of the politician. It requires finding agreement among previously disparate and possibly conflicting individuals and groups. It demands finesse in convincing the participants that their varying desires will be served. Long demonstrated this skill (though only in part) by bringing conservatives into government to ward off criticism and expand support, by encouraging Negroes to participate and by being flexible about the form of various policies, such as accepting the housing formula which would win the most widespread support and the vote according to investment on the OID.

A sense of strategy is helpful to anyone who participates in collective life. It can be used to create opportunities and to seize upon the favorable moment. Opponents may be maneuvered into untenable positions. The kinds of strategies which Long pursues are rather simple and direct. His study of game theory has not, of course, resulted in any direct applications to the real world. But it has further sensitized him to thinking in terms of alternative approaches and different kinds of pay-offs. When a policy arises he asks himself which person or body has the formal right of decision. (On occasion, as in the Gibson case, he may try to alter the locus of decision if the outcome seems destined to go against him.) From his store of past information he will calculate the position of some key people and concentrate on those necessary to make a majority. Knowing he cannot coerce, he will seek to persuade. If that fails, or he has reason to believe that it will, he will try to find someone on his side who has a better chance of approaching the key individuals. (Note his choice of workers on the anti-petition petition.) He is not averse to rumors suggesting that he has inordinate power because this leads to a sense of fatalism on the part of his opponents—he cannot be beaten—and makes him seem more powerful than he really is. He maintains that certain issues will always be fought tooth and nail by a handful of conservative people, that the job is always to force these people to give reasons for their positions, and that if this is done their arguments will fall apart and they will then be defeated. Long is concerned not only with the immediate present but with future decisions and seeks to recruit a corps of personnel who share his general orientation. He is tireless in suggesting that this or that person serve on a committee or commission and rarely misses an opportunity to draw a person into more active participation. Sometimes, as with Blanchard and Nord, people who were already on city commissions when he was elected, and who were also well known as conservative Republicans, he urges them to move from the commissions and run for the council seat. To be better prepared than his opponents, to move first and fast, at the right place and time, to come early and stay late, represents his mode of operation.

The multiple activities of Bill Long provide an example *par excellence* of the pyramiding of resources. Long first used his energy to build up the Co-op. His solid position there was used to gain contacts, information and popularity. These resources were then parlayed into a Council victory which was used to gain further popularity and respect. Legitimacy and respect were used to further the cause of industrial development; some success here increased his ability to raise funds to promote a shopping center which, in turn, increased his chances of fostering the type of community development which he preferred. While it is conceivable that Long might have done even more than he has, there can be little doubt that he has exploited the resources available to him at a higher rate and with greater efficiency than anyone in town with the possible exception of the City Manager. Since there are inevitably vast reservoirs of resources which may be tapped when their possessors feel sufficiently concerned to make this worthwhile, Long's pyramiding was eventually answered by increased and more intensive opposition.

What kind of a person is Bill Long? In attempting to answer this question, we do not intend, even if it were possible, to provide a psychological case study. Knowledge of political psychology is not sufficiently advanced to permit us to say that under "X" conditions certain characteristics will probably lead an individual to "Y" political activity and under "A" conditions to "B" activity. Instead of relying on this fascinating but inconclusive procedure, let us seek out politically relevant aspects of Bill Long's personality based on depth interviews lasting several hours, observation over an extensive period of time, and a questionnaire he filled out and made available.

Bill Long is an activist. He cares deeply about local and national politics, though not state politics. He votes in all elections, talks incessantly about public affairs, writes to public officials, expresses opinions frequently, is a Democratic precinct committeeman, contributes to campaigns, asks others for political support, and is approached to give his in turn. He has joined five organizations and is active in all to which he belongs. On anyone's index of political participation, he would score 100 percent.

Long evidences a high degree of civic obligation which is probably deeply internalized. He believes that what governments do is very important and that every citizen has an obligation to participate even if (though he is inclined to hedge a bit here) he really does not like it. He disagrees strongly with the notion that it is best to stay out of community affairs, and thinks it is probably true that participation in Oberlin politics raises one's prestige in the community.

Far from being a pessimist, or exhibiting feelings of impotence in the public arena, Long has an extremely high sense of political efficacy. Governmental decisions are by no means too complicated for the citizen to understand. Politicians do care about what he thinks. They do not really manipulate people very much. The community arena is open and subject to change by the citizenry.

Long may be described as a person who is sociable, aggressive and confident. He likes to meet people, to argue with them and to convince them, and he is rarely at a loss for words or possessed by feelings of awkwardness. He utterly rejects the notion that he should not take sides in arguments between people he knows even though he recognizes that a person might lose friends by such actions. He believes that one must be aggressive to succeed in politics, that this is a risk which must be taken. Ultimately, he is confident that things will turn out well.

Everything that Long does demonstrates a tremendous need for achievement. The objective of man, he believes, is to strive and achieve. But he does not believe that he seeks achievement for the accumulation of power, prestige or wealth, but rather for an idealistic end which he would clearly define as being to obtain the best interests of the community. Long relates how, in discussion with Leonard Barr, one of the most successful of the out-of-town businessmen who eventually gave him support, he was prodded as to what he was really up to and responded with a now favorite saying of his: "There is a bit of the creator in every man, an urge to put something where nothing was, a desire to be able to say 'this happened because of me'." Long says all this without embarrassment.

Linked with this drive toward achievement is a characteristic which could be described as a need for control over events. He insists that planning ahead is indispensable. He vigorously objects to the idea that an individual's success or failure is dependent on the operation of uncontrollable outside forces. On the contrary, he believes that the individual is responsible for his success or failure. He would stand with Cassius in proclaiming that the fault lies not in our stars but in ourselves.

Like most people in our society, Long is ambivalent about exercising power over others. He agrees somewhat with the notion that people should not exercise control over others but he is convinced that politicians have to exercise control over others in order to do their jobs. Thus he uses the legitimacy of public office to resolve this dilemma.

On the basis of some roughly comparative findings by others, it appears likely that the portrait of Bill Long we have presented is quite similar to that of other activists. They also tend to feel that they are effective, to internalize civic obligation, to enjoy socializing, to have a high need for achievement, to believe the individual is responsible for his own fate.[2]

Why is Long so active? He would say that he thinks people *ought* to be active and that he is an active type of person. He would also stress the importance to the community of the goals which he has set out to achieve. The question arises as to whether his temperament is such that he would be active regardless of the content of the goals. Perhaps. But the goals are really inseparable from the activity. He might find it difficult to live with himself without the sustaining belief that his activity was useful for others besides himself. A desire to be of service may well be fused with a need to achieve.

It has occurred to Long that Oberlin may be too small an arena for his talents. Yet he feels that in a small town an individual can do concrete things and see the results in an immediate way that might not be possible, say, in Washington. There are many matters on which others are more proficient than he is, as he readily acknowledges. But in the realms of community development and the solving of civic problems he has yet to find anyone whose talent matches his. He would like to find such a person, to compare notes, to pit himself against him. Once, when his wife asked what he would most like to do for a vacation, he suggested attending one of those seminars for business leaders which he had read about in *Fortune* so that he could see if these leaders really were superior to him in solving problems, Long's few contacts with big businessmen have not convinced him that this is so.

There is in Long a joy in civic combat which few others share. He does not get involved in every possible combat—he has refused to become involved in controversies at the golf club and over welfare policies. He likes opposition, likes to overcome it, to outmaneuver it, to defeat it. Exercising his skills, picking the crucial element in a problem, solving it, brings him considerable satisfaction. If he can be accused of being insensitive on occasion to the feelings of particular individuals, he is acutely aware of group sentiments and has a feeling for dealing with them. Not given to introspection, Long is happiest when engaged in many activities. Where other men would wilt under the strain, he appears to thrive.

In conclusion, it is well to point out that the purpose of these comments has been to focus attention on a single individual whose leadership qualities mark him off from the mass. A sympathetic view has been taken in the belief that his qualities could be best appreciated in that way. Yet the writer is aware, and the reader can hardly have failed to notice, that many of the characteristics which make Long a leader also produce antagonism. His brash manner, informal attire, and generally aggressive behavior result in opposition and negative criticisms. An elderly lady once commented, "I could forgive him a lot if he would just button his shirt collar." The wide scope of his interests and activity make him an obvious target for hostility which he might not suffer if he were more specialized. The advantages he accrues from being manager of the Co-op are partially offset by the suspicion engendered by that organization and its label as a center of radicalism. His insistence on moving forward sometimes overpowers his awareness of the importance of timing, as when he brought up zoning ordinance difficulties about apartments over local stores just before the 1959 election, thus intensifying the opposition to him. His ability to pyramid resources has led to charges of conflict of interest and some uneasiness even among those who normally consider themselves supporters. It has led to his withdrawal from the Council and enforced circumspection in some areas where the city is involved in industrial development. To say all this, however, is to signify that he has the defects of his virtues. For if he did not have these disabilities it is unlikely that he would be the kind of person he is, an outstanding leader in the community.

18   WHO RULES IN OBERLIN AND WHY

The essential purpose of the case histories and role studies presented in the previous chapters was to present evidence which would enable us to decide what kind of political system exists in Oberlin. We have described every major decision (education is described briefly in this chapter), during the period from January, 1957, to June, 1961. Following the method proposed in chapter 1, we agreed in advance on how to interpret the evidence. If we find that the same participants exercise leadership in nearly all significant areas of decision, that they agree, and that they are not responsible to the electorate, we conclude that a power elite rules in Oberlin. If we discover that a majority of citizens are influential in all or most cases, the proper conclusion is that Oberlin is ruled by the people as a mass democracy. And if we find that the leaders vary from one issue area to the other, with such overlap as there is between issue areas concentrated largely in the hands of public officials, we must conclude that there is a pluralist system of rule in Oberlin. Once having arrived at the correct conclusion, it will become possible for us to attempt to explain why this particular power structure exists, to account for such changes as have taken place since the 1930's, and to go into the dynamic aspects of how decisions are made in the Oberlin Community.

Following Dahl's procedure, we set up a Leadership Pool consisting of all those who participated in a particular decision and could conceivably be candidates for leadership. Then we separate out those who lost, who got nothing of what they wanted. This leaves us with a Leadership Elite—those who in some way helped secure an outcome they deemed to be favorable. Within this broad category, we seek to distinguish among those who initiated, vetoed, or gained consent for a policy proposal.

Rarely is it possible to trace the first origins of an idea. To initiate a policy in our terms means to seize upon an idea, develop a policy proposal, and pursue it to a successful conclusion. To veto a proposal means either to secure its defeat entirely or to modify or reject a part. To gain consent one must secure the assent of others for a favorable policy outcome. These categories are further divided in order to give some idea of the degree of leadership. This is inevitably somewhat arbitrary and we have sought to do as little violence to reality as is possible by restricting ourselves to three broad degrees—high (implying a major role in initiating, vetoing, or gaining consent), low (a discernible but minor role), and moderate (a residual category).

For analytical purposes the case histories are divided into seven issue areas—housing, utilities, welfare, industrial development, zoning, education and nominations and elections. After describing leadership in these decisions, we shall compare them to discover the extent of overlap between issue areas and the kind of individuals who exercise influence in more than one area.

The adoption of the housing code was the work of many hands and no one individual or group stands out alone and all-powerful. The major part in initiation was taken by the City Council, the City Manager, and the members of the Housing Committee who were active in this area: Mrs. Goldberg, Mrs. Stewart and George Simpson. Other members of the Housing Committee took some part as did college student John Tropman, to a lesser extent. Together, these people appointed the Housing Committee, acquired the necessary information, and wrote the code which was eventually adopted in somewhat modified form. Consent was gained pre-eminently by Fred Comings, who proposed the formula for enforcement that cleared the way for passage, and by Long, Ellis, Mrs. Goldberg, and Simpson who carried the affirmative case to the townspeople. Other Councilmen (Gibson, Zahm, Stofan, and Hellmuth), gained some consent by explaining the code to citizens and by bargaining for changes to make the code acceptable to each other and to interested citizens. The Housing Committee also did a little persuading among their fellow citizens. A moderate amount of vetoing was done by Gibson, Comings, Zahm and Stofan as they plugged for changes to make the code more widely acceptable. In this work they were prodded to some extent by citizens like Fred Holloway, Chris Oliver, Arthur Salo. The results are outlined in Chart F.

While it may appear strange to give prominent mention to an event, rather than a person, there can be no question that the fire overwhelmed all else in responsiblity for initiating and gaining consent for enforcement of the housing ordinance. There was virtually no enforcement until the fire. City Manager Dunn pushed enforcement as much as he felt able and utilized the citizens mobilized by the fire to give added impetus to his quest. Long, Dunn, Nord and the *News-Tribune* were most active in gaining consent, followed by the aroused citizenry. The only vetoing was done in a minor way by Long, Ellis and Hellmuth when they blocked a proposal to evict, after inspection had shown serious faults.

Little need be said about the attempt to integrate Willowbrook Farms. The management simply refused to meet with city representatives or to discuss the problem in any way and thereby succeeded in vetoing the proposal. The proponents were not even able to force the issue when there was a misunderstanding about who was to make the down payment and the Negro "test case" backed out. The fair housing ordinance and the attempt to get federal housing are in the works but have not been finally decided yet. Inclusion of these two decisions would not further concentrate the ranks of leadership but would tend to spread them out even further.

The total citizenry has not been mentioned but this does not mean that they were unimportant. The leaders would not have done precisely what they did, and failed to do other things, if they had only themselves to please. In both passing the code and enforcing it, the formal decision-makers were sensitive to the possible uproar that might take place if too many citizens were adversely affected all at once.

Turning to the area of utilities, we find Dunn, Long, and the PUC (especially Blanchard) as those most responsible for creating and persevering with the new water system. The other Councilmen played an important but more modest role and the engineering firm of Burgess and Niple gets a nod for developing the tech-

CHART F. *The housing code*

	High	Moderate	Low
Initiate	Mrs. Goldberg Simpson Mrs. Stewart Mrs. Hawkins Council Dunn	Other members of Housing Committee*	Tropman
Gain Consent	Comings, Long, Ellis, Goldberg, Simpson	Other Council members (Gibson, Zahm, Stofan, Hellmuth, Dunn)	Other members of Housing Committee
Veto		Gibson, Comings, Zahm, Stofan	Oliver, Salo, Holloway, few other indi- vidual citizens

Enforcement of the housing code

	High	Moderate	Low
Initiate	The fire	City Manager Dunn	A hundred or more indi- viduals, Council
Gain Consent	The fire	*News-Tribune*, Mosher, Nord, Long, Dunn	A hundred or more indi- viduals

Integration of Willowbrook Farms

Initiate	
Gain Consent	Management of Willowbrook
Veto	Farms

* Mrs. Van Atta, Mrs. Tumbleson, Richard Lothrop, Ted Wigton, Bur-
rell Scott, Chalmer Davidson, William Jackson, Rev. Joseph King, Marshall
Morrow, Mrs. Ernst Hoffman, Douglas Johnson, Mary Rainbow, Dr. James
Stephens, Mrs. Helen Sperry, Don McIlroy, Richard Haller, Orlando Shilts.

nical data and supporting the victorious alternative. Long stands by himself as a gainer of consent. He took the lead in defending the project before the community and at Council meetings, and was instrumental in quashing the water petition with the anti-petition-petition. Ellis and Blanchard defended the project and Ellis participated in planning the anti-petition-petition. Dunn had some part in this and, more important, was a prime mover in arranging the minor concessions to small and larger users which made the project somewhat more attractive. The *News-Tribune* actively supported the proposal and condemned the opposition. Solicitor Severs and the various helpers who volunteered or whom Long recruited to conduct the anti-petition drive may properly be placed at the low end. A minor role in vetoing may be assigned to three local businessmen (none of whom were active in housing or the United Appeal), and Tower for their efforts contributing to the pressures which resulted in slightly more favorable rates for large users.

The case of the light plant engine is one which is almost wholly confined to specialists. Although a considerable sum of money was involved, and the decision could affect the services provided by the light plant, it would be unreasonable to expect citizens to be interested in this technical problem. The initiative came from members of the Public Utilities Commission, who acted in response to demands for power from the FAA, and secured the consent of the Council and City Manager for the victorious four-cycle engine. The Cooper-Bessemer Company and the Daverman organization helped convince Council that this was the proper move and are credited with a moderate part. No one vetoed though several light plant employees and competing companies tried.

A different group of specialists undertook leadership in the United Appeal. Organizational changes of considerable moment were introduced by Don Pease and Douglas Polhemus, men who volunteered their participation. But since there was virtually no opposition we will not formally consider these decisions. Instead, we will concentrate on the decisions to grant or to withhold funds from the recipient agencies. The lead in instituting new financial forms, making the agencies justify their positions, and cutting a number of them was taken by Don Pease with other members of the Executive Committee playing an important but moderate role. The Committee as a whole helped gain consent from the General Committee. The Center for the Sightless, the Visiting Nurses Association, and the Family Service Association gained consent in their areas by convincing the Executive Committee that part or all of the cuts made should be restored because of the desirable nature of the programs affected. Vetoes were exerted by Ira Porter, John Cochrane, Frank Van Cleef and Ken Roose as they persuaded the General Committee to restore amounts for the agencies they favored.

The unquestioned leader in getting new industry to settle in Oberlin has undoubtedly been Bill Long. He was instrumental in

CHART G. *The great water controversy*

	High	Moderate	Low
Initiate	Dunn, Long, PUC (Blanchard, Howe, Ben Lewis, Trautz, Bruening)	Ellis, Hellmuth, Gibson, Zahm, Stofan, Comings	Burgess and Niple
Gain Consent	Long	Ellis, Dunn, Mosher, Blanchard	Mrs. Aschaffen-burg, Mrs. Walker, Mrs. Thomas, Mrs. Baker, Mrs. Davidson, Fowler, League of Women Voters, Severs, Comings
Veto			3 local businessmen, Tower

The light plant engine

	High	Moderate	Low
Initiate	PUC (Howe, Pease, Trautz, Griswold, Bruening)	Council (Nord, Blanchard, Hellmuth, Ellis, Comings, Long) Dunn, Daverman	FAA
Gain Consent	PUC	Cooper-Bessemer, Daverman	

CHART H. *Distribution of funds in the United Appeal*

	High	Moderate	Low
Initiate	Pease	The Executive Committee (Polhemus, Clark, Singleton, Mrs. Carpenter, Haller, Severs)	
Gain Consent	The Executive Committee	Center for the Sightless, Visiting Nurses Association, Family Service Association	
Veto		Porter, Cochrane, Van Cleef, Roose	The General Committee

moving quickly to meet the FAA's requirements and in overcoming the qualms of specialists in education concerning the impact of increased enrollments. He was the prime mover in establishing the OID, which facilitated the entry of Gilford Instruments and Muller Packaging. As usual, he was dependent upon convincing others—Council, Board of Education, financial contributors—to give their assent. He was deliberately shut out of the Off-Street Parking Corporation by John Cochrane, Ira Porter and the other leaders in that enterprise. Where Long could not persuade, he could not exercise influence. In the realm of private enterprise, no one group has all the resources, no one can coerce the other successfully, and the field is open for those who can muster the necessary capital and skill.

The Gibson apartments have not been built; the delaying tactics of Dunn, Long and their associates have proven successful. Thus the ability of Gibson, to gain favorable court, Zoning Board, and (on occasion) Council decisions is not formally scored under our method because it did not lead to the outcome he desired, but rather, to the one preferred by his opponents. Nevertheless, it should be noted that a single citizen won several skirmishes (if not the final battle) against a group of public officials and compelled them to continually increase the rate at which they used their resources in order to triumph. In the end, it was not the overwhelming power of his opponents but Gibson's own inability to move fast enough after he won in the courts that led to his defeat.

The requirements for nomination (which may be considered the initiation stage of elections) are so small (only 28 signatures are necessary) that virtually anyone can run if he or she feels like it. Willingness to run being quite limited, however, leadership may be exercised in this sphere by making a decision to run and, to a greater extent, by persuading others. Initiation is therefore shared by the promoters of the Solid Six, the planners, the other nominees, and to a lesser extent by those who did something to persuade people to run. Consent may be said to be gained by the active supporters of the winning slate and a veto exercised by citizens who failed to vote for the losers. There can be no doubt that the voting citizenry exercised a high degree of influence not only over the personnel of government but also over the general direction of future policies. While the water decision probably could not have been reversed, enforcement of the housing and zoning ordinances would undoubtedly have been pursued less vigorously, the City Manager replaced by a person with less pronounced planning tendencies, the future of the electric plant thrown into doubt, and many other changes made, if the Solid Six slate had won. The policies of the planning coalition had generated such serious opposition that they required at least indirect legitimization by the populace at the polls. If this does not provide a convincing demonstration of the profound importance of free elections in Oberlin, no reasonable operation of a democratic society can meet that test.

With only two vacancies to be filled on the School Board, and a heated election for City Council taking place, there was no great amount of activity in the 1959 nominations and elections for the Board.[1] Cowling, Vance, Wood, Lothrop and Haller put themselves forward mainly on their own initiative and easily secured the 28 signatures on their nominating petitions. Approximately 25 people, none of whom had any great impact, urged one of the candidates to run. The voters (including those in Russia Township who are in the school district) chose Cowling and Vance and thus vetoed the other candidates. Campaigning was minimal except for statements in the local newspaper and Roose's sending of cards to rural voters.

CHART I. *The Oberlin Industrial and Development Company*

	High	Moderate	Low
Initiate	Long, Roose	Mosher, Anderson	Bronson Clark, Kenny Clark, Barr, Severs
Gain Consent	Long	Roose	
Veto			Barr, Kenny Clark

The coming of the FAA

	High	Moderate	Low
Initiate	FAA	Long	Council, Hill, Mosher
Gain Consent	Long		Council
Veto			

The Off-Street Parking Association

	High	Moderate	Low
Initiate	Cochrane, Molyneaux	Board of Directors (Fauver, Klermund, Stetson, Sable, Powers, Carpenter, Porter, Murphy, Hopkins, Warner	
Gain Consent	Molyneaux, Cochrane		
Veto			

CHART J. *The Gibson Case*

	High	Moderate	Low
Initiate	Dunn		
Gain Consent	Dunn, Long	Stofan, Comings, Hellmuth	
Veto	Long, Dunn	Murphy, Arnold, Bronson Clark, Hellmuth, Schwartz, Severs Comings, Ellis	Stofan, Zahm

The five mill levy decision (the Board receives most of its funds from real estate taxes) was clearly initiated by Superintendent Duncan and Board President Kilmer with assistance from the

CHART K. *Nomination and election in 1959: City Council*

	High	Moderate	Low
Initiate	The Arnolds, the Fauvers, the Moly- neauxs, the Smiths, Long, Dunn, Comings, Stofan, Zahm, Gibson, Tumbelson, Gaeuman, Scott	Pease, Mosher, Anderson, Simpson Vance, Barr	Perhaps 25 indi- vidual citizens
Gain Consent	Same as above	Same as above	Same as above
Veto	(None of nominations) Citizens opposing defeated candidates	Election veto exercised	

School Board, the Teacher's Committee and the Principals. Consent was gained by the above together with the Campaign Committee led by Dr. Piraino. The proposal of the citizens committee for a ten mill levy (which may only have been half serious) was vetoed by Duncan and the Board because they feared that voters might reject it. The levy was passed overwhelmingly.

The 2-2-2 plan, which occasioned heated controversy, revolved about a proposal to regroup elementary schools so that each one would contain only two grades. The desirability of neighborhood schools, transportation problems, the advantages of specialization in teaching and equipment, and racial considerations (the plan implied a higher degree of integration), were all involved. After prolonged and sometimes bitter discussion, the plan was vetoed by Mrs. John Strong, Robert Schreiner, and allied parents, and a majority of the School Board. Mrs. Strong, who was not usually active in public affairs, was concerned about the impact on her children and worked furiously and incessantly to block the proposal. Superintendent Duncan and his allies were defeated.

The alternative plan—two elementary schools with grades one to four and one with grades five to six—was initiated by the Superintendent, with the approval of the Board. The participants on both sides of the 2-2-2 controversy had created such an uproar that no one was disposed to quarrel about a reasonable alternative. Redistricting was accomplished almost as an administrative measure by the Superintendent with the assistance of several school principals and school psychologist Wonderly. They gained the consent of the Board and no one was disposed to open old wounds by challenging them. The effect of this decision was to secure total integration by altering the boundaries for attendance at the schools.

Looking at the area of education as a whole it is apparent that most of the participants are not active or influential in other areas of community decision. The separate election and functioning of the Board, its separate financial base, undoubtedly helps secure these results as well as the differential interest of citizens, teachers and administrators. Although the educational arena is capable of arousing much passion among the citizenry, far more than most

CHART L. *Nomination and election in 1959: School Board*
(2 vacancies)

	High	Moderate	Low
Initiate	Cowling, Vance Wood, Lothrop Haller		About 10 teachers, Roose, Samuel Goldberg, Dr. & Mrs. Stephens, Mrs. Douglas Johnson, Mrs. Chamberlain, Dr. Hoover, several school principals, Parsons
Gain Consent			
Veto	Voters in Oberlin and Russia Township who vetoed Wood, Lothrop and Haller		

The Five Mill School Levy

	High	Moderate	Low
Initiate	Duncan, Kilmer	School Board (Cowling, Chamberlain, Hoover, Boase) Teachers Committee	
Gain Consent	Duncan, School Board, Piraino	Campaign Committee	Teachers, Principals

263 *Who Rules in Oberlin and Why*

The 2-2-2 Plan

Initiate

Gain
Consent

| Veto | Mrs. Strong, Schreiner, Cowling, Mrs. Chamberlain, Dr. Hoover | | Citizens, who wrote letters, spoke to Board members, and agitated against 2-2-2 (none active in any other case so far as we can tell) |

The Substitute Plan

Initiate	Duncan, Board of Education		
Gain Consent	Same as above		All participants in the 2-2-2 conflict accomplished this by making an alternative seem highly desirable. To those named above we add Anderson, Mrs. Schwimm, Elders, Barenbaums, Dixon, and other supporters of 2-2-2

Redistricting

	High	Moderate	Low
Initiate	Duncan, Principals, Wonderly		
Gain Consent	Same as above		
Veto			

areas, most decisions are handled by the officials directly concerned—the Superintendent, the principals and teachers organizations. When the consent of the voter is required, or meteors like Mrs. Strong appear who actively contest an issue, then participation is broadened to include almost anyone who cares to take part, with the likelihood that parents of school children will predominate. The voice of the people, mute on most occasions, may be amplified and, more important perhaps, taken into account by decision makers, as the decision to reject a ten mill levy shows.

In the charts expressing the distribution of leadership, we find a clear outline of a pluralist system in accordance with the theory stated in the first chapter. There is no person or group which exerts leadership in all issue areas. To the extent that overlap between issue areas exists, it is held predominantly by public officials —the City Manager, Mayor Long, City Council—who owe their positions directly or (in the case of the Manager) indirectly to expressions of the democratic process through a free ballot with universal suffrage. The one exception is Don Pease, co-editor of the *News-Tribune*, who owes his prominence in the light plant issue to membership on the Public Utilities Commission, who has the kind of dispensable occupation which permits time for leadership, and whose job encourages, if it does not demand, rather wide participation in community affairs. Innovation comes from individual specialists, such as members of the PUC, elected officials such as Long, an administrator charged with innovation (City Manager Dunn), meteors in a single case such as Mrs. Goldberg and Mrs. Stewart, and a self-selected activist like Pease.

Although men like Long, Dunn and Comings, who combine public office with unusual activity, are clearly outstanding leaders, none of them has all the influence there is to have in any case. They all require the consent of others. Only in the OID case is it clear that lack of participation by a single person—Long—would have changed the result, and he certainly required a corps of auxiliaries.

The number of citizens and outside participants who exercise leadership in most cases is an infinitesimal part of the community. This is necessarily the case since the total number of all those who participate at all in any way is quite small. Meteors who participate in only one or two cases (and that sporadically), and specialists, who confine their participation to one or two issue areas, make up the bulk of influentials. The ability of citizens who devote much time and effort to a single case or issue area to become leaders is clearly indicated as is the initiative and support provided by generalist public officials.

Some Councilmen, though not the most vigorous, may be given a higher rating than they deserve. This is likely because it is often difficult to tell who is merely going along with others and who is acting independently when they are all agreed. (In cities where a leader possesses coercive authority, we would not face this difficulty.) The same is true for bodies like the Housing Committee, the PUC, and the UA Executive Committee. At the same time, it is possible that the City Manager has been rated down somewhat because his quiet words of prodding, encouragement, and opposition may go unrecorded and unremembered by himself and other participants. It is extremely doubtful, however, that any gross errors have been made by omitting high or moderate leaders.

In order to provide a double-check on our observations, a series of studies were made of the activities of Oberlin's service organizations (Rotary, Kiwanis and the like), its churches, and the College to see if their officials or the organizations themselves had engaged in community activities which failed to show up in the case studies. Members were interviewed and asked to describe the activities of the organizations and its members. The results were completely negative. No activity turned up which was not found through the case studies and mentioned in this volume. The attentions of College administrative personnel are attuned to the institution, not to the town. They wish it well, help it out when they can, but avoid controversy unless their interests are directly affected. The service organizations engage in non-controversial support of worthy causes like providing scholarships, school equipment, and funds for charitable causes. The churches typically do not engage in the controversies of this world in the local community. (The major exception is some support for Negro candidates by some Negro churches at election time.) Most active is the Social Action Committee of the First Church, the most prestigeful religious institution in town by all accounts. It sponsors meetings on subjects like aid to education without taking a stand. When a course on family relations and sex was presented in the Sunday School, committee members hoped that eventually it might be presented in the public schools. But the program was never fully evaluated and has not been presented to the Board of Education. The closest the committee came to public affairs was a discussion of candidates for the 1961 elections for City Council and the Board of Education. As a result, one or two members approached some individuals to run, all of whom refused. The one issue on which there has been even minimal participation by some churches occurred when several ministers supported an Open Housing Ordinance from their pulpits and collected supporting signatures on petitions. The issue has not yet been resolved.

Although quantification suggests a precise accuracy which we do not claim, it may be helpful to attach some numbers to our calculations. It seems reasonable to give high leadership five points, moderate three and low one. The totals for the first three issue areas are given in Chart 8.[2] After viewing this table one could make reasonable inferences as to the probability that given individuals would be influential in the specific issue areas, though the inclusion of the meteors would lead to error; they might not be active in the next case. This would be nothing, however, compared to the error of generalizing from one issue area to another or from all three to any single one. Long, Dunn, Comings and Ellis would be credited with influence over the United Appeal where they do not have any, while members of the Housing Committee would be expected to lead in utilities and would not. False appearances of success might be obtained by generalizing Long and Dunn's influence from housing to utilities, but the attempt to generalize the PUC's from utilities to housing would be disastrous.

When we add the educational issue area to those we have been considering, the diffusion of leadership is greater. Only on rare occasion, as in the decision to bring the FAA or on a parking problem, do people active in education participate in the other issue areas. Some overlap exists but it is very small.

Although leadership is diffused in Oberlin, the outcomes of

CHART M. *Degree of influence in three issue areas*
(High-5; moderate-3; low-1) *Housing* (3 decisions)

15............Long
14............Dunn, Comings
12............Ellis
10............Simpson, Mrs. Goldberg, Zahm, Gibson, Hellmuth, Stofan
 5............Mrs. Stewart, Mrs. Hawkins, Willowbrook
 3............Mosher, Pease, Williams, Housing Committee
 1............Tropman, Oliver, Salo, Holloway, approximately 100 individuals

Utilities (2 decisions)

15	Howe, Trautz, Bruening
13	Long
11	Blanchard
11	Dunn
10	Griswold
9	Ellis
6	Comings, Hellmuth
3	Gibson, Stofan, Daverman, Cooper-Bessemer
1	Burgess & Niple, 3 local businessmen, League of Women Voters, FAA, Aschaffenburg, Walker, Thomas, Baker, Davidson, Fowler, Severs

United Appeal (one year, many decisions)

10	Pease
8	Polhemus, Clark, Singleton, Buck, Mrs. Carpenter, Haller, Severs, Salo
3	Porter, Cochrane, Van Cleef, Roose, Center for the Sightless, Family Service Association, Visting Nurses Association
1	The General Committee

community decisions are not merely random occurrences but fall instead into a rather well-defined pattern. From inspection of the leaders in the cases we have described it appears that a rather broad coalition of interests, though its members occasionally disagree and suffer defeats, has been victorious on most issues of importance. This combination of the Co-op, some college people, out-of-town businessmen, and Negro leaders has, for the sake of convenience, been called "the planners."

The major analytic tasks confronting us are, first, to account for the success of the planning coalition and, second, to explain why the more oligarchic power structure of the thirties gave way to the pluralist system we have found today. The explanatory factors we shall employ include differential rates of participation, the structural conditions created by the non-partisan ballot, the existence of several independent centers of influence, and, most important, the more active and skillful exploitation of key bases of influence by the planners.

The planning coalition was in part consciously created—Long, Dunn, Hellmuth, Comings, Blanchard and Ellis set out to recruit commuting businessmen, Negroes, and college people—and partly the result of engaging in conflict and discovering who was on what side. As the various planning policies were debated it became obvious that the cost involved and the constant use of government had led to a split among the activists. Many of the local businessmen were directly affected by the increased water rates, threatened by the possible influx of competing enterprises, and generally fearful of change which might upset the accustomed patterns of affairs in the community. From conversations it appears that some felt that their middle class status was threatened by increased costs which might compel them to become wage earners and reduce their hard-won standard of living. Others objected to changes in the community introduced without their consent, changes which foreshadowed a deprivation of their customary influence and the deference they felt to be their due. At the same time, the commuting businessmen and college people welcomed policies which had the magic label of "planning" and which showed promise of improving community services. The taxes they paid on their houses did not seem onerous to them and they were more than willing to sacrifice a little cash for rewards in terms of better schools, and more attractive housing areas and streets. Negro activists like Wade Ellis made common cause with the planners not only because of a general sympathy with them but also because they saw new industry and a housing code as means of improving the conditions of their race in Oberlin. Their eminence within the Negro sector enabled them to overcome some opposition from Negro homeowners who had low incomes and objected to higher costs. Skill in coalition building was exercised by Dunn and Long as they proposed policies meeting widespread preferences, recruited personnel to promote them, provided a rationale for those who chose to agree, and modified opposition where necessary without giving up essential elements of their program.

If its members had to run together as Republicans or Democrats however, the planning coalition probably would have been impossible. Take the case of Charles Mosher, publisher of the *News-Tribune*. He was a Republican State Senator, a career legislator, a person who worked hard at his job and looked forward to advancement within the party. He would have found it exceedingly difficult, if not impossible, to justify supporting Democrats as Democrats in Oberlin city elections. His allegiance to the party and the expectations of party officials would have been violated by such an action. Under a non-partisan system, however, Mosher could and did support Bill Long and other Democrats on the ground that their party affiliation was not relevant to local affairs. Men like Eric Nord and Homer Blanchard and other commuting businessmen, most of them Republicans, would also have felt uncomfortable at being formally allied with Democrats. Moreover, as is common among middle and upper class individuals, they tend to shy away from active participation as partisans, preferring to avoid the tones of political hostility associated with party strife. They were much more easily recruited under the banner of non-partisan good citizenship than they would have been under party labels.

Central leadership for the planners was provided by tandem, cooperative arrangements between Councilman Bill Long and City Manager Richard Dunn. They helped set the general direction, provided huge amounts of energy, initiated proposals of their own, vetoed some they did not like, and helped gain support for the policies of others with which they agreed. Allied with them on the basis of shared perspectives and mutual agreement were active out-of-town businessmen, the editors of the local paper, some college faculty, a few Negro leaders, members of the Co-op, and a sprinkling of others. The point is not that all people falling within these categories gave their support, but that they provided a corps of activists, mostly specialists, who shared the task of developing policies and gaining public approval. It is doubtful, for example, that the category of out-of-town businessmen numbers more than one hundred individuals. But they provided two-sevenths of the 1959 Council (Nord and Blanchard), four of the eleven candidates for City Council in 1961 (Nord, Blanchard, Griswold, Johnson), and a vastly disproportionate share of commission and committee memberships appointed by the Council.

College people like Ken Roose, George Simpson, and David Anderson performed similar functions. It is probably true that the traditionalists had a substantial minority of support in the faculty, but except for a brief flurry in the 1959 election, these people were not especially active.

Why was the planning coalition successful in getting most of what it wanted? One answer could be that it possessed resources which were superior to those of its opponents. Another answer could be that resources were employed more actively and with greater skill. A third possibility is that it met with no appreciable resistance because others agreed or did not feel strongly enough to bother to challenge the coalition. Let us, then, survey the major resources (bases of influence) which were employed to control decisions in Oberlin and appraise their degree of dominance over others and the rate and skill with which they were employed. We will see that the planning coalition was superior in its possession and use of time, energy, official position, knowledge, persuasion and political skill. And that resources commonly thought to be dominant, such as money, control of credit, jobs, social standing, and the like were not crucial or were mainly in the hands of the losers.

As is only natural, money was most important in private ventures such as the OID and the Off-Street Parking Corporation. But no one side had a monopoly, none was able to deny it to the other, and none was willing or able to interfere with the other. Moreover, organizational ability, the skill required to get many people together for a common purpose, was also of considerable importance. It was not Long's wealth (which he did not possess) but his ability to organize, persuade, and persevere which was most responsible for the establishment of the OID.

The local banks might refuse to lend the Co-op money, but this was not a critical factor in view of its ability to borrow out-of-town and to raise funds through internal subscription.

In the public realm, by far the most significant use of wealth was by Bert Gibson who utilized his funds to make his housing appeal to the courts and to secure favorable decisions there. Without several thousand dollars, he could not have done this. In the end, however, failure to move quickly enough cost him the prize for which he had fought and the ever-vigilant planners won out. The amount of money necessary to run elections is so small that virtually any group of people can raise it. Actually, if more than a minimum amount had been spent, it might have led to diminishing returns, as citizens became annoyed at soliciting or wondered if someone was trying to buy an election. Long's ability to raise a small sum for a plane trip did enable Blanchard to run. It is difficult to find additional uses of money other than such minor things as being able to spend or raise five or ten dollars to mimeograph a petition. Indirectly, of course, some wealth is essential to run a newspaper. And it is most instructive that threats to remove advertising did not deter the editors of the *News-Tribune* in the election campaign, partly because the paper received a considerable portion of its revenue from printing jobs for the College, a separate social center unwilling to use its resources to intervene in community decisions which do not affect it directly.

Most of the wealth that exists in Oberlin is not used for any political purpose at all. Hence, those who have little but use what they have are not necessarily disadvantaged. And since all participants (except those at the barest margin of financial existence) have a little cash to spare, wealth is not terribly important. No doubt the existence of financial obligations may help in getting a few signatures on a petition or in obligating an individual to do some work. But these are effects easily obtained by other means. In the secrecy of the ballot box, no one need fear reprisal. There may be some who fear to participate actively lest they incur the displeasure of the wealthy. Yet we know of no such cases and, if they exist, they have not prevented blatant opposition to policies favored by presidents of both banks and wealthy merchants. The victorious planners are in no position to exert financial sanctions over anyone (College faculty and commuting businessmen hire few townspeople, lend no money) unless it be a few employees of the Co-ops who are not noticeably active in town politics.

Social standing appears to be an insignificant base of influence in Oberlin. No doubt there are deference relationships in Oberlin but these do not appear to translate themselves into the political realm. There are some families who frequent a Country Club in Elyria and who hold dances in auspicious surroundings. But most of them are not active at all in the community and the few who do take part are rather equally divided between the opposing factions. Eric Nord and Robert Fauver may gain something from high social standing, but Bill Long, Richard Dunn, Ira Porter or John Cochrane do not. If these activists receive deference, it is due to something other than their social position. To be sure, high social standing may predispose individuals toward activity but no one political group has anything like a monopoly of that resource.

Friendship is a valuable resource which is widespread in the community. Dunn's good relationship with Tower, the College Business Manager, makes life easier for the City Manager. Long's close association with Roose and the latter's with Leonard Barr helped smooth the way for the OID. The friendship between Cochrane, Molyneaux and Fauver helped get the Solid Six organization going. While it is difficult to say that anyone made much better use of friendship than others, it does appear that the planners had more success in getting their acquaintances to become active in civic affairs than did the traditionalists, with the exception of the 1959 election.

One reason for the greater activity of people identified with the planners is a consequence of another resource at their disposal—officiality, the holding of elected or appointed public office. This enabled the planners to recruit kindred spirits for positions on the many city commissions and special committees formed to promote policies like the housing ordinance. As these people began to participate, conversations with many of them reveal that they became more interested and engaged in additional activity. They came to know what was going on, developed new friendships, a taste for political "gossip," and even saw some positive results now and then which further solidified their interest.

The most obvious advantage which officiality brings to a Councilman is his vote and to the City Manager, his formal authority. There being few or no effective means of coercion in Oberlin (such as patronage), Councilmen are relatively free agents and can dispose of their votes to secure their preferences. This is evident in the many votes establishing and enforcing housing and zoning ordinances, a new water system, continuing and expanding the light plant, and also in internal bargaining whereby individual members receive concessions, such as modifications of the housing code, in return for their votes. The many examples of the City Manager's use of his office include blocking the Gibson apartments, exercising discretion in enforcing the housing code, and presenting information unfavorable to the Elyria offer to supply water. Officiality is limited, of course, by the official's perception of community sentiment and by desire for re-election and reappointment. Indeed, it would be extremely difficult for any faction to secure its preferences in most areas of community policy unless they were able to occupy public office and they are sensitive to the need for popularity which this entails. Nevertheless, in regard to the general run of decisions which do not occasion much interest, officiality is a crucial resource. This is all the more true when it is recognized that officiality provides access to other resources—knowledge and information, popularity, friendship, development of skills, the expectation of activity and the legitimization of attempting to exercise influence.

In a democratic political system, officiality is largely dependent on popularity with the voters as the 1959 election demonstrates. The planners proved to be more popular. But why was this so? Although this question cannot be answered conclusively, it does appear that the traditionalists were considerably less skillful, and less continously active. Their decision to run as a group concentrated their popularity and enabled Long to tar them all with the same brush as hidebound and against progress. Time after time they were caught with less than full knowledge of a particular issue and made to appear uninformed. They did not foresee their weakness among college people and Negroes and did little to appeal to these sections of the population. The major difficulty here, it seems, was that they started too late. Their burst of activity at election time could not make up for the continuous activity among the planners to pursue policies which would appeal to college people and Negroes, and, possibly more important, to recruit leaders from among these groups. The opinion leaders in the two communities were overwhelmingly for the planners long before the election, a circumstance which may have made it extremely difficult for the traditionalists to make an impact at election time, as their precinct workers discovered. By contrast, the program of the planners appeared to be considerably more positive and received favorable notice from activists in college and Negro quarters. The slate which the planners put forward was deliberately chosen to make a broader appeal through inclusion of Blanchard and Nord who were known to be conservative businessmen. As the election returns show, the planners appealed to a much wider section of the community than did their opponents.

As the planners were more popular, so were they more persuasive in a context where ability to persuade others is perhaps the chief resource available to anyone who wishes to influence a community decision. Whether it was Dunn and Long on the water system, Blanchard on the light plant, Comings on the housing ordinance or Nord on enforcement of the housing code, the planners seemed better able to convince others. Long was particularly outstanding in persuading Council and the Board of Education to go along with the FAA, persuading the *News-Tribune* to back the water system, persuading a series of investors to form the OID. When he could not persuade, as when the members of the Zoning Board interpreted the Gibson case as the individual against the state, he lost that round.

In part, the greater knowledge of the planners was a function of their officiality—the City Manager, Councilmen and Commission members had a right to demand information, were in an advantageous position to receive it, and were required by their positions to be knowledgeable. The advantages this knowledge confers are evident in virtually all the cases under discussion from the water and light plant decisions, where members of the PUC had little difficulty in showing that opposing proposals were ill-informed, to the City Manager's ability to help block the Gibson apartment and to further recreation goals by knowing what was happening. To a considerable extent, however, the superior knowledge which the planners possessed was a product of their greater effort to inform themselves. Long's mastery of detail in many areas, his willingness to do research into the past to show up alleged inconsistencies in the positions of his opponents and his general knowledge of what to do in business, finance, and government were notable. Part of Long's persuasiveness can be traced to the awareness he creates among his listeners that his knowledge is much greater than theirs, greater, in fact, than anyone else they have heard. Where so few trouble to inform themselves, even a little knowledge can be a potent weapon. On a number of occasions the author has personally witnessed Long make a seemingly futile effort to convince another person only to discover a few weeks later that this individual was using Long's arguments in discussion and finding no effective counters.

Day-in and day-out there can be no question that Long, Dunn,

Comings, Blanchard and other planners devoted far more time and energy to civic affairs than did anyone else in the community. Whether one considers the efforts of Mrs. Goldberg to write the housing code and Comings to negotiate its passage, Long and Dunn's extraordinary persistence in blocking the Gibson apartments, or the determined activity which brought success to the anti-petition-petition, the superiority of the planners is evident. Yet time and energy are resources available to all (though not in precisely equal amounts), and capable of considerable expansion. That the prizes in democratic politics tend to go to the interested and active should surprise no one. The success of the planners was due in no small measure to the fact that they backed up their concern with activity while others did not.

When the energy of the planners was met by nearly equal activity they experienced difficulties. A "meteor" like Mrs. Strong—suddenly and enormously active in one case—was able to help defeat the 2-2-2 plan. Bert Gibson made the planners sweat hard. The Off-Street Parking Corporation froze them out. An individual like Fred Holloway received consideration in the housing code as did others who voiced complaints. Activists like Ira Porter and John Cochrane may get their way from the United Appeal because of their known willingness to make an issue.

While raw energy is undoubtedly important, the skill with which the activity is carried on obviously makes a difference. The rival petition campaigns in the water issue may serve to reveal differences in skill. Porter arranged to get some signatures but failed to check them carefully and went off for a vacation. Long sought expert legal advice and determined that the petitions were almost certainly invalid. But he decided, correctly, that a mere technical invalidation would not have as favorable an impact as an anti-petition campaign. He organized this with meticulous care. He persuaded people to do the work who would be able to best approach those, mainly Negroes, who had signed the original petitions. He was constantly in touch with his organization and kept prodding them until the job was done.

It would be wrong, however, to think of skill as something esoteric or a composition of various tricks. For the most part, in Oberlin, it consists of rather simple kinds of actions. First, the collection of information so that one is better informed than others. Second, the development of a rationale for approaching those who make the decision. Third, the use of citizens committees and Council Commissions to test community sentiment, to gather support, and to ward-off opposition. Fourth, open meetings to give opponents a chance to vent grievances, to convince the doubtful, and to comply with feeling of procedural due process so that no one can accurately say that he was not given a chance to present his views. Fifth, ceaseless persuasion through personal contact, the newspaper, and official bodies. Finally, and this is perhaps most subtle, an appreciation of group dynamics and a general sense of strategy which includes pinpointing the crucial individuals and persuading opinion leaders of important groups such as Negroes. A good example is the choice of a slate in the 1959 election which was designed by the planners to blunt criticism of their alleged radicalism.

The point is not that this general approach reveals the presence of some mastermind but rather that the opponents of the planners had nothing to match it. The traditionalists never quite found a way to combat the use of committees and commissions as strategic instruments. To do so would have required a recognition of the danger they posed and the recruitment of a corps of specialists to compete with them. Only by matching the interest and activity of the planners could they have competed with them on the level of knowledge and persuasion. They did not do so, it appears, partly because they did not think the effort was worthwhile and partly because they could not adjust their thinking to a new type of situation in which participation in public affairs, however limited it might appear, had been significantly enlarged. The planners had pyramided their resources by using officiality, knowledge, skill, time and energy to gain popularity, using this popularity to promote policies expanding their base of support, using this increased support to win an election, using the additional personnel to promote new policies, using time in office to develop more knowledge and skill, and so on. At any time, however, the planners could be defeated by losing a majority on Council or in a referendum. They won the 1961 election handily (five to two) but suffered an important defeat in 1962 when the voters overwhelmingly rejected a proposed one percent income tax.

What emerges most clearly from this discussion of resources is the accessibility of the most effective ones. Most people have time and energy if they care to use it, most can obtain knowledge if they work at it, all have a vote to help determine who holds public office, and virtually anyone who feels he can get support is in a position to run for office. Only a small number take advantage of these opportunities but they are there. Presumably, if sufficient numbers of people felt sufficiently unhappy about the existing state of affairs they would find these resources available to them and could quickly increase the rate at which they were being employed. True, there are some whose socio-economic position or low education have not provided life experiences which would predispose them toward effective participation. There is reason to believe, for example, that members of the Negro community could benefit themselves if they expanded their participation, even though their responses to the questionnaire do not show that there are issues they would like to promote which are not being debated in town. It is true also that interests they have are being promoted by a few of their leaders and by white people who identify with them so that the benefits they receive are greater than their participation *per se* would justify. Should a number of new leaders— men who would help formulate and interpret their demands and explain the connections between what they want and what happens in community affairs—arise from within the Negro community, the disabilities they may suffer today might be lessened.

The basic answer to the question of why the planning coalition was successful is that it utilized commonly available resources at a much greater rate and with considerably more skill than its opponents. Time, energy, knowledge, persuasion and skill were all available to others in quantity. The only resource the planners came near to monopolizing was officiality and that for only a limited two-year period, subject to approval by the electorate.

What about "other factors" in the situation which may have been significant but which we have not mentioned? It is hardly possible to exhaust the total range of conceivable explanations. But it is desirable to consider at least three others: rule by businessmen, social changes, and the presence of a "great man" who molded local history in his own image.

Regardless of our previous analysis, it may be said, the fact remains that most of the influential planners were businessmen and this alone may account for their victory in a capitalist society. Yet as we observe the opposing forces over a wide range of decisions in Oberlin, several issues splitting the community from top to bottom, it becomes strikingly evident that the term businessman is woefully inadequate as a predictor of common interests, complementary strategies, or mutual support. The fact is that men who can all properly be called businessmen have taken opposing sides on most of the controversies in Oberlin. Otherwise, it would be exceedingly difficult to account for the conflicts over the past several years, since most of the activists (with the exception of the City Manager and a few college people) are businessmen of one kind or another. It is essential to distinguish among different kinds of businessmen. Bill Long, with his base in the Co-ops, and Eric Nord, with a factory out of town, have quite different ideas and environments than do John Cochrane of the Ben Franklin Store and Ira Porter of the People's Bank, who are downtown merchants, or identify with them. Even the downtown merchant category is by no means solid, as the planning proclivities of photographer Andrew Stofan and bookstore owner Fred Comings testify. The Chamber of Commerce, run by the downtown merchants, has not in recent years been able to get together on anything except the Off-Street Parking Corporation and that only after well-justified fears that new businesses might come in and take away their customers by providing parking facilities. In view of the splits in the business community it is not so surprising that Porter and Warner, heads of the only two banks in town, have been defeated on every major issue in which they participated during the period covered by this study.

In an attempt to show whether the change in power structure between the 1930's and the later 1950's could be related to changes in the social composition of Oberlin, an investigation was made on census returns since the turn of the century. What they reveal is that Oberlin appears to be a remarkably stable community. Population grew slowly with the largest increase coming after World War II and undoubtedly due to the national phenomenon of "war babies." The percentage of Negroes and foreign born remained remarkably constant as did the division between the sexes, the types of employment, private versus rental housing and income. This does not rule out the possibility that the census returns do not pick out the crucial social variables. The increase in out-of-town businessmen, to which old-time residents attest, is not apparent in the returns. A study of the College was also undertaken which shows that the student body grew by a quarter from the sample years 1938, 1958, the faculty by one-third, and the administration by approximately two-thirds. The faculty is younger and contains fewer Oberlin graduates but does not appear to have markedly different origins than was the case in the thirties. The straw polls taken among faculty at election time do indicate a considerable switch to the Democratic Party, a conclusion in which older members concur, and from this we may infer a greater probability that faculty members would be receptive to a planning program. The safest conclusion would appear to be that although social changes may in some degree be responsible for the success of the planners, the available evidence does not suggest that we can lean too heavily on this kind of explanation.

The role of the individual in history has long been the subject of inconclusive debate. Is he a true maker of history or is he merely a manifestation of deeper social currents? The case of Lenin's relationship to the Bolshevik Revolution is instructive on this point. Lenin did not and could not have accomplished the first October Revolution which was a result of such factors as mass upheaval due to a bloody war, breakdown of the Czarist system, and the work of many revolutionaries not including the Bolsheviks. Yet it can be said that without Lenin there would have been no Bolshevik (November) Revolution. For he was the only prominent Bolshevik who was in favor of making the attempt and it was he who convinced his fellow conspirators to go ahead. It can be said, then, that while Lenin could not have created the conditions for Revolution, he was able to seize the strategic moment in a vast cataclysm and turn it to his own advantage. Probably the best that can be done in this famous "chicken-and-egg" controversy is to look upon the conditions of the time as setting broad limits within which the remarkable individual can move, that is, to look upon the remarkable individual as thwarted or assisted in varying degrees by these circumstances.

Had Bill Long come to Oberlin in the 1930's he probably would not have been as successful in community affairs as he was at a later date when his opportunities for gaining allies and pursuing change through planning were greater. In the 1930's he would have found college and town more united in a conservative direction, the Negro sector even more quiescent, poverty a greater problem, far fewer out-of-town businessmen, and hence much less disposition to undertake costly ventures like a new water system or a housing code which might involve considerable remodeling. The idea of planning and its accompaniments—zoning and housing ordinances, parking areas, industrial development, unification of the downtown area—would not have been so much part of the national climate of opinion. To say this, however, may be no more than to suggest that Long might not have tried to do in the thirties what he found feasible in the fifties.

Yet it does appear that if Long had not moved to Oberlin, a number of developments like the OID might not have taken place. At least, and this seems to be a safer statement, the changes that he helped bring about might well have been delayed. It is true that housing and zoning ordinances, a new water system, industrial development and similar matters had been discussed before he came to Oberlin and became active. Yet if he had not participated in hiring a person like City Manager Dunn, nor used great quantities of energy, knowledge and skill in bringing these items up for decision, nor persisted where other men might have stopped, much less would have been done. Of course, Long could not and did not do it alone. But he seized upon and created opportunities which might otherwise have come to naught. Without his presence, Oberlin's political system probably would have been much more fragmented; the existing central direction might have given way to relatively autonomous specialists.

Thus far we have confined ourselves to observations based on community decisions made in Oberlin over a three year period. Our attention was focused on the behavior of leaders in a variety of circumstances and on the resources they used to accomplish their purposes. Now let us consider a number of possible ways in which leaders may be distinguished from other people. The means for doing this are at hand in the questionnaire which was administered to a random sample of citizens. This questionnaire was also given to twenty people who were leaders in the cases we studied, thus enabling us to compare their responses to four other sets of people: the general population, activists, voter-observers and apathetics. Responses were gathered from those leaders highest in influence in the various issue areas. While the sample of 20 is undoubtedly representative of the leaders, its small size dictates that we look for only the most outstanding differences between leaders and other people. Two rules have been followed in this connection. First, the magnitude of difference in response has to be at least 10% to be considered; it is usually far greater than that. Second, if the first rule is to be violated, this may be done only in cases where the direction of differences is uniform from apathetics to voter-observers to activists and to leaders so that it is clear we are on to something. It should be kept in mind throughout that the two samples are arrived at in radically different ways: one is a random sample of the population, the other a sample of leaders derived from the case histories.[1]

Leaders are activists. More precisely, they are the most active activists. Only one of them engages in less than eight kinds of activities. Leaders are overwhelmingly found in the seven per cent of the population which manifests the highest degree of political participation in the community—eight to twelve kinds of activity (Table 35). That this should be true in regard to local activists is hardly surprising (Table 36); these respondents were designated on the basis of their activity. What we wish to emphasize here is that their activity, while greater at the local level, extends to other arenas as well. The activities of leaders in the local sphere are not something apart from but are integral to their overall participation.

T A B L E 35. *Political activity in Oberlin by the number of kinds of activities*

	% of General Population Sample	% of Leaders
No Activities	29	0
One Kind of Activity	18	0
Two Kinds of Activity	15	0
Three and Four Kinds of Activity	16	0
Five, Six and Seven Kinds of Activity	16	5
Eight to Twelve Kinds of Activity	7	95

T A B L E 36. *Political activity in Oberlin by kinds of activities*
(*Yes* answers given by leaders and non-leaders)

	% of General Population Sample*	% of Leaders†
1. Have you ever been asked to vote for a candidate in a local election in Oberlin?	43	90
2. Do you talk to people during political campaigns and try to show them why they should vote for one of the candidates in elections for City Council in Oberlin or in elections for the Board of Education?	42	85
3. Has anyone ever asked you to support his or her candidacy in a local election in Oberlin?	35	85
4. Have you ever been asked to serve in any organization in Oberlin?	34	95

* All the data in these and other tables dealing with citizens are based on a random sample of 101 names on the Municipal Electric Bill list of Oberlin, Ohio, as of April 1961.

† The 20 leaders chosen at random from those selected by the case history method.

5. In the past year or so have you had any written or spoken contact with political or governmental officials in Oberlin?	30	100
6. Did you ever try to get someone to run for office in Oberlin or encourage a person to run?	22	100
7. Do you go to political meetings, rallies, dinners, or things like that in respect to local elections in Oberlin?	21	80
8. Have you given money or done other things to help in campaigns for local political office in Oberlin?	16	90
9. During the past year or so have you yourself done anything actively in connection with some local issue or problem, political or non-political?	16	85
10. Have you ever been asked to serve on a City Council Commission?	5	90
11. Have you ever held public office?	5	80
12. Have you ever held an office or had a job in a political party?	4	25

Let us offer a small part of the available evidence. When a random sample of citizens is asked whether they talk to people during local, state, and national campaigns to show them why they should vote for one of the parties or candidates, the least difference between them and leaders is 23% in the national sphere. In the local arena, leaders are 51% ahead in this kind of participation (Table 37). When it comes to giving money or helping in state and national campaigns, leaders are two to three times as active as the general population (Table 38). On the national level, leaders do much more than activists and more than seven times as much as apathetics. Wherever we turn, whether it is writing or talking to local officials or Congressmen (Table 39) or attending national campaign meetings (Table 40), leaders do a great deal more than others. Leaders not only say they like to join organizations somewhat more than do the general population

(Table 41), they actually join many more and are officers in more. In the general population only seven per cent belong to more than five organizations compared to 45% of the leaders (Table 42).

To some extent the higher level of activity on the part of leaders may be accounted for by their greater interest in community af-

TABLE 37. *"Do you talk to people during political campaigns and try to show why they should vote for one of the parties or candidates in local elections?"*

Group (D)	Yes %	No %	Blank %
Leaders	95	5	0
General Population Sample	44	52	4

"in state elections?"

Leaders	75	20	5
General Population Sample	34	52	15

"in national elections?"

Leaders	75	20	5
General Population Sample	52	34	15

TABLE 38. *"Have you given money or done other things to help in campaigns for state political office?"*

Group (D)			
Leaders	55	30	15
General Population Sample	22	62	17
Activists	57	35	8
Voter-Observers	15	63	22
Apathetics	6	78	16

". . . in campaigns for national political office?"

Group (D)			
Leaders	95	0	5
General Population Sample	30	54	17
Activists	57	30	13
Voter-Observers	28	48	24
Apathetics	13	78	9

285 How Leaders Differ From Other People

"Have you ever written or otherwise contacted any local public officials or politicians to let them know what you would like them to do on something you were interested in?"

Group (D)	Yes %	No %	Blank %
Leaders	95	5	0
General Population Sample	31	63	7

"Have you ever written or talked to your Congressmen or Senator to let either of them know what you would like them to do on something you were interested in?"

Leaders	95	5	0
General Population Sample	29	67	4

T A B L E 40. *"Do you go to political meetings, rallies, dinners, or things like that in respect to national elections?"*

Leaders	60	30	10
General Population Sample	23	58	20

T A B L E 41. *Attitude toward joining organizations.*

Group (D)	Blank %	Like to Join Many %	Like to Join a Few %	Don't Like to Join %
Leaders	0	0	80	20
General Population Sample	3	5	63	30

T A B L E 42. *"Do you belong to any organizations?"*

Group (D)	% of Leaders	% of General Population
No organizations	10	49
Less than 5 organizations	45	45
5 or more organizations	45	7
Officer of more than 1 organization	50	23

fairs. Almost twice as large a percentage of leaders (85%) felt they were very much interested in public affairs at the time they were interviewed than did the general population (44%) (Table

43). As we would expect, the disparity is even greater when the question is phrased to refer to interest in or talk about Oberlin politics and local affairs (Table 44). The general population is much more concerned with personal affairs, and less with public affairs, than are the leaders (Table 45).

As is compatible with their far greater interests in public affairs, leaders are much better informed than are other sectors of the population. Not only are they more accurate in naming the Mayor and Representative in Congress, with virtually perfect scores, they are the only ones who come remotely close to naming their State Senator (Table 46). They all know there are factions in Oberlin though only 41% of the general population perceives

TABLE 43. *"Thinking about events in the last month or so, would you say that you have been very much interested in political affairs, somewhat interested, or not interested at all?"*

Group (D)	Very Interested %	Somewhat Interested %	Not Interested %	Blank %
Leaders	85	15	—	—
General Population Sample	44	45	5	7

"Would you say that you were very much interested in local affairs, somewhat interested, or not interested at all?"

	Very Interested %	Somewhat Interested %	Not Interested %	Blank %
Leaders	95	5	0	0
General Population Sample	42	45	10	4

TABLE 44. *"When you and your friends get together, do you ever talk about Oberlin politics and local affairs?"*

Group (D)	Yes %	No %	Blank %
Leaders	100	0	0
General Population Sample	72	20	8

"Do you talk about Oberlin politics and local affairs a great deal?"

Leaders	70	20	10
General Population Sample	26	60	14

this elemental political fact (Table 47). Leaders read and subscribe to more newspapers and a greater variety of them than do non-leaders (Table 48).

When the question is phrased to ask whether the individual cares a great deal about what happens in state, local, and national politics, a substantial majority of the general population, as well as of the leaders, say that they do care (Table 49). Why, then, does the felt concern of the general population not manifest itself in activity? Why, to put the question in terms of our current analysis, do the leaders follow through with activity to a much greater extent than others?

So far as the questionnaires provide clues to the answers to these questions, these clues appear to lie in the higher degree to which leaders feel adequate and confident.[2] Feelings of adequacy in social situations may be inferred from the fact that leaders are

T A B L E 45. *"What things are you most concerned with these days?"*

	Leaders %	General Population %
Personal Affairs	20	52
Public Affairs	40	17
Both	10	14
Blank	30	18

T A B L E 46. *Name of Mayor, State Senator, District Representative in Congress*

Group (D)	Mayor % Correct	Mayor % Incorrect	Senator % Correct	Senator % Incorrect	Representative % Correct	Representative % Incorrect
Leaders	95	5	50	50	100	—
General Population Sample	46	54	4	96	50	50

T A B L E 47. *"Are there any political factions in Oberlin?"*

Group (D)	Yes %	No %	Blank %
Leaders	100	—	—
General Population Sample	41	21	39

far more likely to disagree with the statement that it is difficult for them to talk to new people (Table 50), and more likely to agree that they frequently have ideas and try to convince others in social conversation (Table 51). Twice as many leaders as non-leaders (55%) enjoy speaking in public (Table 52). Leaders are also far more willing to risk the hostility involved in taking sides in arguments between people they know (Table 53).

Confidence is indicated in several ways. Leaders disagree both

TABLE 48. *Reading papers*

Group	Leaders %	General Population %
Either major out of town paper (Cleveland Plain Dealer or Elyria Chronicle Telegram)	90	22
Either major out of town paper and local paper	80	29
Both major out of town paper and local paper	45	13
Only local paper	0	7
Neither major out of town papers nor local paper	0	20
New York Times Readers	25	12

TABLE 49. *"Generally speaking would you say that you care a great deal about what goes on in local politics?"*

Group (D)	Yes %	No %	Blank %
Leaders	95	5	0
General Population Sample	65	32	3

"in state politics?" *

Leaders	65	30	5
General Population Sample	61	28	12

"in national politics?" *

Leaders	90	10	0
General Population Sample	83	14	4

* Not significant at the .05 level.

How Leaders Differ From Other People

strongly and somewhat more than do all other categories in response to the idea that an individual's future depends on factors
outside of his control (Table 54). The notion that it is unwise to
plan ahead calls forth more disagreement by leaders than by others
(Table 55). The contrary opinion, that the individual can make

TABLE 50. *"It is hard for me to find anything to talk about when I meet a new person."*

Group	Agree Strongly %	Agree Somewhat %	Disagree Somewhat %	Disagree Strongly %	No Opinion %	Blank %
Leaders	0	0	60	35	0	5
General Population Sample	6	20	37	28	5	5

TABLE 51. *"In social conversation I frequently have definite ideas and try to convince others."*

Group (D)	Agree Strongly %	Agree Somewhat %	Disagree Somewhat %	Disagree Strongly %	No Opinion %	Blank %
Leaders	45	50	0	5	0	0
General Population Sample	21	42	14	8	13	3

TABLE 52. *"Do you enjoy speaking in public?"*

Group (D)	Yes %	No %	Blank %
Leaders	55	25	20
General Population Sample	27	65	8

TABLE 53. *"I prefer not to take sides in an argument between people I know."*

Group (D)	Agree Strongly %	Agree Somewhat %	Disagree Somewhat %	Disagree Strongly %	No Opinion %	Blank %
Leaders	0	20	30	30	20	0
General Population Sample	31	29	19	11	7	4

plans work when he devises them, is most strongly supported by the leaders (Table 56).

There are some objective reasons why leaders might feel more adequate and confident than non-leaders. Using an accepted scale of occupational prestige, leaders have more prestigeful occupations than do all the other categories of people. Taking mobility to signify difference in occupation between the respondent and his father, leaders are the only category which shows upward mobility (Table 57). The occupation ratings of their fathers are lower than those of any other category except apathetics, a sign

TABLE 54. *"An individual's success or failure depends largely on circumstances over which he has no control."*

Group	Agree Strongly %	Agree Somewhat %	Disagree Somewhat %	Disagree Strongly %	No Opinion %	Blank %
Leaders*	0	0	50	40	10	0
General Population Sample	3	22	29	28	8	11

* One leader wrote in "at times" in the box labeled "No Opinion." This answer was counted as "No Opinion."

TABLE 55. *"It is not wise to plan too far ahead."*

Group	Agree Strongly %	Agree Somewhat %	Disagree Somewhat %	Disagree Strongly %	No Opinion %	Blank %
Leaders	0	5	45	50	0	0
General Population Sample	13	27	25	28	1	7

TABLE 56. *"When I make plans, I am almost certain I can make them work."*

Group	Agree Strongly %	Agree Somewhat %	Disagree Somewhat %	Disagree Strongly %	No Opinion %	Blank %
Leaders*	40	50	5	0	0	5
General Population Sample	27	36	20	4	7	7

* One leader answered this question twice. He is not counted.

of how far the leaders have come. They rate themselves as belonging predominantly in the middle classes, and occupy the upper three dimensions of the class scale to a greater extent than does any other group (Table 58). Their incomes are higher than that of the general population with 55% of the leaders over $10,000 a year and none making less than $5,000 (Table 59). They feel

TABLE 57. *Occupations and Occupational Mobility**

	Leaders	Activists	Voter-Observers	Apathetics
Occupational average	77.5	73.3	69.3	63.2
Father's average	71.5†	75.5	72.4	69.2
Average mobility	+6.0	−2.2	−3.1	−6.5

* These prestige ratings of occupations refer to the North-Hatt scale found in Mosow and Form, *Man, Work, and Society*, pp. 277-80. Where specific occupations were not listed, the average for general classes of occupations was used.

† Two blanks not counted.

TABLE 58. *Class self-ratings: "although you might not think in these terms, we would appreciate it if you told us which social class you most nearly belong to."*

Group	Upper Class %	Upper Middle Class %	Middle Class %	Lower Middle Class %	Working Class %	Blank %
Leaders	10	55	30	5	0	0
General Population Sample	6	15	31	7	25	17

TABLE 59. *Average Annual Income Estimated by Participant* (Those failing to answer excluded)

Group	Less than $3000 %	Less than $5000 %	Less than $7500 %	Between $7500 and $10,000 %	Between $10,000 and $15,000 %	Over $15,000 %
Leaders	0	0	15	30	30	25
General Population Sample	17	26	24	18	11	4

healthier (Table 60). They are better educated, containing twice as many college graduates as the general population (Table 61). And 70% of them believe they are leaders, whereas 87% of the general population believe that they themselves are not (Table 62).

In view of the preceding analysis, we should expect that leaders would manifest a higher sense of efficacy than other citizens. They are generally more confident, feel more adequate, have better life chances, are "up" or on the way up, and (as the case his-

TABLE 60. *"Would you say that you were in good health?"*

Group (D)	Good Health %	Fair Health %	Poor Health %
Leaders	95	5	0
General Population Sample	77	23	0

TABLE 61. *Education of activists and non-activists*

Group (D)	Leaders %	General Population Sample %
Did not complete High School	0	18
High School Diploma	0	27
Did not complete College	20	6
College degree	45	21
Graduate work	5	9
Doctorate	25	10
Business Education	5	6
Registered Nurse	0	1
Music Education	0	2

TABLE 62. *"In your own view do you believe that you are a leader in the Oberlin community?"*

Group (D)	Yes %	No %	Blank %
Leaders	70*	20†	10
General Population Sample	5	87	9

* a response of "sometimes" was counted as a "yes."
† a response of "They tell me I am, but I honestly can't see how" was counted as "no."

293 *How Leaders Differ From Other People*

tories demonstrate) have undoubtedly had visible signs of their ability to affect the course of events. Far more than others, leaders disagree with statements that politics are too complicated for them to understand (Table 63), and that public officials do not care what they think (Table 64). Almost three times as many leaders as non-leaders disagree strongly with the belief that governmental decisions do not importantly affect a person (Table 65). Though leaders are split on the question, 50% of them disagree somewhat or strongly that people are frequently manipulated by politicians compared to the general population's 15% disagreement (Table 66).

Leaders are not Pollyanna types. They are under few illusions as to the potential costs of community activity. They are as aware

TABLE 63. *"Sometimes politics and government seem so complicated that people like me can't really understand what is going on."*

Group (D)	Agree Strongly %	Agree Somewhat %	Disagree Somewhat %	Disagree Strongly %	No Opinion %	Blank %
Leaders	5	5	15	75	0	0
General Population Sample	19	33	17	19	11	2

TABLE 64. *"Public officials do not care much what people like me think."*

Group	Agree Strongly %	Agree Somewhat %	Disagree Somewhat %	Disagree Strongly %	No Opinion %	Blank %
Leaders	0	5	50	45	0	0
General Population Sample	10	19	22	35	11	4

TABLE 65. *"A person's life is not affected very much by what the government does or does not do."*

Group (D)	Agree Strongly %	Agree Somewhat %	Disagree Somewhat %	Disagree Strongly %	No Opinion %	Blank %
Leaders	0	5	80	15	0	0
General Population Sample	8	13	47	21	7	5

that participation in community issues might lose them friends as is the general population (Table 67). Leaders disagree slightly more than do the rest with the statement that participation in government and politics raises a person's prestige in Oberlin (Table 68). Yet their sense of civic obligation is high (Table 69). When an obligation question is stated in direct terms—it is best to stay out of community affairs—90% of the leaders disagree, while the general population is much lower with a 40% disagreement (Table 70). Their feelings of confidence and adequacy enable leaders to take the acknowledged risks of involvement much better than do ordinary citizens. More highly motivated to engage in public affairs to begin with, they have sufficient internal resources to overcome the expected disabilities of participation.

TABLE 66. *"People are very frequently manipulated by politicians."*

Group	Agree Strongly %	Agree Somewhat %	Disagree Somewhat %	Disagree Strongly %	No Opinion %	Blank %
Leaders	15	35	5	45	0	0
General Population Sample	19	47	4	11	10	10

TABLE 67. *"A person might lose friends if he gets too involved in community issues."*

Group	Agree Strongly %	Agree Somewhat %	Disagree Somewhat %	Disagree Strongly %	No Opinion %	Blank %
Leaders	25	40	15	15	0	5
General Population Sample	16	41	19	12	7	6

TABLE 68. *"Participation in government and politics raises a person's prestige in Oberlin."*

Group	Agree Strongly %	Agree Somewhat %	Disagree Somewhat %	Disagree Strongly %	No Opinion %	Blank %
Leaders	10	40	20	20	10	0
General Population Sample	25	34	9	4	19	10

TABLE 69. *"Whether he likes it or not a person ought to take part in community affairs."*

Group	Agree Strongly %	Agree Somewhat %	Disagree Somewhat %	Disagree Strongly %	No Opinion %	Blank %
Leaders	45	40	0	0	10	5
General Population Sample	36	35	9	8	9	4

TABLE 70. *"It is generally best to stay out of community affairs."*

Group (D)	Agree Strongly %	Agree Somewhat %	Disagree Somewhat %	Disagree Strongly %	No Opinion %	Blank %
Leaders	0	0	10	90	0	0
General Population Sample	6	10	29	40	10	6

We have found that leadership is associated with greater interest in community affairs, stronger feelings of adequacy and confidence, and a resulting high level of activity. It seems likely that these factors reenforce one another. Confidence leads to activity which increases confidence through experience. Interest leads to activity which, in turn, stimulates greater interest. The reverse type of syndrome may help to account for low or non-existent community activity. Low interest results in low participation which never enables the individual to develop the confidence to encourage activity which might have stimulated his interest further. Low feelings of adequacy or confidence prevent interest from being translated into activity which might generate increased confidence through experience.[3]

Relatively high social and economic status may be a general conditioning factor which gives people in these categories an advantage. They have the education and background which encourages interest and activity as an obligation. They develop the social and communication skills which facilitate activity. And this increases the confidence they already have. Some individuals with less social and economic status can and do break out of the cycle which keeps their participation in community affairs low, as is demonstrated by a vast amount of evidence on their assumption of leadership. But this break probably requires a special effort—securing higher education, for example—or special circumstances —a party, church, labor, fraternal or other organizations which caters to them and which gives them the requisite experience and encouragement to participate. There are no unions based in Oberlin and none of the other groups supplies this kind of training now.

Another hypothesis would be that leaders are characterized by an overwhelming need for achivement which propels them into the public realm. What evidence we have does not support this hypothesis. If anything, leaders agree to a lesser extent than do non-leaders with the statement "nothing else that life can offer is a substitute for great achievement" (Table 71). What does seem to be true is that leaders are more willing to do what has to be done to accomplish things in the community. They disagree somewhat more than does the general population with the statement that no one should exercise control over others (Table 72), and they agree in greater proportion with the belief that public officials have to exercise power over others in order to do their job (Table 73). Again, leaders are distinguished by an expressed willingness to act which is borne out in practice as the case histories show.

TABLE 71. *"I feel that nothing else that life can offer is a substitute for great achievement."* *

Group	Agree Strongly %	Agree Somewhat %	Disagree Somewhat %	Disagree Strongly %	No Opinion %	Blank %
Leaders	15	10	20	25	20	10
General Population Sample	10	16	24	27	19	5

* Not significant at the .05 level.

TABLE 72. *"No one should exercise power or control over others."*

Group	Agree Strongly %	Agree Somewhat %	Disagree Somewhat %	Disagree Strongly %	No Opinion %	Blank %
Leaders	10	10	35	20	20	5
General Population Sample	30	21	24	12	5	9

TABLE 73. *"Public officials have to exercise power over others in order to do their job."*

Group	Agree Strongly %	Agree Somewhat %	Disagree Somewhat %	Disagree Strongly %	No Opinion %	Blank %
Leaders	30	35	25	10	0	0
General Population Sample	11	37	22	16	8	7

Another alternative explanation would be that leaders are people with a special need to compensate for personal defects by publicly recognized activity. On balance, for distinguishing leaders from other people, this hypothesis does not seem useful. One difficulty is that almost everyone seems to have a need to compensate for something or other; the question would be why some people choose community affairs for this purpose while others do not. A second difficulty is that there would seem to be less reason for leaders to require outlets for compensation than for non-leaders. After all, leaders are higher up on the socio-economic scale, have moved faster on the occupational scale, and have other features like feelings of good health which put them ahead of their fellow men. It is the non-leaders who might require compensation if anyone does. In view of their relative lack of feelings of confidence and adequacy, special efforts may be required to enable them to overcome, first, their disinterest and, second, their fears of the consequences of participation.

There may, of course, be other factors we have not considered which may be more important in distinguishing leaders from non-leaders. A search for other factors, however, did not turn up significant results. Leaders are not distinguished from other people by their party affiliation. They reflect the Republican preponderance in Oberlin, although they tend to consider themselves as "independent" slightly more than does the general population (Table 74). Like activists, a greater proportion of leaders are married (Table 75); and have a larger percentage of their children in public schools (Table 76)—factors which may encourage their involvement in the community. There is too little difference in average length of residence to say much except that apathetics have noticeably been in town for fewer years and leaders have not been there the longest period of time (Table 77). Leaders are slightly older than the general population averaging 47.6 years (Table 78). They are predominantly male (Table 79), and white (Table 80), reflecting differences in social roles among the sexes and the relative lack of leadership among Negroes. It is true, however, as we have seen, that Negro leadership appears to be increasing.

In general, leaders have many of the same characteristics as activists. But they are by no means identical. As we traverse the path from category to category leaders consistently score in the same direction as activists but to a greater degree. Leaders intensify the

TABLE 74. "Do you consider yourself a Democrat, Republican, or some other political affiliation?" *

Group	Republican %	Democrat %	Independent %	Other %	Blank %
Leaders	35	25	40	0	0
General Population Sample	41	23	27	1	9

* Not significant at the .05 level.

TABLE 75. Marital status of leaders and non-leaders*

	Married		
Group (D)	% of Yes	% of No	% of No Answer
Leaders	95	5	0
General Population Sample	80	19	1

* Not significant at the .05 level.

TABLE 76. Average number of children per family and percentage of families with children in public schools*

		% of Children in Public Schools†	
	Average Number of Children	% with	% without
Leaders	2.35	60	35
General Population Sample	2.52	39	42

* Not significant at the .05 level.
† Based on all participants, but some failed to answer.

attributes of activists and bring into bolder relief the differences between themselves and the rest of the adult population. Considering that leaders were chosen by a different method (the use of case histories), the consistent direction of the findings suggests that we are measuring something real and definable. Hopefully, similar studies in other communities would enable us to compare characteristics of leaders, take note of the variations from place to place, and attempt to relate differences in leaders to the social and political systems in which they operate.

TABLE 77. *Number of years in Oberlin**

Group	Average Length of Residence—Years
Leaders	19.4
General Population Sample	21.2

* Not significant at the .05 level.

TABLE 78. *Age difference between leaders and non-leaders**

Group	Average Age
Leaders	47.6
General Population Sample	45.3

* Not significant at the .05 level.

TABLE 79. *Sex of leaders and non-leaders*

Group	% of Males	% of Females
Leaders	95	5
General Population Sample	51	49

TABLE 80. *Racial differences between leaders and non-leaders*

Group	% of Whites	% of Negroes
Leaders	95	5
General Population Sample	77	24

One cannot emphasize too much the consideration that the features which distinguish leaders from non-leaders tell only part of the story of community decision-making. The danger of making unwarranted inferences should be avoided. For some the data in this chapter may be taken as confirmation of the proposition that the upper and middle classes rule Oberlin in their own interest. This is false. It rests upon assumptions which are not found in the data. A most unfortunate assumption would be that the upper and middle classes are united within themselves, that people who fall into these statistical categories agree on what are their interests. The case histories fully refute this notion. The course of community affairs in Oberlin is inexplicable without the knowledge that the contestants on both sides are composed of people from the higher economic strata (as well as a sprinkling of others) who disagree on what is good for the community as well as for people like themselves. Failing agreement among themselves, they fought out their conflicts in the public arena by seeking support from the general population in free elections. Each side attempted to mobilize lower income elements, the planners drawing largely (though by no means entirely) from Negroes and the traditionalists from whites. Even in an arena like welfare activities in the United Appeal, knowledge of the distribution of wealth among participants (economic class) would in no way enable anyone to explain the outcomes. The fact of conflict over objectives in all strata of the population is central to an understanding of the exercise of power in the community.

Leaders in Oberlin sought many policies—industrial development, expansion of the publicly owned power plant, housing and zoning codes, greater employment opportunities for Negroes—whose benefits were certainly not limited to any one section of the population. A policy like that of the Off Street Parking Corporation has not deprived low income people or anyone else unless it turns out that those merchants who pay for it do not get a reasonable return. Nor is it always evident who will or will not be benefited or deprived by a policy. There is room for much doubt, for instance, about the precise effects of the coming of the FAA to Oberlin. No doubt people in the more substantial houses do not have to make expenditures to bring them up to the standards in the housing code. Yet it is by no means clear that those who have had to make some changes have been disadvantaged thereby.

There is perhaps no need to say that upper and middle class people did not enter into any conspiracy to harm their fellow citizens. Yet some may argue that if they wanted to, and if they agreed, they could have done so. Since both statements are contrary to fact we do not really need to consider them. They hide an assumption, however, which it is important to bring out into the open. This is that other citizens would have done nothing to stop them if these hypothetical upper and middle class individuals had actually tried to put through a series of policies from which they gained and others lost. It is difficult to test this assumption for many reasons, the most important of which is that the events it refers to do not occur. It does seem reasonable to suppose, however, that when citizens find themselves deprived they are more likely to accept the risks of participation in order to do something about it. In the absence of evidence, it is wrong to assume that one class of citizens can step up their rate of activity in ways adverse to others without incurring resistance.

Alchemy is always a temptation. Just as the alchemists sought a shortcut to wealth by converting base metals into gold, so students of power have sought a magic key which would open up its mysteries. Politics being harder than physics, as Bagehot said, it is no wonder that seemingly simple ways of dealing with complex realities have an overwhelming attraction. Yet a shortcut is not of much use if it does not take you where you want to go, a fast train is worse than a slow one if it goes in the wrong direction.

Imagine a situation in which an individual's reputation for leadership was an accurate index of his actual exercise of leadership. Imagine, further, that finding the reputation of individuals for leadership, together with a little interviewing, would enable a researcher to determine the distribution of leadership in a community. Granted these assumptions, the problem of power would become amazingly simple. For if reputation pointed to the underlying reality, there would be no need to painstakingly study many decisions in order to observe leadership in operation. One would have the far simpler option of asking who are reputed to be leaders, charting their policy preferences, and inferring from this data the realities of the structure of power in the community.

Since a controversy has arisen over the merits of what is called the "reputation" or "power attribution" method of determining community power structure,[1] it seems worthwhile to subject it to an empirical test by observing how individuals reputed to be influential in Oberlin differ from those observed to be influential. In doing this we hope to illuminate the broad problem of the adequacy of perceptions of leadership. We will attempt to answer such questions as: Who do people think rules in Oberlin? What accounts for perceptions of leadership? What is the connection, if any, between a person's reputation for being a leader and his actual exercise of leadership? Does a reputation for leadership, even if presently undeserved, help gain future influence for the individual?

The reputational method

The field of community power has seen the rise of a school of social scientists, led by Floyd Hunter, who stress the study of reputation for leadership and who assert that reputation is an excellent index of reality. They begin by finding a panel of citizens believed to be knowledgeable about the community. These judges are then asked either to rank the names on a list supplied by organizations like the Chamber of Commerce or the League of Women Voters, or to themselves name people who would be influential in getting a project adopted, or to follow both procedures. Hunter submitted four lists to his panel of judges and ranked (attributed power to) the ten who were most often chosen by the judges on each as the top leadership in Regional City (Atlanta, Georgia). By following this "reputational method" the power structure of the community was alleged to be pyramid shaped and run by crowds of economic dominants.

The reputational method has been subject to withering criticism by Polsby, Wolfinger, and Dahl. A brief list of a few of the major criticisms will help set the stage for the empirical test of the reputation method which is to follow. Hunter and his followers ask their judges questions like, "Who is the 'biggest' man in town?" and "If a project were before the community that required decision by a group of leaders—leaders that nearly everyone would accept—which *ten* on the list of forty would you choose?" A first criticism of this approach is that the questions are ambiguous. One has no way of knowing whether the judges have in their minds criteria like popularity, social prominence, official position, willingness to serve, or something else. Furthermore, the questions hide a basic assumption that power is a generalized phenomenon which is the same for the different areas of policy in the community. The critics suggest (and cite some evidence to demonstrate) that if the judges are given questions limited to specific issues-areas—education, welfare, utilities—the answers will be quite different. Power is tied to issues, the critics claim, and they show this is true of New Haven and several other cities.

A second major criticism is that there is no reason to believe that the judges picked at the beginning of the inquiry will have accurate perceptions of leadership in the community, and much reason to believe that they will not. They may not be in a position to know, may distort what they do observe, may be the victims of implicit theories like "the bankers run this town," and so on. The point is not that use of informants is bad *per se* but rather that the information gained from them must be crosschecked with that of the actual participants, documentary evidence, and the like, in order to have confidence in the results. This leads to the third major criticism: premature closure. If a researcher knows that there are only forty influentials in town and that ten are top leaders before he begins his research he has assumed most of what he was supposed to find out. Everyone has to begin somewhere; the criticism is directed at the arbitrary decision to stop at some number like forty. Yet if the reputational researcher does not pick the cut-off point he must leave this up to his respondents, and there is no reason to believe that they are capable of such a task.

Finally, the critics of the reputational method assert that the mere listing of perceived influentials, even if it were proved to be correct, would not tell enough about the community. One could not know whether top leaders were united, whether small amounts of influence on the part of many could overwhelm larger individual amounts held by a few, whether those who have resources potentially useful in politics will actually use them and at what rate, and whether the distribution of influence might not be changed by events such as elections.

In comparison with the reputational approach the case history method has the disadvantage of requiring considerable time and resources. It is necessary to gain an intimate knowledge of the community, to study numbers of case histories intensively, and to observe the process of decision over a period of years. The advantage which the reputational method offers in this connection is that the questionnaires are easy to administer, only a short time is required, comparison with other studies is facilitated, and the researcher need not get involved in the grubby task of compiling case histories. But if the reputational method leads to fallacious results, and the case history method does not, the fact that the latter requires considerably more effort is not serious by comparison. On the other hand, if reputation for leadership is an adequate index of the exercise of leadership, then the economy of the reputational approach might lead to its being preferred.

We propose to submit the reputational method to an empirical test by comparing reputational leaders in Oberlin (chosen through asking Hunter-like questions to supposedly knowledgeable respondents) with those turned up through the case history method. If it turns out that perceived reputation is virtually synonymous (or has a very high correlation) with the reality demonstrated by the case histories, then the reputational method may be said to have been validated, at least in Oberlin. If, however, many leaders are left out and individuals who are nominated as leaders are not in fact leaders, our conclusion will be that reputation is not an adequate index of leadership. In order to push the analysis further, answers to reputation questions have been collected for a sample of the population as well as for apathetics, voter-observers, activists and leaders. Activists more than meet the qualifications of knowledge set by Hunter in that they are chosen on the basis of engaging in five or more activities in the community. Perceptions by leaders provides a more stringent test because it is difficult to conceive of any other group who would be presumed to know more about what is going on than these men. Inclusion of apathetics, voter observers and a random sample of the population permits us to note differences in perception in the various categories, check on whose perceptions are most nearly correct, and discover what it is that the respondents think they are naming when they are asked reputational questions.

We addressed two kinds of reputational questions to our random sample of Oberlin citizens and our sample of leaders. The first was: "Who do you think are the most important, most powerful men in Oberlin?" The respondent could write in as many answers as he saw fit to this general question. No assistance was given in interpreting it lest this prejudice the result. The results were tabulated for the population, leaders, activists, voter-observers and apathetics according to the number of times a name or a group designation was mentioned. The same procedure was followed in recording answers to the following three questions: "If there was a project before the Oberlin Community in the field of housing and zoning ('water services and rates') ('local education') which individuals do you think would have the most to say about (the most power over) it?" For purposes of convenience, we have required that a person or a group be named at least twice in order to qualify as a reputational leader. This procedure guards against the possibility that reputational leaders were left out by setting the requirements for agreement on them too high. The results in these tables were then compared with the case history leaders in the various issue areas covered by the questions (see Chapter 18). Again, for convenience, we have called all those who scored three or more in each area a major leader and all who scored only one a minor leader. For purposes of comparison with the general reputational elite, we have used the list of leaders for all the issue areas studied. Now we are ready to present our findings.

Looking over the results (Table 81) it is clear that the reputational elites differ from one area of policy to another. Whether the attribution of power is made by leaders or by a sample of the population, by far the largest number of individuals and groups are named in only one area; a much smaller number are common to two, and a very few to three. When the leaders do the nominating, Long, Dunn and Nord score in two policy areas and only Long scores in three out of a total of 29 possibilities. When the nominating is done by a sample of the population, there are 59 possibilities of overlap, and only Long, Dunn, Council, and Comings are listed in all three areas. All these men are public officials. The overlap between the general and issue-area elites is very small. The number of individuals and groups who are nominated in both the general and the issue-area elites (taken separately) is much less than the number included in the general elite but not in the issue elites, or in the issue elites but not in the general elite. Indeed, when the leaders do the nominating, the amount of overlap is never half as great as the number of cases which do not overlap (Table 82). If we attempted to predict the reputational issue-area elites from the general elite, we would (among many other errors) find that Long and Dunn would be rated too high in education,

TABLE 81. Reputation elite in Oberlin including general elite (G), housing elite (H), water elite (W), and education elite (E); nominations by sample of population, leaders, activists, voter-observers, and apathetics.

Reputation leaders	Sample (101)				Leaders (20)				Activists (23)				Voter Observers (46)				Apathetics (32)			
	G	H	W	E	G	H	W	E	G	H	W	E	G	H	W	E	G	H	W	E
Long	26	24	26	9	7	3	8	3	14	6	7		23	13	14	6	13	5	5	3
Dunn	24	19	14	3	4	6	3		7	5	11		11	13	8	3	6			
Nord	20	8	14		7	5	4		8	4	7		9	3	6		5			
Porter	17	4	4		2		5		6	2	2		7	2			4			
Ellis	10		9				2		5		3		5	4	5					
Mosher	10				2				5				3				2			
Carr	9								5				4							
Warner	8								4								3			
Council	7	18	22	4	2		5		8	8	8		6	9		3			3	
Hellmuth	7	7	7	3			3		4		4		2		2	2				
Tower	6				4				4				2							
Bill Davis	6	2	11				5				5		3		6		2			
King	6	3							3	2			3							
Murphy	6								3				2							
Comings	5	2	4	2			3				3		3	2			2			
Pease	4	2					3		2				2	2						

Name								
Love	4					2		
Kilmer	2	8	5	2		5	3	
Goldthorpe	2			2				3
Williams	2					2		
Duncan	2	29 2	9	2		11	15	3
Spitler	2			2				
Jones	2			2				
Blanchard	2	6	6	2	3			
Stofan	2		2					
Roose	2							
Sable	2							
Cochrane	2	4						
Faculty	2	2						
Zoning Board	6	8		4		2		
Mrs. Crosby	5		2			2		
Simpson	2							
Scott	2							
Housing Commission	2							
Herm Davis	3				2		2	
PUC	3		8					

TABLE 81. Continued

Reputation leaders	Sample (101)				Leaders (20)				Activists (23)				Voter Observers (46)				Apathetics (32)			
	G	H	W	E	G	H	W	E	G	H	W	E	G	H	W	E	G	H	W	E
Zavodsky			2												2					
LWV			2					2												
Consumers of water			2																	
School Board				15				8	2	6						7				2
Dr. Hoover				7						3										2
Mrs. Chamberlain				5						4										
Competent townspeople				2											2					
Cowling				5						4										
Parents				4												4				
Vance				3				3												
Betty Martin				3																
Mrs. Johnson				2						2										
Voters			2																	
Fauver	4																			
Oberlin College																				
Johnson	2																			

Arnold	2
Planning Commission	6
Berger	2
Holmstead	2
Mrs. Schwinn	2
PTA	3
Carpenter	2

TABLE 82. *Overlap between general and issue-area elites based on nominations by population and by leaders*

Number included:	Population* (101)	Leaders† (20)
In both the general and the housing elites	9	3
In the general but not the housing elite	20	7
In the housing elite but not the general elite	5	5
In both the general and the water elites	12	5
In general but not the water elite	17	5
In the water elite but not the general elite	6	8
In both the general and the educational elites	6	2
In the general elite but not the education elite	23	8
In the education elite but not the general elite	9	6

* Based on radom sample of 101 Oberlin residents.
† Based on sample of 20 leaders chosen through the case history method.

Superintendent Duncan and the School Board too low, and that banker Paul Warner and President Carr of Oberlin College would erroneously appear in the housing and water elites. The obvious conclusion is that compilation of a general reputational elite is not useful for selecting out those individuals and groups who are reputed to have the most power in the various policy areas in the community.

A direct confrontation between reputation and reality is made in Table 83 where the general, water, housing, and educational case history elites are compared with those reputed to be influential. Column I, at the far right, shows that at least some members of the reputation elite turned out to have actually exercised influence in a particular issue area. Reputation is sometimes in tune with reality. Turning to column II, however, we discover that approximately the same number of people who were nominated as reputational leaders did not actually exercise influence in the issue areas concerned. Hence the reputation method appears to have about a 50/50 probability of naming leaders who actually are leaders. Simply choosing the public officials designated to deal with these areas would have scored as well if not better. Since the reputation method does not contain any mechanism for permitting us to know which half of its nominations are the correct ones, it would be impossible to use it with confidence.

The most notable failure of the reputational method, however,

TABLE 83. *Reputation and reality*

I. Number of Reputational Elite "leaders" who were in fact successful in the issue-areas studied:

II. Number of Reputational Elite leaders who were NOT successful in the issue-areas studied:

III. Number of "real" leaders for whom there was no consensus of 2 votes or more in the Reputational Elites: *Major* (receiving a rating of more than 1 or—the rest—*Minor*

	III-B	III-A	II	I
A. General Elite (checked for *all* issue-areas)				
1. Population	16	22	13	16
2. Leaders	14	25	3	9
3. Activists	16	22	9	9
4. Voter-Observers	16	20	6	12
5. Apathetics	17	25	2	6
B. Housing Elite				
1. Population	4	9	8	7
2. Leaders	4	13	6	3
3. Activists	4	13	5	2
4. Voter-Observers	4	11	5	5
5. Apathetics	4	14	1	1
C. Water Elite				
1. Population	13	4	7	8
2. Leaders	13	4	6	7
3. Activists	13	5	5	6
4. Voter-Observers	13	7	4	4
5. Apathetics	13	10	1	1
D. Education Elite				
1. Population	7*	9*	9	6
2. Leaders	7*	6*	4	5
3. Activists	7*	6*	2	5
4. Voter-Observers	7*	6*	9	5
5. Apathetics	7*	6*	0	5

* There would be many more if members of the Teacher's Committee, the Campaign Committee, and the Principals were counted separately.

lies in the fact that it misses many people who were in fact leaders in the areas designated. The two sections of column III show the number of major and minor case history leaders for whom there was no agreement of two or more designations in the reputational study. In every case but one (the general elite on water) the number of real leaders left out exceeds the total of those named correctly or incorrectly as reputational leaders. Except for the water area, the number of major leaders omitted from the reputational elite (column III-A) exceeds the number correctly nominated as leaders in every category (column I). These figures emphatically point out the major weakness of the reputation method, at least as applied to Oberlin. It is not so much that people are named as leaders who are not, though this is serious enough, but that a substantial proportion of those who are leaders do not receive mention.

Centering our attention on respondents who were leaders and activists, we discover that their nominations for reputed influence do not meet the mark. They leave out about the same number of leaders as everyone else, doing just a little better in the water area. Nor except in the water area are they noticeably better at naming real leaders. Leaders and activists are slightly ahead of others in naming people who were not leaders in housing and slightly behind in this dubious distinction in the water issue. Leaders did better in naming "general leaders" who were influential in some issue areas. But in housing, for example, leaders picked twice as many wrong as right and in water and education the right choices barely exceed the wrong ones. It seems doubtful that any group of respondents would do better in meshing reputation with reality than our sample of leaders. Where leaders and activists do come out ahead is in filling in the spaces when asked reputation questions. As we would expect because of their greater interest and activity in public affairs, leaders, activists, voter-observers and apathetics score in descending order in completeness. While it is true that leaders and activists are more accurate respondents for reputational purposes, this advantage is overwhelmed by the fact that neither they nor anyone else comes reasonably close to reality through reputation.

The ambiguity of general reputational questions poses a real problem. Although we do not believe in the utility of a general list of influentials, we have put one together by adding the various issues areas in order to have a basis for comparison with the responses to the "big man" question. This device is open to question, however, on the grounds that the respondents may have had other things in mind when they answered their questions. They may have nominated the Reverend King because they considered internal decision making within the First Church or the Religious Affairs Council as of paramount importance. They may have nominated bankers and college officials because they believe internal decisions in these realms to be most significant. Assuming for the moment that these men are leaders within their respective institutions,[2] the responses of those who nominated them cannot be said to be erroneous. It is also possible, however, that the respondents did not have this or only this in mind, and believed that the men they named exercised influence to some extent in community decisions. Such would appear to be the case because these holders of institutional positions are erroneously named as leaders in the various issue areas. Yet we cannot be certain. For our purposes, it is sufficient that the nominations for the specific issue areas where the problem of ambiguity is not so serious justifies the conclusions that have been made in regard to the reputational approach.

The answer to why so many real leaders were left out of the reputational elites lies in the kind of people who were omitted. The most outstanding category is the "meteors," people who are not normally active or influential but who happen to be so on a particular issue or cluster of issues that interests them. Thus Mrs. Stewart, Mrs. Hawkins and Mrs. Goldberg were uniformly left out of the housing elite as were Mrs. Strong and Mr. Schreiner in education. When people think about who is a leader they apparently consider those who have been continuously and prominently active. Yet the elimination of meteors hides from view a significant aspect of leadership and democracy in the local community. For if citizens who do not normally participate can intervene successfully when highly motivated, then not only their considerable actual power but the possibility that they might act have to be taken into account by other leaders. A second category includes those whose leadership would be known to only a very few engaged in a particular issue. Although the general designation of City Council was given, the work done by members like Zahm and Gibson in the bargaining on the Housing Code was not recognized by individual designations. Well-known specialists like Professor Simpson in housing and Homer Blanchard in utilities do receive some recognition, though not enough. But less advertised specialists like Professor Howe, Tom Griswald and Carl Breuning in utilities are not designated by name.

Taking the reverse approach, we can look at the problem by asking who are named as the reputational elites. Suppose that citizens who lack precise knowledge are asked to nominate leaders. After they have exhausted those few people they might know something or have heard something about, they might take one of two tacks or both. They might name people in official positions (the less informed would choose organizational titles) or they might rely on some *a priori* reasoning which seemed common sense to them. If one believes that wealth is a controlling aspect of the community, then one might name bankers and rich men or organizations with wealth like the college. Indeed, this is precisely what appears to happen. Respondents uniformly name occupants of formal positions like the City Manager, Councilmen, Superintendent of Schools, bankers, and College. In addition, they name people who are talked about like Bill Long and Ira Porter. Leaders and activists name both formal decision-making organizations like the Zoning Board of Appeals and individuals known to have an interest in a particular area. The voter-observers, and especially the apathetics, present a more general and more "Marxian" list. They give single designations as "bankers," "businessmen," "Chamber of Commerce," "College administration officials," and "white upper class." They also include some prominent people in these categories like President Carr and Business Manager Tower of the College, Ira Porter and T. O. Murphy, a banker and a wealthy businessman. The respondents go wrong when official position is an inadequate guide to power, when men who control wealth or occupy an institutional position do not control decisions, and when a local celebrity turns out not to be influential.

A list of those most frequently misnamed as actual leaders (during the period of time covered by this study) is quite revealing. They include Ira Porter, Bill Davis, Paul Warner, President Carr, T. O. Murphy, Eric Nord, and Joseph King, Pastor of the First Church. They fall into various categories depending on which of their roles we choose to stress. Porter, Davis, and Warner are high bank officials. The fact that not one of them was successful in a single issue during the period of this study (except for the restoration of a $500 allowance by the United Appeal) seems not to have bothered anyone who nominated them. Porter's reputational prominence is easy to understand. He did indeed deserve it —in the 1930's when he was the most active and probably the most influential individual in Oberlin. And he led the opposition to the water system which kept him in the news even though he failed. Inclusion of heroes of the past is likely to be an inherent defect of the reputational method. Warner, Nord, Carr and King undoubtedly enjoy high social status due to their institutional positions and/or their wealth. Yet Carr and King are only peripherally involved in most of the decisions we have studied, Nord and Warner were on opposite sides, and there is no evidence of any common purpose or alliance among them as would affect community decisions. Murphy and Nord are businessmen of some wealth. Nord had received the largest number of votes in the 1959 Council election, was becoming more deeply involved in controversial community affairs, and was beginning to push the idea of an income tax for Oberlin (which was later defeated) when this study was cut off. He may represent the case of a person with some actual leadership, and a lot of apparent potential, but one whose performance would have to be evaluated in the future to satisfy our criterion of exercising influence. Community myths as well as community realities evidently play a part in determining reputation for leadership.

One other error in perception of power deserves special attention. Bill Long who was correctly named in housing and water was also erroneously included in the educational elite. No one can say that his reputation for leadership in many sectors was undeserved. But during the period of this study he was not active or influential in setting educational policy except possibly for some conversations with school officials on the impact of the FAA on the educational system, discussions which did not lead to any action so far as the schools were concerned. The leaders (who did nominate Long) and the activists (who did not) might possibly have known about this peripheral activity but the voter-observers (who gave Long the most designations) and the apathetics (who rate him equally with the Superintendent of Schools) almost certainly did not. It is apparent that Long's extraordinary rate of activity and his high visibility led many respondents to assume that he must also have been a leader in education. A tendency to generalize from one scope of activity to another and to give too much credit (or blame if you like) to the well-publicized are prime disabilities of the reputational approach.

But the question still remains as to whether the very fact of being reputed to be influential, deserved or not, helps gain influence for a person. The answer is "yes, with qualifications." Bill Long assiduously cultivated his reputation for being powerful, feeling that some who might have opposed him might not try because they believed it to be hopeless. Evidence on an anticipated reaction of this kind is terribly difficult to gather. While Long's reputation was not an unmixed blessing—opposition began to center around him even where his proposals might have been acceptable —it undoubtedly helped him win allies and recruits who would consult him and respect his preferences. Porter's reputation for being influential may have helped him in an operation like getting signatures on the water petition, and his deserved reputation for kicking up a fuss when he thinks the public interest is not being served certainly helped gain the restoration of the United Appeal contribution to the Village Improvement Society. Yet reputation alone, or in combination with the other resources he possessed as a banker and activist, did not enable Porter to triumph in any other local arena. A holder of an important institutional position such as College Business Manager Lewis Tower wields considerable influence within his own domain. Because the College and the town share the same physical space at times when it is presumed to affect the College he is consulted. This might also bring him in on such matters as whether to sell the light plant, in which the College has at best a slight interest. Yet, as we have seen, College officials are oriented inward towards their institution, not outward to the community, and they do not ordinarily choose to take great interest in matters of controversy. In any event, there is no record to suggest that the President or others in the College get their way in cases of controversy like the light plant; they are more likely to be resources in the strategies pursued by others— say the City Manager—for whom the municipal arena is of prime importance.

Though they may have been erroneously listed in the educational elite, Long and Dunn were certainly influential in several other areas and the reputational method may be given credit for bringing this out. But why were they listed? The most direct and possibly the most correct answer is because their reputation was justified by their leadership. It is also possible, however, that some respondents chose them because of their official positions or their notoriety. Even when a reputation listing corresponds with reality we cannot be reasonably certain that the right response was not made for the wrong reason.

This is as good a note to end on as any. For what our study shows is that reputation for influence is a curious compound: part reality, part myth; part guess, part knowledge; part what one does, part the position one holds; part observation, part assumption. If one wants to gain a reputation for leadership, he might first gain wealth and social position, or head a prominent institution, or advertise his activities, or even earn it by demonstrating actual exercise of influence. The hard way may be the best way but it is not the only way. On this rock if no other the use of reputation as an index of power must founder. Reputation itself is a worthy object of study and attention. Curiosity aside, it is worth knowing how reputation is related to the exercise of leadership.[3] But those who follow this path must make clear to themselves and to others that it is reputation and not reality they are studying.

21   ON THE ADVANTAGES OF
      LIVING IN A MASS SOCIETY

The literature on the debilitating consequences of living in a mass society[1] seems to be the social science equivalent of existentialist pessimism. If to Sartre "man is a thorn in the flesh of the universe," then to the theorists of the mass society man is a natural born victim of the forces unleashed by industrialism. Alienated from his fellows, at the mercy of forces he can neither understand nor control, man disintegrates into the "sickness unto death" (Kierkegaard's existentialist version) or the psychological collapse of "anomie" (social science version).

A good deal of the writing on power structure has been permeated with the spirit of despair over the fate of man in a mass society. Works like C. Wright Mills' *The Power Elite*, the Lynds' *Middletown in Transition*, as well as Vidich and Bensman's *Small Town in a Mass Society*, see man as helpless before industrial, military or economic elites who will destroy him while serving their own selfish purposes. The few particles of hope that are implicit in these works are best viewed as counsels of despair. Whether it is the Lynds' insistence that the "better elements" ought somehow to come to rule in Middletown or Mills' plea to the intellectual elites in all countries to join together to prevent world holocaust, it is difficult to take their solutions seriously. It is as if they were saying "things would be better if they were different" to the very people who are presumably caught in the toils of the mass society which is the true culprit of the author's indictments.

We take a different view. We believe that what is called the mass society, i.e., industrialization, has many advantages for the individual in democratic societies, advantages which enhance his creativity, his ability to direct his future, and his capacity to resist those who would use him for their own ends. What is said here, however, should not be regarded as a thoroughgoing criticism of theories of the mass society but only as a corrective of what has for too long been a one-sided presentation.[2] We begin with a brief critique of the mass democracy model of the community held by few scholars today but serving to highlight differences with other descriptions of the power of the mass of people in the community. A discussion follows of two of the outstanding contemporary models of power structure—the power elite of the United States and Mr. Big of Middletown—which are intimately connected with theories of the mass society. The very term "mass society" suggests a dichotomous view of the community; there is "the elite" and "the mass" and one must have the upper hand. Finally, a critique of the idea of the mass society can be made with examples from the literature and the Oberlin experience.

Mass democracy

A theory of mass democracy (equality of influence among citizens) fails to take into account basic inequalities in society. This is not only the "natural aristocracy" of which Jefferson spoke, the unequal distributions of talents, knowledge, skills. Nor is it merely the large differences in the "life-chances" of different individuals based on relative wealth and social position. It is also the vastly different interest and activity in public affairs which individuals manifest. If only a few individuals care enough to participate in community affairs, it would be vain to expect their more apathetic neighbors to be as influential as they. Many citizens do not even vote. Those who do often have no clear idea of the policies they prefer, and parties have a stake in blurring issues as well as making them. Many decisions never reach the electoral arena, others are made without any clear idea of popular preferences, still others come up anew. Furthermore, we hardly need Michel's "Iron Law of Oligarchy" to inform us that parties, like almost every other large organization, are run by a small number of activists. The fact that most decisions are made by a relative few is an inescapable conclusion of our political life.

Power elite

There is an enormous difference, however, between influence by
many small groups who compete with one another, and influence
by a single group (a power elite) which can enforce its desires
without considering the preferences of others. The conception of
the power elite rests upon two basic assumptions: 1) there is a unified group of men (military and industrial leaders) with similar interests and training who want to rule in all significant areas, and
2) these men actually succeed in their desire through their possession of resources which dominate all others which might be
used against them. Neither of these assumptions happens to be
correct.[3]

Businessmen in this country are united, if at all, on tax policy
though not on tariffs, and on little else. The fissures in labor, the
military, agriculture, politicians, bureaucrats and other likely candidates are evident to anyone who keeps up with current events
and are well documented in the academic literature. If wealth
were truly dominant one could hardly explain the New Deal,
high taxation, or most of the nation's social legislation. No one
group monopolizes effective resources.

Some insight into the requirements for a ruling elite may be
achieved by taking a brief look at the extreme case of totalitarian
regimes. They are not content to rest on their monopoly of
force as the one dominant resource. One of their first acts is to
destroy all competing centers of solidarity which might protect
the individual. They ban unauthorized meetings, control the flow
of information, and eliminate free elections. A secret police is established to ferret out dissent and a propaganda monopoly pushes
the party line. None of these moves is possible in the American
environment where there is a great diversity of independent
groups, freedom of assembly, competing sources of information,
and competitive politics in most areas.

The outstanding characteristic of ruling elite theory is its im-
perviousness to evidence. It cannot be contradicted because it is
not formulated so as to be capable of verification. That the
"power elite" does not rule in areas such as labor, civil rights,
agriculture, housing, and many more does not faze Mills at all.
He simply ignores these areas or claims that they are unimportant

issues on which the elite does not care to rule. On what issues does the elite rule? The important ones. What are the important issues? Those on which the elite rules. The combination is unbeatable. Even by defining military and foreign policy issues as crucial, as Mills does, we do not arrive at his conclusions. Mills cites no issues which would support his thesis. If we take such cases as the decision to intervene in Korea, or not to intervene in Indo-China, we find that they were made by the President upon advice from the Secretary of State and the top military men, results which even naïve versions of democratic theory would lead us to expect.

It cannot be denied that the public did not directly make these decisions. In our times, when great decisions may have to be made in a few hours time by a few tired men, this is a sobering thought. But if the decisions are made by public officials elected or appointed for that purpose, men who are subject to the sanction of electoral defeat or dismissal, who are part of the current of opinion that we can help create, this may be the best we can get. How can it be otherwise unless we reject the technological revolution and with it the modern world? When have the ordinary citizens of larger countries had a more direct say or a wider range of choice? *The Power Elite* is more of a romantic protest against the elemental facts of political life in industrial societies than a reasonable description of power structure in the United States.

When all else fails, the proponents of the ruling elite may resort to an explanation in a "capitalist indoctrination," by means of which it is alleged that the wielders of capital get other people to want what they want through control of the media of information. It is quite impossible to disprove this directly because when people say they want the same things, the observer cannot separate the leaders from the followers even if there is such a distinction. Recent literature on voting behavior,[4] however, suggests an indirect and convincing refutation of the indoctrination thesis. Party identification has turned out to be much stronger than we had previously thought, an important conclusion in the light of the fact that some seventy percent of the voters make their decisions on a party basis. Changes in party identification occur slowly except under the impetus of events such as the civil war and the depression which have overwhelming impact which directly affect the individual. Propaganda from any side may serve to whip up the believers but it changes few votes. Most people are marvelously impervious to arguments against their party; they tune out what they do not want to hear. The result is that by far the most important determinant of voting—party identification—is not basically within anyone's control. Unless, of course, one wishes to claim that big business got us into the depression so that there would be a mass turn toward the Democratic Party which would make that the majority party for decades to come.

Mr. Big

What we may call the "Mr. Big" model of the Lynds' Middletown studies holds that a single family, with Mr. X at the top, used its outstanding wealth, control over credit and jobs, to run Middletown as it pleased.[5] As we shall see in Chapter 22, on the basis of the evidence presented, Middletown appears to be a pluralist community in which the X family is only one of a number of leaders (or leadership groups) which get their way on decisions of importance. The fact that the poorer citizens, through their elected representatives, sometimes prevail over the expressed wishes of Mr. X does not register on the Lynd's theoretical instruments. If one assumes that a single resource like wealth is dominant, then it would not be necessary to study behavior, for one could merely discover what the possessors of this resource wanted to do and it would follow that this would be done. When we recognize, however, that there is no dominant resource and that some effective resources are widely available, a less pessimistic picture emerges than one in which a helpless citizenry is victimized by a controlling family. Middletown is not just another example of the sorry state of man in industrial society.

Mass society

There was a time, a much better time it seems, when a man was truly a man and not a dispensable tender of machines. He had roots, deep into the soil of his community. He knew who and what he was and was at peace with himself and his God. The rulers and the ruled had clearly defined relationships which no one thought to transgress: each man had his place and there was a place for each man. To escape from freedom man once had to be free, and, if not in a state of nature, this was apparently sometime in what is loosely called the Middle Ages, though the exact location is not important. Anxiety, that dread disease of the modern world, comes from doubt and choice: since no doubt was allowed and no choice was permitted there was no suffering. All was perfect, creative, and static in this integral community.

The advent of industrial society, however, brought untold disaster in its wake. Ordinary man found himself at the mercy of vast, impersonal forces directed by wielders of predatory capital or unscrupulous panderers of utopia. He was dehumanized. He no longer found personal satisfaction in work which was not his personal product and in community life from which he had been uprooted. Atomized and alienated, he was an easy prey for exploitation by totalitarian elites who no longer recognized a responsibility for stewardship of society and wielded the mass of helpless humanity for their own lust and profit.

Politics was a sham, a crooked game by which the ruling elite hid from the masses the true causes of their misery, the government but an engine of despotism, the ruling body of the bourgeoisie, to use Marx's term.[6] Politics was "superstructure" while the really important events took place through fundamental economic changes, or in conspiracies "behind-the-scenes," as mysterious to the ordinary person as the movements of the stars. No hope then for peaceful change, lest the economic forces unaccountably move in that direction, because the ruling elite would not give up its power.

A few revolutionary leaders see through this fraud. Through blood and fire and cataclysm the evil which the modern world has cast upon innocent man is purged as he returns to his former goodness. Man is to be re-integrated through a great humanizing bureaucracy.

Mass society and the small town

In a famous article on "The Factory in the Community," by W. Lloyd Warner and J. O. Lowe,[7] we can see how theory of the mass society is applied in interpreting events within a locality. The essential facts to be explained are clear. The workers of Yankee City (Newburyport), a town where there had been few strikes and no successful ones, engage in a strike and win all their demands after a lengthy struggle. One might think that the authors, clearly sympathetic to the employees, might raise a few cheers. This is not what happens at all. Instead, we are treated to a prolonged lament over the passing of what the authors call " 'The good old days' " (p. 43). This nostalgia deserves lengthy quotation:

> In the early days of the shoe industry, the owners and managerial staffs of the factories, as well as the operatives, were residents of Yankee City; there was no extension of the factory social structures outside the local community. The factories were then entirely under the control of the community; not only the formal control of city ordinances and laws, but also the more pervasive informal controls of community traditions and attitudes. There were feelings of neighborliness and friendship between manager and worker and of mutual responsibilities to each other and to the community that went beyond the formal employer-employee agreement (p. 35).

> In learning to respect the skill of the master craftsman, the apprentice learned to respect himself. He had security in his job, but he had even greater personal security because he had learned how to respect it. And because he was a member of an age-graded male fraternity made up of other men like himself who had the knowledge and necessary skills to make shoes, he possessed that feeling of freedom and of being autonomous that comes from leading a disciplined life. He spent his life acquiring virtue, prestige, and respect. . . .

> Slowly this way of life degenerated and the machine took the virtue and respect from the workers. . . . There was no longer a period for young men to learn to respect those in the age grade above them and in so doing to become self-respecting workers. The "ladder to the stars" was gone and with it much of the fabric of the "American dream" (p. 33).

In the past, it seems, a worker could have his grievances re-dressed through direct, personal contact with the factory mana-gers. Now all that is over as the shoe industry has passed out of local hands to outsiders in New York City. This explains why labor carried the day. "The management of industry was no longer directly tied in with wider life of the community. This split be-tween management and the community made it possible to mo-bilize the workers into an organization to fight management. Be-sides exerting economic pressure, the union gives the workers a new sense of strength and becomes a powerful weapon to force management to recognize their worth as men. To compensate for their loss of status and their anxieties in a changing industrial civilization, workers have been trying to find status and security in union organizations" (pp. 43-45).

One may be pardoned for remaining skeptical about the glories of the past in the absence of any evidence other than a few rose-colored reminiscences. We do not, however, wish to challenge this account on the point of accuracy. We do wish to observe that a system of noblesse oblige, in which workers depended on the good will and sense of responsibility of owners and managers, has been replaced by one in which the workers themselves, through their union leaders, succeed to some extent in controlling their destiny. Even if the silvered past would not turn green under a critical gaze, it seems likely that the individual worker's ability to protect himself would be greater while he, rather than others, was doing the protecting. There is surely no reason to prefer the strength of ascribed position in a traditional hierarchy to that of self-help in a more mobile industrial society. The fact that a community exists in an industrial society, whatever disadvantages that may entail, clearly has its positive aspects. Without the geographical dispersion of ownership and residence, it might have been much more diffi-cult for the workers to protest, and to gain allies in the com-munity.

A rather interesting view of mass society is found in Vidich and Bensman's *Small Town in a Mass Society:*

The illusion of democratic control over his own affairs given by the formal structure of government stands in sharp contrast to the ac-tual basis of local politics which is controlled by external agencies. . . . The belief and illusion of local independence and self-determination prevent a recognition of the central place of national and state institutions in local affairs. The reality of outside institutional dominance to which the town must respond is given only subliminal pragmatic recognition. The community simply adjusts to mechanisms which are seen only dimly and rarely understood (pp. 286-87).

But the people of Springdale are unwilling to recognize the defeats of their values, their personal impotence in the face of larger events. . . . By techniques of self-avoidance and self-deception, they strive to avoid facing issues (pp. 313-14). . . .

The small town citizen has apparently replaced the proletarian at the losing end of the socio-economic system.

Advantages

No one who is familiar with the many difficulties facing our cities is likely to be too sanguine about the future. But neither is there reason for despair. The existence of independent forces outside the local community, however, far from being merely a cause for complaint, has significant advantages for enhancing democratic self-expression and for preventing the formation or perpetuation of ruling elites with their abuse of power.

The integral community may have its attractions but it also has serious drawbacks, though these are to be found more in the works of novelists like Sinclair Lewis and Hamlin Garland than in the writings of social scientists. The ties that bind certainly give one support of a kind, but they also enclose and limit the individual. Imagine a community which is self-contained, generates its own special culture of a sort, has few ties with the outside world, a law and an existence unto itself. The internal restraints upon the traditional rulers must be powerful indeed for there is little else to limit them. No doubt those who are advantaged members of the society feel safe and protected. But what about the others? Where is there room for the man who wants to "buck" the system or challenge any of its features? There is literally nowhere for him to go; if he escapes he is lost in a new and alien culture. If he does not please the bankers, he may get no credit. If he does not please the employers, he gets no job. He is either "in" or an outcast.

A community in an industrial society, by contrast, has many ties with the outside world and feels the restraints imposed upon it. There is much more room for individual and group action against the prevailing tides. Many citizens live in one place and work in another so that their jobs cannot be used as a control against them. If corporations are disposed to do this, they are checked by labor unions which can gather resources from a wide area. A bank which refuses credit knows full well that a person who is a good risk can probably get the money out of town. The individual is part of the community, but he also shares common values with fellow professionals, legionaires, sportsmen, who reside elsewhere. He can move into a similar culture, appeal to a broad legal tradition. In brief, the pluralist community offers less opportunity for pressure on the individual and more opportunity for resistance.

Bill Long's rise to leadership in Oberlin may be taken as a demonstration of the open and fluid nature of the pluralist power structure. For here is an outsider in terms of residence, occupation, political style and policy preferences, who managed to prevail despite the opposition of bankers, local merchants, and other citizens of substance. Indeed, if we were to take the position held by many students of community power, we would have concluded that he had little or no chance to accomplish anything. The "economic dominants" were against him. He appeared to be just the kind of radical whose challenge to the existing system is bound to come to naught as he is crushed by countless indications of hostility and by sanctions applied to job, family, and friends. On the contrary, by inference, his ability to defend himself and to use commonly available resources to challenge the going system tells us much about the more hopeful aspects of the "small town in a mass society."

It is difficult to find any important instance in Oberlin in which one individual controlled the behavior of others through the imposition of sanctions or the fear that sanctions might be applied. Oberlin is not a closed, integral community in which the citizens are dependent on a few employers or bankers or merchants or rich men for their sustenance. The city, despite its small size, is part of the larger society and its citizens draw benefits from and can appeal to the world outside for support if they are threatened. The fact that all their lives are not bound up in the community, while possibly depriving them of some sources of satisfaction, also presents opportunities for defense against coercion. Rewards denied in the locality may be achieved elsewhere; resources which might be monopolized in a small town may be obtained in the larger world. If the individual feels less integrated into his community, there is also much more scope for him to exercise his skills and capacities against opposition or in areas no one occupies by prescriptive right. The development of the individual and his ability to express himself creatively, long accepted as one of the desirable goals in a free society, has more scope in a pluralist system than would be possible in the more rigidly defined roles of the integrated society.

The sharp and sometimes open display of hostility which took place in Oberlin may be traced in part to the somewhat independent existence of the several social groups. In other small towns the prevalence of face-to-face contacts and interdependence of the populace might have acted as a sharp brake on conflicts, but these factors did not operate as strongly in Oberlin. College people, out-of-town businessmen, local merchants, though they have some contact with one another, are not really part of a fully integrated culture. They receive their livelihood from different sources, have rather different career aspirations, find their friendships in different circles, and do not have to be overly concerned about the opinions of others. The College faculty member probably has tenure and, in any case, need have no fear that anything he does in the community will react unfavorably upon him in his College life. If he is a "local" (to use Merton's term)[8] he may seek his rewards within the administrative world of the College; if he is a "cosmopolitan" his gaze may be outward to the profession of which he is a member. The need he may feel to mitigate the friction with his colleagues, which is so clearly evident in faculty meetings, is not at all apparent in local affairs. An individual like Bill Long, who is personally not disposed to flee from conflict, gets support from this position by maintaining friendships with college people and commuting businessmen so that he is not isolated. The case of the commuting businessman is self-evident; he spends his working hours literally in another world and is hardly amenable to local pressures. He might be much less willing to risk conflict if he lived where he worked and his fellow citizens were also his business associates. The same factor, however, may serve to mitigate the most severe type of conflict because the individual need not be wholly engaged as if "his life depended on it." In any event, the basis for a politics of independence from blatant coercion is evident. And this independence is clearly part of the essential requirements for a democratic politics.

WHY AMERICAN CITIES ARE PLURALIST

We are talking about communities in which the rules of democracy are operative. There are free elections with universal adult suffrage, a secret ballot, some approximation of majority rule, and competition for office. Citizens are permitted, indeed encouraged, to organize themselves into what De Toqueville called free associations. Information is available for the interested participants and may be freely communicated. A community in which a substantial body of citizens are effectively disenfranchised or which is populated by migrant laborers without citizenship would be less likely to manifest a democratic structure or pattern.

We seek to explain the structure of leadership, power, influence, control (they are equivalent terms) over community decisions. In its most general aspect, we conceive of control over decisions within a democratic context as the result of low but (as among people) highly disparate amounts of interest in public affairs; the high costs and comparatively low returns from activity in public affairs; the unequal but dispersed distribution of resources; and the independent, conflicting relationships among leaders. Interest, activity, and access to effective resources are separately viewed as necessary and together as sufficient conditions of leadership. Conflicts among leaders supply the dynamics of the system. These variables, the factors affecting them, and their inter-relationships, form the basis of our discussion.[1]

Most people are not interested in most public issues most of the time. They simply do not care. Why should they? An individual in the United States can get a wonderful job, marry, have a happy family, and do creative work without ever taking an interest in the public realm. His primary satisfactions do not ordinarily lie in political life; basic needs are met or thwarted on the job, in the home, through friendship circles and the like.

Community affairs are remote. They are complex and usually unrelated to the individual. Before a person can understand them and relate himself to them, he needs a sensitive perceptual mechanism, a capacity for considerable abstract thought, equipment which most people do not have. This is especially true as one descends the educational ladder, for education not only indoctrinates one in the value of political participation, but also prepares one to make connections between apparently remote events. It is not easy to perceive that a new waterworks may attract more industry which will affect local merchants, and then consequently the service in stores and employment opportunities in town. It is difficult to maintain an interest in what one cannot understand.

And is it worth understanding? To take an interest means to spend some time which might bring greater returns on the job or through a hobby. The cost of interest is obvious, but the return is not, particularly if one does not believe that what the government does is important or that one can do anything about it. Study after study has shown that interest is related in a high and positive way to a sense of efficacy. The usual propaganda, of course, has it that every vote is crucial. But one vote out of millions or even thousands rarely changes anything and from the limited perspective of the individual he may rationally believe that nothing he would do could really be efficacious. This feeling may be overcome by a deep sense of civic obligation, but many people do not have this sense.

To be interested in some issues some of the time is one thing; to be interested in most of the issues most of the time is quite another. If time were free and unlimited, those with an inclination to be interested might gorge themselves. But this is not the case and even the most avid partisan of public affairs must be selective. What, then, can we say of the many who are not disposed to be interested when they are confronted with a vast and confusing array of subjects about which they might conceivably know something.

Let it not be thought that most people will remain disinterested under almost any provocation. Imagine a law which separated parents from children or which forbade citizens to watch television. Then one would really see what mass participation was like. There is no need to retreat into realms of fancy; policies adopted in the Soviet Union since World War II will serve to demonstrate the point. In 1946 the Soviet Government announced an exchange of currency—to fight inflation it said—which reduced the value of savings by about 90 percent. A decade or so later the regime, in effect, repudiated the national debt by announcing a moratorium on the payment of government bonds which workers had been compelled to buy to the amount of 20 percent of their salaries. Can anyone imagine a democratic government thinking of such a policy, let alone promulgating it? The participation engendered by it would be immense, but the experiment is hardly likely to be made.

There are a few people, a very few, who are continuously interested in a wide variety of issues. They usually are public officials, newspaper editors, academics, people whose occupations require this interest. There also are people who have specialized interests in specific policy areas. These may include public and private officials, members of civic organizations, and pressure groups, citizens who are directly affected, and a sprinkling of others who make a hobby out of being interested, including seekers after causes, club women, and people who like to get their names on letterheads.

The fact that individuals do vary enormously in their degree of interest has profound implications for political life. If interest is a necessary condition of leadership, then the disinterested remove themselves from consideration, and leadership is concentrated in the small population which does care. Yet the number of interested people, small though it is, is large compared to the number of active people. The factors which limit activity are of cardinal importance in understanding political affairs.

Activity is costly. It eats up time and energy at an astounding rate. To be active on strategic problems in nuclear politics or on the operations of a municipal electric plant is not a matter of a few moments of reflection; many hours must be spent. One must ordinarily attend meetings, listen to or participate in discussion, write letters, attempt to persuade or be persuaded by others, and engage in other time consuming labors. This means devoting less time to the job, to the children, and to hobbies. Yet these activities, rather than public affairs, are the primary concerns of most people, and so the cost of participation in public affairs seems greater than the return. Only a few issues, at best, induce most citizens to participate in politics.

Activity may be costly also in terms of ego involvement. The goal of the activity may not be achieved, leaving the participant with a sense of failure. If he is not especially skilled, his seemingly bumbling efforts may provoke ridicule, which is hard to bear. The hostilities incurred in controversies over policy may rebound in the form of personal invective.

The active person leaves himself open to social and financial retaliation, or thinks that he does. Hence some businessmen believe that "politics is bad for business." All the more reason, then, for not following up an interest with dangerous overt activity.

Activity depends on the possession of certain skills which usually are products of a middle and upper class subculture. People in academic life, because these skills are part of their job, tend to underestimate the extreme difficulty others have in speaking in public, in writing down their ideas coherently, and in defending them in argument. Unless a citizen is willing to confine himself to more routine operations, like addressing envelopes, he finds that lack of these skills is a tremendous handicap. Lower class individuals who are trained in these skills in labor unions, churches, or social organizations provide an important source of leadership in defense of their interests. But only a few take this path.

A sense of civic consciousness is more deeply ingrained in upper class than in lower class mores. The explanation may rest in part upon class-based experiences of relative autonomy, of actually "making a difference" by one's actions. The result is that a person with higher income and more advanced education is likely to feel more obliged to participate, and to have this feeling reinforced by social pressure. These are statistical tendencies, of course, and there are people on the "wrong" side of the percentages.

Activity varies considerably with the nature of the issue. Some issues—an end to the Korean War, a tax increase, unemployment —have a more obvious impact on large numbers of people than do others. Some issues are selective of participation in that they bring out people with a special concern who would not be active in other areas. Thus the relatively few people active on farm issues tend to be different from those few concerned with labor, air pollution, or sewerage.

Participation is affected by the activities of leaders who have a stake in decreasing or increasing it. Their ability to "make an issue," to broaden the interested public, increases their bargaining power. The task of the leader is to show the connection between the events he is concerned about and the lives and fortunes of at least some segments of the population. The general lack of public attention and inability to make the desired connections turn issue-making into one of the most valuable components of the art of leadership.

There are many types of activity and some are much less costly for the individual than others. This is particularly true of voting, which is done in secret and requires but little time and attention. Party labels and factional alignments serve as a means of cutting information costs, enabling the voter to express a generalized preference without too great attention to the issues.

The universally low participation in civic affairs does not mean that the citizen who wishes to become active finds that others block his path. Just the opposite is usually true. The demand for participants is almost always greater than the supply. Those who are or would be leaders require followers of all kinds to spread propaganda, ring doorbells, engage in research, and perform a multitude of other tasks. Entry into public affairs is so free and easy, in fact, that many individuals become participants by self-selection, by simply appearing and showing that they are willing to work.

With these comments in mind, we can proceed to classify political participation (interest plus activity) in a way which will prove useful for analytic purposes. We will distinguish between four types of participants according to the rate and scope of interest and activity:

1. The *apathetics* who neither vote nor participate in any other way.
2. The *meteors* who vote with some regularity, and engage in a few activities sporadically.
3. The *issue specialists* who vote regularly and who continuously

participate in a particular issue area but are not active in other aspects of community affairs.

4. The *generalists* who vote regularly and participate extensively in many though not all issue areas.

The generalists compose an infinitesimal percent of any community, their number is easily counted on the fingers. The number of specialists is larger but is unlikely to include ten or even five percent of the people in most communities. The largest group of citizens is the meteors, with the apathetics making up from 20 to 60 percent of the population.

Routine issues, which do not involve innovation or challenge to established interests, may be decided by an administrator or a small number of specialists. Somewhat more controversial issues are likely to bring out a few meteors. Highly controversial issues increase the participation of meteors and may even arouse some of the normally apathetic. Elections bring out all but the apathetics and some meteors, depending on circumstances. Mass participation in which virtually everyone engages in a variety of activities other than voting is practically unknown.

One conclusion is obvious: the prizes in politics go to the interested and the active; people who do not try to influence decisions do not have a direct impact upon them. If the preferences of a large number of citizens are met, therefore, it is not because they ordinarily participate but because they might participate, because relationships between participants are arranged so as to secure this result, and because of the particular ways in which effective resources are distributed and used.

As everyone knows, resources which may be used to affect public decisions are unequally distributed. Some people have much more wealth, credit, control over jobs, information and social standing, than do others. But effective resources are also widely dispersed. No one has all of them and few have none. No single resource is dominant, so that use of it overwhelms attempts to wield others. The wealth of businessmen may be offset by soliciting small contributions from many workers. The popularity of a leader like Franklin Roosevelt may counter the hostility of the media of information. The skill of a Lyndon Johnson may smite enemies with higher social position. The bureaucratic positions of a Robert Moses may prove too much for elected leaders. And aroused citizens may overcome Moses by forming a barricade of carriages around a threatened playground in Central Park. There are, then, many different kinds of resources, not all tightly concentrated, nor useful for the same purposes, nor employed with similar effectiveness.

That resources exist does not mean that they will be used fully, skillfully, or at all. Most people use their resources sparingly, with varying degrees of effectiveness. The cost in terms of time, energy, money, and ego damage usually seems too great in comparison to the benefits which appear remote and uncertain. As a result, there is a vast reservoir of resources lying untapped by people who prefer not to use them. When and if they become conscious that things are going badly, and feel that participation in the community area may provide an answer, the meteors and (under great provocation) the apathetics may step-up their use of resources.

An exhaustive discussion of resources is literally out of the question. A few central points must suffice. Which resources might conceivably dominate over others in our society? Wealth comes readily to mind; its relative concentration is established, and there can be little doubt about its usefulness under many conditions. But it is not, as is commonly supposed, a universal solvent in the civic arena. It often cannot buy popularity with the electorate as many wealthy men have learned to their sorrow. A minimum sum for electoral purposes is a necessity, but a hundred times that sum may not bring additional returns and may actually bring resentment against the spender. Other resources may be converted into wealth; a politician may use patronage to fill the party coffers, or his continued tenure in office may demonstrate the advisability of contributing to his campaign fund. If an organization like the Cooperative Stores in Oberlin can raise funds by internal subscription or through outside sources, the local banks cannot effectively use against it their ability to withhold credit. It sometimes is said that politicians may be bought; but they are not worth buying unless they remain in office, and they may not be able to do that if they so consistently please the wealthy as to antagonize the more numerous citizens of moderate income. No doubt money may control some decisions in some issue areas just as superior information, skill, and even physical force may control in others. But money does not control in all decisions nor necessarily in any which are deemed vital by others who possess some wealth and other resources with which to engage in conflict.

Many who possess wealth do not in fact employ it to influence community decisions. If there was an X family in Middletown which sought to influence many decisions, there also was an extremely wealthy Y family which was not interested in most community decisions. Most large corporations are extremely wary of direct political participation, fearing adverse publicity. Since many who possess wealth do not attempt to employ it, and some who have but little do use what they have, it is not at all clear whether wealth *per se* confers an advantage. There is little point in arguing that the potential influence of the wealthy is great, should they care to employ their resources, for there are many individuals and groups who could employ more of the resources in their reservoir to considerable effect. Instead of the oversimplified notion of the billiard ball effect—asking how far can A influence B—we say that it depends on A's involvement, his willingness to use his resources to the limit, B's ability to expand his use of resources, the costs involved, and the activities of other participants.

While resources are subject to diminishing returns, we would like to suggest that those which are capable of the most effective expansion are either widely diffused or most readily available to public officials who are subject to restraints of the electoral process. Time, energy and skill (to which least attention is paid) are among the most important resources. Merely by putting in a great deal of time, coupled with considerable energy and a modicum of skill, most participants can increase their influence over specific areas and, more important, increase their access to other resources. Politicians do this by devoting full time to public affairs, making friends, doing favors, and working with amazing energy, and it is not surprising that their experience increases their skill. The ensuing popularity can be converted into votes; public office can then be used to win more friends; this good will can be turned into contributions; increased wealth can be applied to buy expert advice; the knowledge gained thereby will provide advantages over opponents; this success can be used to recruit more followers. This process, which Dahl has called the pyramiding of resources, is not readily available to those who lack the legitimacy of public office, which carries with it a publicly recognized right to be active and the necessary time to do it.

It is conceivable that all the interested and active individuals might agree on most policies. They would then monopolize the resources which were being used to affect policies, thus reserving influence to themselves. If the rest of the population shared these preferences, the result would be an end to conflict and the millennium of total harmony spoken of in utopian novels but never seen on earth. If the participants used their resources to compel the obedience of nonparticipants, a ruling elite would result. But there is no ruling elite in Oberlin or any other city for which we have a full account. What is wrong here is the assumption of unity among the participants. How else can we explain the occurrence of conflict in our communities?

It is difficult to think of a community of any size which does not have its share of disagreements. This is true for many reasons. Issues have a differential impact. Different individuals and groups stand to lose or gain from a tax increase, from one type of service rather than another, and from a zoning ordinance. School issues may pit those with school children against those without. The "ins" versus the "outs" create another basis of rivalry as do personality conflicts. Members of different professions are likely to have somewhat different values. A category like businessmen has certain utilities as a statistical shorthand but it fails miserably as a predictor of unified interests and goals, as the Oberlin study should show to anyone's satisfaction. Those who stand to lose by industrial development may take different positions from those who stand to gain. When leadership depends on a few, the fact that some businessmen are opposed to others may assume critical importance.

Social class in the United States has not proved to be an efficient ground for organizing conflict, and we do not find monolithic alignments of the classes against the masses. We do find ethnic, religious, and racial grounds for conflict as well as liberal and conservative orientations and varieties of preferred political styles which cut across class lines. Our conclusion is that the interested and the active are not unified against the rest of society. Of course, they do agree on the "rules of the game," the procedural aspects of democracy; this places limits on their conflicts without doing away with the conflicts themselves. This has far-reaching implications for the problem of political change.

There are two simple answers to the question of how change takes place in the community. One is that a unified set of leaders is able to impose its will on all others. Either the elite decides and it is done or the elite is opposed and it is not done. Only a revolution can impose change against their will in the short run. Another easy answer invokes mass democracy; change occurs when a majority of citizens or voters decides that it is desirable. What can be said, then, of the infinitely more complex situation in which most people are uninterested and inactive; there are conflicts among the leaders; and no one of the leaders has sufficient resources to prevail most of the time?

To a limited extent a leader may introduce change into a community without encountering significant opposition. This is, in part, a consequence of the generally low interest, activity and use of resources. Most individuals and groups do not find it worthwhile to calculate precisely how they might be helped or hindered by a change. The leader's skill is important because issues may be so constructed and explained as to persuade some that they stand to gain. Indeed, it is sometimes possible to arrange things so that few in the community suffer and many gain as when funds are procured from other levels of government. Policies may be framed so that their impact is not immediately apparent—taxes may be hidden—or segmented in impact so that only limited numbers are adversely affected at any one time—enforcement may be selective. Because people do not always know what they want, the skillful leader may also create demands which he then fulfills. This is not possible when people are adversely affected in a recognizable way. There are strict limits to deception, especially when other would-be leaders are prepared to exploit it. The leader may use his popularity, support from those to whom benefits have been distributed, to weather storms which arise over objectionable innovations. But this fund of resources is not inexhaustible. He may be able to afford antagonizing some people part of the time but not most of the time. He has to pick and choose among policies with this in mind.

In his brilliant pamphlet, "What Is To Be Done," Lenin argues that revolution is not a task to be accomplished by amateurs devoting spare time and weekends but only by professionals devoting all their time to the job. We might phrase his argument in our own terms by saying that innovation in the community, like revolution in the nation, is most likely to be accomplished by interested and active participants who utilize their resources at a high rate and devote a great deal of time to the task. The most likely innovators, then, are participants who work full time at some aspect of community affairs—city managers, bureaucrats, elected officials, heads of private agencies and civic associations. Next, perhaps, are newspaper editors, businessmen, and attorneys who have "dispensable" occupations which permit them to devote considerable time to civic affairs or are especially related to them. The editors are more likely candidates because they are supposed to be concerned whereas only the occasional attorney or businessman has work which justifies his attention.

While innovation is possible it ordinarily does not go too far because there are persuasive reasons for leaders to minimize conflicts. The formal structure of government, with its emphasis upon free elections and separation of powers, frequently means that cooperation from others who cannot be coerced must be obtained. The chances are that the ordinary social division of labor in society also makes crucial individuals immune to pressure. Those who control jobs, for example, unless they are politicians, are engaged in different pursuits with different aims and rules. The leader who possesses resources dominant in one issue area often finds that they are not similarly effective in another. It soon becomes apparent that the opponent of today may be the indispensable ally of tomorrow, and that it is most unwise to alienate other leaders for the sake of one policy to the extent that agreement on other policies is precluded. Finally, competing sets of leaders have a stake in not pursuing policies which will lead to the entry of new participants who will make a bid for leadership that may upset prevailing patterns. The more extreme the policy, the greater the departure from the *status quo*, the more likely that interest will be created and potential leaders motivated to make their bid, thus threatening the powers that be.

Severe conflict is so costly that a multitude of techniques have evolved for avoiding or mitigating it. Perhaps the easiest way for a leader to avoid conflict is to limit his activities so that his goals and strategies are largely independent of those of other leaders. This appears to be the approach which is taken in most cities. Where this is not possible, his policies may be framed to accommodate values held by other leaders. Mutual agreement, granting rewards in one area to offset deprivations in another, compromise through bargaining, all are techniques leaders use to limit strife. They may narrow and segment conflict so that it does not become all pervasive. Issues may be blurred or ignored. They may confer symbolic rewards by designing an euphemistic cover for an unpalatable decision. Instead of "calling a spade a spade," so that losses and gains are immediately apparent to the contestants, leaders call it something entirely different. Only when the normal channels for limiting conflict have broken down, as in a bitter intra-party feud such as the one between the "reform" and "organization" Democrats in New York, are all the stops pulled out. Then the disputants fight for their political lives. At such times, it is necessary to have a commonly agreed arena—a primary, an election, or a convention—with clearly defined rules for waging the combat and registering the decisions considered legitimate.

We have now presented the four variables—interest, activity, resources, conflicts among participants—which we will use to explain the pluralist structure of power in most American communities. The time has come to draw the appropriate conclusions using these variables and the factors affecting them.

No one person or group is powerful in all or most of the significant areas of community life. Different individuals and small groups of participants typically make decisions in different issue areas. Specialists and generalists use resources more frequently and to a greater extent than others most of the time. It should come as no surprise, therefore, that they frequently prevail in their own domain, especially when the decisions they make are largely routine or do not interest others. (These people may not feel deprived because they are not influential; they just may not care.) When decisions are made which adversely affect others, or which alter established practices in which others have a stake, participation normally increases. Frequently, electoral sanction is necessary and this requires support or at least acquiescence from voters who may be mobilized by opponents. Other leaders must be pacified. Since this normally cannot be done by coercion (in the absence of dominant resources and in the presence of a reservoir of resources), it must be done by bargaining, or granting rewards in other areas, or recourse to the ballot. Leaders take care, under democratic conditions, not to systematically violate the preferences of the ever-present "others" who may challenge even their routine supremacy. This accounts for a great deal of the informal consultation, the formation of citizens' committees to secure widespread support, and the many compromises that take place. Leaders must ordinarily choose goals which permit coalitions with other leaders.

One type of pluralist system may be described as a multitude of independent centers manned by specialists whose goals and strategies are substantially nonconflicting. When conflict threatens it is settled by bargaining among leaders who find this method preferable to the risk of breaking up the system from which they all gain. Only small changes in policy are made so that the chances of severely depriving others by any one move are considerably reduced. When the policies pursued by one center adversely affect that of another, the difficulty is handled by "fire-truck" tactics, that is by dealing with each small difficulty in turn in whatever center of decision it is. The city of Chicago may be described in these terms.

Another type of pluralist system, represented by New Haven and Oberlin, has central direction. Policy is effectively coordinated by a center of power. The leader or leaders are likely to be public officials with time, skill, energy, and ability to pyramid resources. While they are the only ones who are influential to some degree in most of the issue areas, they are not wholly influential in any area. They must share influence with specialists, meteors and other leaders who may threaten to or actually do mobilize against them. They are not equally effective. They are defeated now and then. They are compelled to husband their resources carefully lest they incur hostility which will deprive them of office. For the most part their success depends on the disinterest of others and their own skill in meeting the demands of the interested and active while serving their own purposes as well.

Conceivably there may be small communities in which a generalized elite, dominant on all or most issues, does exist. Perhaps there is a single employer who monopolizes wealth, jobs and credit to such a degree that no one can challenge him if he seeks to exert himself. Possibly there is a sharp educational difference between social classes so that a small, upper class group monopolizes political skills. Lower class members may wish to contest decisions, to make issues, but they do not know how. Never able to begin participating in the civic arena, they do not acquire the experience and confidence. Their sense of efficacy remains permanently low. Yet the ruling elite may not ignore them. There is still the possibility that the arrival of new citizens, defections from the elite, conflicts within it, or a bid for leadership by an exceptional lower class person might change the situation. Therefore the elite places self-imposed limits on actions which might disturb others. It seeks to maintain friendly contact with lower class individuals and goes so far as to seek approval from them before trying a new policy that might raise sufficient concern to upset the pattern of community power. Lower class persons do not lead, but neither are they led very far against their will.

Pluralist theory is supported not only by the Oberlin experience but also by a growing body of literature on American cities of various sizes and complexions. In *Governing New York City* (New York, 1960), Wallace Sayre and Herbert Kaufman conclude:

> No single elite dominates the political and governmental system of New York City. . . . Most individual decisions are shaped by a small percentage of the city's population—indeed, by a small percentage of those who engage actively in politics . . . the city government is most accurately visualized as a series of semi-autonomous little worlds each of which brings forth programs and policies through the interactions of its own inhabitants. . . . New York's huge and diverse system of government and politics is a loose-knit and multicentered network in which decisions are reached by ceaseless bargaining and fluctuating alliances among the major categories of participants in each center, and in which the centers are partially but strikingly isolated from one another. (Pp. 709-16.)

Edward Banfield's description of Chicago politics in his *Political Influence* (New York, 1961), follows the pluralist lines of New York quite closely. He also describes an interesting political style that has evolved in Chicago which we may view as a result of the pluralist factors in the environment.

Chicago is too big a city, and the interests in it far too diverse, to allow of quick and easy agreement on anything. By approaching an issue slowly, the political head gives opposing interests time to emerge to formulate their positions and to present their arguments. . . . According to the Chicago view, a policy ought to be framed by the interests affected. . . . The political head should see that all principally affected interests are represented, that residual interests (i.e., 'the general public') are not entirely disregarded, and that no interest suffers unduly in the outcome. (Pp. 270-71.)

Lorain, Ohio is a steel manufacturing city just a few miles away from Oberlin. James McKee, a sociologist, set out to study the community in order to test the hypothesis that management was the new ruling group in our society. He found that by organizing and mobilizing the votes of the previously conflicting ethnic groups in Lorain's polyglot population, CIO labor leaders forged a coalition with the Democratic party and the Catholic Church which controlled decisions in the city's educational system and government. McKee concludes that

First, there is no single locus of decision-making, but rather a number of loci, each differently structured. . . . Second, a number of groups may have varying effects upon decision-making in any given locus. . . . Hence, the pyramidal model of the social order, with power and authority located at the apex, is inaccurate and misleading. Third, the organization of political power in the community provides a striking and contradictory contrast to the system of power and authority within the corporation. . . . In the community decision-making is more democratically structured. This is not to assert that what goes on in the community fully epitomizes democracy. But it is to assert that a share in decision-making in the community is now more easily attained by citizens of low status. (McKee, *op. cit.*, pp. 369-71.)

In New Haven, reported in the studies by Dahl, Polsby and Wolfinger, the political style is quite different as the diverse centers have been unified under the forceful leadership of Mayor Richard Lee. The city's politics are unmistakably pluralist, however, for though Lee was the only participant who was influential in most of the issue areas studied, his degree of influence varied from area to area, and he was sometimes defeated. As Dahl puts it,

The Mayor was not at the peak of a pyramid but at the center of intersecting circles. He rarely commanded. He negotiated, cajoled, exhorted, beguiled, charmed, pressed, appealed, reasoned, promised, insisted, demanded, even threatened; but he most needed support and acquiescence from other leaders who simply could not be commanded. Because he could not command, he had to bargain. (Mimeo draft.)

The various reputation and stratification studies of community power do come up with different conclusions. But the evidence presented in them suggests that the communities they studied were probably pluralist. The Lynds report that power in Middletown (Muncie, Indiana) was held almost entirely by the X family through its control over jobs and finances. Yet we learn that an insurgent Mayor was elected over the opposition of the X family and that he successfully opposed a policy of relief payments which was desired by the X's. The Mayor also "forced the Chamber of Commence [said to be dominated by the X family] to side with him in a WPA project favored by Middletown's working class before he would approve the pet project of the business class (opposed by the South side) for an interception sewer." (P. 329.) Coming closer to home, a river flowed through the upper class districts, right by the X house, which was so noxious that Mr. X had to close his windows in the summer time. The river did not, however, pass through the working class area in the South side. As a result, the workers' representatives on the City Council blocked the use of funds to clear up this nuisance because they did not want to tax themselves for the benefit of the wealthy. We also are given examples where the X family prevailed on public policies against opposition. Insofar as the limited evidence permits us to judge, there appear to be several centers of influence in town, no one of them uniformly successful in all areas.

Floyd Hunter studied Atlanta, Georgia and found it dominated by business leaders. It does not take long, nevertheless, to discover other participants who exercised leadership. There was Truman Worth, "The boss of a large suburban development," a reputed power in the state legislature, without whom, Hunter says, no move on a metropolitan wide basis was made. For years he successfully opposed a proposal favored by some businessmen to coordinate services on a metropolitan basis. There was Calvert

Smith, a Negro leader, who used the substantial Negro vote to bargain for advantages for his people. "Everyone politically inclined," Hunter tells us, "is aware of the power of the Negro vote to swing elections within the city . . ." As our last example we have labor leaders. "In recent years public solicitations have reached down into the worker groups," Hunter reports, "and there is a growing tendency for some of the labor leaders to have a voice in the management of purely civic expenditures." The existence of several independent centers of leadership suggests that bargaining among leaders rather than coercion by businessmen is the order of the day.

Pluralist power structure is clearly visible in Harry Scoble's study of leaders and issues in Bennington, Vermont.

> The Bennington study, with its recognized limitations, indicated that no single power structure existed in the community. The data suggest that 'a community' is in fact to be characterized by a multiplicity of power structures to be empirically determined among different decisional areas. For example, the monolithic, flat-surfaced pyramid, with the empirical features: a small number of power-holders, acting in pre-determined concert, and with wealth as the dominant power-base, this seems appropriate to Bennington's hospital decision but not to the other, non-charity, public policies examined. For in the latter cases the data indicate consistent central factions which compete to control necessary public offices and/ or to produce desired policy outcomes depending on the issue involved. Finally, lacking a formal governmental mechanism for coordination (which does exist in larger communities), we may infer from the data on office-holding that there was intent—somewhat self-limited and frequently unsuccessful—to achieve informal coordination through overlapping personnel and through controlling focusing of public attention. But in the last analysis coordination was achieved by the nonleaders. (Morris Janowitz, Editor, *Community Political Systems* (Glencoe, 1961), p. 141.)

In summing up the results of the massive inquiry into power in Syracuse, New York, Frank Munger writes as follows:

> Only three over-all conclusions seem warranted by the materials examined. First, the myth that significant decisions in Syracuse emanate from one source does not stand up under close scrutiny.

Second, there tend to be as many decision centers as there are important decision areas, which means that the decision-making power is fragmented among the institutions, agencies, and individuals which cluster about these areas. Third, in reality there appear to be many kinds of community power, with one differing from another in so many fundamental ways as to make virtually impossible a meaningful comparison. (P. 311.)

It would be difficult to find a more direct description of a pluralist system than is found in *Decisions in Syracuse* (Bloomington, 1961).

Thus, evidence from cities as diverse as Lorain, Ohio, New Haven, Connecticut, Chicago, Illinois, and Atlanta, Georgia bears out our thesis that the contemporary city is likely to have a pluralist structure of power.

Appendix to chapter 22

This chapter was written in order to present a theory which, while consistent with the Oberlin experience, would also be applicable to the growing body of literature on other American communities. A bibliographical essay, therefore, describing the major sources from which the elements of this theory have been taken, would seem more appropriate than the usual string of footnotes. The key variables used in the theory—interest and activity in public affairs, conflicts among leaders, and the distribution and use of effective resources—each come from a different body of thought to which I am deeply indebted.

Theory on political participation goes back at least to Aristotle who demonstrated keen awareness of the consequences of different rates of political activity in his *Politics*. My major debt, of course, is to the recent studies of voting behavior: Campbell, Converse, Miller and Stokes, *The American Voter* (New York, 1960); V. O. Key, Jr., *Democracy and American Public Opinion* (New York, 1961); Berelson, Lazarsfeld, and McPhee, *Voting* (Chicago, 1954); Seymour Lipset *et al.*, "The Psychology of Voting: An Analysis of Voting Behavior," *Handbook of Social Psychology*, ed. Gardner Lindzey (Reading, 1954); Lazarsfeld, Berelson and Gaudet, *The People's Choice* (New York, 1944). The study of interest and activity in Oberlin, reported in this volume, produced results highly consistent with the national findings.

Conflict among leaders is an outstanding element in what might be called the pluralist literature describing American national politics as it has developed from Woodrow Wilson's *Congressional Government* (Boston, 1885) through David Truman's *The Governmental Process* (New York, 1951), and the various editions of V. O. Keys' *Politics, Parties and Pressure Groups* (4th ed., New York, 1958). An outstanding source of pluralist theory is Pendleton Herring's *The Politics of Democracy* (New York, 1940). Limits on leadership, the lack of coercive authority, the stress on bargaining, emerge from such works as Herring's *Public Administration and the Public Interest* (New York, 1936), Charles Hyneman's *Bureaucracy in a Democracy* (New York, 1950), Richard Fenno's *The President's Cabinet* (Cambridge, 1959), and the present study. Methods of achieving agreement may be observed in the many case histories published by the Inter-University Caset Program, T. C. Schelling's *The Strategy of Conflict* (Cambridge, 1960), and the seminal works by Charles Lindblom, "On the Science of 'Muddling Through'," 19 *Public Administration Review*, 79-88 (Spring, 1959), and *Bargaining: The Hidden Hand in Government*, the RAND Corporation (Santa Monica, 1955).

Comments on the use and distribution of resources are found in Robert Dahl's *Who Governs?* (New Haven, 1961), Lasswell and Kaplan's *Power and Society* (New Haven, 1950), case histories and newspapers, and the Oberlin study. Economic concepts like information costs, diminishing returns, discounts, and pyramiding of resources are derived from Anthony Downs, *An Economic Theory of Democracy* (New York, 1957), Dahl, *op. cit.*, and Dahl and Lindblom's *Politics, Economics and Welfare* (New York, 1953). Truman, Herring, and other pluralist writers cited above also have much of interest to say about resources in the American context. The extensive literature on "bossism," (see D. W. Brogan, *Politics in America* [New York, 1954] pp. 123-73, and Robert Merton, *Social Theory and Social Structure* [Glencoe, 1957], pp. 73-84) containing implicit theory of an exchange relationship between politicians, voters, and businessmen, should also be mentioned.

Conceptualization was aided by the following community studies: Dahl, *Who Governs?*; Sayre and Kaufman, *Governing New*

York City (New York, 1960); Edward Banfield, *Political Influence* (New York, 1961); Harry Scoble, "Leadership Hierarchies and Political Issues in a New England Town," in *Community Political Systems*, Morris Janowitz ed. (Glencoe, 1961), pp. 117-45; James McKee, "Status and Power in the Industrial Community: A Comment on Drucker's Thesis," 58, *American Journal of Sociology* (January, 1953), 364-70. Useful general analysis of local power structures include James Coleman, *Community Conflict* (Glencoe, 1957), and Norton E. Long, "The Local Community as an Ecology of Games," 64, *American Journal of Sociology* (November, 1958), 251-61.

That the opportunities for expression and protection provided by a pluralist political system exist does not mean that they will be used. Those who cannot see the connection between what governments do and their own welfare are not likely to inform themselves or to act. Those who lack a sense of efficacy are unlikely to translate any concern they may have into action. In the absence of training in the skills of participation—speaking, communicating, organizing, understanding—these people are dependent upon leaders who will represent them. Rival parties, factions, personalities have an incentive to provide this leadership in order to obtain office in a competitive political system. But no one can be certain that leaders will arise who can articulate and pursue the interests of those ordinarily unwilling or unable to protect themselves. While the political system places limits beyond which citizens cannot be deprived, it by no means guarantees them against deprivations. We all take our chances and it is no secret that the less well endowed in the requirements of our political culture can expect to suffer more than most.

What of those citizens, however, who do possess the necessary skills, who do wish to participate, but who find the prospect overwhelming? Participation may seem to them to require so much effort that the very thought is fatiguing as well as defeating. In this chapter we propose to discuss the situation and to suggest a strategy through which the individual can make himself effective in a pluralist context.

What would life be like, we may ask, if the citizen fulfilled even a small part of the endless injunctions given him to be interested, knowledgeable, and active? One can hardly devote less than two evenings a week to master local problems, another two to state affairs, one to the United Nations, and two to national domestic issues. All evenings are now present and accounted for. Yet there is no time for war and peace and a host of international issues. Perhaps Saturday and Sunday must also be given up. But where is the time for family activities, for social life and friendships, for hobbies and reading and just plain relaxation? There isn't any. To sacrifice all this at the altar of citizen participation seems excessive, to say the least. No wonder there are few truly political men.

These comments may seem like sacrilege coming from a political scientist who devotes his life to the study of public affairs and who would be thought to desire the widest possible citizen participation. Although there is much to be said for emphasizing the quality rather than the quantity of participation, there being citizens whom one might wish to remain apathetic, we hasten to assure the reader that we do teach and advocate citizen participation. The point of the remarks thus far has been that the usual exhortations to do everything are quite impossible to fulfill. All they really succeed in doing is to inculcate guilt at having failed or a sense of utter futility in view of the magnitude of the task. They may actually harm the cause they set out to advance by setting sights so high that more manageable goals are not even attempted. If we are interested not merely in the amount of participation but in its effectiveness and its reasonable relationship to the whole life of the individual, then we must suggest a goal and appropriate strategies which take into account both genuine interest and competition from other essential activities.

The goal is to become a specialist and the major strategy is to specialize. It is vain to think that anyone of us can become generalists. We don't have the time and even if we did we probably wouldn't be willing to devote it solely to this purpose. Even an extraordinarily active person like Bill Long is a generalist only for local affairs and not on the state or national level. But it is possible for any reasonably intelligent person, with a high school education or its equivalent in experience or ability to read, to become an effective issue specialist. This goes for issues as far apart as disarmament and whether to sell the local electric plant. The first question is how to decide what single issue or two or three issues to specialize in.

We can all find the time to read a decent newspaper and perhaps a good supplementary weekly for local affairs. If such a paper is not available in a particular region, it is easy enough to get a subscription to something like the *Christian Science Monitor* or the news magazines. By making a quick survey of the news day-by-day, aided now and then by news broadcasts, the citizen can decide what it is that interests him most. Soon he builds up a small fund of information on a variety of issues which should better enable him to choose his specialty. If there is no paper which contains even the barest account of local events, it may be necessary to attend a few meetings and find out who is well-informed so that these people can be approached from time to time for a résumé of happenings. Having chosen a specialty, the next question is how to become sufficiently informed to develop one's own preferences about what needs to be done.

Where to begin? This is not easy because the citizen does not yet have the background which enables him to pinpoint the literature which best meets his needs. There are, however, a number of ways to proceed which may help to cut information costs. If the citizen is fortunate and knows someone whom he respects and regards as informed, he can ask that person for recommendations as to what to read. Once having begun with something decent, there are almost always additional references to other highly regarded works. Occasionally, the citizen may develop a liking for a columnist or news commentator who suggests appropriate reading. If these resources are not available, a foraging expedition to the local library is indicated. Leaf through several books and articles on the subject of interest and see which has the most immediate appeal. The point is to begin somewhere and keep at it. For there are few issues which cannot be mastered once the citizen has discovered the relevant literature.

In the realm of local affairs there may not be literature which appears immediately relevant to the problem at hand. But the chances are that this is not so and that at least some comparative experience on housing, planning, education, and the like is readily available. To be informed on local differences, however, may require reading special reports and attending meetings devoted to the issue. Take heart! There may be many meetings on many issues; there are rarely an inordinate number on any single one.

There is always the danger that the unwary citizen may be submerged by a flood of material on a well-known issue without being aware of how to extricate himself. He will soon discover, if he is careful, that after two or three books and a half dozen articles, the amount of repetition rises rapidly and he can get by more than adequately with his newspaper, a book, and a few articles every year. It is necessary to know when to stop as well as when to begin.

While it is difficult to imagine the citizen doing this kind of research constantly, it is not utopian to believe that he can do it from time to time if he specializes. There is no point in being in a great hurry and if the project takes six months or a year little harm is done. Suppose there is an emergency or the issue comes up for a decision right away? The obvious way to handle this is to plunge right in yourself. But a few plunges will prove tiring if not tiresome. The optimum strategy here is to specialize not only in specific problems—shall we teach Russian in the high school or shall we put a sewer in on X street—but in a broader area such as education or utilities or defense. Then one will always have a store of information by which to judge events when they turn up.

Specialization increases the fund of information in many ways. The citizen may find that he gets acquainted with people who share his interests, who attend the same meetings and join the same organizations, and who welcome discussion in the area of their mutual concern. Each participant may pick up pointers from the others. When some new development takes place, the specialist is more likely to be informed because his interest has become known. After a while, his right to know is likely to become established through usage and public and private officials inform him as a matter of course. The better acquainted he is with the material, the more agile his mind is likely to become in making the required associations, thus increasing the efficiency of his efforts to acquire information.

The need for participants is so great in most public organizations that anyone who manifests interest is likely to be co-opted. By attending meetings, speaking up on occasion, volunteering his services, or just letting it be known that he cares, the citizen can vastly increase the probability of being asked to take part. The more time and energy he has to devote to this issue area, which is partly a function of his specialization, the greater the likelihood that he will be asked to do more. And the more he does the more likely he is to do still more. Patience is required, however, for it must not be thought that the moment the citizen shows that he is interested, people will flock around demanding his services. A period of time must elapse to demonstrate his genuine interest and for others to judge that he has taken the trouble to become informed.

There can be no guarantee, of course, that the preferences of the citizen who actively specializes will actually be met. There may be others who are equally active and who possess superior resources which he cannot match. Unless the citizen finds himself isolated to the point where few other interested persons share his preferences, however, he does have a good chance to become influential. The probability of his exercising an impact upon decisions will certainly be much greater.

In pluralist political systems where the prizes go to the interested and the active, and where so few others bring their resources to bear, the specialist has great advantages. Most other people do not possess his information, knowledge, and skills in this area and they certainly do not match his rate of participation. Routine decisions are likely to be made by specialists because no one else is concerned. Some decisions which are a bit out of the ordinary may not get to the attention of anyone else. Even when a controversy arises which tends to broaden participation, the specialist has a much better chance of knowing the disposition of forces, the intentions and capabilities of leaders, the degree of solidarity or agreement among them, the kinds of other people who might be mobilized, and similar political data. He will be looked to for leadership by others who are novices in this area compared to him.

In the national arena, particularly in regard to foreign policy, the difficulty which the informed specialist has in making his views felt may be greater because the locus of decision is further removed. The specialist cannot normally expect to have personal contact with the formal decision makers nor secure access to their secret sources of information. Where the specialist might be one of a handful in his local community, he inevitably counts for a smaller proportion of the activists on a national scale. Nevertheless, he does have considerable scope for effective activity. He can help to create a climate of opinion favorable to proposals he prefers by convincing others and propagating his views. Though the effect is difficult to measure, there is little doubt that decision makers in foreign policy do make attempts to sound out opinion and are likely to be influenced by what they think the interested publics will accept. There are pressure group organizations of all kinds which can bring the citizen's preferences directly to the attention of those in power. Letters to Congressmen which are individually expressed may have impact if there are many; such campaigns can be run. Activity in nominations and elections of national officials can have an indirect effect on foreign policy. To become a local opinion leader on foreign affairs is no small accomplishment.

The case histories included in this volume clearly demonstrate the value of specialization. Most decisions are made by a relatively few people who specialize in just one or a few issue areas. The citizen who specializes can find himself writing a housing code, leading a movement for integrated housing, helping to decide whether to sell the municipal light plant and what kind of engine it should have, making decisions on zoning against the wishes of other leaders, changing the operations of the United Appeal, and influencing decisions as to which agencies get how much money. To be sure, the cases also demonstrate the value of superior re-sources possessed by a newspaper editor, a city manager, elected officials, or a businessman. Yet the most useful of these resources—time, skill, energy, and legitimacy—are widely available. Specialization can match the time devoted to one issue area by those in a superior position, and the skill as well if the specialty is pursued long enough. The legitimacy which comes with public office can overcome advantages in other resources and is indirectly available to specialists who are appointed to committees. The ballot is widely distributed. Specialists can make themselves more effective by devoting time during elections, which come but once in every two years, to securing candidates who reflect their views.

We have seen that pluralist societies reduce the probability that some citizens can effectively coerce others in the public realm, thus removing a potentially insuperable bar to participation. If an individual does feel himself constrained in some issue areas, he can specialize in others where he is not open to reprisal or where those who might coerce him do not feel that the outcomes are salient to their interests. There is more than room enough for the citizen to specialize in an area which will give him space to expand his influence. The notion of America as a land of opportunity is certainly valid in this respect.

A remarkable book, *The Great Impostor*, which has interesting implications for many aspects of social life in America, tells the story of a series of impersonations enabling Ferdinand DeMara to assume positions of leadership in several organizations and communities. He draws from his experiences the lesson that there is leadership sort of lying around the streets to be had for the asking. But he enters a persuasive caveat: always be certain that you are not stepping on someone's shoes; avoid this elemental conflict and you can expand your resources considerably before anyone else finds it worthwhile to try and stop you. By implication, DeMara suggests that ours is a society in which there are many unused and inefficiently exploited resources. These, however, are available to many people. For this reason he recommends following a strategy in which your moves do not immediately conflict with those of others, since there is in any event plenty of room to expand your operations in a narrow sphere without running into opposition. It would not be out of place to suggest that those who would be community leaders might find the same rationale convincing.

Granted that specialization is a useful strategy for increasing the influence of the citizen, doubts may arise as to whether it is socially desirable. Is it desirable for citizens to limit themselves to a narrow segment of community affairs? An immediate retort might be that they can hardly do anything else, since considerably increased participation is wholly unrealistic. But this smacks of a debater's trick and we will offer additional arguments. Specialization need not imply total neglect of other areas and we have already advised attention to the general picture through newspapers, broadcasts, and other media of information. It does require the use of various techniques to cut the cost of making one's preferences as effective as possible without large scale participation. The party system, for example, serves as a mechanism for registering an important general preference and does not require knowledge on all issues. The citizen can simply choose the party which on past knowledge he believes best reflects his views. He can see how well the parties operate in the area of his specialization and make deductions from that. He can try to get in touch with specialists in other areas whose opinion he respects and trade information. There are well known commentators in the public media who express their views for all to see. If things go badly in his opinion, the citizen can always decide that it is worthwhile to switch his specialization or temporarily take on a new one until he is satisfied.

To say that the specialist need not suffer overly in other areas because of his particular strategy is not to demonstrate that his mode of operation results in a political system which meets preferences widely held in society. We propose to argue that it does under pluralist conditions providing that one gives up the belief that it is realistic to expect or essential to achieve a political system in which most decisions are made in accordance with the active will of a majority of citizens.

For most citizens most of the time most community affairs are not of active concern. They may have reason to know that things are going well from their point of view and see no reason to participate. It is more likely that the negative is true; they have no reason to believe that things are not going well and it is not worth the cost in time and energy to establish beyond any doubt that this is so. From time to time events do occur which lead them to take an interest and perhaps participate sporadically on a few matters of great concern. If citizens are able for the most part to bring the leaders in these areas into a responsive position on these few matters, so that their preferences are taken into account, then in large measure the community may be said to be ruled in accordance with their wishes or, more accurately, the wishes which are important to them. If the specialists who predominate in each issue area are representative of and can be made responsive to those who care the most about it, then we have a situation in which different minorities rule in different areas and the same result ensues. Given the reservoir of resources which most citizens possess, their willingness to use them at a higher rate in the few areas of their concern, and the interest rival leaders have in taking their case if they are dissatisfied, the rule of minority satisfaction should apply. This is not majority rule in the sense that all or most community decisions accord with the preferences of a majority of citizens; it is majority rule in the special sense that the minority who feel intensely about an issue make up a majority of those who receive consideration and some satisfaction from the outcome. In this way specialization serves the public interest in contributing to a political system which comes closer than others to meeting the widest range of preferences.

Nor are the minimally active without resources to protect interests they deem vital in a community in which the democratic process is highly effective. Leaders, whoever they may be, know that they must at some point take into account the preferences of those who might be activated by severe deprivations and that the citizen, when aroused, has ample means to make his will felt. As the leaders rule, they are influenced in turn by their expectations of what the community will accept. A greater approximation of justice would undoubtedly occur if leaders arose to protect the interests of those whose previous deprivations have left them without the attributes—education, sense of efficacy, self-confidence— which would lead to participation. This process has begun in Oberlin and may be expected to continue as the advantages of activism—made so obvious by the planners—become more apparent. All in all, there is good reason to regard Oberlin as a successful endeavor in self-government. Those who participate in its affairs, whether they gain their immediate objectives or not, have every right to feel that they are making a notable contribution to self-government in which the clash of interests provides a reasonable approximation of justice and makes the will of the people, realistically defined, a major element in community decisions.

✤🏚🏚✤ NOTES

Chapter One

1. Richard McKeon, ed., *Basic Works of Aristotle* (New York, 1941), pp. 1185-87, 1212-24. See also, Norton Long, "Aristotle and the Study of Local Government," *Social Research* (Fall, 1957), pp. 287-310.

2. Arthur W. Kornhauser, *The Politics of Mass Society* (Glencoe, 1959).

3. Robert A. Dahl, *Who Governs? Democracy and Power in an American City* (New Haven, 1961); Nelson W. Polsby, *Community Power and Political Theory* (New Haven, 1963); Raymond E. Wolfinger, *The Politics of Progress*, forthcoming; and, especially, Polsby's "How to Study Community Power: The Pluralist Alternative," *The Journal of Politics* (August, 1960), pp. 474-84.

4. For a critique of the approach pursued in this volume see Peter Bachrach and Morton Baratz, "Two Faces of Power," *American Political Science Review* (December, 1962), pp. 947-52, and Thomas Anton, "Power, Pluralism, and Local Politics," *Administrative Science Quarterly* (March, 1963), pp. 425-457. The major points in these articles are dealt with in the course of Polsby's *Community Power and Political Theory*, *Op. Cit.*, especially pp. 95-97, 132-38.

5. The methods used for purposes of historical inquiry are described in Chapter 3.

In order to keep the volume at a reasonable length, detailed case histories in education will not be presented. Instead, capsule descriptions will be presented in Chapter 18 in order to facilitate comparison with other areas of decision.

Chapter Two

1. The numbers in this survey are too small to permit excessive confidence in their precise reliability. Measures of statistical significance have not been used because this would be highly misleading in a chapter designed to develop rather than to test hypotheses, and because, as Lipset, Trow, and Coleman, argue so persuasively, such tests are not useful for distinguishing among categories of a single, limited sample. (See S. Lipset, M. Trow, and J. Coleman, *Union Democracy* (Glencoe, 1956) pp. 427-432.) When we compare leaders with a sample of the general population (Chapter 19) it will be more appropriate to test the significance of the comparisons between the two sets of respondents.

2. Dahl, *Op. Cit.*, pp. 276-81, 342-43. For further data on political participation see Bernard Berelson, Paul Lazarsfeld and William McPhee, *Voting,*

(Chicago, 1954); Angus Campbell, Phillip Converse, Warren Miller, and Donald Stokes, *The American Voter* (New York, 1960); and V. O. Key, Jr., *Public Opinion and American Democracy* (New York, 1961).

3. Dahl, *Op. Cit.*, pp. 298-300.

4. See Key, *Op. Cit.*, pp. 324-26, and Robert Lane, *Political Life* (Glencoe, 1959), pp. 157-61.

5. See Campbell, Converse, Miller and Stokes, *Op. Cit.*, pp. 515-19, and Lane, *Op. Cit.*, pp. 147-55.

6. Dahl, *Op. Cit.*, pp. 289-93, Lane, *Op. Cit.*, pp. 155-62.

7. "The Fear of Equality," *The American Political Science Review*, LIII (March, 1959), pp. 35-51.

Chapter Three

1. *The Biographical Encyclopedia of Ohio of the 19th Century* (Cincinnati, 1876).

James H. Fairchild, *Oberlin: The Colony and the College, 1833-1883* (Oberlin, Ohio, 1883).

Robert Samuel Fletcher, *The Government of the Oberlin Colony* (Reprint in Oberlin College Library).

Robert Samuel Fletcher, *A History of Oberlin College From Its Foundations Through the Civil War* (Oberlin, Ohio, 1943), 2 vols.

General Catalogue of Oberlin College, 1833-1908 (Oberlin College, 1909).

Rev. Delavan L. Leonard, *The Story of Oberlin, the Institution, the Community, the Idea, the Movement* (Boston, 1898).

Ohio Roster of Township and Municipal Officers and Members of Boards of Education.

Wilbur H. Phillips, *Oberlin Colony, The Story of a Century* (Oberlin, Ohio, 1933).

Scrapbook of Obituary Clippings, 1901-06 (Oberlin College Library).

C. S. Van Tassel, ed., *The Ohio Bluebook or Who's Who in the Buckeye State* (Toledo, Ohio, 1917).

C. R. Camp, *Camp's Directory of Oberlin, 1873-74* (Oberlin, Ohio, 1873).

J. W. Holton, *Holton's Semi-Centennial Directory and Guide to Oberlin for 1883* (Oberlin, Ohio, 1883).

Oberlin City Directory, 1886 (Oberlin, Ohio, 1886).

Oberlin City Directory, 1888 (Oberlin, Ohio, 1888).

C. S. Williams, *Williams' Medina, Elyria & Oberlin City Directory, City Guide, and Business Mirror*, Vol. 1 (1859).

2. James H. Fairchild, *Oberlin: The Colony and the College, 1833-1883* (Oberlin, Ohio, 1883), p. 205.

3. Robert W. Tufts, *Municipal Ownership of the Light and Power Industry in Oberlin* (Typescript, 1940) in the Oberlin Library.

4. A perceptive review of the literature is contained in Eugene C. Lee, *The Politics of Nonpartisanship* (Berkeley, 1960). See also Charles Adrian, "Some General Characteristics of Nonpartisan Elections," 46 *American Political Science Review* (September, 1952), pp. 766-76 and his "A Typology of Nonpartisan Elections," 12 *Western Political Quarterly* (June, 1959), pp. 449-58. Recent work of interest includes Charles Gilbert and Christopher Clague, "Electoral Competition and Electoral Systems in Large Cities," 24 *Journal of Politics* (May, 1962), pp. 323-49; Gilbert's, "Some Aspects of Nonpartisan Elections in Large Cities," 6 *Midwest Journal of Political Science* (November,

1962), pp. 345-62; and Oliver Williams and Charles Adrian, "The Insulation of Local Politics Under the Nonpartisan Ballot," 53 *American Political Science Review* (December, 1959), pp. 1052-63.

Chapter Five

1. At this time the members of the PUC were Carl Howe, a Professor of Physics, Don Pease, co-editor of the *Oberlin News-Tribune*, Edward Trautz, Vice President of the Oberlin Savings Bank and manager of the Amherst Branch, Thomas Griswold, Manager of the Pfaulder Company in Elyria, and Carl Breuning, an official in the Buildings and Grounds Department of Oberlin College.

Chapter Six

1. George Simpson, Chairman, Mrs. Marion VanAtta, Mrs. Marcia Goldberg, Mrs. Blair Stewart, Mrs. Ruth Tumbleson, Richard Lothrop, Ted Wigton, Burrell Scott, Chalmer Davidson, William Jackson, Rev. Joseph King, Marshall Morrow, Mrs. Ernest Hoffman, Douglas Johnson, Mary Rainbow, Mrs. Bruce Hawkins, James Stephens, Mrs. Helen Sperry, Don McIlroy, Richard Haller and Orlando Shilts.

2. Long had previously been successful in setting up the Smith Street Sewer Fund, a program by which the residents of Smith Street contributed as much as they could to the cost of their sewer, and borrowed the remainder of their assessment from a fund to which other private citizens had contributed. This fund was the sort of arrangement Long and Ellis hoped to set up. They travelled to Philadelphia to see a wealthy woman whom they hoped would be interested in financing such a program because of her previous association with Oberlin, but failed to raise the necessary funds.

Chapter Eight

1. Harold Peterson, Eric Nord, Mrs. Charlotte Baker, a Negro employee of the Co-op, Milton Yinger, a sociology professor, and Robert Tumbleson, who operates the Oberlin School of Commerce, were elected directors. Peterson became president, Tumbleson, vice-president and Mrs. Baker, secretary. Dr. Warren Sheldon, a physician, was elected to the board, and Richard Huber, an attorney, was named treasurer.

2. Fred Owens, a compositor at the *News-Tribune* printing plant, Lawrence DeMott, an instructor in the Geology and Geography Department of the College, Bruce Hawkins, a physics professor, Richard Huber, his wife, Nancy McMurray, a nurse for the Lorain County Health Department, and Mrs. Walter Reeves, wife of the Assistant Director of Development at the College, became members.

3. They were Paul Hamlin, an employee of Clark Brothers, General Contractors, Mrs. Don Pease, wife of the co-editor of the *News-Tribune*, Robert Scott, a foreman of the city street department, Suzanne Vance, a high school student, and Connie Bracey, Pat Joslyn, Elizabeth Lester and Margaret Morris, Oberlin College students.

4. The members were: Reverend Edward Jones, Bill Long, Don Pease, Donald McIlroy, Principal of Pleasant School, Richard B. Huber, a local attorney, his wife, a teacher, Eric Nord, Council Chairman, Burrell Scott, a Negro ma-

son, David Anderson, a physics professor at the College, Reverend Joseph King, Pastor of the First Congregational Church, Harold Peterson, an instructor in education at the College, Robert S. Thomas, a Negro reporter for the *Lorain-Journal*, Thomas Griswold, Division Manager of the Pfaudler Company in Elyria, his wife, Reverend W. K. Hogg, Pastor of the First Methodist Church, H. R. Von Dorster, an advertising manager, William Miller, a Negro employee of the Ohio Turnpike Authority, his wife, Arnold Schwartz, an out-of-town businessman, Cornelius Wright, a Negro moulder at General Industries in Elyria, Mrs. Marlin Butts, a social worker and wife of a sociology professor at the Graduate School of Theology, Milton Yinger, a professor of sociology at the College, Edward Long, Jr., a professor of religion at the College, Mrs. Eva Mae Crosby, a Negro attorney and school teacher, and Dr. James Stephens, a physician. Thus was formed the Open Occupancy Housing Committee.

5. Reverend Joseph King, of the First Congregational Church, John Strong, leading Republican and insurance agent and writer of the sports column in the *News-Tribune*, John Baum, an associate professor of mathematics, Dr. J. R. Bay, a physician, Edward Long, Jr., a professor of religion, George Simpson, a professor of sociology, Mrs. Louis Berger, wife of a business management consultant, Mrs. Margaret Baker, wife of a Negro factory worker, Dewey Ganzel, professor of English, Richard Wolf, professor of church history in the Graduate School of Theology, Lee Ross, former proprietor of the Ross Lumber Company, Reverend Fred Steen, of the Mt. Zion Baptist Church, a Negro, L. A. Owen, associate professor of pastoral theology, and Luther Palmer, a mason.

6. One Negro who made an emotional speech about discrimination in the community was an air traffic controller at the new FAA installation. He told how pilots entrusted him with their lives, and how he was considered capable to control equipment worth $1,000,000; but complained that when he asked to be shown houses in Oberlin, he was taken down below the tracks. He intimated that he had been looking for a $25,000 house, but had not found anything fit for his wife and children to live in. After the meeting, Bill Long, who it will be remembered was Chairman of the Placement Committee, spoke to the FAA employee and informed him that he knew of a $25,000 house on the west side of town in a fine neighborhood, which a Negro could buy. The FAA man replied that he was "just looking" and walked away. He later asked to buy a much less expensive house in all-Negro Gladys Court, down below the tracks.

Chapter Nine

1. The passage of a revised zoning ordinance in 1959 occurred without incident or opposition. For this reason, it is not especially useful for the determination of community power structure. Nevertheless, it does illustrate one type of decision where all that is necessary is to overcome inertia. Accordingly, a brief account of the revised zoning ordinance is included in an appendix to this chapter.

2. In addition to members of the Commission, Harold Gibson, son of Bert Gibson and a member of Council, Allyn and Bert Gibson, Bill Long and the City Manager attended the meeting.

3. The other members were H. A. Broadwell, a former city clerk, now proprietor of the Janby Oil Company and a member of the Lorain County Planning Commission, W. E. Parker, proprietor of the Time Shop, Dr. George Hoover, an osteopath, and G. Cervone, a title examiner.

4. By this time the composition of the Board had changed. Broadwell was now chairman, and W. E. Parker was still a member. New Members were Tom Flanigan, a business executive in Grafton, Saul Gilford, owner of Gilford Laboratories, which is located in the Industrial Park, and Harry Hicks, a Negro dental technician. Gilford was a friend of Long's and Hicks was recruited by Nord.

5. Its members were Paul Arnold, representing the Planning Commission, H. A. Broadwell for the Zoning Board of Appeals, Richard Dunn, as City Manager, Larry Severs as City Solicitor, and Andy Stofan, representing the City Council.

Chapter Ten

1. See James March, "The Business Firm as a Political Coalition," 24, *The Journal of Politics* (November, 1962), pp. 662-78.

2. At the time of the events described here, the agency was known as the Civil Aeronautics Administration. The name was changed to the Federal Aviation Agency at a later date, and to avoid confusion, this name is used throughout this chapter.

Chapter Eleven

1. For biographical material on Long see Chapter 17.

2. Oberlin Stores consisted of Eloise Fowler, a language teacher; Orlando Shilts, principal of one of the public schools; Fred Foreman, a geology professor; David Anderson, a physics professor and Long's next door neighbor; and Long's mother-in-law.

3. Brad Williams, co-editor of the *News-Tribune*; Paul Warner, president of the Oberlin Savings Bank; Ira Porter, president of the Peoples Banking Company; Frank Van Cleef, resident trustee of Oberlin College; Lewis R. Tower, business manager of Oberlin College; Senator Mosher, Roose, Fred Comings, co-owner of Comings Book Store; John Cochrane, owner of the Ben Franklin Store and T. O. Murphy, owner of a plumbing construction company, came to the meeting.

4. The potential investors were Eloise Fowler, who already had a share in Oberlin Stores, Don Pease and Brad Williams, co-editors of the Oberlin *News-Tribune*, Mills Clark, a retired real estate developer; Samuel Goldberg, a professor of mathematics at the College; Andrew Stofan, owner of the local photography shop; Douglas Johnson, an architect; Orlando Shilts, who already held a share in Oberlin Stores; Grover Severs, city solicitor; Frank Locke, a nurseryman; Ben Lewis, an economics professor, Chuck Smith, owner of Smith Floor Coverings; Fred Comings, co-owner of Comings Book Store; Bronson Clark, Kenny Clark, Mosher, Roose and Long.

5. Actually, OID sold land to Clark Brothers who built and leased it to Guilford. Two years later Clark sold it all back to OID which then improved the property.

Chapter Twelve

1. This joint body was made up of Jim Molyneaux, Ira Porter, Orren Hillman, Richard Dunn, Norris Ryder, C. A. Barden, Don Pease, Phip Zahm, Karl Augenbaugh, Leonard Barr, Bill Tower, and Bill Long, Wade Ellis, and Harold Gibson representing the city council.

2. The committee was to consist of Harold Gibson as chairman, along with Wade Ellis, John Cochrane and Paul Warner, with Orren Hillman and Richard Dunn, in their capacities as city engineer and city manager, as advisers.

3. The officers were John Cochrane, president; Jim Molyneaux, vice-president; Robert Fauver, secretary; and Henry Klermund, treasurer and manager. The Board of Directors included Cochrane, Molyneaux and Fauver and Stetson.

Chapter Thirteen

1. Ruth Tumbelson, active in many civic organizations, was urged to run by those who appreciated her work. She was interested in serving the community. William Gaeumann, a local builder, and Gerald Scott, a Negro barber-shop proprietor, gave no reason for their decisions.

2. Eleanor Cooley, former Mayor John Kutscher, Carl Spitler, an officer of the Peoples Savings Bank, and Ruth Lampson, were co-chairmen. Sue and Bud Arnold were placed in charge of membership; Ester Sperry, a public stenographer, and Bill Close, Editor of *Where* magazine in Cleveland, were the publicity chairmen; and Ira Porter, President of the Peoples Savings Bank, headed the finance committee. A core group of Bill Davis, Bob Fauver, Sue and Bud Arnold, John Cochrane, Mrs. Mabel Tobin (widow of a former businessman in town), George Dudley, an insurance agent, the Cooleys, Burt Gibson, Bill Close, and the other candidates and their wives formed policy for the Citizens' Committee. They set a budget of $400, which Ira Porter raised by soliciting contributions in small amounts from the Citizens' Committee.

3. When the writer first arrived in Oberlin, September 1958, he immediately was informed that Ira Porter ran the town and that election returns could be deduced from this assumption. If it was not Porter, then it certainly was the banks and the downtown merchants with their control of credits and jobs. Victories by Stofan, Gibson and Comings in the 1957 election led to caustic remarks to the effect that all you had to do was have your name on a prominent store-front and you were in office. The election of 1959 certainly disproves all of these hypotheses, if this kind of speculation can be dignified by that title.

4. See Robert Dahl, *Preface to Democratic Theory* (Chicago, 1954).

Chapter Fifteen

1. Ira Porter, William Davis, Donald Love, T. O. Murphy, Lester Ries, and C. A. Barden.

2. A few others asked to have their names withheld but they were not active on the United Appeal.

3. S. Douglas Polhemmus, Director of the Alumni Association at Oberlin College; Mills Clark, a retired developer; and Robert Singleton, vice-president of the Nelson Stud Welding Company in Lorain.

4. Mrs. Walter Carpenter, an elementary school teacher; Richard Haller, a company manager; Don J. Pease, co-editor of the *News-Tribune*; and Grover L. Severs, City Solicitor.

5. It would not be surprising if a few large contributors made the decisions on how to allocate funds for private welfare programs. If there are also many small contributors, however, as is almost always the case, and they have a joint spokesman, such as a labor union council, then they may have a strong voice in these decisions. Many small contributions may give greater weight than a few large ones. For a demonstration of this point see James McKee's account of

how labor unions in Lorain, Ohio, gained leverage in community welfare programs. ("Status and Power in the Industrial Community: A Comment on Drucker's Thesis," *The American Journal of Sociology*, LVIII (January, 1953), pp. 364-70.)

6. For a discussion of the concept of "fair-shares" in budgeting see the author's forthcoming *The Politics of the Budgetary Process* (Little, Brown, 1964).

Chapter Sixteen

1. For an excellent study of city managers see Gladys Kammerer, Charles Farris, John DeGrove, and Alfred Clubock, *City Managers in Politics, Analysis of Manager Tenure and Termination*, University of Florida Monographs, Social Science, No. 13, Winter 1962.

2. Richard Dunn graduated from Dartmouth College in 1951, received a Masters degree in City Planning at Cornell two years later, worked in Rhode Island for a year, and then returned to Cornell to receive a Masters in public administration. In 1955, he obtained a job as assistant city manager in Oak Park, Illinois, and came to Oberlin in 1958. He is a Catholic and a Republican, married and has two children.

3. Wallace Sayre and Herbert Kaufman, *Governing New York City* (New York, 1960), pp. 224, 227.

4. *Ibid.*, p. 252.

5. This was the only labor dispute in Oberlin during the period covered in this study. It involved a handful of employees in a supermarket. After some recrimination and picketing, elections were held under the supervision of a Professor of Economics. Management won and the net result was that two of the four employees originally dismissed for poor work, as one side would have it, or union activity, as the other side would have it, lost their jobs.

Chapter Seventeen

1. Members included the Arnold Schwartzes, the Saul Gilfords, Doctor and Mrs. Robert Bay, the Reverend Ted Jones, the David Andersons, and the Tom Griswolds.

2. See Robert Lane, *Political Life* (Glencoe, 1959), Chapter 11, " 'Strength,' Happiness, and Morality in Politics," pp. 147-62.

Chapter Eighteen

1. Because of limitations of space, these case histories are presented in the briefest possible space. They omit a great deal but they do include just enough information to accompany the charts which are used for comparison with other issue areas.

2. The conclusions would be the same if we took the space to present all the issue-areas.

Chapter Nineteen

1. In the tables in this chapter the number of respondents in the General Population Sample is 101 and the number of leaders is 20. The number of Activists is 23, Voter-Observers 46, and Apathetics 32. Together, these three sets of people exhausts the Population Sample. Wherever the figures mentioned

for Apathetics, Voter-Observers, Activists, and Leaders increase or decrease in the same direction, this is indicated by the letter "D" in parenthesis after the designation "Group." The Chi Square test was applied to determine whether the differences between the leaders and the General Population Sample might have occured by chance. We find that all tables are significant at the .05 or .001 level or less except for several specifically labelled as not significant. In a few cases (Table 36 "in state elections," and tables 56, 66, 72 and 73) the numbers were too small in certain columns and a two-tailed or four-tailed division was made in order to obtain more reliable results. Tables 72 and 73 are marginal cases leaving room for judgment as to whether the results are significant at the .05 level.

2. See Robert Lane, *Political Life* (Glencoe, 1959), Chapter 11, " 'Strength,' Happiness, and Morality in Politics," pp. 147-62.

3. Robert Dahl, *Who Governs?* (New Haven, 1961), pp. 289-93.

Chapter Twenty

1. Extensive bibliographies of this controversy may be found in Nelson Polsby, *Community Power and Political Theory* (New Haven, 1963) and Lawrence Herson, "In the Footsteps of Community Power," *American Political Science Review*, 55 (December, 1961), pp. 817-30. The major work using the reputational method is Floyd Hunter's *Community Power Structure* (Chapel Hill, 1953). For other examples see Delbert Miller, "Decision-Making Cliques in Community Power Structures," *American Journal of Sociology*, 64 (November, 1958), pp. 299-310; Robert Schulze and Leonard Blumberg, "The Determination of Local Power Elites," *ibid.*, 63 (November, 1957), pp. 290-96; Ernest Barth and Baha Abu-Laban, "Power Structure and the Negro Sub-Community," *American Sociological Review*, 24 (February, 1959), pp. 69-76; and David Booth and Charles Adrian, "Power Structure and Community Change," *Midwest Journal of Political Science*, VI (August, 1962), pp. 277-96. Criticisms may be found in Herbert Kaufman and Victor Jones, "The Mystery of Power," *Public Administration Review*, 14 (Summer, 1954), pp. 205-12; Polsby, *op. cit.*; and Raymond Wolfinger, "Reputation and Reality in the Study of 'Community Power'," *American Sociological Review*, 25 (October, 1960), pp. 636-44. Defense of the reputation method appears in Herson, *op. cit.*; William D'Antonio and Eugene Erickson, "The Reputational Technique as a Measure of Community Power: An Evaluation Based on Comparative and Longitudinal Studies," *American Sociological Review*, 27 (June, 1962), pp. 362-76; and Howard Ehrlich's, "The Reputational Approach to the Study of Community Power," *ibid.*, 26 (December, 1961), pp. 926-27. The battle is joined between the same covers in two symposia: Robert Dahl and Delbert Miller joust in a book edited by D'Antonio and Ehrlich, *Power and Democracy in America* (Notre Dame, 1961); Polsby and Wolfinger contend with D'Antonio, Erickson, and Ehrlich in separate essays in the *American Sociological Review*, 27 (December, 1962), pp. 838-54.

2. Of the College it may be said that the President has secured some of his objectives and not others. Any description of his leadership would have to include limits beyond which he cannot go and defeats as well as victories.

3. Let us consider a few hypothetical suggestions. Reputation might provide a clue as to why certain individuals are asked for assistance in handling community problems. Reputation might be related to morale. It is possible that morale would be higher in a community where power was perceived to be

more widely shared. Indeed, this approach might be used in studying industrial organizations. Reputation studies might be stood on their heads by inquiring what the designations of the respondents tell us about themselves. What kind of people see conspiracies and what kind name formal officials? What people think about the exercise of power may tell us something important about how they relate to the political arena.

Chapter Twenty-One

1. The best guide to this literature is found in William Kornhauser, *The Politics of Mass Society* (Glencoe, 1959). Basic writings include Erich Fromm, *Escape from Freedom* (New York, 1945); Hannah Arendt, *The Origins of Totalitarianism* (New York, 1954); Karl Mannheim, *Man and Society in an Age of Reconstruction* (London, 1940); Robert Nisbet, *The Quest for Community* (New York, 1953); and A. Vidich and J. Bensman, *Small Town in a Mass Society* (Princeton, 1958).

2. For another attempt at correction which procedes from a somewhat different viewpoint, see Joseph Gusfield, "Mass Society and Extremist Politics," *American Sociological Review*, 27 (February, 1962), pp. 19-30. In addressing himself to the problem of culture in a mass society, Edward Shils also departs from the usual extreme pessimism. "Mass Society in its Culture," *Daedalus*, 89 (Spring, 1960), pp. 288-314.

3. For critiques of Mills' *The Power Elite* (New York, 1956), see Robert Dahl, "A Critique of the Ruling Elite Model," *American Political Science Review*, 52 (June, 1958), pp. 463-69; Daniel Bell, "The Power Elite—Reconsidered," *The American Journal of Sociology*, LXIV (November, 1958), pp. 238-50; and Talcott Parsons, "The Distribution of Power in American Society," *World Politics*, X (October, 1957), pp. 123-43.

4. See, especially, Campbell, Converse, Miller and Stokes, *The American Voter*, (New York, 1960).

5. Robert and Helen Lynd, *Middletown* (New York, 1929), and *Middletown in Transition* (New York, 1937). A searching critique may be found in Nelson Polsby, "Power in Middletown: Fact and Value in Community Research," *The Canadian Journal of Economics and Political Science*, XXVI (November, 1960), pp. 592-603.
The Comments which follow also apply to Floyd Hunter's *Community Power Structure* (Chapel Hill, 1953), with its theory of crowds of economic dominants running things to suit themselves.

6. Marx's view of the city under capitalism and socialism can be found in *The Paris Commune* (New York, 1920), especially pages 70-76.

7. William Whyte, Editor, *Industry and Society* (New York, 1946), pp. 2-45.

8. Robert Merton, "Patterns of Influence: Local and Cosmopolitan Influentials," *Social Theory and Social Structure*, (Glencoe, 1957), pp. 387-420.

Chapter Twenty-Two

1. See the Appendix to this chapter for the sources of this theory.

🌲🏛🏛🌲 INDEX

Abolitionism, 14, 34-36
Active participants,
    definition of, 15
    social characteristics of, 16-31, 282-302, 321, 340
    and Negroes, 111-112
    and city planning, 127
    and 1959 elections, 177-178
    and Commissions, 195, 199, 355
    City Manager as, 215, 217, 233-235
    Bill Long as, 235-252
    in education, 263-265
    and coalition of planners, 270-271, 273-280
    on reputational leaders, 306-319
Activists,
    See Active participants
Administration, 237, 246
    See also Decision making, techniques
Age,
    and participation in politics, 19-20, 299-300
Allen Hospital, 206, 207, 211, 213
American Civil Liberties Union, 238
American Missionary Society, 35
American Public Health Association, 86
American society, 26
Amherst, Ohio, 60-62
Anderson, David,
    and housing, 105
    and community development, 152, 157
    and 1959 elections, 170, 172, 174
    and planners, 270
Apathetics,
    characteristics of, 15-31, 284, 336

and Negroes, 111-112, 125-126
and reputational leaders, 306-313, 316-319
and political activity, 337, 338
Appointments,
    by Council, 93-94, 195-199
    and City Manager, 215, 218-222
    and Bill Long, 248
    and individual participation in politics, 355-356
Architectural Forum, 240
Aristotle, 4-5, 349
Arnold, Paul B.,
    and building permit controversy, 130-132, 138
    and Zoning Ordinance, 140, 142
    and parking signs, 165
    and planners, 168
    and 1959 elections, 172
    and downtown redevelopment, 227-228
    as reputational leader, 311
Arnold, Sue, 177
Artino, Joseph, 155
Artz, Frederick, 176
Aschaffenburg, Walter, Mrs.
    and petition on water issue, 65
Atlanta, Georgia, (Regional City), 304, 347, 349

Backus, W. H., 37
Bagehot, Walter, 303
Baker, Margaret, Mrs., 65, 104
Ballot,
    levy on, 44
Banfield, Edward,
    Political Influence, 345-346
Bankers, 316, 318, 329

and 1959 elections, 172, 176, 177,
182
as City Solicitor, 185
and downtown redevelopment, 229
social status of, 272
and decision making, 273
as reputational leader, 310
Federal Aeronautics Administration
center, (FAA), 155, 156, 301
and water supply system, 54, 56,
181
and electric power plant, 75, 76,
257
and housing, 120, 121, 144, 145
efforts to bring center to Oberlin,
143-149, 153, 259
and leadership chart, 261
and school expansion, 275, 317
Federal Housing Administration, 118
Finance Committee, 222-223
Fire,
death of children by, and enforcement of Housing Code, 101, 255
Firemen's relief and pension fund, 40
First Akron Corporation, 135, 136
First Church, 315, 316
First National Bank, 35
Flanigan, Thomas, 137, 138
Ford Motor Company, 54
Fowler, Richard, 59, 65, 66
Friedrich, Carl, 10
Friendship, 273-274
See also Decision making, tech-
niques
Fund raising, charitable, 11, 200-203

Gaeuman, William, 59, 121
Garland, Hamlin, 328
General Motors, 241
Generalists,
political activity of, 337, 343-344,
353
Gibson, Allyn, 127, 136
Gibson, Bert,
and building permit controversy,
127-142, 247, 259-260, 271, 275-
276
and leadership chart, 261
Gibson, Harold, 47
and non partisan elections, 44, 48
and Housing Code, 90, 92, 94, 96-
97, 254, 315

and building permit controversy,
127-128, 131-135
and Zoning Ordinance, 141
and downtown parking, 161
and 1959 elections, 170-171, 174,
175, 187
and Commissions, 195
Gilford Medical Instrument plant, 76,
155-157, 259
Gilford, Saul, 137, 155
Girl Scouts, 200, 201, 209
Goldberg, Samuel, 174, 237
Goldberg, Samuel, Mrs., 84-90, 93-94,
97, 254, 265, 276, 315
Goldthorpe, David, 309
The Great Impostor, 358
Green, Frank, 59
Griswold, Thomas, 198, 270, 316
Gruen Plan, 47
Gruen, Victor, 240

Hall, Charles Martin, 207
Haller, Richard, 84, 260
Hawkins, Bruce, 105
Hawkins, Bruce, Mrs., 85, 88, 97, 315
Haylor, R., Jr., 176
Health,
as resource for political activity, 28-
29, 243, 293, 298
See also Resources for leadership
Health Commission, 209, 210, 213
Heart Fund, 201
Heidelberg College, 236
Hellmuth, William,
election to Council, 47
and water supply system, 59-60
and water rate schedule, 68, 70
and Housing Code, 89, 90, 94, 106,
108, 254-255
and building permit, 131, 133, 134,
138
and FAA, 144, 146
and 1959 elections, 170, 174, 175,
187, 189-192
and Commissions, 195, 219
and budget, 223
and construction contracts, 232-233
and City Manager, 234
and Bill Long, 237
and planners, 268-271
as reputational leader, 308
Hendry, Samuel, 35, 37

Occupations,
of leaders, 291-292, 298
Office of Air Navigation Facilities, 143
Office of Air Traffic Control, 143
Ohio Bell Telephone Company, 145
Ohio Edison Company, 75-76, 77
Ohio Electric Power Co., 39, 73-74
Ohio Exchange Club, 40
Ohio Farm Bureau and Cooperative Association, 236, 237
Ohio Municipal League, 224
Ohio Public Service Company, 43, 74
Ohio Society of Professional Engineers, 55
Ohio State Department of Health, 56
Ohio, State Highway Director, 41
Ohio Supreme Court, 135
Ohio Water Resources Board, 55
Ohly, P. H., 176
Oldfield, John, 87
Oliver, Chris, 57, 92, 255
Olmstead, Richard, 176
Open Occupancy Housing Committee, 112, 119-121
Open Occupancy Housing Ordinance, 122-126, 267
See also Housing, Housing Code,
Owens, Fred, 105

Palkovic, Anthony, 136
Parents Teachers Association, 311
Parker, W. E., 137
Parking,
meters, 43
downtown, 159-166, 229-230, 241
school, 231
Parsons, Frank, 168, 192
Pease, Don, 117
and 1959 elections, 170, 178, 187
and Commissions, 195, 198
and United Appeal, 204-213, 257
and recruitment of teachers, 231
and Bill Long, 243
leadership of, 265, 308
Polhemmus, Douglas, 206, 257
Peoples Banking Company, 38, 40, 57, 63, 123
and employment of Negroes, 64
and Housing Foundation, 115
and Bill Long, 237

Pepperidge Farms Bakery, 153, 155, 156
and water supply system, 54, 56, 65
and electric power plant, 76
Persuasion,
and decision-making, 246-247
and Housing Code, 254
and Council, 260
and planners, 271, 275, 277, 278
and leadership, 284
and political activity, 334, 357
Peterson, Harold, 104, 114
Petition,
for referendum on water supply, 62-66, 257, 276
Phillips, W. H., 37
Piraino, Thomas, 129, 262
Planners,
as active participants, 46, 268-280, 360
and Council, 47, 260
and water supply controversy, 99
and building permit controversy, 128, 131, 133-134, 140-142
and 1959 elections, 167, 171, 189-194, 260
opposition to, 168-170
and Commissions, 197, 199
and City Manager, 218
supporters of, 301
Planning,
belief in, and participation in politics, 29, 46, 239
and individual rights, 83, 127, 132, 133, 139
and Zoning Ordinance, 140-142
and 1959 elections, 177-178, 186-187
and City Manager, 216-217
and Bill Long, 240, 250, 281
and coalition of planners, 269-271, 273-280
Planning Commission, 311
during 1945-1955, 42
and extension of city services, 114
and building permit controversy, 128, 130, 131, 139
and Zoning Ordinance, 140
and appointments to, 196, 198
Plumb, Samuel, 35, 37
Pluralist political system,

Water (*cont.*)
reputed leaders in decisions, 307-317
Water Department, 54
See also City services
Weisbrod, Fred
and water supply system, 54
Welfare activities,
and decision making, 7, 254, 266, 301
and United Appeal, 200-201
Williams, Brad, 178, 187, 309
Willowbrook Farms, 117-119, 121, 255-256
Wolfe, Joseph, 37
Wolfinger, Raymond, 8, 304, 346
Wonderly, Donald,
school psychologist, 263
Wood, John, 87, 91, 97, 260
Wood, Ted, 219
Worth, Truman, 347
Wright, Cornelius, 97

Yinger, Milton, 117, 118
Yocum, J. D., 37
Young Men's Club, 40

Zahm, H. V., 39, 40
on annexation, 42
on city services, 42-43
and water rate schedule, 68, 70, 71
and Housing Code, 88, 90, 91, 94, 254
and building permit, 131, 133, 134, 315
and FAA, 146
and 1959 elections, 171, 174, 187
Zoning,
issues during 1945-1955, 42
and building permit controversy, 128
and decision making, 254, 260, 301
reputed leaders in, 307
Zoning Board of Appeals, 309, 316
and rezoning, 40, 42
and building permit controversy, 128-132, 136, 138-139, 275
appointments to, 199, 259
Zoning Ordinance, 233, 252
and Gibson building permit, 128, 130, 132, 138
revision of, 140-142